A JOURNEY TO LEAVE YOU WITH...

ODD SHAPED BALLS

By Tom Hudson

&

Jodie Burton

ISBN-13: 978-1468184297

ISBN-10: 1468184296

Published in 2012

This is dedicated to everyone in the 'Global Rugby Family' without whom it would have been a long lonely journey choosing a quite pointless method of transport. Also, to Stefan, who without his gentle push in the right direction, we would have no one else to blame.

PROLOGUE

'Shhhh,' I whispered into Jodie's ear, as I reached across and placed a single finger on her lips. Jodie didn't move an inch, she had heard it too.

Just moments ago, we had strapped up our panniers and settled down for the night, but now our senses were more alert than ever before. We lay side by side in the darkness, dead still in our tiny tent, listening intently in just our underwear.

The noise came again, this time closer, an identifiable grunt of an animal much larger than we had ever had visit us before. Then footsteps, heavy laboured footsteps, cracking twigs immediately beside the tent. By now we could hear its breathing, almost feel every single breath as it stopped only inches from my side.

'Huffff... ' the deep grunt shook the tent as the steps slowly paced around to the tent doorway. We lay frozen, not making a sound.

Shhhiiiii-iiiiiit! What the heck was that?

We hadn't seen a town for many kilometres, and it was therefore quite unlikely to be a pet on the loose. An animal this large could be livestock, maybe just a stray cow, but then again this wasn't farmland, we had cycled up into dense woodland and were now perched in a small rest area. It wasn't a great start to my investigation, and given the current state of my pants, I would have happily accepted either situation.

We were deep into the hills of Romania, a long cry from civilisation, and we had camped up on some flattish grass next to an old table. Scattered around us was the rubbish from many previous picnics, not a great choice in the wild, but the fading light and endless procession of hairpin turns had given us no other option. My mind was blank with panic, I had only just read about bears and wolves in areas of Romania, but had we reached those parts yet?

'Jo,' I whispered again, 'where are we?'

'What do you mean?' she whispered back terrified, 'You're lying in the tent in your fucking pants, where do you think?'

'I'm trying to picture that flyer of Romania,' I answered quietly.

The unwelcome creature began to disturb rubbish in front of our tent.

'We're in Transylvania,' she replied, staring straight ahead to the entrance. It seemed like an odd moment to roll out the jokes, and I was far too scared to see any comedy. I turned to look at Jodie and hoped for a more sensible answer.

'No, seriously, where are we?' I asked again, I knew Transylvania wasn't a real place and she really needed to work on her timing.

'Tom, we're in Transylvania, it's here in Romania.'

Now that *was* funny, she didn't appear to be joking.

A crisp packet now rustled a few inches from our tent flap.

Shit! Why did all these people have to leave their rubbish? I'm about to be eaten in my pants, this is such a crap way to die!

As I lay there sweating, I began to envisage the predictable international news headlines. Two more stupid English travellers die out in the real world. Would anyone even sympathise with us? Not likely, they even gave out awards for that kind of thing. I think it's called Darwinism.

Anyway, why was there so much rubbish?

It seemed a bit unusual seeing how clean most of the country had been. What if all these picnics had been disturbed by someone, or something? Did vampires eat crisps? I had no idea. I had never noticed vampires snacking in-between meals. No, this had to be an animal, we could still hear it snuffling away, it could be a bear, or maybe a wolf.

A wolf in Transylvania? Oh God! Our situation wasn't getting any better at all.

'Please let it be a bear,' I whispered over and over again, realising the irony of praying for a bear to be outside our tent.

'Jo,' I whispered, possibly for the last time, 'what were we thinking?'

CHAPTER 1
BIG DECISIONS, TINY COMMITMENTS

'So Tom, please tell us,' the Romanian broadcaster joked a few days later in Bucharest, 'how *did* you persuade Jodie to come with you on this bike ride?'

I laughed nervously and turned to Jodie. I was definitely within elbow distance and her patience with this question was now getting thinner than the crotch of my primary pants. I specify 'Primary Pants' as my other pair, 'Pants B' were in a much more stable condition - usually saved only for radio interviews and for wearing while I washed my 'Primary Pants'.

At first it had been difficult to adjust to life on the road, especially with the new pants schedule. Back in London I would change my pants two, maybe three times a week, but now found the rotation had reduced to once every two or three countries.

Reading other touring accounts the advice had been consistent, mostly suggesting a short practice cycle to iron out your equipment selections. Fully loaded, we had followed instructions, pedalling off for a wobbly five day practice, then returning to sort our equipment into the three advised piles;

1) Items that we used all the time
2) Items that we used sometimes
3) Items that we never used

The voices of experience encouraged us to be ruthless and discard the last *two* of these piles. It sounded obscene but when really forced to question our selection, we made some rather alarming discoveries. I learned that life could go on without a wind up radio, that deodorant didn't make you a better cyclist, and that carrying a 10 kg first aid kit was probably more likely to cause an accident. Basically speaking, we were told to keep our equipment to a minimum, then halve it again.

Personally, I had decided that two pairs of pants were necessary, and that if this was halved, that the number in our relationship might also follow suit. One inspirational English adventurer and cyclist, Alastair Humphreys, had pedalled for four years around the globe carrying not three pairs of socks, but literally just three socks. Two socks were for wearing as he washed the third, before cleverly integrating it back into his cyclic sock rota. The spare sock would rarely remain idle, either being used to filter out segments from his homebrew 'bicycle wine', or pulled over his head during bank raids necessary to fund his ever continuing journey.

3

'Oh you know, she's a good girl, she does most things I tell her,' I joked again, wearing my metaphorical skirt under the table. Jodie gave me a sharp glare and I realised that this response had now exceeded its use by date.

The real inspiration however was a little too coincidental and ill-conceived for radio, emerging instead from reading a Cross-Atlantic rowing story called 'The Crossing', a book which had sat beside my bed for a year.

It was in a Lincoln bookshop, two years previously, that I had decided to take a leap of faith and purchase a book for *my* side of the bed. This particular bookshop had a quaint, unassuming entrance with an almost inconspicuous village doorway, but more relevantly to me it was located at the top of a very steep hill.

Most visitors would be forgiven for not noticing it, but after walking up the very steep hill I was now moving so slowly that the artist sitting outside included me in his charcoal sketch. Jodie, my book devouring girlfriend, didn't need a second invitation and was through the door like a little white rabbit into a burrow. Inside, she scampered off while I enjoyed a good long rest in a very comfortable leather chair. Eventually, becoming hungry for a pub lunch I stood up and began the search for Jodie.

It was an unusual shaped shop, the aisles were narrow and the shelves were crammed with seemingly random authors and topics. Despite its small appearance, the shop soon became a thick maze of literature, as I tried to negotiate my way through the crazy paperback corridors.

With visibility now reduced to just a few metres, I explored deep into the aisles before facing a standoff with a customer trying to move in the other direction. Trying to pass side by side in such circumstances would be seen, by many, as entirely socially unacceptable. There would certainly be contact made in squeezing through, and it was odds on that the groin or buttock region would be involved. Very simply, in this situation only one could prevail, the other would have to reverse all the way back to 'Autobiographies' and start again.

Continuing a life of pitiful weakness, I backed down, reversing to the till, then sloping off and waiting for Jodie in the 'Kids and Travel' corner. In hindsight, I believe that these were two independent sections, but at the time I did consider the problems that such a combination could cause.

Finding myself once again sitting down, surrounded by books and with no sight of the white rabbit, I finally conceded. I was such a lazy reader that even the thought sent me to sleep, but here I was in a fantastic book shop and I was flicking through at a kids book of flags - it was time to grow up. I looked up at a book shelf and spotted an intriguing title: 'The Crossing - Conquering the Atlantic in the World's Toughest Rowing Race'.

'That'll do!' I thought to myself, firstly because I loved indoor rowing, and secondly because it was only £3 and I could reach it from my chair. After reading the first chapter I decided to buy the book, feeling remarkably grown up for doing so, it wasn't the first time I had spent £3 in a bookshop, but it *was* the first time I had bought a book from one. Normally, I would head upstairs to buy Jodie a skinny latté while she skimmed through novels about detectives, chimney sweeps and neurotic killers in pre-Victorian England - her questionable genre of choice.

Jodie left the shop with a pile of books but predictably, when we returned from our Lincoln break, I placed my solitary purchase next to the bed where it lay undisturbed for months, as piles of magazines collected on top.

At work, a long and drawn out redundancy situation was finally baring its teeth, and suddenly I found myself with two weeks of gardening leave in our flat. The herb pots on the small paved roof were long dead and as such, my gardening responsibilities had subsequently been revoked. It was time to look for alternative entertainment - I decided to book a scuba diving holiday in Gozo.

I searched the apartment for a token 'holiday' book to take with me, realising that I would need something to do while she read her seventeen novels about dead chimney sweeps. I was faced with two choices, 'The Crossing', my Lincoln purchase, or '101 Funny Anecdotes from the Daily Mail'. To my own surprise I rather maturely opted for the former.

We sat on our balcony overlooking the sea in Gozo, sipping Maltese wine and reading the parallel but diverse accounts of the two rowers. James Cracknell, the Olympic Gold medallist and ever present professional striving for victory, with Ben Fogle, the wife of the partnership, trying to live up to James' expectations, then trying even harder to maintain peace when he couldn't.

The pair endured relentless shifts of two hours on, two hours off, suffering storms, a capsize, equipment failure, but aside from James' blistered bottom, all their problems had been overcome. I hadn't even finished the book but I was inspired - all I needed was to find my own Olympic champion rowing partner and raise £70,000 to hire the boat and equipment. Sadly, after a surprisingly short discussion with Jodie, it emerged that my dream would be quite short lived.

'If you're looking for a ridiculous challenge,' she said, 'why don't you consider one that involves the girlfriend you're having this ridiculous discussion with?'

I sensed that rowing was already out of the question, but with a second bottle of the local wine now open she *reminded* me of her own ideas for a challenge. Having sat quietly, while she recalled accounts of people who had cycled the world, travelling cheaply and living in a tent, I began to question the definition of 'remind'.

Over the first bottle we had agreed to start a new life in Australia, but by the third we now seemed to be entertaining the concept of pedalling there. Whatever the truth, the next morning I took down the four empty wine bottles, and when I got back Jodie was humming 'Swing Low, Sweet Chariot' with a huge grin on her face.

*   *   *   *   *

Most boys love sport, in my case rugby and cricket, but oddly it equally seems that most girls love writing lists. One morning, the stars aligned, and as I lay on the couch throwing a rugby ball, Jodie grabbed a pencil and wrote a list of jobs. At this stage it was a fairly generic list, and held open the possibility that some items may require further discussion.

Cycling To The Rugby World Cup
Item 1:   Choose route
Item 2:   Buy bicycles, buy things to survive

I looked at the list and congratulated her, it seemed to cover everything. I still clung to the hope that she would lose the list and forget about her idea, but if discussing it made her feel better then I was willing to listen. Worryingly, the discussions developed and it quickly emerged that further items would need to be addressed. The list started to evolve.

Cycling To The Rugby World Cup
Item 1:   Choose route
Item 2a: Research bicycles and things to survive
Item 2b: Buy from 2a

The finer details of Item 2 were now becoming a little overwhelming, and I really wasn't sure whether this trip was for me after all. Granted, making rash decisions had always been one of my fortés, but this level of meticulous planning seemed to be jeopardising everything I believed in.

Rather than fight the system, I decided to keep a low profile and allow Jodie a couple of months to research everything from bike tyres to 'sporks', and saddles to stoves. Considering the stretch between England and Australia was also a bit of a mystery to me, I handed over 'Item 1', waiting for something to crop up that was more suiting to my abilities.

'What about a website?' I suggested, as Jodie scribbled it on the list.

Cycling To The Rugby World Cup
Item 1:   Choose route
Item 2a: Research bicycles and things to survive
Item 2b: Buy from 2a
Item 3:   Get website

After six long years of personal debt I had finally finished paying off my failed website franchise, so armed with my rich experience I rushed off to tackle my item.

Minutes later we had a website and I had achieved 'Item 3'. I hurried back to show her my achievement, Jodie *would* be pleased.

'Where is it?' she asked, scanning the page.

'That *is* it!' I remarked.

'Who are those people?' she continued, pointing to a family throwing a beach ball.

It was a fair question under the circumstances, they were not directly relevant to our journey, nor was the Latin text that filled the narrative beneath - these had come with the website template I had chosen.

'Okay, I will update the list of jobs,' I added, scribbling as I spoke.

Cycling To The Rugby World Cup
Item 1:   Choose route
Item 2a: Research bicycles and things to survive
Item 2b: Buy from 2a
Item 3a: Get website
Item 3b: Get website name, give website content

Two months later and a very rough plan had begun to form. Jodie had now mapped out a potential route from Twickenham Stadium in London, to Eden Park in Auckland. She unearthed a selection of maps and walked me through the path - even for me this now sounded pretty exciting.

Using her finger, we wove our way through Eastern Europe, squeezed through Turkey into Asia, continued through Iran and Pakistan, before cutting across China, down into South East Asia. Within minutes I was ferry hopping across Indonesia, presumably swimming to Darwin, before dashing down the East coast of Australia in time for a flight to New Zealand. What a holiday!

After the initial jubilation, there was one thing nagging at my mind, something that Jodie had clearly not considered - didn't it seem quite a long way? Jodie had made me join her for a 100 km charity walk the year before, and I had got bored 110 times - once after each kilometre, and once more each time a food break had finished. If I was going to motivate myself along 28,000 km, I needed something *seriously* distracting to work on.

I added something that I didn't mind spending my time doing.

<u>Cycling To The Rugby World Cup</u>
Item 1:   Choose route
Item 2a: Research bicycles and things to survive
Item 2b: Buy from 2a
Item 3a: Get website
Item 3b: Get website name, give website content
Item 4:   Explore rugby across the world

In our final weeks in London, we both committed ourselves to breaching as many work policies on personal e-mail as we could. Together we began sending messages to the rugby world, from small rugby communities in Laos all the way up to the IRB. We informed everybody we could think of about our journey, even the inspiration himself, Ben Fogle.

```
From: 'Jodie and Tom'
To: 'Ben Fogle'


'Dear Ben,


Jodie and I read your rowing book last year and we
want to say a big well done indeed. We also want to
say thank you for inspiring us on our own journey.
Now we are going to cycle 28,000 km across the world
to explore rugby.
```

Well done and keep up the good work at the zoo.

Tom and Jodie'

* * * * *

Item 5:   Budget

'Tom, there's one thing we haven't talked about,' Jodie said to me.

My mind went blank. *Dear God what was it?* We had enjoyed so many diverse topics over the years I really thought we'd covered them all. Would either of my answers be enough this time? 'I'm just looking after them for someone!' or 'I swear, it was like that when I found it!'

'How much have you saved for the trip?' she enquired carefully.

'Oh that, of course!' I replied, relieved that we'd finally talked about *everything*. I referred to my bank balance.

'About £3,000,' I proudly announced. This was genuine pride, in the ten years I had slaved away in the city, this was the highest my bank balance had ever reached. For years, all I could do was watch the large negative numbers get gradually smaller.

'£3,000, that's great honey. Have you already put money aside for your bike and equipment?' she asked, almost rhetorically.

'Not aside as such,' I explained to her. 'At this point I thought it'd be safer all together.'

I had stayed clear from 'Item 1' and 'Item 2' believing that I could pick up a load of cheap gear from eBay just before getting on the road. As long as it had remained out of my sight, it had stayed a long way out of my mind, but that was all about to change.

'So anyway, how much do you think it will cost us?' I queried, trying to act casual.

'You can probably get a decent bike for £1,000,' Jodie suggested, 'and I've already bought most of our equipment off eBay, it came to about £500 each.'

I tried to half laugh it off, half scoff in defiance, but trying not to display too much arrogance I now appeared to have paralysed my vocal chords, letting out a feeble whine.

'Are you okay?' Jodie asked, with genuine concern.

'Yes, I'm fine,' I rallied, 'it's just that you said that the bike will cost £1,000. I'll get it much cheaper than that second hand, don't you worry!' hoping my confidence in the matter would appease her.

'So, err, what sort of bike do I need then?'

'I'm glad you asked,' she answered, almost in anticipation.

Jodie continued to treat me to a lesson in bicycle touring, showing me the results of her extensive research. Double-butted chromoly steel frames, Brooks leather saddles, Schwalbe Marathon tyres, choices of bars, brakes, gears, chains and racks. Even the wheel sizes seemed important, apparently I needed to choose a size common throughout Asia as well as Europe. I stopped listening at spokes, this was getting far too much.

It seemed I had a lot to learn, but still I was confident I could use my internet skills and source whatever I needed for £500. I played around, put in some bids, sent some enquiries and waited patiently. Two weeks later, I handed over my £1,000 to the lovely staff down at Brixton Cycles. To my surprise, Jodie didn't say a word, she didn't need to.

The spending was finally complete, and a quick and painful review of the bank account saw my life savings standing at £1,500. Even to the untrained eye this might seem a tad short for such a long vacation, but secretly I was still enjoying the novelty of having such a chunky pool of cash.

'Perhaps a little under what I had targeted!' I offered as positively as one could in the situation, 'But Asia will be cheap,' I added, having performed absolutely no research on the matter.

'Okay, so I will lend you some money and we can set our budget at £6,000?' she replied to me calmly, and in complete control.

'Woo there missy! I'm not borrowing any more money,' I was clearly on the back foot. 'There is no way I am going to do this and get back in debt! I will just have to make it stretch.'

It did seem to be a ridiculous budget for such a long journey, and on several occasions Jodie attempted initiating an adult conversation to discuss it. Thankfully, with a strong track record in immaturity, I managed to hold strong and block her attempts with childish noises. In the end, stubbornness prevailed, and she reluctantly agreed. We had our shared budget, £3,000 for 540 days on the road. If Jamie Oliver could 'feed a family of four for a fiver' what sort of feast could I expect for nearly six quid!

After only three short weeks I logged on to find a message back from Ben Fogle's team.

From: 'Ben Fogle'
To: 'Jodie and Tom'

'Dear Tom and Jodie,

We passed on your message, Ben says 'Good luck!'

Regards, Dianne (Personal Assistant)'

Ah, thanks Ben!

CHAPTER 2
A HOOLIGAN'S GAME

In all my ten years of playing senior rugby I have never accepted why so many people choose to play soccer over rugby. I knew why they did, I just didn't accept it. There were many things I didn't accept, like why girls sometimes held you to your word when you'd had a few drinks. Taking the English as an example, why did we play so much soccer when we clearly struggled so much at the international level?

Soccer is 'the working man's' game, the 'beautiful game' and rugby is a sport for those too fat to play the beautiful game, or for those born into so much wealth they never need to work. Although probably true, thankfully this stigma has slowly disintegrated since the introduction of professionalism, but still, in a country whose side has competed in three Rugby World Cup finals already, I doubt that the average Englishman would answer appropriately when asked where you might find a hooker.

I hoped that out there in the unknown we would find cultures that *had* embraced the game, and if not, maybe we could do our bit to help force it on them.

Although we knew what we wanted to achieve, many people encouraged us to carry a symbol of our journey, something more tangible than just a story or a blog. It needed to be something that the rugby world could somehow hold and interact with, and therefore something that could literally be delivered to the Rugby World Cup as a unified global message from the community.

'What about a rugby ball?' I suggested to Jodie.

'It's an idea,' replied Jodie, letting me know politely that it was not a particularly good idea. 'Besides, we are already carrying a rugby ball. We need something a bit more interesting.'

I was out of ideas, and so we put an e-mail out to all of our friends and contacts:

'SUBJECT: Help! Interesting ideas requested'

Luckily for us, on our list was an ideas man, Tom Griffiths, the founder of 'Gapyear.com'. Only minutes later we had a response. 'Hi guys, there are a thousand ideas, you are only limited by your own imagination.'

'Wow, what a positive start!' I said to myself, it was certainly encouraging to know that such a large and specific number of ideas were in existence. Perhaps though, by mistake or just irony, he had then chosen to remind me why I probably wouldn't access any of these ideas. In just a few words, we appeared to have come full circle. But wait, there was more!

'This is an old fashioned journey, and you are carrying a message to the Rugby World Cup. How did messages used to be carried?'

I don't know Tom. Pigeon? How did he expect us to feed ourselves and a pigeon on six quid a day?

'Written on a scroll!' he answered on the next line.

'A scroll?' I considered with one raised eyebrow. 'Now why didn't I think of that!'

I realised fairly quickly that the bottom had long since fallen out of the scroll market, having been replaced first by letters in bottles, then e-mails, then more recently *'tweets'*. The scroll was a good idea though and because it was so obviously old, people might not suggest that we could have used a more updated method. It'd probably be better received if we galloped up to Eden Park on a white horse, but all things considered cycling half way across the world on six pounds a day, I think they'd have to be grateful for a bit of rolled up parchment.

Once Jodie's dad had got to work with some curtain rail, drawer handles, varnish and a cut of painting canvas we were set to go. I was impressed, it almost seemed a shame to write on it.

'It needs a name,' I said to Jodie, 'something representative of the global rugby community, as well as the Rugby World Cup.'

'Okay good, that's a start. Well, what's the general theme of the Rugby World Cup?' she asked, teasing out some suggestions.

'It's the World in Union,' I announced triumphantly, 'but what I want to do is get a message out there that the whole world is standing together as one community.'

'Right, well what's another word for a group of people standing together with a common purpose?' she asked, putting the kettle on in case the process took longer than she was hoping.

I gave it some thought.

'A rally?' I shouted. 'No, a protest!'

'You think the best way to promote rugby is to carry a message of protest?' Jodie poured some water into the teapot.

I pondered names over and over again, maybe I'd go back and check with Tom, he was the ideas man.

'No, I'm sure there'll be something better out there,' I assured her, 'something that shows the world standing together, in union.'

'We'll if you're sure!' she concluded and brought me a cup of tea.

'Jo! I have it!'

'Is it the *World in Union* scroll?' she asked, without looking up from her newspaper.

'How did you know?'

*   *   *   *   *

'Be ambitious!' Tom replied, once we'd updated him on the scroll progress. 'Don't aim low and certainly don't *ever* settle for second best. If you are going to do this, do it properly and go right to the top. I tell you what, if you manage to get a Head of State on there, I'll buy you both a curry.'

With our new incentive and buoyed by Tom's relentless positivity we decided to get a few squiggles on the 'World in Union' scroll before we began.

'Right, England captain to start us off!' I proudly announced, as if the job was already done, 'Then the Queen.'

'Let's just start with the England captain Tom. We're leaving next Saturday and I imagine getting through to Buckingham Palace might take a bit longer.'

'Fine, buy your own curry then.' I replied, a little disappointed.

Clearly not the fan I thought myself to be, I wasn't entirely sure who the current England captain actually was. Since the 2007 Rugby World Cup, the England captaincy had changed hands more times than a naughty magazine on a school bus. There had been four separate captains during the six week tournament alone, and subsequently it had been handed to Phil Vickery, Martin Corry, Lewis Moody and Steve Borthwick depending on who was fit and available.

A quick Google search confirmed that Steve Borthwick was indeed the current captain, although he was presently injured and unavailable for selection. Good for us, because the Saracens training ground in St Albans was only a short train ride away. I wrote the Saracens team an e-mail and to our surprise Simon, their Media Manager, wrote back and invited us down to a training session the following week.

Simon welcomed us into the clubhouse as the squad came in from their morning training session. While the rest of the guys shovelled down huge bowls of pasta, the Saracens and England captain, Steve Borthwick, came to join us at a separate table, so too did Wales and British & Irish Lions legend, Michael Owen.

These two giants had not only played international rugby but had also captained their country to a Six Nations title, Michael even to a Grand Slam in 2005. To suddenly be sat beside them was so exciting that it almost helped clear the monstrous hangovers from the previous night. As Steve kicked off the 'World in Union' scroll signing he asked if we'd also like some other national signatures.

14

Over came Fijian star and former Fiji captain Mosese Raulini to add his name. *Three national captains already!* I was beginning to wonder whether Queen Elizabeth would have any space left to sign.

'Jacques! Over here will you,' called Simon, before a large and curly looking 'Cousin It' made his way across the floor. Underneath the mop of hair, avoiding attention was Jacques Burger, national captain of Namibia - now our fourth national captain in as many minutes.

'What's going on here guys?' Chris Wyles, the USA 7s captain said, as he popped over to check out the commotion.

'Sign their scroll Chris!' Jacques said, 'They're doing something for charity. What are you doing again?'

'We're cycling to the Rugby World Cup!' Jodie told him again.

'No way! That's awesome!' Jacques said, remembering the previous minute's chat.

Chris leaned over the table and grabbed the pen, but before putting pen to parchment he paused in contemplation, as they had all done. Perhaps the historical significance of using a scroll had somehow made this signature *more* meaningful than any of the thousands of autographs they'd given over the years. Maybe one day this scroll would be treasured like the Dead Sea Scrolls and other famous parchments like the United States Declaration of Independence.

'Listen, really, the best of luck with your trip.' Chris said as he handed the pen to the next curious player.

'Sorry, just national captains for the moment please,' Simon explained to the deflated unidentifiable youngster.

Overwhelmed by the success of our visit, we prepared to roll up our precious scroll when a stocky looking guy made his way across the room.

'That's Cobus Visagie!' Simon said, 'I'd get Cobus to sign it if I was you.'

'Great, was he national captain too? I replied.

'Er no, but he's played tight head for South Africa, the Barbarians and the World XV and I wouldn't want to be you if he finds out you *didn't* ask him!'

We left the Saracens' clubhouse with a bicycle pannier safely housing the six national signatures from the rain. I suddenly reflected on how small I had felt standing next to Michael Owen. I bet nobody has ever wondered why *he* started playing rugby - these boys had literally never stopped growing!

Being a fairly average performer in even the lowest of English leagues, people rarely felt the need to ask why I started playing. It's usually assumed that I was tricked into it, and like most youngsters in the game, this was a largely accurate assumption. Okay, so an entirely accurate one. Despite this, after ten years in the game I have only shown glimpses of improvement and therefore I feel that I should justify my sporting decision.

'If you're so rubbish, why *did* you play rugby?' Jodie just asked, reading over my shoulder. Well, thank you Jodie, allow me to explain.

I was never interested in rugby as a boy, to put it simply, it was far too rough. People would say that rugby was a hooligan's game, played by gentlemen, and that it would separate the men from the mice. It was, and it certainly did, and as such, I would spend my Saturday mornings scratching around the field hiding from contact, before scurrying back to my parent's car.

Unfortunately for me, I was attending a traditional all boys grammar school and 'soccer' was not on the school menu. Your dishes were simple, rugby (meat course) or athletics (vegetarian). Personally athletics sounded pretty good to me, I fancied the javelin, maybe a bit of high jump, maybe even an indoor discipline that took us over to the girl's gymnasium.

I was twelve years old, and on day one, we stood on the sports field and were presented with our choices. I like to think, that of the 120 boys in my year, at least 119 of them were thinking the same as me. My voice hadn't yet broken and the guy at the end of the line was sprouting a beard. We didn't need a sport to separate the men from the mice, we could separate ourselves thanks very much. I watched as the boys tentatively shuffled between rugby and athletics groups until our rugby teacher played his ace.

The first twenty boys to compile the athletics group were dispatched indefinitely around the grass field for what was described as 'cross country practice'. The subsequent rugby subscription was unprecedented and suddenly our coach had a full six teams.

So there I stood, a pipe cleaner of a boy, held together by a pair of cotton hot pants, and a rugby shirt made from 3% polyester, 97% itchy crap. I was now officially a rugby player, although like most boys, I still had no idea of the rules.

Thankfully for me I was a half decent footballer, and our coach decided I could be a 'fly half'. Today the position has been made glamorous by the likes of Johnny Wilkinson, Carlos Spencer and Daniel Carter, but at school it felt like an entirely different game. Like most school fly halves, I quickly identified the opportunity to kick at *every* possession, it was 'Plan A' in a fly halves' armoury of self-preservation. A variant on 'Plan A' was offloading a hospital pass to anyone wearing the same school jersey.

This strategy got me through four years of schoolboy rugby, notching up numerous undeserved points in conversion kicks along the way. I managed to sneak through largely without question, though most Saturdays I would have to explain to my mum why my brave tackling friend Ben had a black eye and split lip, and how even my knees were still clean. I didn't have an answer that I was proud of so I simply argued that a teenager shouldn't have to justify his or her own cleanliness.

As the years passed, my fellow classmates grew stronger and gradually more hairy. Tragically, my puberty had been put on ice and my strength was now becoming inversely proportional to my height. I was fast approaching 6 foot and weighed in only slightly heavier than my pet guinea pig. By this point, I had been gently demoted to the 'B team' where I could put my kicking to even more frequent use. Despite the lower competition, my tackling continued to degenerate, and soon I was compared to one of those turnstiles you find at the local supermarket - by my own mother. It was time to quit and face the cross country music.

At the tender age of fifteen, I hung up my boots and spent my remaining school years dodging PE classes, playing snooker with Ben. Ben's promising rugby career had been cut short early, not from rugby, but from a pane of glass he had collided with in a game of 'British Bulldog'. I still can't understand why they banned that game.

In 1999, I went on my first cricket tour to the Isle of Wight. Many of my team mates played both cricket and rugby, and naturally it didn't take long before inquests were made into my winter activities. I had recently finished playing youth football and was weighing up the option to pursue the aggravation of adult leagues. Having watched my final season at youth level disrupted by whinging parents, I was adamant I wanted something else.

'There's no pressure,' Jake would say, 'just come down to training at Footscray and see if you like it.'

Jake Cakebread was a fine specimen of a man, physically intimidating, and with a stare that could cut you in half. A fireman, national swimmer, water polo player and county rugby player, he was a man not born, but welded together from pieces of iron. Despite being a caring family man and grandfather, he bore a fiery moustache, had hands like shovels and shoulders like a grizzly bear. Even affectionately, I would describe him as a cross between Arnold Schwarzenegger in 'Kindergarten Cop' and Daniel Day Lewis in 'Gangs of New York'. He was certainly not a walking advert for people like me to start playing rugby, yet his son, Neil, had become a close friend and the whole family had already taken me under their protective wing. I felt comfortable in my new surroundings and wanted to spend more time with these people, but rugby? No thanks.

Another man, John Chandler, had also asked the same question. It was like watching a party of fishermen casting their lines, sitting patiently until they had you hooked. I assured them that I was the one fish in the sea that would die of hunger before playing rugby and they politely left it at that, or so I thought. The next morning John found the island sports shop and bought a pair of rugby shorts clearly 16 sizes too small for himself. As I padded up in the changing room, he revealed his purchase, casually tossed them onto my bag and informed me that training was Tuesday night.

'You only have to come for one session,' he added innocently, 'then you can decide for yourself.'

I searched for a way out, surely there had to be one. I was now almost a grown up, had I not left behind the days of bullying and peer pressure?

'John doesn't even reach into his pocket for his own beer!' Jake joked. 'He must really want you to play.'

I didn't want to offend John so I packed the shorts away. It was *only* the one training session after all.

I never looked back.

CHAPTER 3
PUTTING ON A BRAVE FACE

```
From: 'Eduard Krutzner'
To: 'Jodie and Tom'


'Dear Jodie and Tom,


I have received you e-mail about your wonderful
bicycle and rugby adventure. I have 75 years in
April and have played rugby in Czech Republic since
1956 and have many rugby friends across the world. I
welcome to you my house near Praga and show to you
my tie collection. I am looking forward to meet you
in our country.


My best rugby regards, Eduard Krutzner Snr'
```

It was our only response, but with that e-mail we finally knew which direction we would be turning out of Calais.

*　　*　　*　　*　　*

We awoke at 6 a.m. on the morning of May 1st 2010 at a friend's flat in Putney. Will King came into the front room to wish us a final good luck before departing early for his rowing training.

'You guys look after each other, and be careful,' he said as we stood embraced in a group hug. 'I'll see you in Brisbane!'

For the sake of masculinity I have left out the numerous 'I love you guys!' and 'I love you too Wills' but in truth, this goodbye had suddenly hit a nerve. I was becoming a little choked by the occasion. Was I really beginning to question leaving behind such good friends, or should I just ask Will to loosen his arm from my neck?

As he shut the front door we were left alone. Normally not shy of a few words, we both struggled to put together a sentence, each trying to assure the other that all was in hand. Thankfully, we only had a short time to pack the last of our panniers before two friends arrived on bicycles to escort us to Twickenham Stadium. If not for Ange and Toby, we may well have been engulfed by that morning's silence.

Moments after arriving at the Golden Lion gate we were met by several of our closest friends, some who had travelled for several hours just to wish us well. As the clock ticked, we tried our best to put on brave faces, but our nerves must have been clear to all. We didn't even know where we would be sleeping that night, and with a £6 a day budget, it wouldn't even be a campsite let alone the Rainham Travelodge.

We needed a coffee, perhaps something stronger, so we walked over to the food and drink vendors. At the first stall we were greeted by two women dressed head to toe in authentic 1940s costume. I say authentic but in hindsight it just looked old fashioned, and my knowledge of housewife fashion in the early 20th century has faded with time. The pair were raising money for 'Help the Heroes' by selling war ration style boxes of tea, in line with the military rugby match kicking off next door.

''Ello there my luv!' one greeted me in her best cockney accent. 'Wanna cuppa tea do you?'

'Err coffee actually,' I muttered, a little taken aback by the surreality of my last brew in the UK.

'Oh no luv. We only do tea 'ere. You wanna cuppa tea?'

With the best of intentions she was now beginning to scare me. Perhaps tea women stared blankly a lot in the 1940s but if authenticity really was in question, I think she should have stopped at the costume.

'I'm really just looking for a coffee right now?' I answered, feeling that she didn't particularly care about my caffeine requirements. 'I'll just go next door.'

'Only £3 a box, supporting Help for Heroes!' I heard, as I marched away with my head down.

As we walked back to the Golden Lion gate, coffees in hand, Jodie looked at me, 'How much were our coffees then?'

I counted the change from our five pound note - £1.10.

'£3.90,' I replied, knowing exactly what this implied about the next 540 days.

She knew it too, and as we sipped our coffees in silence we both hoped that somehow things would just work themselves out. Now back with our friends we waited for 11 a.m. and with it, our cue to start the 28,000 km. The conversation was minimal, but at this point their company alone was our best medicine.

At 11 a.m. on the dot, the gates opened and the RFU President, John Owens, came to help us turn the confused dream into reality. Slowly and a little wobbly, we cycled away from the Golden Lion Gate at Twickenham Stadium surrounded by 50,009 cheering rugby fans. Nine of these fans had come *specifically* to wave us off, while we assume the other 50,000 had turned up just to watch the Army vs Navy match.

On their swift road bikes, it didn't take Ange and Toby long to catch us again, and after a little pedalling and conversation I called for everyone to pull over.

'What's wrong?' Jodie asked, 'Is your bike okay?'

'Yep, it's just, erm, well,' I pointed to the bike computer. In all the excitement of the morning, I had forgotten to start the bike computer at the stadium.

'I'll start it from here,' I said, 'we'll just add a couple of kilometres on at the end!'

We had expected the voyage to present us with problems; torrential rain, punctures, fatigue, depression, poor road signs and Neanderthal-like humans yelling incomprehensible garbage at us, but we *had* hoped to get past Dover before experiencing them *all*.

*   *   *   *   *

Perhaps it was the curry, the wine, or just the knowledge that there would be no more hotels, but neither of us slept much that night. When the alarm went off at 6 a.m. we had been staring at the ceiling for many hours, wondering what lay ahead for us in the unknown. We pulled open the curtains to see the Dover rain still hammering down outside. It was not in the least bit inviting and a stark reminder for what might come.

We sloped downstairs to meet Jodie's dad, Ian, for breakfast. Jodie and mum, Pat, had said their goodbyes the previous evening, knowing that an early start and final moments together would be too much to handle the following morning.

Jodie struggled to stomach even a small bowl of muesli, while I, knowing that this was my final chance at a decent breakfast, ordered the full English, compliments of Ian. Conversation was very light and completely without purpose, much like at Twickenham Stadium when the uniqueness of the situation had stripped us of our familiar instincts and trails of thought.

Looking back on things now it's easy to reflect on those times, but in the midst of the situation the brain was unable to rationally comprehend such a barrage of feelings. Separation from friends and family is not a natural part of human or animal nature, why on earth would it be? Animals don't just wander off out of pure curiosity for the world, burning calories for 'fun' or leaving the protection of a safe environment. They would only do this in desperation to find food, or at a push, to avoid producing cross-eyed offspring. Even today, many towns around the world seem not to find *either* of these items a necessity and so it remains, separation is both an uncommon and bizarrely difficult concept to process.

The departure time came imminently closer, and as it did, the conversation became more and more strained. We all knew what was about to happen, and with this unspoken knowledge, we each grew gradually more nervous. There would be another unnecessary glance at the watch followed by a small sigh, 8:02 - a minute before it had read 8:01. The countdown had began, these were the final few minutes together ahead of an eighteen month journey that would leave us placed on the opposite side of the planet.

With breakfast stomached and the boarding time now arrived, we prepared for the final push. Ian began to run ahead through the rain, whilst we returned to our rooms to collect the bicycles and bags. We reconvened down by the ferry port and stood in the morning drizzle to say our final goodbyes.

Next Christmas, if not for the whole film, tune in for the final few minutes of ET - the Extra Terrestrial, it's probably the closest comparison I can draw to your attention. Over a very emotional final three and a half minutes together, Elliot and ET manage a pitiful eight words between them, you might otherwise have mistaken it for a silent movie.

The reality of our goodbye meant a similar complexity of conversation, but without the luminous finger and musical arrangement from John Williams (that was ET's luminous finger and not John Williams' by the way, to my knowledge all of John's are just regular fingers).

As we boarded the ferry to the unknown, we turned and waved to Ian, now stood alone on the docks, rain pouring down his cheeks and his eyes red from tears. His heart was crying out for Jodie to stay but I'm sure the tears were more in sympathy for the young man at her side.

Celtic Sea

North Sea

Mediterranean Sea

1. England
2. France
3. Belgium
4. Germany
5. CZ Republic
6. Austria
7. Slovakia
8. Hungary
9. Romania
10. Bulgaria
11. Turkey
12. Georgia

CHAPTER 4
A NO-BOOZE BOOZE CRUISE?

The ferry ride was fairy uninspiring, a handful of passengers looking to venture across to Calais despite the conditions, most in search of cheap alcoholic pleasures. Once upon a time I would have relished every minute of this little journey, instead I now paced around the seating deck as if I had just poured diesel into a petrol engine. We talked it through over and over again during that two hour crossing. I wanted a coffee but I couldn't afford one, I'd have to wait to set up the kettle on French shores. Jodie felt the same I was sure, but having pulled through an emotional morning already, it was taking all her strength of will to keep herself together.

I looked at our situation once again. We were trying to begin a rugby themed journey that would explore the sport all the way to the opposite end of the planet. We had one solitary lead, a seventy-five year old man with a tie collection somewhere in Prague. We didn't even have his address!

Even looking at the bare logistics, we were about to start an eighteen month, 28,000 km journey, without proper maps, without a phone and trying to jointly survive on £6 each day. It was fucking ridiculous and I became frustrated that nobody had tried to point that out to us. Then I remembered, they had - everyone had.

Maybe they were right all along. It sounded like an amazing adventure, but in the damning light of day it was now clearly evident that we had become too caught up in our own hype. Too many leaving parties, pre-cycle articles and a cushy four week ease-down from work, even a deceptively pleasant five day training ride. We'd talked about it for so long, that I'd started to think we'd *already* done the journey. I cast my thoughts back to a friend in London, his name was Layth.

Layth, had three passions in life, for ease we can just refer to them as A, B and C. Passion A was soccer, B was travelling the world, and C was his ever expanding family - his wife and three young children. As an avid supporter of Arsenal and England, he found that he was able to regularly indulge in A and B, but as C had grown, he'd noticed their quite rapid demise.

On occasions, he had attempted to achieve B by requesting permission from his wife to attend A. Although permission for a ninety minute activity was often granted, what usually landed him in trouble was the two day delay in getting home from the match in Buenos Aires - a portion of match detail that had traditionally slipped his mind.

Layth was a man that everyone wanted in their corner, whatever the occasion. He was a human pillar in the pub and an absolute commodity in the pub quiz. Not only was he a walking encyclopedia of sport, history and literature but a substantial unit of a man, who seemed not only to get smarter as he got older, but develop substantially bigger biceps too. It was fair to say that everyone wanted to be Layth's friend, but as the great man himself explained it wasn't always that easy for him to make room.

'No honestly guys,' he'd explain, having shared a drink with another Arsenal fan, 'he really is a nice bloke, but I've already got enough friends.'

It seemed the book was closed, and we realised what a huge privilege it was to be Layth's friend. I wondered, had I managed to squeeze in before the book shut, or had I stepped into a slot created by an irreparable disagreement? Not many people could say they had a friend called Layth, and under the current friend recruitment plan, it was unlikely that many more would get the chance. Layth's friendship soon became such a widely sought after asset that financial traders across the world started dealing in 'friendship options'. Layth now has friends he hasn't even met yet, and I myself have purchased a 'Layth-friendship future' in case we fall out after he reads this book.

He said many memorable things during our time in London, but one thing in particular, mainly to Tottenham Hotspur fans whenever they brought up the subject of Champions League qualification. It was a fairly damning statement;

'Boys! Do it, *then* talk about!'

I had talked about it, Jodie had talked about it, our friends had talked about it, but now that it boiled down to choosing a side of the Channel, it was the British side that had the most appeal. I felt completely out of my depth and overwhelmed by the challenge. We could turn around and go home couldn't we? Nobody would be disappointed in us, we'd be home with our friends the next day and with a bit of grovelling, we could probably walk back into our old jobs.

The captain came on the tannoy, the weather was clear in France, the sun was shining and we'd be pulling into port in thirty minutes. A strong wind was coming in from the northeast but otherwise conditions were fine.

'Come on, let's just do it and see what happens,' Jodie said, sensing my hesitation.

Despite the captain's warning, the battering we took from the freezing northeasterly wind was enough to remind us of the challenge that lay ahead. The moment we free wheeled down the ferry ramp, my admittedly feeble two day 'traveller's beard' was painfully whipped from my face.

Our better judgement said to follow signs towards the 'hypermache' and seek comfort amongst aisles of French cheeses and wines. Instead we ignored the instincts and fought on against a soaring headwind for 30 km. We made such slow progress that I immediately wondered whether 500 km a week was ever realistic.

Settling into our new life on the road was no easier in France than it had been in Kent. The cycling had been a little slower than expected, but it was as the sun began to set that reality once again slapped us with a wet one round the face. Where were we going to sleep that night?

Trying to remain hidden from view, we searched high and low for a protected spot, but after blindly exploring side roads and housing estates, we were soon prepared to take any spot at all. It was only when looking for an area to wild camp that we came to notice how much of the country was either fenced off as farmland, dense woodland or sold off for housing.

Eventually, the only thing we could find that first night was a patch of overgrown grass on the wrong side of a thicket of brambles. Together we laid down the bicycles and stamped down a path through the scratchy bush. Desperately trying not to tear the tyres or panniers, we took everything separately, making several trips back between the grass and the road. Physically and emotionally exhausted we trod down some grass and threw up the tent.

Houses around us had potential 'line of sight', a term we would use many times on our journey, but the laws of averages suggested that we wouldn't be disturbed by anyone that night. Despite this comfort of mind, our dinner was still a cold tin of baked beans for fear of giving off smoke signals from our petrol cooker.

As I flicked off dozens of tiny slugs from our tent, I thought back to the Saracens and wondered why I had not received a response from my e-mail to the Lille Metropolitan Rugby Club.

'Bonjour!' I had started, 'I hope you speak English...'

There had been no reply. Lille was the first main town on our route, and from our limited path through France it had represented our only shot at really *exploring* French rugby. For what it was worth, I had doubts whether our two day French cycle would throw up any revelations that a heavily scrutinised history of over one hundred years hadn't already. Nevertheless, we were going to be heading through the town, and while we were there, we would visit the ground and get some photos, at least then it might feel like the rugby project had started.

We arrived in Lille and tried to use the compass to plot a path to the southeastern suburbs. More difficult than it seemed without a proper map, we came unstuck a few times, often finding ourselves on the wrong side of a complex network of rail tracks. After eventually making it through to the right suburb, an old man squeaked past us on his bicycle. He couldn't have looked more French if he had been balancing a baguette on his beret. Now behind me, he murmured something in French.

'Tom!' Jodie called after me, 'That man just asked us if we wanted a coffee?'

'How do you know that?' I asked her. 'Ah yeah, I forgot, you speak French don't you! Tell him yes! Hang on, why didn't *you* write the e-mail to Lille Rugby Club…?'

Nevertheless, we gratefully accepted and so it became that on our very first morning on foreign turf, we had been welcomed in by a complete stranger. The kind man's name was Pierre, who had started his own online business selling second hand children's novels. He showed us around his house, gave us coffee and asked so many questions about our journey that I almost expected him to follow us out. Having gone from being on our own in the damp French air to sipping fine French coffee at his breakfast table, he had broken our panic, and we both had a chance to absorb what it was that we were trying to do. The challenge wasn't to pedal across the world, it was to open ourselves up and truly embrace it. Pierre's kindness that day set the tone for how great human beings can be.

Online book sales were slow that morning and so he found time in his morning schedule to guide us to the Lille Metropolitan Rugby Club. We said our goodbyes and strolled onto the first overseas pitch of the tour, but even today it's a little difficult to describe how we really felt about that moment. Part of us believed that this was just the very first step in a possibly monumental rugby tour, uncovering the very soul of the sport across the world, and helping to promote the game in places a ball has never reached before. The other part of me wondered how standing on an empty bit of grass was ever going to make a difference. It did make a difference however, mainly to a very aggravated grounds man, who had walked over 400 metres to come and kick us off. Jodie explained something about 'velo' and a 'coupe de monde', he wrinkled his nose like he'd trodden in something on the way over, grunted, threw an arm up in the air and stormed off. This was the French I was waiting for, little Pierre was nothing but a distraction.

*   *   *   *   *

We pedalled on from Lille, heading mostly east following signs towards the market town of Tournai. 'Tournai 8 km' the first sign read.

'Great nearly there Jo, let's stop there for some lunch. Celebrate a job well done.'

One kilometre further, the next sign read 'Tournai 9 km'.

'Hang on a minute, have we gone past it?' I asked.

'No, we shouldn't have, it still looks ahead of us on the map,' Jodie checked.

We carried on another kilometre further and the sign read 'Tournai 8km'.

'Okay,' I said, 'but surely we're another 2 km closer to Eden Park?'

Neither of us really knew. Maybe we were, maybe we weren't, or maybe on a bicycle the only real distance was the one you thought it was. Was it really even 28,000 km to Eden Park? Probably not exactly, but we would still use that number as a target and count down every kilometre pedalled along the way.

The next sign for 'Tournai 5 km' was followed by another sign for 'Tournai 5 km' and then another 'Tournai 5 km', each kilometre, for the remaining five kilometres. It soon became obvious that we had to completely ignore the distance markers, assuming that we were far, far away from the town, until we could *actually* see it.

That evening's camping was a lot more successful and we found privacy in some woods by a horse paddock. We fired the cooker up and enjoyed our first homemade meal. Jodie had always been a fantastic cook, and even under such rationed circumstances, she still managed to make the menu at least sound appetising. If I hadn't known better I might have ordered it in a restaurant!

'Smells lovely Jo,' I said, I was starving. 'What've we got?'

'We're having Italian style spaghetti, topped with diced French red tomatoes, flakes of Atlantic skipjack tuna, drizzled with dolphin friendly soy bean tuna oil. To be eaten with a spork!' she added with a flourish.

In case you've never been put in such a situation, a 'spork' is a flimsy plastic spoon with a forked end and a blunt serrated side used for a knife. It was designed by the same *complete plank** that brought us the solar powered torch and the flame resistant match.

Author's note: A *'complete plank'* by definition is someone who not only has a half-arsed idea, but actually takes the time to see them through, e.g. I once read about two complete planks who cycled between rugby clubs to get to the Rugby World Cup...

'Wow, who'd have thought?' I said, 'I was just expecting tuna spaghetti with half a tomato. You're spoiling me with …'

Jodie placed the dinner on my lap.

'Oh no, you're not spoiling me, this *is* tuna spaghetti with half a tomato.'

'Bon appetit!' she smiled, sucking up a piece of spaghetti.

CHAPTER 5
LES TROIS PHILIPPES

The next morning we resumed our journey and suddenly began to feel more positive about our chances. We had pedalled less than 400 km since Twickenham, but had already visited my first club, Footscray RFC in Kent, and an empty pitch at Lille. Not only that but we'd also been invited into a house. I was almost struggling to keep up with all the excitement.

In the morning sunshine, the little French towns looked quite magnificent. The cobbled streets made for crap cycling but we were happy just to push and soak up the journey. We stood in the middle of a square at Mons, taking in the stunning architecture and relaxing in the peaceful atmosphere, as a handful of people slowly made their way to work around us. The grand shadows of a clock tower and museum retreated back across the stonework and soon we were reclining on a bench absorbing the warmth.

'Hey guys!' came a voice from behind us. 'Where are you going?'

'Ah hello,' I opened my eyes, 'well, it's a bit of a long story really.'

'That's okay, I should have been at work twenty minutes ago, it doesn't really matter now!'

We introduced ourselves to our new friend Laurent, who was very complimentary about our journey and of our intentions to explore rugby.

'So you like rugby?' I asked him, a little surprised to hear so far to the northeast of the country. I hadn't noticed any clubs nearby in any of my searches.

'Yes, I do actually. It isn't very popular here though, I just like it because my friend at work plays.'

'No really?' I asked again, I was very intrigued. 'Who does he play for?'

'He plays for the national team,' Laurent replied, with a degree of pride. 'Do you want to come upstairs and meet him?'

'National team?' I said, 'Sorry, I think I've missed something here. How can your friend play for France *and* work in your office during the day?'

'But he plays for the Belgian national team of course?' Laurent laughed.

'Ah I see, but he works in France?' I was determined to get to the bottom of this.

'No,' he replied with admirable patience, 'he works here with me!'

'Okay, I give up,' I said, 'I don't know how the rugby works here.'

'Tom,' Jodie finally decided to speak up, 'I think Laurent is trying to tell us we are in Belgium already! We just didn't realise it!'

Laurent paused and absorbed our confusion, then laughed. 'You know that his club are playing in Brussels next weekend, it's the grand final, you should come!'

'Ah no way!' I exclaimed, overwhelmed by so much new information. 'We're meeting the rugby club in Liège in two days time. We have to keep going.'

'Oh well, no problems,' said Laurent, 'but hey, please stay in touch, I'm really interested to see how your travels go. Maybe one day I could also do such a trip!'

*   *   *   *   *

The weather was filthy as we pushed up the steep hill to Royal Liège Rugby Club. Worse still, we were early and nobody had come to open up the clubhouse. We tried to shelter under a grated set of stairs leading to the bar but it was about as effective as eating soup with a fork. Finally, a lady arrived and quickly changed our mood, opening up the clubhouse and an extra changing room so that we could have a well needed hot shower. It was our first wash since Dover.

Even though the weather was more fitting for a swimming lesson, the turnout was good and soon the bar was bustling with squad players from both the 1st and 2nd XVs. A broad shouldered prop, heavy set and thick with stubble, entered the room, blocking the entire doorway as he did so. He was dripping wet and clearly in a foul mood, probably due to being caught in the downpour outside. I watched him storm past me, throwing his bag onto the pile of others and made for the bar.

'I wouldn't want to get in his way Jo!' I said. 'He looks like he's about to punch someone.'

A second row saw his turbulent mate coming and put down his glass of juice to greet him. The two men came face to face, one with rain still pouring down his cheeks, clearly incensed at being caught outside without a raincoat. The room was filled with pre-training testosterone, and yet despite the circumstances, the two bruisers still paused for a delicate cheek to cheek kiss. This was very different from my experiences back home, I never got that close to my props.

While the boys went outside for training, the clubhouse lady cooked us up an omelette. We looked outside as raindrops thundered against the window and felt relieved to have a roof over our heads. If not for rugby, we would right now be searching for a place to hide in the middle of Liège, not an easy task.

After training we mixed with the players and coaching staff. They spoke enough English to hold a good conversation and were able to explain a bit about themselves, even that they were preparing for their own plate final the following weekend. Their star man was back in town, a fly-half who had moved across to France to train with the Montpellier U20s.

As beers were poured, someone passed round a set of Belgian rugby songbooks. This prompted an evoking rendition of the club song, followed by a whole hour of probable lewdness, all belted out in passionate French tongue. I had never seen such enthusiasm after a training session before, and wondered whether this was just a sign of things to come. I thought that us English were quite a passionate rugby community. We still sang songs at the club, but these guys would sing *before* they got drunk and weren't even ashamed of a little smooch in public.

After the show, and much spilled beer, I tried my luck with finding a representative for our scroll. This was our only scheduled rugby club in Belgium and I hoped that there would be a link back to someone with a big history in Belgium rugby. It emerged that there was not just one, but three, and they were all called Philippe.

The *'Trois Philippes'* were all former Belgian national players from varying eras and since retiring, they had all gone into coaching. In the haze of Belgian beer, it was very difficult to choose between them, so they insisted we continue the evening down at the karaoke bar in town, to find the true icon of Belgian rugby. With such generous hospitality, we ignored the 7 a.m. departure the next day, and accepted their invitation.

By midnight, all positive effects of rugby training had been thoroughly negated and we ourselves were contemplating some drunken cycling, at least until lunchtime when the hangover would sink in. The karaoke did nothing to separate our Belgian legends apart, and despite a late display of impromptu break dancing from the Belgian U20 coach, we decided to do the right thing. We'd spent a fantastic evening with the Royal Liège guys, and it had become evident that all three Philippes were integral to the sport in many ways, not least for being role models for the young players coming through the club and national structures. We got them all to sign our scroll.

Next morning, there was no time to lose. We'd done our very best in Belgium and had been rewarded for a week of cycling in the rain, but we were now just a few hours outside of Germany and we'd still not established a contact. We stood outside McDonalds and downloaded our e-mails on the free wifi, before sending another e-mail to the 'Deutscher Rugby-Verband' - the German Rugby Union. We were heading for Heidelberg, one of the two main rugby centres, and desperately hoped that someone would get back to us with a personal contact, or help us with an introduction. We had no idea when they would train or whether they would have a home or away match that weekend. Without this information, it was difficult to budget our next 550 km to arrive on the right day, and at the right hour.

Into Germany we went, and as we pedalled through each town we stopped by the McDonalds to check for a response. Although we were grateful for the opportunity to communicate without using our food budget, the smell of fries and cheeseburgers was mouth watering, and having to stand outside in the rain, sheltering the laptop with our coats over our heads, only reminded us of the extent of our sacrifices. Our budget was not enough even to justify a coffee on the road, let alone a 'Happy Meal'.

Then, to our delight, we received a positive response from the Chairman's secretary. Claus-Peter Bach, the Chairman himself, would like to meet us on Friday lunchtime for a chat, and would even open up the German Rugby Museum for a private tour. This was beyond our biggest hopes, but what an invitation. We'd pedal extra hard to get there on time, sod it, we'd get there Thursday night just to make sure!

*   *   *   *   *

'Where's Gilbert?' I shouted to Jodie in a panic.

Our Gilbert ball had gone from the back of my bike and was nowhere to be seen.

'I didn't see it fall,' explained Jodie, who had been riding in front of me for some twenty minutes. 'Try and think when you last saw him?'

'*Fuck!*' I shouted in frustration, 'I can't believe I've lost Gilbert. We were supposed to carry him across the world and I couldn't even get him across Germany!'

'*Gilbert!*' I wanted to cry out, and against all common sense I turned around and pedalled frantically searching for my fallen companion.

Jodie followed behind, concerned not just for the welfare of Gilbert, but that she'd stepped foot in a scene from 'Castaway'.

With no sign of the rugby ball anywhere, we continued to re-trace our route until finally we reached a train crossing.

'Maybe he fell off when I crossed over the tracks?' I suggested in desperation.

'Look Tom, I know you want to find our ball, and I *know* that you'll hate me for saying this, but we've already cycled seven kilometres back on ourselves. We're going to have to make a decision on it soon.'

'If we don't find Gilbert then it's as good as over isn't it, we've failed already!'

'Don't you think you're exaggerating just a little bit?' she asked.

'Our aim was to carry a ball across the world and explore the sport Jo. *Half* of the mission has gone already!'

'Okay, come on, let's have a quick look, if it fell off here it can't have... Look, there it is!' she said, pointing to a patch of grass at the side of the railway line.

'Gilbert!' I shouted with relief. I lay down my bike and ran to collect him. He was a bit wet from the long grass but otherwise seemed unfazed.

'I'm not letting you out of my sight again,' I said, before placing him inside a black bin liner and tying it onto my rear bag.

'Tom,' Jodie said, after a little time had passed, 'things *are* going to go wrong on this journey, and we *are* going to have to find a way to get through. You do know that, don't you?'

It wasn't so much a question, more a gentle hand on the shoulder, but I had to admit, if I couldn't handle losing a rugby ball, how would I cope losing something we depended on?

'Yes, I know,' I conceded, 'it's just a lot harder than I had realised.'

CHAPTER 6
THE HARSH REALITY OF DAFT CONCEPTS

I waited outside Nettos and stood by the bicycles, in the rain. Jodie strolled towards the door, but not in time to avoid a group of German pensioners who waddled very casually in front of her. In slow motion she passed through the sliding doors, picked up a basket, and made directly for the fruit and veg section. I watched her through the large shop window as she ducked and dived between the stalls, first tomatoes, lettuce, celery, cucumbers before returning back to tomatoes. She'd still not picked up a single thing, but now she was heading over to the bread.

'What is she doing?' I muttered to myself, 'It'll be a crap sandwich if there's nothing in it.'

I was starving.

Back home I'd have been tearing into my daily feast by now. Usually 500 g of pasta, a tin of tuna, packed with spinach, spring onions, tomatoes, cucumbers, mayonnaise, pine nuts and a little seasoning to complete the mini saga. With the first course finished I'd have an apple or two, then wash it all down with a gigantic coffee accompanied by a Yorkie bar. Yes, I'd normally feel quite sick, but I had a desk job, and in my book the afternoons were purely there to allow your stomach recovery time before dinner.

By now Jodie had progressed to the biscuit aisle, still empty handed. The rain had eased outside, but I was growing weaker by the second and judging by the lack of items in Jodie's basket, lunch was still a long way off. One of the waddling penguins was already queuing at the checkout. With a complete circuit of the Netto track completed, she returned to the entrance and looked to start a second lap, it was killing me.

In all my despair I must have missed the green flag, but thankfully the safety cars were now gone and Jodie was powering round the store, snatching at items mid-flow and flinging them into her basket. Judging by the average age of the Nettos' customer base, this was undoubtedly the quickest lap ever to be set.

'Finally!' I thought to myself, 'Come to papa!'

'Sorry I took so long,' Jodie apologised, 'I had to work out what we could afford first.'

'How much did you spend?' I asked.

'€8.76.'

'And that's all we got?' I gasped, looking at the tiny bag of shopping, 'What are *you* having for lunch then?'

'Don't worry, there's plenty of food,' she said, 'let's just sit here and I'll make you some sandwiches.'

Jodie opened the loaf of bread, pulled out her Swiss-army knife and carved up a solitary tomato. I turned away and checked on our laptop. With the rain having stopped, I'd decided to test the effectiveness of our solar charger. It was still very cloudy, but maybe it would extract a little juice anyway. I leaned over and checked the LED charging light. It was off.

'Here you go,' Jodie said as she handed me a sandwich.

'Lovely, thanks,' I replied, relieved to finally receive some lunch.

'I'll make you another one in a minute,' she quickly added, before I needed to ask.

I glanced down at my sandwich for a moment, there was something not quite right. I opened it up for inspection, inside there was a layer of processed cheese, the type you put onto a beef burger, and some sliced tomato. It wasn't the type of sandwich to set the world alight, but yet at the same time, there was nothing to suggest raising the alarms. I closed it up again and stared at it in my hand.

'Why does it look so far away?' I said, suddenly realising what was wrong.

'It's just a bit smaller than usual,' Jodie started to explain, 'the normal size bread was too expensive for our budget, so I bought the smaller one.'

'But it's about half the normal size? I thought we were trying to cut back on cost, not the amount of food!'

I demolished my little morsel, worried that a gust of wind might take it out of my hand, but if anything I only felt hungrier than before.

'I'll make you another one, don't worry.'

'What else did we get?' I asked, a little nervously.

'I got four apples and a pack of chocolate bars.'

'What else?'

Jodie paused.

'A receipt,' she replied after careful consideration.

Ordinarily I would have applauded such a witty reply, but I'd made two rules in life - never to say nice things about the French, and never, *ever* to joke about food.

'But we overspent didn't we? We're only supposed to spend €6.80 per day.'

'Yes, but the cheese will last for two days and so will the chocolate.'

'How will the chocolate last for two days?'

'There are six bars. We can share three today, and three tomorrow.'

I stopped to gather my thoughts. It appeared that Jodie had missed the point. An A-level in maths and ten years working in a bank had taught me how to halve the number six, it was the reality of the answer that led me to question our situation. How was sharing three little chocolate bars and eating a postage stamp sized sandwich going to fuel me through 100 km of cycling each day?

'What do we have for dinner?' I asked, 'And breakfast tomorrow?'

'We still have pasta left, and a tin of tuna,' Jodie answered confidently, 'and we've got a pack of oats.'

I started to run through the numbers in my head. We had put together around £1,500 each for living expenses on the trip, this had to last for the 540 days until the Rugby World Cup final, in other words just £2.77 each per day.

On current exchange rates this got us just over €3, or three meals a day at an average of €1 per meal. It wasn't much, certainly not enough to survive in Germany for eighteen months. In fact, given that we'd pre-bought some of our food in the UK to get us through the first few days, I estimated that we were already spending at double our daily allowance. This meant that halfway across China we would have blown our entire budget for the journey.

'Look Jo, I know there's no point in banging on about the budget this early on, but we're going to have to keep an eye on things.'

'How do you mean?'

'Look, I'll give you a very rough example. Fifty cents might not sound much, but it is about 15% of our daily budget. If we over spend by 15% each day, we will do our budget with just under 15% of the journey left, in other words, *seventy* days of cycling with no money at all!'

Saying it out loud was just my way of letting it go. There was only one thing in life that bored Jodie more than statistics, and that was listening to me talk about statistics. At the mere mention of 15% she had noticeably switched off, but sat there quietly and let me finish my little speech.

'Like you just said Tom, it's too early to be worrying about the budget, we know that food will be cheaper in Asia, and we'll be spending a lot more of our time there than in Europe.'

That was good enough for me. It was probably too early to start worrying about the budget, and I really couldn't consider eating sandwiches any smaller. For all we knew, the bikes could get stolen that night and the whole thing would be over anyway.

As we cycled out of the Nettos' carpark I heard what sounded like my mudguard rubbing on my rear wheel. I looked down to identify the noise as it happened again, this time I realised, it was just my stomach grumbling away in a sulk.

*   *   *   *   *

'Well done Jo!' I said, 'I can't believe we've made it, with time to spare too!'

We were already in Heidelberg, and it was only 4 p.m. on Thursday afternoon. Even despite the relentless rain and rolling hills, we'd polished off the 550 km cycle in six and a half days.

'There are loads of places to camp here,' I pointed out, with relief. The previous three nights had been extremely difficult to find hidden spots. Urban German towns seemed to be well designed, with footpaths allowing dog walkers access to nearly everywhere, and good lighting meant few dark areas. Fortunately, on the first two evenings, we had been found by couples out for a walk and taken in by the families.

On the left there was a huge field, which although currently busy with a farmers market would make an ideal camp spot later. We decided to use the extra daylight to duck into Heidelberg for a quick explore. By coincidence, we took a road towards the main river which grabbed my attention.

'Hang on Jo, that sign just said TierGarten Straben!'

'Yeah, so what does that mean then?' she replied with every right, I'd never mentioned it before.

'For some reason, I remember seeing that name when I looked up the German Rugby Museum. There's a rugby club there.'

Jodie viewed me suspiciously, I never remembered place names, not even English ones.

'Okay, well should we check it out?' she suggested, 'It might be an even better camp spot too!'

'Let's do it!' I said, not needing a second invitation.

Only minutes later and we had found the entrance to the SC Neuenheim Rugby Club, home to the German Rugby Museum. Wasting no time at all, we pushed the bicycles down the gravel path and were confronted by an enormous chalk sketch of Jonah Lomu. Outside the clubhouse, a large group of guys were enjoying a beer on the patio.

'Hello, can we help you?' a small Indian man said to us as we approached, he didn't sound very German.

'Ah, we've come to meet Claus-Peter Bach,' I said, 'he's the Chairman of German Rugby, do you know him?'

'Yes,' he replied hesitantly, 'I know Claus-Peter very well. When are you meeting him?'

'Well, not until tomorrow actually,' I answered, suddenly feeling a bit daft, 'but we got here early and thought we'd come and have a look at the club. We're cycling to the World Cup.'

By now, several of his friends had come to investigate the situation and they stared down at us from the raised patio.

'Guys,' came an English accent beside him, 'you know that the World Cup starts next month don't you? You're going to be a bit late.'

There was a general air of agreement as they collectively waited for our response. Perhaps from our appearance they could guess we had no bad intentions, but our unscheduled arrival at their hidden club had certainly asked a few questions.

'Not the soccer World Cup!' I answered, 'The Rugby World Cup in New Zealand! We're trying to explore rugby across the world as we travel.'

'You're exploring rugby?' the Indian man replied, with an entirely new complexion. 'Well, you two will have to come through with me.'

'My name is Rama and I'm the club manager here,' he said, introducing himself. 'Now, what are you going to have to drink? Any friend of Claus-Peter is a friend of mine.'

Rama was an enthusiastic and friendly character, and chatting with him over a strong German beer we learned that before he had become the club manager, he had been one of the club's most capped players too. Despite looking considerably younger, the little scrum half was already retired, and had played rugby in Germany for the best part of twenty years. He pulled out a giant laminated album and placed it on the bar. As he did so, one of the elder members voiced his pleasure and opened it up for us. Inside were newspaper cuttings of every photo and match report dating back through thirty years, many showing the athletic Indian distributing from scrum half.

'When you see Claus-Peter tomorrow, please tell him that Rama says hello,' he asked. 'Claus-Peter and I played together for many years. He was a very fine second row.'

Listening to Rama's stories brought me huge encouragement for the project. I had never really known that rugby existed in Germany, but I could now picture the nippy Indian running round tormenting his opposition. The whole idea seemed so far-fetched that I would never have envisaged such a situation before meeting him.

'I need to take you outside and introduce you around,' he offered, 'I love that you guys are exploring rugby around the world. I'm delighted to have you here.'

Outside we met with some of the team, a hugely diverse pool of rugby talent from all over the globe. Firstly US soldiers based in Germany, then Italians, South Africans and even a student from

Argentina. Why had I never heard of Germany as a hotpot for international rugby?

'You were asking about national players earlier?' Rama reminded me. 'These three guys have all played at national level.'

The three players relaxing after the Thursday afternoon fixture were Sean Smith, former Zimbabwe scrum half, Marten Strauch the current German Schlussmann (Final man or Fullback), and our English sounding companion Adam Taylor, a former centre for the Spanish U20 side.

Adam was a multilingual student of English and Spanish heritage and was a particularly big fan of travel and culture. He had learned German for six months so that he could relocate to Heidelberg for an extension to his degree. Although he couldn't offer us any floor space in his apartment he insisted we come back to his for the after party and use his garden to put up our tent. It solved the issue of wild camping and meant hanging out with the rugby boys whilst testing our livers for a little longer.

While we still had the power of speech, we decided to add the three new autographs to the World in Union scroll but by midnight, and many shots of unidentifiable alcohol later, I collapsed into the tent as Adam, Sean and a small handful of the others pressed on and headed back out to a club.

The following morning appeared from nowhere, and with a throbbing head, I reached painfully for my bottle of water - it was empty.

'Argh,' I sobbed quietly, 'I don't feel very well.'

'I'm not surprised,' Jodie said, 'you were guzzling that beer like it was water.'

'You weren't allowed to hold two beers at once,' I tried to explain, but it was no use. Girls appeared not to understand such strict regulations.

'Do you remember spilling petrol and setting fire to Adam's garden table last night?' she asked. Suddenly I woke up.

'Oh shit! I do remember something like that actually. What happened?'

'Don't worry,' she explained, 'luckily it was still raining so most of the petrol just washed onto the grass. You nearly lost your eyebrows though.'

I was desperate for two things, firstly some water to fix my dehydration, and secondly to take a leak and make it even worse. I peered through Adam's window to see if I could wake him, but his bed appeared empty and he was nowhere to be seen. I couldn't bear it any more and despite being overlooked by many surrounding windows, I marked my territory, as discreetly as possible, in the corner of his garden. As I did so, I spotted a garden hose coiled round the leg of his patio table, it retraced to an external tap by the side of the house. I twisted the tap and ran back to the end of the hose just in time to point it away from the tent doorway. A flow of chilled water poured from the green hose and I guzzled as much as I could stomach.

'I've become a tramp,' I thought to myself, as I began to indulge in post-drink self loathing. This was all Stefan's fault.

I took a couple of aspirins and lay back down. We still had four hours until our appointment with Claus-Peter so I took the opportunity for another hour to process the drink, with my eyes closed. Jodie, on the other hand, was using our day off to attend to general maintenance and kit checks. I managed to get a little sleep but soon she had made her way through all twelve bags.

'Excuse me Mr. Hudson, but what are *these*?' Jodie exclaimed, holding up the offending item.

'Oh no,' I thought as I looked up at her, 'she's found them.'

'Erm... ah, yes honey, I think they might be Pants C,' I said, fumbling for an excuse.

'*Pants C*?' she said with a face suggesting that I had been smuggling tiger cubs. 'So what happened to carrying just two pairs then?'

Pants C, or 'Contingency Pants' was a precaution I had taken in case of a PPC scale event - 'Potential Pant Catastrophe'. To Jodie's face I had obediently conformed to the strict clothes allowance, but behind closed doors I had tucked my contingency pants into a zipped compartment with the bicycle tools. We were less than two weeks into the trip and I had already been rumbled.

'I didn't want to say anything before,' I tried to reason with her, 'but I had concerns over Pants A before we left.' My explanation had done nothing to change Jodie's expression.

'You'd probably have described them as threadbare already and as it turns out, these two weeks have pretty much seen them off. Tell you what, I'll bring Pants C into the clothes pannier and chuck this pair out.'

Jodie sighed with clear disappointment at my logic. 'If they already had holes in them, why did you bring them?' she asked anyway.

I felt that Jodie deserved an answer. 'Well, most of my pants had holes in anyway, but these ones had Scooby Doo on, I couldn't just leave them behind.'

'Okay never mind,' she decided, 'but am I going to find any other stowaways lurking in our gear?'

'Not if you stop looking,' I thought to myself silently, but instead I shook my head solemnly to demonstrate my utmost regret.

'Come on, I think we should be heading off to see Claus-Peter,' she said, 'I think it's fair to assume we won't remember the way back to the club!'

By lunchtime we had managed to retrace our steps thanks to piecing together our fractional memories from the previous night. The petrol station the boys had bought a second crate of beer from, the traffic light that Sean had climbed, the patch of grass that Adam had fallen off my bike onto, slowly it had all come back. We sat in the rugby club car park and continued to drink our bottles of hose water.

The tall figure of Claus-Peter Bach stepped out from a car, accompanied by a much smaller man carrying a large camera.

'Welcome Tom and Jodie,' he called to us, 'you found the club okay then?'

'Yes, thank you!' Jodie replied, trying to ease the pressure off my hangover. 'We actually found it last night! We met with Rama too, he sends his regards!'

'Oh excellent!' Claus-Peter responded, 'Isn't he a fantastic character! Please come through and I'll show you the museum. I hope you don't mind but I arranged for our photographer to come and take a few photos.'

We didn't mind in the slightest, but with a stinking hangover and a permanent expression of disbelief, it's questionable whether he got any good photos that afternoon. Having been explained the history of German rugby, I wouldn't have looked more surprised if Claus Peter had turned to us and said, 'Tom and Jodie, I am your father.'

There could be no better tour guide than Claus-Peter Bach. His father had been the captain of the German rugby team, and even Claus-Peter himself had been a national player and vice-captain, before becoming chairman. More importantly, he had also gone on to investigate and publish a book translated as '100 years of the German Rugby Union'.

It is believed that rugby in Germany started as early as 1850 with some interest from British students in Heidelberg, but by the late 19th century there were many clubs, and rugby was growing in popularity. In 1900 the German Rugby Federation was created, winning silver at that year's Olympics before organizing an official Test match against France in 1927. Although they lost this first encounter, they went on to defeat the French 17-16 in the return match in Frankfurt, and again in 1938.

As World War II broke out in 1939, Germany was ranked second in mainland Europe, only behind France. It was to be the last time they held such a position. The war is thought to have killed almost the entire national team and it marked a turn in the sport that it would never recover from.

Progress had been made however, and there was such a significant increase in interest, that both Claus-Peter and the Federation had set out their stall to qualify for the 2015 Rugby World Cup in England. Sadly, after a winless season in the FIRA top flight, they were demoted, and almost with an air of personal sadness, he revealed that this had killed off any hope of fulfilling their vision. Nevertheless, the country still sees over one hundred clubs in competition and nearly twelve thousand registered players, which in comparison is about twice the number playing rugby in Georgia, the highest ranked European FIRA side.

'I'm going to write about your visit,' Claus-Peter said to us. 'I am a sports journalist for the regional newspaper and I always try to push for more rugby presence. So, where are you heading to next?'

'We're off towards the Czech Republic tomorrow,' Jodie answered, 'to see a man called Eduard Krutzner near Prague.'

'Oh Eduard!' he replied. 'I've known Eduard for a long, long time. When you see him, please pass on my best regards.'

'You know him?' I piped up.

'Yes, of course Tom. You know, the rugby community is very large, but the family is very tight. You'll see that soon enough.'

CHAPTER 7
THE GODFATHER OF EAST EUROPEAN RUGBY

To our genuine astonishment the weather didn't ease up, but got steadily worse as we cycled east. Now three weeks into our trip and we'd only had a single day without rain. The terrain was becoming increasingly difficult to have rest breaks, and finding any suitable spots to wild camp was nearly impossible.

We were soon forced into situations that became categorised as 'Military Off' where we would sneak into official camp spots after dark, then leave early the next morning before we were sprung. The price to pitch a tent inside these parks was between €12-15 per night, which was too much for our budget, but did make the camping experience a little bit more exciting. Our favourite thing to do at the end of the day was to scout out the campsite procedures. How people entered, how they left, what workers were around, 'line of sight' from the reception area and anything else we could think of to remain undetected overnight. We'd normally enter through the exit late in the evening, as the light was dimming, and fire up the cooker behind our tent. In three consecutive days, and three consecutive 'Military Off' evacuations, we managed to negotiate over 300 km of soggy river bank and woodland, taking us to the border of the Czech Republic.

Crossing a border on foot is always an experience I've found very revealing, giving you an insight into many aspects of the two countries. The obvious and visual differences in the buildings will give you a quick lesson relating to the history, affluence and maybe religion of the country, but if you talk to people at these borders, you'll also sense something about their relationships with each other. Better still, if you can observe the border guards or passport control interact with citizens of the opposite country, you might see signs of things to come as you progress.

Most of Europe's borders are now nothing more than a colourful sign, but that's not to say you don't enjoy the experience of entering the Czech Republic. From the quaint, almost fairytale German border villages, it would be just far too easy to gaze across at the slightly seedy Czech border and pass comment. With a more sympathetic attitude, the giant beer bottles might just indicate their proud local refreshments, whilst the fluorescent lights of ladies, teasingly waving their legs in the air, could hint towards a developing appetite for synchronized swimming.

Either way, whatever you see on the other side of the border, you must remind yourself of one thing - who is it really for? By doing this, you might find out more about the country that you are leaving, than the one you are about to enter. Those cheeky little Germans.

*   *   *   *   *

In some parts of the world, most in fact, your house can be located through an address. This is usually a fairly unique indicator, so that any given individual may know exactly which of the world's seven billion beds you tend to sleep in. The basic information required in an address might be the country, region, town, road and street number. Any further derivation and you could probably find the right door by yelling their name loudly enough in the street.

Over the years, this simple five step guide has allowed for governments to monitor taxes, the men at TomTom to turn a handsome profit, and most importantly, for your postman to finish his round in time for a pub lunch.

In other parts of the world, life is frustratingly more centred around the works of J.R. Tolkien.

'Okay, I think we're close, 202, 206... 237... 194,' I paused as if to contemplate the new system, 'why aren't the numbers in order?'

'I don't know, it's stupid,' Jodie analysed the system for me.

'202... 317... 84... 202... hang on, pull over a minute,' I stood with hands on hips, not sparing a thought for how camp my posture might have been. We'd had a very tough day on the saddle, and I was trying to work out how the last step could be going so wrong at the end of another 125 km cycle.

'There are three houses with the same number in this road, and they're not even next to each other!'

'Let me see the address again,' Jodie asked.

I pulled out the e-mail from the handlebar bag. It read:

'Hi Jodie and Tom,
After the crossing of Czech border Germany, you must to seek the town BEROUN, about 100 km from border and here you must to find the river Berounka. This river you will bring to me. Around this river is very good cycling-road. LETY is my village. You must go around the river and will pass some houses and when you will see on the right side the high trees, 100 m after you will see big wooden house with my garden. The first way on the left, 40 m on the right, 40 m on the right and you will come to me, 378 with the lime tree. I wait your news.

```
Good luck!
Eduard'
```

'It just says number 378, in Lety, next to the lime tree,' I read out.

'Do you know what a lime tree looks like?'

'I do if it has limes on.'

'Let's just hope he hasn't picked them all then. Isn't there a road name?'

'This is the Czech Republic, maybe it's the road with the lime tree?'

'What's Czech for lime tree?'

'Dunno.'

One hour later, and on the fourteenth road that we tried, we eventually stumbled upon success.

'375, 376, 377... Jo look, see what it says!'

'Beware of the dog?'

'No, next to that.'

'Eduard Krutzner Snr' etched onto a shiny bronze plaque shimmered in the early evening sunshine.

'We've done it!' I clapped my hands, becoming less manly by the second.

It was now 6:30 p.m. and although we hadn't been able to confirm an arrival time, we hoped that he would be home. If not, it would be a very brief visit as he was booked on a flight to Austria the next morning.

Just then, a man dressed in a blue sports tracksuit came out onto the first floor decking. He was definitely in his 70s but skipped down the stairs with an incredibly youthful agility.

'Tom and Jodie! Welcome to Czech Republic!'

'Eduard!' we both greeted him with a hug, 'it is *so* nice to finally meet you.' At last we had met the man who had breathed life into our project.

'Please come into my house and meet Maria, then we will go to my favourite Czech restaurant! You must be hungry!'

Eduard Krutzner Snr is like the 'Don Corleone' of East European rugby. Wherever we went, and whoever we spoke with, the name Eduard Krutzner Snr would be recognized and tributes would be paid. Some people didn't even know him, they just knew *of* him. I was seriously impressed, especially as the distances between him and these people increased across many borders.

Eduard's rugby career started in 1956, when already playing in the Czechoslovakia national basketball team, he went to work at a car garage called 'Praga'. As a young sportsman, it didn't take him long to be persuaded to help represent the garage rugby side in the local Czech competition. He started in the 2nd XV and the next season was promoted to the 1st XV. Unbelievably, after only two seasons in the game, he was selected as back row for the national team, in one of the historical Eastern European 'Tournament of Peace' competitions. This particular tournament featured powerhouse Romania, East Germany, Poland and Czechoslovakia, and he impressed so much in this first outing that it wasn't long after that he was named national captain.

Blessed with a fine rugby talent, the sport opened up many doors for Eduard, none more so than when the German Rugby Federation arranged a fixture against a European Select XV. The match was scheduled for 26 August 1968, with Eduard the only Czech National to be selected. On 21st August, just five days before the match, Soviet tanks rolled into Prague and the occupation of Czechoslovakia had begun.

Eduard, with wife Maria and young son Eduard Jnr (now coach of Slovakia), boarded the first available train to Germany to make the fixture. Following the match, he received many offers to remain and play rugby in Germany, but with his friends and family left behind in the unstable climate, he chose instead to return to Prague and see how the situation would unfold.

A year later, in 1969, the Czechoslovakia national XV travelled to a small town in France to play against a French XV, with Eduard as their captain. Although they lost 34-14 to the French, his performance made quite an impression. So much so, that before heading home he was approached by the President of the Olympique Besançon Rugby Club to come back to France and play for their team. This time he would be persuaded to explore his options.

It took two more years to secure the necessary documents to officially leave Czechoslovakia, and when he arrived at Olympique Besançon in 1971, they had just gained entrance into the French National Division III. Eduard subsequently became part of a very special period in club rugby history. Winning the Division III at their first attempt, they gained promotion to Division II where, after a thrilling final match, winning 9-8, they achieved promotion into the top flight of French national rugby. This victory marked an astonishing achievement, taking the club from regional rugby to the highest national level in three straight years, a feat never to have been repeated in France, or perhaps anywhere in the world, even today.

Eduard enjoyed a final season competing in the French top flight before returning to Prague and raising another three children. He took on coaching roles at Praga Bears and the national XV, then became a member of the FIRA-AER executive committee, before finishing as

President of Czech Republic Union. Even in his mid 70s, he still travels the world to catch up with the hundreds of friends he has made during his lifetime in the game.

Although Eduard was our only active contact in the Czech Republic, it soon emerged that it wasn't just his own travel that he had been planning. The next afternoon he had advised his club side, Praga Bears (derived from the original car garage), to welcome us to the 7s tournament occurring at Tatra Smichov Rugby Club in Prague.

We completed the short cycle to Prague and eventually located the rugby ground, a quite spectacular location, high on a hill overlooking the city. Although the Praga Bears went undefeated in the tournament, they were extremely reserved in their post-tournament celebrations, most having to drive back across the city and wake the next morning for a XVs fixture. They were a good group of young boys and before leaving, their skipper kindly chatted with the Tatra team, arranging permission for us to camp on their pitch for a couple of days. A very hospitable team, but with little English, the Tatra boys nodded enthusiastically to us in agreement. We had cycled to Prague with only a solitary day's rest, so due a break, we set out our stall for the rest of the weekend.

The sun was still bright, but with no money and the Praga Bears now dispersed, we very sheepishly took our water bottles into the club to fill before relaxing back at the tent. As we strolled back out onto the grass, a voice called from behind us and a bare chested boy with dreadlocks ran over.

'Hello you guys!' the boy said, as his team watched on from the doorway, 'Please excuse my poor English, my team would like to give you a present of Tatra Smichov.'

He handed us a club polo shirt each and invited us inside to join them for some beer and food. Suddenly our tuna pasta had turned into Czech sausage, chicken, bread and salads - I was ecstatic.

The dreadlocked lad was called Vitek and he had been voted by the team to deliver the shirts because of his better English. He was only 21 years old but due to his strong physique and heroic tackling skills, he'd been a feature in the senior side for several seasons. Bringing over two ice cold Czech beers he officially welcomed us to the club. The sun was still shining, the Czech Republic were playing an important ice hockey match on the big screen, and it was clear that the Tatra boys were going to make an evening of it, they were in great spirits.

'Hey you guys, would you like another beer?' Vitek asked, after I'd washed down my third sausage sandwich.

'Hey Vitek, I'd love one,' I replied, 'but whose paying for it? We need to thank them.'

'You don't need to worry about that,' he insisted, 'after today, we have much money for beer.'

'What do you mean, *after today*?' Jodie asked.

'Every time somebody makes a mistake in the match, they must pay some money into the glass.'

'Ah, like a fine system,' I explained, 'we have that back at home too.'

'Yes, a *fine* system,' he agreed, 'it is a very good system! I like this system very much!'

He laughed and raised his glass, and then we all did. It soon became apparent that many of the boys could understand enough English to follow our conversation, but just lacked the confidence to try. In contrast to this, Vitek's English got better and better with each beer, and by the end of the evening his grammar was noticeably better than our own.

To the delight of the entire clubhouse, the Czech Republic went on to win the ice hockey game, and another round of beers was ordered in celebration, accompanied by an evil looking bottle of Czech spirit called Stara Myslivecka. On the bottle was the image of a moustached man in a red bow tie and green jacket. I didn't trust him one bit.

'Hey Vitek, is this still being paid for by the fine money?' I asked.

'Guys,' he laughed again, he started most of his sentences in this way, 'I told you already, you don't need to worry about money. Every time somebody makes a mistake in the match, they must pay some money into the glass. Today we all played like... '

He paused as he considered his English vocabulary.

'Dog shit!' Vitek collapsed in laughter on his chair, 'And now we can drink for two weeks!'

The Tatra Smichov boys were also playing a game the following day, and we were eager to see how they would face up to their opposition on tour from Wales. At least we could guarantee that getting slaughtered the night before was not going to be a disadvantage, one had to assume a Welsh side in Prague would still be drinking come kickoff.

We walked down into Prague the next day and met up with Vitek again, who gave us a guided tour of his city, then took us back to his family house for some much needed coffee. Vitek's father, Vladislav Petras was no ordinary rugby man, he was actually the founder of the Tatra Smichov Rugby Club in 1958. Not only that, but even into his 70s, he was still turning out as fullback for the Tatra veterans.

Vitek was hugely proud of his father, as his father was of him. Ever since Vitek was a young boy, Vladislav had collected a scrap book of Vitek's rugby successes, photos of him playing and any articles from the local papers. Since Vitek had competed at many of the national youth levels too, he was able to recount many fond memories from his teenage years. Now Vitek himself has taken on the album and proudly keeps his rugby career updated each season. We both felt very honoured to see such a private and personal collection, and it reminded us once again that you could grow up into a rugby family anywhere in the world.

After a second strong coffee, we hurried back to the clubhouse where Vitek joined his young squad in preparation for their fixture with Rhigos RFC. Rhigos itself is a very small Welsh town formerly known for it's mining, and although it now only competed in the lower Welsh leagues, was once a home to the back row legend, Williams David 'Dai' Morris. As predicted, a huge coach of singing Welshmen disembarked into the car park, and whereas twenty of them staggered to the changing room, at least as many again went straight to the bar.

As the teams lined up, I boldly voiced my approval of the Tatra side. Although much slighter in build, they were a young, athletic and smart outfit, in contrast to the rabble of Welsh, who looked as if they would never struggle for front row replacements. Sadly, during the first half, the boys from Rhigos RFC dealt us all a harsh lesson in reality. Sometimes there is just no replacement for strong direct running and fierce contention at the breakdown. In doing these basics well, the shorter, more rotund men, stormed to a three try lead and it looked like curtains for the lighter Czech boys.

The Rhigos social members kept in fine choir voice on the far side of the pitch, and returned to the bar to refill at halftime. Perhaps their players wanted to as well, because by the early second half minutes, their legs were finally adhering to the unforgiving laws of gravity. As the Tatra boys sensed their opportunity, they turned quick ball into a fast running game and got it wide at every opportunity. As expected from the start, this line of attack quickly proved to be their best strength, and with only a handful of minutes remaining, they had squared up an exciting encounter at three tries a piece. If not for the young cannonball of the Rhigos number 8, Tatra may well have gone on in-betweento clinch the match, but after another barraging run, breaking many failed tackle attempts, the Welsh side went over in the far corner to secure a narrow victory.

The Tatra heads were low following the final whistle, perhaps with the late realisation that they possessed enough skills to defeat a UK side. Jodie and I heaped praise on their efforts, especially on the electric leg speed displayed by the young Tatra back three, and the monstrous defensive effort shown throughout by the courageous Vitek. A couple of beers later and Vitek's boys were smiling and laughing once again. Firstly, when a naked Welshman took off round the pitch on Jodie's bicycle, and again when the moustached man in the red bow tie notched one back for the Czechs.

*   *   *   *   *

With another Czech hangover to process, we had over 100 km to cover for a reception at Přelouč Rugby Club, our third appointment in the country. Eduard had arranged for his good friend Tomas to welcome us at the rural club, and although we had been treated to a dry Sunday, the rain clouds were now congregating above our heads in a more than ominous way. We stopped only for a very short lunch and lucky too, because as we spotted a sign, 'Přelouč 5 km', the sun had long since vanished.

'Oh shit Jo! Look at those clouds,' I cried, 'I don't think we've got much time!'

Spots of rain began to splash off the waterproof map casing and the sky darkened with each rotation of our pedals. We had been on the saddle for over seven hours and as the wind picked up, our pace slowed to a frustrating 10 k.p.h.

'I really don't think we want to get caught in this one,' I said, stating the fairly obvious, 'it's looking pretty messy!'

Jodie clearly agreed and reluctantly we began to force the pace. 'Okay, come on Tom, thirty minutes hard work, let's just get there and we'll keep dry.'

The road wove around some farmland, then through another village, but by now the sky was as murky as my memory of the last Earls Court Real Ale Festival.

'Two kilometres left!' I yelled over the wind.

'Then what?' Jodie called back to me, 'We don't have a map or an address do we?'

'We hopefully don't need one, it's just a small village. Eduard has already spoken with them. He said they'll be waiting for us at 6 p.m.!'

'Okay, but how do we find the club?' she shouted back to me.

'Přelouč surely can't be that big, hopefully we'll just find it,' I added, suddenly realising that wishful thinking did make up the majority of my planning.

'I don't think we have very long!' Jodie answered as the drops of rain started again, 'Hang on, what's that?'

'What's what?'

'Look, there, on the lamppost. It's says 'rugby', and there's an arrow. Straight ahead at the junction!'

'No way! How good is that? Come on Jo, we can get there!' I announced, basking in the glory of wishful thinking.

At each junction there was another carefully placed piece of paper guiding us home. Some were taped to posts, others on fences, some even tied to trees but all with the simplest of international messages: 'rugby (right arrow)', 'rugby (left arrow)', 'rugby (arrow ahead)'. On the final turn, we took a small alley by the side of a church and entered through an old rusty gate next to a hand painted board, 'Přelouč Rugby Club'. As we dismounted and pushed up the narrow dirt entrance, the sky buckled and an explosion of rain began to hit the pitch. We dashed towards the waiting clubhouse, and as we arrived at the pavilion a crowd of people stood to applaud us under the veranda. It was precisely 6 p.m.

The mayor of the town himself had come down to officially welcome us, as had another twenty men and women from the club, they were a hugely hospitable community. We were bustled inside by the mayor and an English man called Steve. Steve had married the daughter of the club chairman, and had been asked to come down to assist with translation, although several spoke enough English to converse. Only minutes into our warm dry indoor reception, we could see an almost tropical storm unleashing its fury on the trees outside. As we stared out of the window, already with a Czech beer in our hands, we began to laugh at our own good fortune, before remembering how we'd managed to find the club so easily.

'Oh, while I remember,' I said, 'thank you for arranging all those rugby signs to help us find you.'

'I think we'd be pretty wet now if it wasn't for those!' Jodie agreed.

'Rugby signs?' one guy replied, 'What rugby signs?'

'All those pieces of paper stuck around the village pointing us to the rugby club?'

They all stared at each other searching for an answer.

'I don't know anything about that?' the first man freely admitted.

'Nor me,' Steve shook his head, 'maybe it was Tomas?'

'Ah Tomas, that's the man that our friend Eduard spoke to!' I looked around the room, 'Which one *is* Tomas?'

'He's the man who brought your bed here!' the first man replied, pointing to the double bed and bright orange duvet by the bar.

'He brought down a bed to the club? Just for us?' Jodie was amazed, 'Where is he now?'

'Oh, he's outside cooking the BBQ!' Steve replied laughing, 'He's very excited that you're here!'

'Someone is outside in this?' I exclaimed, as I looked back outside the window, 'Jo, come on, we'd better go and find him.'

As we made our way across the clubhouse, Frodo's stunt double stepped in through the doorway clutching a tray of sizzling barbecued sausages. The brawny little hobbit was saturated from head to toe, dripping all over the floor as he called for someone to carry the sausages to the table. He stood in the corner shivering as he calmly waited for someone to bring him a towel. We rushed over to greet him.

'You must be Tomas,' I said, 'we are really honoured to come to your club and meet you.'

His little face beamed as he smiled, and when he shook our hands, we could see only warmth in his eyes.

'Thank you so much for doing all this for us,' Jodie said, as she pointed outside, pulling a face at the weather.

'I am very happy you are here,' Tomas spoke softly and with admirable integrity, 'please, it is nothing, this is rugby. We are family.'

He changed into some dry clothes and the mayor said his goodbyes to the group, clearly with no interest in the bright orange sausages. When Tomas returned wearing a Toulouse rugby jersey, we tucked into a pile of potatoes, salads, bread and most importantly, the aromatic Czech sausages. Not for a girl watching her weight, these sausages were the type that left you with stained lips and bits of gristle stuck in-between your front teeth. Real *man* food.

As we feasted with Tomas and the team, we spent the time learning about our new rural hosts. Tomas Cerny was a fantastic individual. He still played scrum half for the club, and despite also having played for every Czech rugby team, he had also found time to gain experience abroad with sides in France and Italy. He had an extremely gentle demeanour and a warm smile, we liked him immediately.

Although his English was a little nervous, we soon realised that there was another way that we could converse more freely, one that thankfully didn't test our abilities at charades. The boys would talk in Czech, through which Tomas would translate into French, and then Jodie would try her best to translate it for me. As effective as this method seemed to start with, it did become a strenuously tested channel as the beers and spirits kept coming. Nevertheless, we learned plenty from our few hours at the bar.

He loved rugby so much that he had stayed with Přelouč, one of the lowest sides in the Czech structure, just to ensure that there would always be a club in his home town. He refused to see it die, and so coached their junior team, captained their senior side, and somewhere in-between, he worked on the ground and clubhouse for nothing.

As the evening flowed, so too did the beers, before Tomas reacquainted me with an old Czech nemesis, Becherovka. My introduction to this spicy little beast had been on a school exchange many years before, and on several subsequent encounters I had been left scratching my head the next day. In the Czech Republic it is seen as an alcoholic cure for arthritis, and is the sort of drink to give 'red bow tie man' a good kick in the nuts. It came as no surprise that the Czechs mixed it with tonic to form a drink called 'Be-Ton' - the Czech word for 'concrete'.

After a few too many toasts made in Czech, I found myself trying to have an extremely deep conversation with their flanker, who understood absolutely no English. It was translated through Tomas, and again through Jodie, that my new friend had found rugby in his 20s, and that it had helped steer him away from serious drug taking in his troubled youth. I was delighted to witness such a strong accolade for the sport, but I was also delighted to see a team of tiny leprechauns dancing on the bar. At this point I began to wonder whether joining the rugby club had actually done anything to improve his health, but we toasted his achievements several more times before I finally lost the ability to speak English - thankfully an already dormant tool.

Nobody seemed to notice my unfathomable drawling, and I suspected that their Czech had similarly disintegrated, but soon it was just Tomas, Jodie and I left alone in the rugby club at 2 a.m. Finally, it seemed it was time to draw a line under Přelouč Rugby Club.

We felt truly humbled by Tomas and his irrefutable love for the game. The club had such little funds and basic equipment, but yet he asked for absolutely nothing from us, and saw it as his duty to support people in the 'rugby family'.

When he came back to the clubhouse a few hours later, we saw that he had even stocked the fridge with items for our breakfast. We felt both deeply ashamed that he'd spent so much of his money on us, but equally honoured by his hospitality. If only we'd get the chance to one day repay the generosity. We couldn't have afforded these items on our tight budget, but we were equally sure that neither could have Tomas on his Přelouč income. Despite our protests the following morning, he insisted that whatever we didn't eat, we carried with us, as he had bought it *all* to help our journey. With our hamper of hams, cheeses, breads, eggs and fruit all packed away, we began the 200 km journey to our final Czech rugby club, Brno Brystc.

*   *   *   *   *

From: 'Paul Duteil'

To: 'Jodie and Tom'

'Dear Jodie, Dear Tom,
Thank you for your email. I have been informed from
Eduard about your visit. I will be glad to meet you
at 6 p.m. on Friday at Schnönbrunn, the national
rugby facility in Vienna.
Best Regards, Paul Duteil [former President of
Austrian Rugby Union]'

*   *   *   *   *

Barely had our livers stopped quaking when we pulled into the Brno
Brystc car park the following afternoon. We seemed to be rattling off
the small targets at a comfortable rate of 100 km per day, but it was
keeping up with the Czech rugby players drinking habits that posed
the biggest problem.

In spite of our fears, Brno presented us with a highly civilised and
pleasant evening, not to mention the opportunity to tour a quite
breathtaking city. Our contact, Daniel Benes, was a former centre for
the Czech national team, but following a serious knee injury, he had
decided to return as a social player at his club, Brno Brystc. At only 28
years old, Dan is one of the busiest people we have ever met. By trade,
he is a genetic research technician at a local laboratory, but in the
evenings he is either helping to coach his senior club side, the Czech
national U17s, or the U15s of his Brno rivals, the Dragons.

After taking us for a long walk around the stunning Brno sights, he
treated us to dinner at a traditional Czech bistro - big tables, big
glasses and big food! Dan had arranged for us to sleep inside the
clubhouse that night, so after dinner we returned to the empty
clubhouse and talked about rugby over a bottle of rum.

Dan had such a mild manner, but a huge passion for rugby,
admitting that he'd often lay awake at night designing training drills
for his various sides. Finally, with the bottle empty, he conceded that
he needed some sleep. The very next morning he was on a train to
Prague, where he was accompanying the national U17s on a sixteen
hour coach trip to France for a tournament. When he boarded that
train, I was still snoring on the clubhouse sofas. It was now Thursday
morning, and with only 135 km to Vienna we could afford ourselves
an easy morning.

CHAPTER 8
DIGGING FOR DNA

I've heard that Hugh Hefner once said, 'If I could die and come back as anyone, I'd come back as *me!*'

If he didn't say that, then I apologise, but I'd like to think it was true. Most people would change something about themselves if they had another chance, I'm sure you would, and I am no different in this regard.

My greatest wish, other than to be able to turn invisible, would be to represent my country in a rugby game, or more accurately, I'd like to be *good* enough to. This doesn't mean getting greedy and coming back as Lomu, Campese or Carter, it would simply be enough for me to have a *realistic chance.* I still believe you should earn your place, as all professionals do, and if you secure a 1st XV national shirt, it's healthy to have another man, or woman, striving to take it away from you. Sadly for me, most women *would* be able to take my position.

Before leaving on our world rugby cycling tour, I had run a poll to test my chances of ever representing my country. It quickly emerged that in England alone, there were an estimated 15,752 full backs that were better than me. I asked the English full back population;

1) Can you kick?
2) Can you pass?
3) Can you catch?
4) Can you tackle?

If you answered with four 'yes', you were better than me too.

Technically speaking, Martin Johnson could get my phone number from the RFU, who in turn could obtain it from my old club, but the statistics were not in my favour, and it would be one very laborious call tree if I was ever to wear the red rose. I suspect that if Martin was to get down to his fifteen thousand seven hundred and fifty-third choice full back, he would probably have pulled on his own boots and squeezed into the jersey himself, quite right too.

If there was a glimmer of hope for me, it wasn't in my ability under the high ball, but in the IRB regulations for eligibility. All I required was a loose 12.5% somewhere in the Hudson DNA to open up the doors to an international rugby opportunity.

8.1 Subject to regulation 8.2 (not having represented another National Rugby side), a player may only play for the Senior National XV, the next senior National XV and the senior National 7s of the Union of the country in which:

(a) he was born; or

(b) one parent or grandparent was born; or

(c) he has completed thirty-six consecutive months of residence immediately preceding the time of playing.

I had been born in England, so too had both my parents, and both sets of their parents. That made me, in the eyes of the IRB, 100% English. There was no hope, other than finishing the cycle, then relocating for a three year work placement in Timbuktu. Admittedly, it already looked too late for me, that was, until I spotted an explanatory guideline accompanying the document.

13. The term *parent* in the regulations is limited to either a blood parent or *a parent that has formally adopted a player* in accordance with the applicable legal requirements of the country concerned.

Adopted a player? Was disowning the Hudson family my chance at a brighter rugby future? I could still visit them on Christmas Day and talk about the good old days when I used to be their son. I briefly ran the idea passed mum, who pointed out that despite the obvious merits, their last will and testament said something along the lines of 'dish it all out between the kids'. With that, the dream had evaporated, but it isn't like that for everyone, as I found out in Vienna where a man was fulfilling his own rugby destiny. First though, we met with our contact, Paul Duteil.

*   *   *   *   *

Paul was a French man, from Brittany, who had relocated to Vienna with his wife Katarina a number of years before. He was also fluent in English and German, and had been the President of Austrian rugby for around five years. He was a busy man, but balancing two jobs, one wife, four children and a rugby union, had caused him to relinquish the voluntary role of President in 2008. I suspect that dropping the latter provided the least consequences, but despite this, his presidency did lay the foundations for some excellent rugby infrastructure, including youth, male and female rugby development.

'Tom, Jodie, let me introduce you to Rudi Glock,' Paul Duteil said to us, as he brought over two cold beers, and the aforementioned Rudi Glock.

'Nice to meet you Rudi,' I articulated slowly and precisely.

'It is narz to mit yu tuu!' replied Rudi, laughing at my mistake.

'Hey, you're not Austrian!' I pointed out, in case this had slipped him by.

'Arm harf orstrian und harf sarfafrikan,' he answered, 'so ikchuly yu are harf corrikt!'

If I have only learnt two things in my life, it's that fat kids always beat me at seesaw and South Africans always beat me at rugby. As most amateur rugby players know, when you arrive at an opposition club house on a Saturday afternoon, you can't help but feel dejected when they tell you there'll be a 'braai' after the game. Not because the food isn't good, it's usually fantastic, but you understand that the chance of being able to chew it in 80 minutes time is fairly remote. They're tough bastards and very strong players.

'Arwarz plee-ing rigby un Sarfafrika, thin un Belfast, win ar dizarded to carm und iksplor mar Orstrian rutz.'

'Tom, just narrate this bit!' Jodie just told me over my shoulder. 'You're making him sound like a Geordie with a hair lip!'

Fine, I totally understand.

Rudi Glock, after a strong background of rugby in South Africa, had decided to use his skills to go travelling, first heading to Ireland where he picked up a semi professional contact with another South African friend. After numerous visits to mainland Europe, Rudi took the decision to explore the Austrian heritage given to him by his grandmother, and searched online to see if there was an Austrian Rugby Union.

He knew nothing about lower league European rugby and sent them an e-mail explaining his situation. If they could help him settle into Vienna life, he would happily come over and assist with their rugby programme, both sides had nothing to lose and everything to gain. Not only had he strengthened their national side with his Austrian ancestry, he had also taken on the U17s coaching position and many other coaching responsibilities with the union.

The Austrian Rugby Union had been particularly observant when it came to utilising the multicultural attraction of Vienna. When a young American lady called Kerry came to spend some time abroad, she was equally well received into the female programme. She now spends the entire rugby season in Austria, working remotely from her new 'office and home', a converted Schonbrunn female changing room. For the next three nights, she was going to have some guests herself.

On Saturday morning, Paul arrived at the club to collect us and show us the sights of Vienna, but first we went to his office in town to chat further about our trip, and to get as many contacts as we could from his database of friends.

In no time, Paul displayed more evidence of the 'rugby family' across Europe as he casually picked up the phone to rugby presidents in Hungary, Romania and Bulgaria, informing them of our trip. He fired out some e-mails to friends in the IRB and FIRA, and after chatting about his rugby experiences around Europe, we even began to plot a new route. On his insistence, we had decided to amend our Bulgarian route, taking in the holiday destination of Varna on the east coastal path. Soon, we were also considering the possibility of adding Georgia and Armenia if time allowed. The trip was truly beginning to take on a life of its own.

*   *   *   *   *

From: 'Jodie and Tom'
To: 'Slovan Bratislava'

'Hi Slovak Rugby friends.

We are the 2 rugby fans from London who are cycling to New Zealand for the Rugby World Cup. We are leaving Vienna today and will arrive in Bratislava today at 6 p.m. Is anyone able to meet with us? We will head to the rugby ground at Trnavska Cesta for 6 p.m. and hopefully meet with you.

Tom and Jodie'

CHAPTER 9
BREAKFAST IN BRATISLAVA

We cycled out of Austria into Slovakia. Then we left Slovakia.

*   *   *   *   *

I feel like I may already have said too much about Slovakia, but I guess the last comment deserves a little explanation.

Throughout the relentless hours of pedalling, I was often hit by random memories leading me to peculiar trails of thought. Although seemingly irrelevant, while I cast my mind back to those situations, it at least provided me with welcome respite from the theme tune to the Smurfs, which by now was on an infinite loop inside my head.

Innocuous conversations with friends, which at the time went under the radar, began to flow back to me with a newfound sense of clarity. I can be sure that most of these individuals would have no memory of what they said, or even awareness that I was paying attention, but many seeds were planted along the way that began to sprout given the right conditions.

Reflecting back on our successful visit in Vienna, I began to feel all the more anxious about the radio silence from Slovakia. I didn't want a rugby failure so early in the trip, but with no responses to my voicemails and e-mails, I didn't know what more to do. I had spoken again with Eduard Snr, father of the coach, and Daniel Benes had chased with his friends in the side, but the day was now upon us and I had nothing but an address scribbled down from their website.

We were still fighting to keep a tight schedule, trying to cover around 600 kilometres per week, and scheduling the rugby visits as part of this process. This meant almost daily cycling of 100 kilometres, and scheduling times and places to meet with teams and individuals in advance. Unless it really pulled us from our intended route, I would not decline a rugby opportunity, and coordinating with everyone so many days in advance was becoming a logistical nightmare. By now, the tight budget was presenting its problems, meaning we had no mobile phone and could only get online by standing in the rain, using the free wifi outside McDonalds.

As we left from Vienna, we both knew Bratislava was a risk to our project. We wouldn't arrive much before sunset, and would have to track down the rugby ground without a map. If no contact was made, we would be unable to wild camp, and then face a decision to continue out of the city at night, or break into the budget for accommodation.

On this particular 100 kilometre stretch I needed motivation, and thankfully I found some in my new sprouting library of inspiration. The author this time was a keen cyclist called Duncan, and appropriately, he was a personal trainer too. One afternoon, similar to any other, we had been discussing methods of improving my 2 km rowing time. For those of you who think this is tedious I won't win you over, but let's just say that it's a standard rowing distance that tests your ability to work extremely hard in a short period of time, but not short enough that it's simply a sprint. I've lost you already, I can tell. It hurts a lot, let's just leave it at that.

I had set myself a new target time and was trying to develop a race strategy to get there. This meant not putting in too much effort early on, avoiding the risk of fatigue, but not to start too slow and then having too much distance to make up when tired. I explained my 'careful start' strategy to Duncan who came at the problem from a slightly different angle.

'Nah, bollocks,' he had said, 'always give yourself a chance!'

I stared at him as he leaned back, quite profoundly, and chomped on a brownie. He didn't say any more.

I considered his words back at my desk, as I worked my way through a kilo of pasta. It dawned on me that he was right, and I had indeed been over thinking the situation. What he had meant was to just go for it. Don't hold back and sit around worrying what may or may not be. If you commit yourself to something, why not throw everything at it and see what happens. What a genius! Unless of course he didn't mean this, in which case I have absolutely no idea what he meant.

As we left Schonbrunn in the rain, his words echoed in my head. Just get yourself there, then worry about whether it works out or not. So, we were off to find Rugby Club Slovan Bratislava with all our fingers crossed that we'd meet someone there.

Rugby Club Slovan Bratislava is the leading rugby club in Slovakia since their creation in 2005. They have *never* lost a domestic fixture, and the majority of their team also represent their national side. Without detracting from these achievements I should also caveat, Slovakia only has the one rugby club, and everyone plays for the national team. This made for a relatively simple league structure, and national trials could also be held at training on a Wednesday evening, killing two birds with one Slovakian dumpling. I couldn't wait to meet with this team and hoped that at 6 p.m. there would be someone there to meet us, sign our scroll, and let us conquer another country.

As the afternoon progressed we realised that the journey was going to be further than 100 km, so we put our heads down and made a dash for it. Jodie took up the lead and we were soon hurtling down the main highway, making good ground and giving ourselves time to find the club before the pre-advised arrival time.

We arrived in Bratislava tired, but ahead of schedule and tried to get our bearings. I didn't expect there to be any signs for rugby, after all with just the single club, the players would already know where their own ground was. As expected, there weren't any signs but despite this, we still located the region, and soon even the road itself. The road was lined on both sides with sporting arenas, stadiums and fields. These venues held the legacy of many generations, but while some remained impressive, others were in disrepair and it seemed had been closed permanently.

The ageing athletics venue was a grand facility, but had now succumbed to nature, and the only life was from the weeds pushing through the cracks in the concrete outside. There were many sports on this road, mostly soccer facilities, but also tennis, basketball, American football and hockey. If there was sport to be played in Bratislava, it would be played on this street.

We cycled from club to club, asking the locals for 'rugby', but it seemed that our pronunciation was not Slovakian enough to recognise the sport. I presented them with my rugby ball to further illustrate our requirements. This seemed to generate acknowledgement, but sadly no directions other than finger gestures back to the American football stadium. Nobody in Bratislava had any idea that there was rugby on their doorstep. We searched every facility twice, and as the hazy sun set, we eventually found some internet connection to aid our quest. From their online map we established the exact blades of grass the team used to train, and we had been inches away all along, an unmarked field back across the road used for multi-sports.

We wheeled our bikes to the correct field and leant them against a small clubhouse, it seemed that at last we'd found the home of Slovakian rugby, and the lights were on. On the wall inside we found several references to the club Slovan Bratislava, but as I scanned the notice boards in excitement, I realised that they only referenced other sports, and not rugby. I asked a few people inside the building if they knew anyone involved in rugby, but nobody could confirm that there was even a rugby team there. It felt as if we were chasing ghosts.

I'm now thankful that I watched the film 'Shutter Island' *after* this whole debacle, or I'm fairly confident that I would have willingly committed myself to an asylum. With no further options left, we simply waited with our bikes in the open air, trying to be as conspicuous as possible. Soon the only people around were walking their dogs and it was getting dark. Reluctantly we agreed that it was time to move on, we were in plain view of the street, and camping here may have attracted unwanted attention.

Slovakia had become our very first failure, but despite the disappointment, it also reminded us how fortunate we had been this far.

We stumbled from hotel to hotel in the rain, asking for prices and discounts, but there was little interest in receiving two wet tourists and three tonnes of dirty luggage for just a single night. Most hotels demanded around € 120 for a room, and wouldn't budge. I felt like reminding them that this was Slovakia, not Switzerland, but I'd already been wrong about the country once and I was still questioning my own sanity.

Eventually, after an hour of traipsing around the city in the rain, Jodie pulled at some heart strings and received a generous discount on the condition that we stopped dripping water over their reception area. We ditched the gear in the room and came down to the bar, then had a couple of beers to put it all into perspective.

We had survived on the road for thirty days, and although it had cost us fifteen days budget for our bed and dinner, we were getting a breakfast in Bratislava thrown in for free. Surely this was the start of a better day tomorrow.

*   *   *   *   *

From: 'Pal Turi'
To: 'Jodie and Tom'

'Hi there,

I've just talked with our General Secretary (Balazs Bohm) at Esztergom Rugby Club. They are happy to host you at their clubhouse! Next, you have 3 nights accommodation in Budapest Exiles rugby clubhouse. I will be in Budapest to meet with you.

The EDF Energy Cup final is on Saturday. Next day, Sunday, there is all day rugby at Kecskemét. You could stay in our Clubhouse of course for the night. It seems you will have a real rugby week in Hungary, hope you will enjoy it.

Cheers
Pal'

CHAPTER 10
THE PERFECT HECKEL

'God, I'm so *Hungary!*' I said to Jodie, who was already busy plotting our route across the next country.

'Go and have another plate then,' she replied, 'it's an all you can eat buffet.'

It wasn't a good enough joke to repeat, and she was clearly preoccupied so I took her advice and helped myself to another grossly loaded plate of meat and eggs. Despite last night's disappointment it was indeed a new day, we did have the chance to cross another border and meet with another rugby club. The only thing unchanged was the miserable European spring. As I feasted on the plush Slovakian breakfast, I decided to be of assistance and help Jodie with her seven day plan.

'Hey Jodie, why are we always looking seven days ahead?' I paused, 'Don't you think that makes for a *week* plan?'

An uncomfortable silence suggested she wasn't biting this morning, so I held back the one about my bicycle being 'two tyred', and quietly listened to her progress.

The short summary reported that we had already established contact with the Hungarian Rugby Union (HRU) through two channels, the new president of the union, Pal Turi, and also through the previous appointment, Lajos. They had both been working hard to organise our visit, and at the last minute had suggested meeting with an extra club on our journey through to Budapest.

Although it was not in our nature to turn down a rugby opportunity, it wasn't always logistically possible to include it *and* remain on course. For a start, we didn't like to set more than a 110 km target on any given day, but furthermore we had to keep an eye on the longer term plan over that country. The reality was that if we were late for one appointment, we'd be late for, if not miss them all entirely.

Our extended offer was to meet with Balasz at his club, Esztergom Rugby Club, situated around 60 km outside Budapest.

'It sounds good!' I decided, wondering what the hesitation would be.

'Okay smart arse,' Jodie replied patiently, 'but when will we visit them, and if so, how will it affect Budapest?'

'Give it here,' I answered, snatching at the European roadmap and getting my sleeve covered in mustard.

I performed my usual calculations and quickly developed a schedule.

'Right Jo, give or take, it's about 180 kilometres along the Danube to Esztergom.'

I paused, waiting for acknowledgement. Although Jodie kept a strict vigil on the overall project, she had never liked numbers and always left these final details to me.

'Is that how you *always* work out the distance?' Jodie looked at me, with a little despair.

'Er, yeah?' I answered hesitantly, 'I thought you already knew?'

'Tom, you just measured halfway across the country using your thumb?'

'Yes?' I decided to stand by my method. 'My thumb is 20 kilometres wide!'

'Please tell me you didn't do that when you calculated our 28,000 kilometre route?'

'Of course not,' I said, 'what do you take me for?' I tried to look hurt by her comments, besides, who would calculate an 18 month bike ride using their thumb? Of course I had borrowed a ruler for that bit.

We were still scoffing breakfast at 10 a.m. so we jointly concluded that we would arrive at Esztergom the following night, probably enjoying a beautiful night's camping under the stars on the way. Balasz had sent an e-mail saying that he would be at the club for the next two evenings, so whenever we arrived we would have a place to stay.

'Okay great,' Jodie agreed, 'we'll do Esztergom tomorrow night, then head to Budapest. Can you log on to their website and get the clubhouse address?'

'Already onto it!'

I found the website and after trawling through twenty illegible Hungarian pages, I eventually found something that resembled an address. I put it into Google maps and took a mental note of where the red mark appeared. It was in the southeast quadrant, but not Esztergom itself, the neighbouring village of Dorog. For a brief moment I considered why Esztergom Rugby Club wouldn't be based in Esztergom, but then I knew that many rugby clubs moved around over the years and decided to get a final plate of bacon and eggs.

We eventually departed around midday with a gentle wind on our backs and our whole week planned. Joking about the terrible European weather, we were enjoying one of only four dry days in our thirty three days on the road. Unfortunately for us, we were cycling along the river when our four dry days turned back into three, with the heaviest downpour yet. With such conditions it wasn't going to be wise to wild camp on the banks, so we chose to press on in search of better grounds. Now cold, soaking wet and hungry, we stopped for a quick lunch break, but worried that we could get sick, we cut it short and pedalled on.

With nowhere to rest we had reached the river crossing to Hungary by late afternoon. This was to be our intended overnight camp spot, but with over 110 km already covered, and every patch of grass under puddles of water, we began to consider the reality of making another 65 km to Dorog in the remaining daylight. The mere thought of having a hot shower and drying our clothes inside was irresistible, and while we didn't exactly commit to reaching the club, at least we would push on and see how much progress could be made.

We fought on to reach Dorog in the dark. The heavy rain was unrelenting, and after 175 km of almost continuous cycling, we were physically and emotionally spent. It was 9 p.m. and only now would we begin our search for the rugby club based on my vague southeast quadrant theory. In the late evening and heavy rain, this theory soon began to display cracks and it quickly appeared that we stood little chance of finding it. Very few people were risking venturing out in the weather, and those that we asked gave varying accounts of where such a club could be found.

One man implied that Esztergom was another 10 km further down the road, but spoke little English, and didn't convince me that he recognised the rugby ball on my bike. He could have been just pointing towards the town of Esztergom. We stepped into the only open premises in the village, an empty restaurant bar. The owner agreed, and pointed us to Esztergom, but indicated that Jodie should wait inside, and that I should follow him around to the back of the building. I was a little nervous to say the least.

At the back of the bar was a small guesthouse, but it looked closed. He rang the buzzer from the gate outside and spoke briefly with a man on the intercom, soon a figure appeared at the doorway and called to him. It was clear that the man spoke no English, but he was very welcoming and even looked a bit amused at my pitiful state.

Despite my hesitation at spending a second night inside tourist accommodation, we had been broken by the harsh weather and were now desperate to get some rest. I collected Jodie, thanked our restaurant friend, and the guesthouse man showed us to our own apartment, before bringing us some towels and bidding us goodnight.

The apartment was very comfortable, but all we wanted was to have a hot shower and collapse into the inviting dry bed. For a second consecutive day we felt utterly defeated by the project. We were managing long distances, chasing after a rugby story on small glimmers of hope, and putting ourselves into such a position that our budget wouldn't stretch to Turkey, let alone New Zealand. If I hadn't needed the towel to dry my drenched body, I would certainly have thrown it somewhere.

The following morning we packed up our things, and went to settle the bill. Using the office computer in his reception, we tried to have a conversation on an internet translation service. We explained our charity cycle and thanked him for opening up so late, then nervously waited for the bill. The man shrugged as if not to understand.

Hungarian is an extremely complex language and I had my doubts over the quality of the translation. I had kept the sentences simple deliberately, but it hadn't prompted the expected response. I tried again, this time typing each bit separately.

'We are cycling to New Zealand.' I looked up at him and he raised his eyebrows in acknowledgement.

'We are raising money for charity.' This time, a gentle nod of understanding.

'Thank you for saving us from the rain.' He responded by opening his palms to mimic the rain.

'How much should we pay to you?' We both waited. There was a pause, and he repeated the exact same shrug as earlier. He *did* understand and he was trying to say there was no bill. The man gestured that he had brought us in because of the bad weather, and he didn't want payment. We were both left staggered by his generosity and set off for the final 10 km to Esztergom with a new belief in our trip.

'Okay, yes don't say it,' I said to Jodie, as we stood outside Esztergom Rugby Club an hour later, in the town of Esztergom.

'There's a reason things need to be researched,' she said anyway.

'Balasz said he'll meet us here at 3 p.m.,' I tried to sound on top of the situation, 'shall we have a look around town first?'

Later that afternoon, and right on cue, the tall figure of Balasz Bohm appeared at the rugby club gate entrance, we were all pedalled out and had been sitting in the sunshine for over an hour.

Balasz was only in his early thirties and was the recently appointed General Secretary to the HRU. He was a very charismatic and colourful character and we felt bad that he had waited until midnight the previous evening, in case we had showed up. It didn't matter to him, and now that we were there, we should drop off our things and come to meet his team.

'Do you have any swimming wear?' he suddenly asked, a bit out of the blue.

'I wish!' I said, 'I would have worn them last night!'

'Why? What happened last night?' he asked.

'Oh nothing, just a little confusion over the address. We ended up searching for your pitch in Dorog,' I admitted, 'I got an address from your website.'

'Oh!' Balasz replied, with wide eyes, 'That would be our secretary's house!'

Jodie stepped into the steam room wearing a sports bra and wrapped in a towel. I followed behind in a spare pair of Balasz's swim shorts but it soon became apparent that we had both come overdressed for the occasion. Perhaps out of courtesy to Jodie, Balasz had followed our lead by covering his genitals, but the remaining Esztergom team were already sat waiting for us in their full birthday suits.

'This is Zoltan Heckel,' Balasz said, as he proceeded to introduce us around the steamy little room.

After we had met with the owners of twenty-eight testicles, we began to chat about our journey. It turned out that several of the players spoke pretty reasonable English. They ridiculed our decision to cycle through Romania, which generated much laughter when we realised that six of the testicles were actually Romanian. They were a good fun group of guys, and once we could handle the heat no more, we made our way outside to relax in the thermal pool.

With the Hungarian dumplings now happily bubbling away and out of our sight, we got chatting to the guys, in particular their star man, Zoltan. The beefy prop was Hungary's most capped national player with over 50 appearances for his country and a pretty handy rugby CV. He had previously played 1st XV for both Portsmouth RFC and Canterbury RFC, before taking up an invitation to play for Abu Dhabi.

Before Zoltan himself opened up the 'Johnny Wilkinson Bar' in town, the team used to get drunk in Slovakia after their home games. It was just a short walk across the bridge and worth every step for the cheap beers on the other side. Now Esztergom itself has become the rugby centre for Hungary, and as we sat relaxing in the pool, the new national stadium and rugby hotel was being constructed only a hundred metres down the road. It had been a fantastic introduction into Hungary and its rugby culture, even if we were a day late.

Fully refreshed and ready to tackle the final 65 km cruise into Budapest, we stopped for a complimentary coffee in the 'Johnny Wilkinson Bar' before making our way casually along the Danube river path. Just 2 km down the road we began to suspect all was not as it should be. Numerous oil drums and roadwork fences had been placed on the junctions with diversion arrows pointing inland, towards the hills.

'Just ignore them Jo,' I called behind, as I squeezed between the hazards, 'it's probably road works further up, we'll be able to push past.'

If there had been any road works further ahead, they'd have needed scuba masks and a tank to get the job done, as the entire road was several feet under water. We backed round and followed instructions. As we took the winding hill route around and into Budapest we noticed more signs and more closed roads. The further we travelled, the worse the flooding got. Being outdoors for most of the time, we had become very observant of the weather, but naturally we tried to remind ourselves that it only 'felt' wetter than usual because we'd normally be inside in the dry. As it turned out, that May had seen record amounts of rainfall across central Europe, and eventually the Danube had burst its banks. At least now we had a real statistic to demonstrate our suffering to our many friends who still maintained that we were 'on a jolly'.

By the time we had arrived at the outer borders of Budapest we were already clocking over 80 km for the day, and with a further 25 km of pedalling across the city still required, we knew that it was going to be another long one. The best and most direct road to dissect the historical city was the river path, which again was now being operated by rowing boats rather than traffic. It took a further three hours before we pushed our bicycles through the thick sludge of the Budapest Exiles playing field.

The Exiles Rugby Club, as the name suggested were once comprised of players from all over the world, but more recently they had become an open club to anyone living in Hungary. We arrived in time to watch a junior Exiles side contest with the soggy conditions, before English coach, Dave Alpert, took us to the ice rink next door for a beer and meal. They had kindly organised for the rugby clubhouse to be our base for the entire weekend while we attended the Central & Eastern European Rugby Cup finals, and much to our horror, a Hungarian breakfast TV show the following morning.

*   *   *   *   *

From: 'Radu Constantin'
To: 'Jodie and Tom'

'Hello Jodie and Tom,

I saw your website and saw you are coming to Romania in your velo trip to NZ. I work for a TV station here in Bucharest and would like to film you and

69

```
take interview. By the way, if you don't have any
accommodation here in Bucharest, me and my wife
would be happy to accommodate you (for free of
course) if you like dogs, because we have a Golden
retriever good dog.

I gave your email address to a very passionate cycle
tourist who stay in Ineu, a little village near the
Hungarian - Romanian border, he would be happy to
escort you on your journey to Bucaresti.

Keep in touch! Have good road!

Radu Constantin'
```

*   *   *   *   *

If my team had asked to play a more competitive fixture, I would have sent them out with 14 players. When Csaba Mezes was asked that by his Hungarian club, Battai Bulldogok (the 'Bulldogs'), he decided to organise the Central & Eastern European Rugby Cup. With some hefty sponsorship from EDF Energy, he created a tournament featuring the top club sides from Austria, Czech Republic, Romania and Hungary. 2010 saw the second season of the tournament, and although further funding had fallen through, it provided a quite unique insight into the subtle differences in levels between the European rugby programmes.

Out of nowhere, as we prepared for the finals, the temperature soared to over 30 degrees and we were treated to an absolute scorcher. As a volunteer official, Balasz had scored us a couple of tickets, so we made our way to the stadium in time for the Wooden Spoon playoff, Dragon Brno (Czech Rep) vs Donau Wien (Austria). Had teams really travelled across Europe to contest a wooden spoon?

'Go on Rudi!' we screamed, as Rudi took to the field with his Austrian club side. It felt odd to see our new friend playing at such an event, although it was Rudi's face that looked the more surprised as he turned towards us. The Czechs took the wooden spoon, and as the bronze match kicked off, Rudi joined us in the stands for a well earned beer. The small crowd settled into their stride as the hosts, the Bulldogs, claimed bronze by defeating Ricany from Czech Republic.

At 5 p.m. the climax of the competition had finally arrived, and as had been heavily predicted, it was last year's champions Timisoara from Romania, playing another Romanian entrant and heavyweight, Baia Mare. Both sides had reached the final with comprehensive wins in every fixture, and one would rightly question whether Csaba had become a little carried away with the event. These concerns were not eased when a parade of white horses, dancers and fireworks contributed to a fifteen minute presentation of the trophy. Baia Mare had walked the event despite most of their 1st XV being away on national duty.

*   *   *   *   *

It was still scorching as we made our way to our next stop, Kecskemèt. There was only the one obvious road, but as it narrowed we spotted the usual frustrating sign, no old men on carts and no cyclists.

'Bloody old men on carts,' I muttered, 'they ruin it for everyone!'

'Should we get off?' Jodie asked me, as she cycled past and ignored the third sign.

'What do you think?' I shouted ahead to her, 'You'd just go round in circles if the road police had their way.'

The very next minute, the bright colours of a police car appeared alongside us. 'Oh bugger,' I thought to myself, 'one of us will have to turn on the tears again.' I tried to ignore the car, staring straight down and pretending to adjust my gears, but the police car slowed down to a crawl, keeping at our pace. The passenger wound down the window and called out to us in Hungarian. No longer able to ignore their immediate presence I conceded, looking up at him, and wondered whether Jodie should use boobs or tears. I only had the one option.

The man in the fancy dress costume smiled cheerily and waved, happy that he had got my attention. He was one of four Hungarians driving a fake police rental vehicle, just like the ones in the American movies.

'That's brilliant!' I shouted, getting Jodie's attention as they sped off into the distance. The Hungarians clearly took their costumes seriously.

'If we get pulled over for real, we can say we're going to the fancy dress party as cyclists!'

In any sport, the best players are the ones who appear to create the most time and space for themselves. They almost effortlessly dictate the pace of the match, and that of others around them. Pal Turi has this exact effect on people, the Hungarian equivalent of Obi-Wan Kenobi. He embodies Hungarian charm, speaking softly and radiating calm that makes being in his company a genuine pleasure. He also had a big hairy face, but that had more to do with a pending grand final than any Jedi teachings.

71

Like many European rugby presidents, he performed his function without pay, balancing his life of project management, with his rugby commitments and wife. We couldn't wait to sit down and have a beer with this man. Well, that wasn't being too presumptuous, we were in Hungary after all!

His teammates had come down to greet us over a traditional Hungarian BBQ, and soon we were all sat around long wooden tables outside the clubhouse. Pal gave a small wave of his hands and almost instantly a tray of hot meat was laid on the table in front of us. A young player at the end called to him, to which he responded by raising his eyebrows. Three beers appeared on the table. It was like watching a hairy orchestral conductor.

'Does he ever need to speak?' I asked myself.

Personally, no matter how tasty the sausages and burgers were, I didn't see much difference between a Hungarian BBQ and any other BBQ for that matter. I was quick to realise my mistake when they reminded me that it wasn't what you ate, it was what you washed it down with. I prepared myself as Pal gestured his pointed finger, and two little padawans ran into the bar to fetch alcohol.

Out came several shot glasses and a clear bottle, containing a distinctively unclear liquid. Minutes later, when I regained control of my facial muscles, I now admitted that I could clearly tell the difference between a regular and Hungarian BBQ.

'Ah, these fat lazy Hungarians!' Gica suddenly piped up, 'This is nothing!'

Gica was the father of Vicentiu, who between them, were coaching the Kecskemèt junior and senior sides. They were both Romanian and previously at the leading club Baia Mare. Gica had now been living in the Kecskemèt clubhouse for several seasons as a full time club coach. He was a hardy and still very athletic old man, with an endearing smile and a sharp tongue, quite the polar opposite of the gentle Hungarians. They loved to have him around, and not just for the rugby coaching.

'They should drink *my* drink!' he laughed, confronting them all at once, 'Then maybe they would not be so *fat* and *slow*!'

Gica gave the nod now to Vicentiu, who walked through to his father's bedroom and collected another clear bottle. Amusingly, someone had stuck on a large sticker, labelled 'Poison'.

The bearded team all sighed in dismay, unable to back down from the challenge, and desperate not to show any signs that their own alcohol could be outdone by a neighbouring rival.

The late sunset did nothing to halt the tide of beer being brought to us from the clubhouse bar, and we chatted about their grand final hopes the next week. They were due to play the Bulldogs, the bronze medallists from the previous weekend's cup. It would be a very tough match, even with the lucky beards. Although Pal had now stopped playing regularly for Hungary, he was still very much an active part of the Kecskemèt 1st XV and was very nervous. The hours rattled away far too quickly, they had all been such fantastic company and we knew that this was our last opportunity to hang out with them.

Before saying our final farewells, we stepped into the clubhouse for one final nightcap and a quick tour around the team photos on the wall. Jodie spotted one from the previous year.

'Hey Pal!' Jodie called out, quite loudly, 'You don't normally have a beard?'

'No, he doesn't!' laughed Vicentiu, 'Go on Pal, show them your driving licence!'

'Yeah, go on Pal, please show us your photo!' pressed a drunken Jodie.

'You don't need to see my identification,' Pal laughed, placing his hand over his wallet.

'You don't need to see his identification,' I echoed robotically to Jodie, suddenly accepting that we didn't.

*   *   *   *   *

From: 'Hasan - Istanbul Ottomans'
To: 'Jodie and Tom'

'Hi Jodie and Tom!
With great interest and admiration, Hakan and I have been reading your website and have seen that you will go through Istanbul as well. We would be more than happy to welcome you and share you our stories, as Turkish Rugby is finally finding its shape and is trying to lift along the momentum the sport in general - Turkey having its first international Rugby Sevens tournament in August 2010.

Best Regards,
Istanbul Ottomans R.F.C.
Hasan Akman'

CHAPTER 11
COUNT DRANKALOT AND THE WEREBEAR

There was nothing more than a customary glance at our passports as we pulled up at the Romanian border control. The guards, however, did take a keen interest in our heavily laden panniers, and especially the rugby ball dangling from the back of Jodie's bicycle. We were about to enter a country with a very strong history in the game.

We were enjoying a short day on the bicycle, having left from Gyula near the border of Hungary, with the intention of staying the night at Ineu with our Romanian bicycle tourer, Claudiu Moga. It was a comfortable morning of 70 km with some good weather, open farmland and very little traffic at all.

Taking any excuse he could to hop onto a bicycle, Claudiu had left at midday to cycle towards the border and meet us. This meant for a nice early afternoon meeting, and we found him leaning against a pub wall in the shade.

'Hey there Claudiu!' we both said without hesitation. He was a tiny framed little man wearing lycra, and aside from the beer in his hand, he looked every bit the hardcore bicycle tourer.

Claudiu gave a nervous cough before he introduced himself in a shaky voice. He paused as we stood absorbing our new surroundings.

'Dulnt ya wanta *bier*?' he spoke with a strong Eastern European accent, emphasising beer with a quiet enthusiasm. It was a fantastically sunny afternoon, but it had never been in our practice to stop for beer halfway through a cycle.

'I would maybe like another *bier*,' Claudiu offered, before we had the chance to respond.

He rummaged through his little bicycle bag and pulled out a small handful of change. He gave another nervous cough before speaking once more.

'I'm so sorry. I only have enough money for just two *bier*s,' he explained apologetically.

'That's okay Claudiu! You don't need to buy *us* a drink!' Jodie said, 'We're just happy to be here relaxing with you.'

Jodie fetched our bottles of water and we sat and got to know our very own Romanian guide. He was an intriguing guy.

From what we could understand, he had never had much of an occupation, but was now training to be a school teacher to help fund his continued life of adventure on bicycle. He was a bicycle tourer the old fashioned way, not like the new breed of explorers, including us, who had suddenly joined the club with a quick shopping spree on eBay. Not that Claudiu would think that, he was in awe of our journey and explained that it would be his greatest dream in life to cycle around the world. His problem, as we expected, would be how to fund such an adventure on a rural Romanian salary.

'I would need to save so very much money,' he explained, 'it is very expensive for me.'

'How long would it take you to save for this Claudiu?' I asked him.

'Maybe I could save my money for three years, then I could try. How much money did you save?'

'We have about €3.50 each per day,' Jodie explained.

'For everything? But this is nothing!' he said, his eyes wide with excitement. 'This is such a great adventure you are having. I would *love* to have this adventure. But it is not possible.'

Claudiu's English got better with confidence, and with every sip of beer he seemed to gain confidence, coming more and more out of his shell. It became clear to us that Claudiu was an extremely nervous character, but yet the mere thought of long bicycle adventures ignited a burning passion inside him.

'I would maybe like another *bier*,' he said, as if he had been waiting to ask.

'Sure, go ahead,' we both agreed, 'it can't be far to your house from here?'

'It is very close,' he confirmed, 'about twenty kilometers.'

'So Claudiu,' I tried to find our more, 'tell us about *your* adventures!'

Every summer since he was a young boy he had taken off on his bicycle, sometimes camping for one night, sometimes a week, and increasingly longer until the entire holidays had been absorbed on the road.

As he grew in confidence, he'd head off to places he wanted to see, usually challenging mountain ranges like the Pyrenees or various sites in the Alps. If he had a smaller budget then he would tour his home country of Romania, of which he claimed there were no longer any uncycled roads.

Asides from only taking the most basic of equipment, the most remarkable thing about Claudiu's tours was that every one of his journeys started, and finished, at the garage behind his house. The Pyrenees were about 2,500 km from his front door through five countries, so if he could cycle there in three weeks, he'd have three or four days to enjoy them, before turning round and pedalling for three weeks back home.

His adventures were incredible, I just couldn't imagine pedalling over 5,000 km for a summer vacation, finishing back where I had started. Often he would pedal so far, that he would run out of money hundreds of kilometres from his home. Many times he had resorted to reciting poetry on the streets to scrape together enough spare change for food. It was true bicycle touring 'on the edge', not rigidly budgeted like our own.

'How far do you think you have travelled so far?' I asked our intrepid new friend.

He thought about it for a little time, possibly recollecting some of the longer tours.

'I think now between 120,000 and 140,000 kilometres,' he concluded very modestly. The poor guy had never left Europe and already he'd technically pedalled enough kilometres to have gone round the world four times!

With all of Claudiu's pocket money now spent on the cheap Romanian beer, we followed him for an hour through the most beautiful of country landscapes, scattered with a handful of unspoiled rustic villages.

That evening we sat in Claudiu's shed and drank beer with the man who was about to guide us through North Romania, down into Bucharest, in time for the Nations Cup. The distance seemed manageable, about 570 km in six days, but the terrain would make for tough cycling, especially with heavy bicycles.

A twelve day cycle was small change for Claudiu, who was happy to make the journey just to pick up a new saddle from a friend in Bucharest. With a distinct love of his own country he explained which route we would be taking, and what spectacular sights we would enjoy along the way. After a few beers we started to get extremely excited, knowing that without proper maps, we would never have considered such a scenic journey.

Claudiu would take us up to Bâlea Lake, situated at over 2 km in altitude in the Făgăraş Mountains. The only way to get there was by a solitary road, the Transfăgărăsan route, considered to be the most dramatic of all roads in Romania. The 90 km former military route crossed the Southern Carpathian mountains, between the two highest peaks in the country, and sounded like one of the best views on earth.

'Tom, that's the road we watched on Top Gear before we left,' Jodie reminded me.

'Are you sure?' I questioned, 'The one that Jeremy Clarkson called *the best road in the world?*'

'Pretty sure,' she said, as Claudiu blindly agreed with everything.

With all the beer drunk, Claudiu snuck a small bottle of his father's gin and we toasted our little mini-adventure together. Knocking back the last stiff shot, we should have called the night over there and then, but I remembered the small bottle of 'Poison' that Gica had handed me for the road. Despite Jodie's protests I dashed upstairs and retrieved it.

'We don't want to be carrying this extra weight all the way up to Bâlea Lake,' I offered, in justification.

'I don't want to be carrying that anywhere!' she answered.

At breakfast, Claudiu looked as pale as a sheet and although we didn't feel too clever either, it was an exciting day. Our first in rural Romania, and with our new guide we could enjoy every minute worry free. His father was a little upset that Claudiu had thieved a bottle of his gin, but his temperament changed minutes later when the 'Gin Man' turned up at the door. He returned to the kitchen with three large label-less bottles of the homebrew. I decided to give him our empty bottle to use for future refills. He accepted the bottle without hesitation, filled it from one of the new bigger bottles, and handed it right back to me.

'No wait, I didn't mean for us!' I tried to explain.

'He wants you to have this, for a gift,' Claudia mumbled, with his face buried in his arms on the table, 'he will be happy if you accept it.'

'Okay, thank you Mr Claudiu, thank you very much!' I said forcing an enthusiastic smile. He gave me a wink and suggested something about it giving me better biceps.

I turned to Claudiu, but he was gone. 'Where'd he go?' I asked Jodie.

'He's gone back to bed!' Jodie said, rolling her eyes. She hated starting late.

'Don't worry honey, he's done this a thousand times, I'm sure he knows what he's doing!'

In the midday heat, we finally began our six day journey to Bucharest. Our bicycles looked fully loaded with bright panniers and our kit bags bungeed onto our professional rack setup. Claudiu, by comparison had only two canvas bags and a tent held on top with a bit of old rope.

It quickly became evident that his natural pace was much faster than ours, and he was forced to stop pedalling almost every minute to wait for us. He didn't seem to mind, and was now quite enthusiastic about joining us on the road. We soon arrived at a neighbouring town, only a few kilometres into the journey.

'Dulnt ya wanta *bier*?' he tried to suggest to us. It seemed as if he was serious.

'Er Claudiu, I think we should try and get the 100 km done first hey?' Jodie stamped her authority on the situation. He seemed quite disappointed,

'I *like* to have a bier,' he retorted, as if to convince her of the suggestion. Nevertheless, he continued in front and described the areas that we would be travelling through. It became clear that he did indeed know Romania like the back of his hand.

He tried several more times for a beer, but both of us were already becoming a little anxious over the schedule. We hadn't appeared to cover much ground, only around 50 km in the first afternoon.

'We can take a shortcut here,' he suddenly said, pointing left to a chalky path. 'This will save us about 10 km.'

'Are you sure Claudiu?' I questioned. Despite having hybrid tyres, they were best suited to surfaced roads. We were carrying heavy loads and the slightest bump would put a great deal of tension through the wheels and frames.

'Yes, I *always* take this road,' he assured us, 'there is a beautiful hot pool I wish to show you here! We can wash.'

'We've only just started!' Jodie whispered to me, but by now Claudiu had already started up the dusty track.

'Come on, if it saves 10 km, then we only need to pedal 90 km today. Let's just trust him.'

The track was awful, only really good for mountain bikes with full suspension. As we ended up pushing in many parts, we both tried to hide our growing frustration with the situation. We had achieved so much already, keeping a strict schedule with disciplined hours and sensible routines, this was not falling into either of those categories. It wouldn't take much for a wheel to become bent, or a spoke to snap, and we would have no budget or opportunity to fix the problem quickly.

True to his word, the track did save us 10 km, but after an hour watching him wash away his hangover in the hot pool, it didn't save us any time. As we finally rejoined the road, it was early evening and the daylight was fading fast. We had managed only 70 km towards Bucharest, even with the shortcut.

Claudiu coughed nervously again, then spoke, 'I know a good place to camp near here.'

'Okay good,' Jodie said, 'we can get an early night and make up for the lost ground tomorrow morning.'

'We should wait until it is dark,' Claudiu now insisted. 'It is much safer to do it this way. We can get something to eat for dinner here,' he said, pointing towards an adjacent building.

'What a surprise,' Jodie muttered, out of earshot, as Claudiu came outside to our table with a large bottle of beer and a giant packet of plain puffy wheat snacks. He offered us to eat with him, and although that wasn't going to constitute *my* dinner, I tried one only because I was now famished. It tasted like a cheesy puff that someone had sucked for an hour before putting back in the packet.

'Is that your dinner?' I asked him, seriously concerned. It wasn't in my schedule to miss my evening meal. He nodded.

'Dulnt ya wanta *bier*?' he asked, looking most upset that we weren't sharing the experience with him.

'I *like* to have a bier!' he cackled crazily, happy that he had been reunited with his bubbly little companion.

What had we got ourselves into? He seemed a very innocent and open individual, but worryingly for someone our age he was still living with his parents, and wasn't taking much responsibility for keeping to our schedule. Even though he was ten times the cyclist we would ever be, it was clear that he had a very different idea of what his travelling would entail.

'Claudiu, we can't cook our dinner here, this is a pub!' I said, tired and getting irritable with hunger.

'We will go to set up our tent soon. I know a very good place,' he promised solemnly.

Patiently we waited, and waited. And waited. By his third two litre bottle of beer we didn't need to ask him to leave, the bar-lady told him as she went to lock up. It was 11 p.m. and we were now cold, sober and very hungry.

As we collected our bikes from the pub wall outside, a scruffy old man took an interest in our situation. The village was empty and dark and he had either got drunk and decided to walk his dog, or had been drinking with his dog at a different pub. Either way he was just off home and asked Claudiu and the bar-lady if we needed a place to stay.

'Tell him yes please Claudiu. That would be perfect seeing as it's so late!'

Claudiu spoke to the man in Romanian, but it was a lengthy conversation and I wasn't sure he had relayed my answer at all.

'Claudiu?' I asked patiently, 'Did you explain to him that we would love to come and stay at his house?'

We pushed the bicycles through the dark village, Claudiu still swigging from his bottle of beer, as he continued to discuss matters with the man.

'I don't trust him!' Claudiu said to us quite openly, 'Don't worry! He doesn't speak English!'

'He seems fine to me Claudiu! Where did he say we could sleep?'

'He says he has a spare bedroom for you two to sleep in.'

'Well, like I told you, tell him thank you!'

'But he says I am not allowed to sleep there.'

'Where do you have to sleep?'

'In *his* bed,' he replied, laughing nervously, 'I think he wants to *bum* me!'

'Sounds fine with me Claudiu,' I replied, willing to sacrifice our drunken guide, 'let's have a vote on it.'

The man didn't seem overly obscure, but after a few more conversations we sensed that something wasn't right, and the dog was walking with a bit of a waddle. We gave Claudiu's rear exit a night off and threw away our hopes of a bed for the night.

'This camp spot better be close Claudiu!' I warned him, 'Or you'll get my foot up your arse instead!'

'Follow me!' he cackled again, swaying from side to side in the dark.

If Jodie and I had been 'frustrated' by the rocky shortcut earlier in the day, we were best described as 'thoroughly fucked off' by the next hour and a half. We were soon cycling through narrow country lanes, with only a single head torch to spot the huge holes in the road, cars whistling passed us without warning.

Claudiu had no light and we would regularly hear a crunch, then a groan, each time he hit a pothole. As he led the way, now many metres ahead, we lost sight of him completely until the occasional car would light up his back as he swigged beer. When we threw up our tents at 1 a.m. we could see nothing of the surroundings, but Claudiu convinced us that he had camped at this spot several times already, and we were too exhausted to care. With a painfully empty stomach I closed my eyes.

The alarm sounded at 8 a.m. and I crawled out of the tent to boil the kettle. We were starving hungry and almost considered a tuna pasta breakfast. Claudiu had not emerged from his leaky little home, and it had rained during the night.

'Claudiu, wakey wakey!' Jodie said, as she strolled over to his doorway. 'Would you like a tea or coffee?'

For a second successive morning we were presented with the pasty faced little Claudiu. He looked quite sheepish and was very quiet indeed.

'I am so hungry!' he stated after a little pensive thought whilst sitting on the grass.

'Us too, come and have some porridge,' Jodie offered.

Claudiu picked up the half full beer bottle and took a large swig, it had been laying in the morning sun for over an hour. We turned away and made the coffee and porridge. Claudiu declined the porridge but insisted he would pick up some food from the next village instead.

As we sat eating our breakfast, I looked around at our surroundings, what did he mean the next village? We were at the village already, camped on a green by a duck pond. There was litter all around us with a sign written in Romanian, it suggested something of a national park area, with photos of wildlife and a list of prices, presumably fineable offences.

We finished breakfast as Claudiu finished his warm flat beer, and packed away the tents, but a utility vehicle pulled up besides us before we could finish. Out stepped a park ranger.

'Brilliant,' I said to myself, 'thanks Claudiu!'

Whether it was our obviously foreign appearance, or that he could smell Claudiu's breath, he chose to approach our little guide first, and not us. He was suddenly very nervous and rambled to the park ranger for many minutes, probably trying to explain the whole story from start to finish. The park ranger was very polite and had enough English to explain to us that we shouldn't be camping in the National Park area without a proper permit. He didn't want to spoil our great trip so wouldn't fine us, but wanted to ensure that we were briefed about the area and the potential hazards.

He gave us a small leaflet and asked if we could take our rubbish away with us, it wasn't ours but we happily obliged, thankful not to have to haggle down a fine on the grounds of 'charity'. He drove off and waved us goodbye.

We turned to stare at Claudiu, who anticipating our response had now packed up his gear with urgency.

'It is fine,' he tried to insist, once the ranger had left, 'I *always* camp here.'

'Well, I'd suggest you don't anymore Claudiu,' Jodie replied. 'Right, we've got a lot of cycling to do today so we'd better get a move on.'

We pedalled into the village and were about to exit through the other side when Claudiu pulled over, and leant his bicycle against a wall.

'I have to eat,' he said, 'I'm so *hungry*!'

He made a very sorry sight and I could sympathise with his condition, it wasn't as if I had never got the munchies the morning after a big session.

'Quick, go and order something then,' we both said to him, accepting the situation. He rushed inside.

'It will be ready in ten minutes,' he said as he invited us to sit down at the table with him.

Reluctantly we got off the bicycles with 150 metres on the clock, and waited for his order. A minute later and the owner walked out to him with a bottle of beer.

'Dulnt ya wanta *bier*?' he asked us, with a genuine face of confusion.

'No Claudiu!' Jodie said, 'I want to cycle to Bucharest, we have to be there in five days and it's still 500 km away!'

He poured a little salt into his beer and gave another little trade mark cough.

'I like to have a *bier*,' he said trying to lighten the subject, he didn't like to talk about the schedule.

'Claudiu, you do understand that we *have* to be in Bucharest on Wednesday don't you?' I asked him directly.

'We have lots of time,' he said, staring into his beer, 'it is so very beautiful on these roads.'

We both decided to leave it alone and just keep an eye on the situation. As his plush Romanian brunch of sausages, spicy soup and bread was served, we took the opportunity to flick through the park flyer. In amongst the Romanian text there were images of beautiful birds of prey, forests, shrews, bears and wolves.

'Bears and wolves?' I thought, 'Jodie hadn't mentioned anything about bears and wolves!'

'Can we stop for a break here?' Claudiu requested. It was very hot, and we'd been on the road for two hours.

'Yep, come on, let's take five minutes,' I decided, although we were only 20 km into the cycle. We sat down on the wall overlooking a stream beneath us, and in a visible 'puff' of smoke, Claudiu had disappeared. He returned moments later with a beer, a packet of salted nuts and an energy bar, and sat with us enjoying the view.

'Don't you think you drink a bit too much beer Claudiu?' Jodie asked him politely.

'I *like* to drink a bier,' came the almost standard giggling response. 'I love to adventure and drink bier. It is my dream.'

I had to agree that his style of touring, however costly, certainly appeared to be much more fun. My only concern was at such a lethargic pace across the planet, he would probably suffer liver failure long before reaching New Zealand. It was with a sense of irony that we noted our poor, unemployed companion living the highlife while his two city-working Londoners scraped through on bread, liver pâté and tomato.

The afternoon continued in the same vein, with Claudiu cycling for an hour, then requesting a rest at every second pub. By 5 p.m. we had reached a restaurant at the foot of a steep ascent into the hills. We had only pedalled 70 km that day and normally we'd have finished comfortably before 6 p.m.

'I have to go inside,' explained Claudiu as he reluctantly walked towards the door.

'Jo,' I said, while he was inside, 'we can't do this anymore. We're going to have to go on without him soon.'

'I know,' she agreed, 'but we don't really know where we're going!'

A distraught looking Claudiu came out of the restaurant and surprisingly he wasn't holding a beer.

'I'm really sorry,' he said, almost with tears in his eyes. 'I'm sorry but I can't come with you anymore.'

'What do you mean Claudiu? Why?' we asked in unison.

'I'm sorry but I won't have enough money to get home. I don't want to beg on the streets again.'

Claudiu had spent almost his entire twelve day budget in only a day and a half on the road. It was enough money to have lasted us both for two weeks. He had gone into the restaurant only to phone his mother and ask for some more money to be transferred to his bank account. Quite rightly, having already given him his budget, she had declined.

It was a very sad affair to say good bye to him so soon, but we were already over 50 km behind the necessary pace and were now under real pressure to get through the mountains. It was not going to be an easy ride.

'Bloody hell!' I said to Jodie, 'That's left us right up shit creek! How on earth does he cycle for three months like that?'

I turned to Jodie, who was now crying as she pedalled. 'It's so sad,' she sobbed, 'I just feel so sorry for him.'

'You should be feeling sorry for us!' I replied to her, 'We have to find somewhere to sleep in these hills tonight.'

*   *   *   *   *

'Jo, I can see it!' I whispered to her as I quietly lifted the bottom of the tent door.

'What is it?' she whispered back, clearly terrified.

'It looks like a small bear!' I replied, quite calmly. For some reason seeing a bear no longer seemed like the worst outcome.

'Be careful!' Jodie pleaded with me, 'We don't want to startle it.'

A noisy engine chugged up the hill and there was a flash of light as it turned past our corner. I looked back out the tent, but the beast had vanished into the trees.

If you count blinking as a very short form of sleep, then we slept very well and very often that night. The rest of the time we were on the lookout for bears, and as we got more tired and delusional, for the caped figure of Count Drankalot to reappear. We barely waited for sunrise before packing up a damp tent and getting up and over the hills towards Sibiu.

It was still about 150 km away and being built at relative altitude, would involve a long day of climbing in the Romanian heat. Determined that we would get back on track we fought hard during a long morning, and an even longer afternoon, but our efforts were rewarded as we arrived at the beautiful town in the late afternoon sun.

'Can we afford a treat tonight?' asked Jodie, voicing both of our thoughts. It had been a pig of a day.

'I don't think it will be that expensive here right?' I agreed, pretending that we hadn't already decided.

'We'll get the very cheapest room in the town!' Jodie added, trying to make our moment of weakness sound like an economical decision.

'But look, if we are going to book into a cheap guesthouse, then we have to do it properly and go out for some food too!' I explained, 'I'm not going to do this half arsed.'

'Okay, but *only* if you say so,' agreed Jodie, with a huge smile.

We probably blew a week's budget on that evening alone, but it was well worth it. We enjoyed a meal, a couple of drinks together and even tried a little sex before we snuggled down to watch 'The Terminator'.

'That was pretty good wasn't it?' I reflected, as Arnie stole a pair of sunglasses, 'It's been a while since we did *that*.'

'I know,' Jodie smiled contently, 'I haven't had a salad for ages.'

If I didn't blame the meal and drinks I'd have a lot of explaining to do, but the next morning I was beginning to feel quite sick.

'It sounds like dehydration Tom,' Jodie sounded concerned, 'here make sure you drink plenty of water, we had a tough day yesterday.'

I took a couple of headache tablets, and took a deep breath. I was feeling dizzy and my stomach was beginning to feel bloated.

'Come on Jo, let's just get going,' I said, 'the earlier we set off, the more breaks we can have.'

Although I guzzled water, the sun was probably stripping at least as much from my skin. We were literally roasting alive as we reached the base of the Carpathian Mountains. I collapsed against a tree and passed out for the best part of an hour. Jodie kept an eye over me while I rested, and when I woke, we talked about the reality of

Bucharest. It was a long way off and would require some intense pedalling to reach there in time.

'We have to carry on Jo, we can't give up now.'

We started the 90 km trail of hairpins and S-bends. Although the summit was only marked around 27 km away this meant a *much* steeper ascent than descent. It proved too hard for me to pedal in my exhausted condition. Even Jodie at full strength was unable to stay above 6 k.p.h. for long.

'We won't make it to the top tonight Tom,' she concluded, 'should we aim for the resort in 15 km?'

'Anything Jo, I don't care,' I wheezed, I was already in a world of pain.

With Jodie's relentless encouragement I finally dragged myself up to the resort and collapsed onto the decking. Jodie went inside to see if there was any chance of getting indoors, but unable to afford any of the rooms, I didn't move. We spent the night outside on the decking, in our sleeping bags.

I felt no better the following morning, and now having not eaten for almost 24 hours, I tried to force down some breakfast. It did no good and my stomach was now doubled over in cramp. We looked up at the final 12 km of hairpins and began to push.

We later found out this section of the Transfăgărăsan is used as part of the annual cycle competition, the 'Tour de Romania'. The difficulty of this section is considered to be very similar to the 'Hors Categorie' climbs in the Tour de France, which quite literally translates as 'beyond categorisation'. Here's a categorisation for you - 'fucking steep'. Try using that Tour de France.

With 10 km still to go, I collapsed by the side of the road before diving behind a rock. As quick as I could drink water, my backside was turning it into Guinness, and I was beginning to fall apart. In desperation I reached into the medical bag and took some tablets; two for anti-sickness and two for stomach cramps - I had already taken paracetamols earlier for my fever. No sooner had they hit my stomach when I realised that something was seriously wrong. With no food inside me, the pills were causing a violent reaction and I suddenly began to struggle for breath. My lungs started to paralyse as if I had been punched in the chest. Jodie panicked and searched for help but the mountain was empty. I did all I could to force my fingers down my throat and bring back up the mixture, thankfully, my relief was almost instant. Two long and enduring hours later and we had reached the top. It broke no 'Tour de Romania' records, but after being on the mountain for over 18 hours, we had finally reached the pass.

'Fuck you Jeremy Clarkson!' I cried, as I lay curled up on the grass.

*   *   *   *   *

'Don't worry Tom, we'll get you fixed up and I'll drop you back off at Pitesti,' Pete the Welshman said to me in the van.

We had pushed on from the summit and had survived one further night on the road, but not able to stomach any food, we had decided the Nations Cup was an unrealistic target unless we got help.

'No thanks Pete, there's not much point in cheating, then still cycling it!'

'If you go back and cycle it, then you won't be cheating,' Radu pointed out, very helpfully but tongue in cheek.

I paused, 'Too late guys, I've accepted it, I think you should too.'

'How does your knee feel?' Radu looked at it with concern.

'It looks worse than it is really,' I answered. After the summit we had cycled through the 'Bâlea Tunnel', Romania's longest tunnel at 884 metres in length. Shortly after completing the longest tunnel in Romania, I had slipped on ice and fallen on my arse.

'And how was the train?' asked Radu.

'It was the best train journey in my life Radu,' I stated quite simply.

By the time we had cycled the final 60 km to Pitesti, I had no hesitation in handing over €6 for the 110 km train journey into the centre of Bucharest. Thanks to Jodie, she had called ahead and found out the times of the trains, the prices, and arranged for Radu to collect us from the station. Radu's friend, Pete the Welshman, was a keen rugby man and had been only too happy to assist us. Whatever the situation, we had made it to Bucharest, and I could now spend a few days on the mend with Radu and his wife Anca. Not only that, but I could still get to see the Nations Cup the following afternoon.

Anca handed me a sausage skewered on a stick, and I immediately began to notice signs of recovery. This was every bit what we had hoped for when Radu had invited us all those days ago from across the border. Thousands of Romanians were now taking their seats, enjoying a day off work and building an atmosphere in the only way they knew.

Despite the temptation to join them, I abstained from the Romanian beers and concentrated on building up my health for our departure a couple of days later. A little splash of sauce dropped onto my lap as the first of the sides, Namibia, took to the pitch in the scorching Bucharest summer.

It was still early afternoon and it was the first of three international fixtures to be played that day, we were sat flush on the halfway line and enjoying the luxury of a shaded grandstand.

The Nations Cup is one of three IRB Tier 2 development tournaments around the world, the others being the Churchill Cup, in North America, and the Pacific Nations Cup. It normally involves Romania and Georgia, and four invitational sides from Europe, South America and Africa. This year, the guest sides were Scotland A, Italy A, the Argentina Jaguars (3rd XV) and Namibia.

'Okay guys, enjoy the game,' Radu said as he stood up and hopped up the concrete steps.

'Hey, where is he going?' I turned back to Peter, 'We've only just got here!'

'He's sitting up there!' Peter laughed, pointing towards the commentary box at the back of our stand. 'He's about the only Romanian who can commentate on rugby.'

'So who's the other man up there in the box then?'

'Let's see,' Peter turned to identify the second man, 'he quite often has rugby guests in with him. Right, have you heard of a chap called Hari Dumitras?'

'Nope, sorry.'

'Well, that's him. Hari is something of a Romanian rugby legend here. He was a very strong back row forward, and captained the side on their *only* victory away in France.'

'I had no idea they'd ever beaten France?'

'They've actually beaten them twice. Most people don't know much about Romanian rugby nowadays, but if you go back to the amateur era, there wasn't much to choose between them and many other top European sides. Hari's boys beat France in '91, and if you can remember the World Cup in 1995...'

'I can't, no!' I interjected before he jumped to any assumptions.

'Right, well, while you were watching Sesame Street, us adults *were* watching it, and the Romanians were a very decent outfit that year. They beat Fiji, and had South Africa on the ropes for a good 70 minutes or so.'

'You sound like a bit of a fan? Have you converted from Wales to Romania?'

'I love all rugby Tom, even England.'

I laughed, 'You're Welsh, you can't like England.'

'No honestly I do, I admire all teams,' Pete smiled to himself. 'If I was to put them in reverse order it would be England, Finland...'

'Hang on, what do you mean Finland?' I had spent enough time on the IRB website to know that Finland propped up the 95 ranked teams.

'Like I said, I do admire the English team, just a little bit less than the Finnish. You know what they say about the English and Welsh don't you Tom?'

'Yes, it's a relationship based on trust and understanding. You don't trust us, and we can't understand you!'

As we listened to the Namibian national anthem I scanned the squad of bright red shirts standing arm in arm across the pitch. At the head, was the familiar mop of hair owned by our Saracens legend, Jacques Burger. As the second ranked side in Africa, they were already heading to New Zealand in 2011, and against them stood a development side from Argentina, the Jaguars.

The match kicked off to a thunderous reception and soon it became clear that the Romanians thoroughly enjoyed their rugby. The match was nothing like the tight affair you might expect from an international fixture, as both sides looked to play a fast, attacking game. The Argentineans were short, stocky and brave, running intelligent lines and keeping the ball alive. The Namibians in contrast played with less structure, and used every opportunity to open up their gazelle-like legs. Finally in the dying minutes, Namibia clinched the match, sending them top of the table.

'Come on Jo,' I said, 'let's go and get Hari Dumitras on our scroll.'

'Who's Hari Dumitras?' she asked.

'Don't you know?' I answered, 'Oh, well while you were watching Sesame Street... '

*   *   *   *   *

```
From: 'Pavel & Stella'
To: 'Jodie and Tom'

'Dear Jodie and Tom,
You don't know us but if you need any support in
Bulgaria, please let us know. By crossing Romanian-
Bulgarian border you are entering rugby wilderness,
so we thought you might need some help :) We can
offer a nice place to stay in Varna, dinner and
drinks are on us too.

Good luck with your journey! Stella & Pavel'
```

*   *   *   *   *

We were now two days into our Romanian break, hilariously referred to as our 'Bucha-rest', but we were already scheduled to depart the very next morning.

My knee was still a bit septic and although I had a healthy appetite back, my 'Coco Pops' bottom was still turning the milk chocolaty. Anca, the polar-opposite of Jodie when it came to open wounds, seemed to relish the opportunity to scrub away at my infected knee. Each morning she removed the green congealed surface with a medical brillo pad, while assuring me that it wasn't the same one she had used to wash the dishes.

It wasn't a pleasant experience, and one that left to my own devices I would have covered up and left out of sight, but as Anca reminded us both, we weren't in England any more and we'd have to start paying close attention to our health as we progressed further towards Asia. Maintaining health was going to be a key factor in arriving at the Rugby World Cup on bicycle, on time.

Many other cross world cyclists had spent weeks or months recovering in far away hospitals, often after coming into contact with contaminated water, and despite the irony of now recovering from illness, our tight budget seemed to be improving our chances of success. Whereas many travellers would purchase bottled water and only drink from filtered taps, we had been glugging from garden hoses, church graveyards and mountain streams. Now in Bucharest, we seemed happy to drink from the water supply, whilst most locals opted to order in large drums of purified water.

'Jodie and Tom,' Radu said gleefully on Thursday morning, 'perhaps you should stay a little longer to rest before you leave.'

'I'd love to,' I replied in total honesty, 'but we're supposed to be leaving tomorrow to keep to our schedule.'

'Yes, but it is the final of the Nations Cup this weekend, after that perhaps you will be well enough to continue?'

I turned to Jodie who seemed to nod unexpectedly in agreement. Although I was officially 'Chief of Schedule', Radu had won me over at 'perhaps you should stay', and the opportunity to watch international rugby under the cloak of recovery didn't seem to deliver any negatives. Still, everyone knew that Jodie was a fidget-bum, and with so many kilometres still ahead of us I was surprised that she didn't at least try to emphasise the need to press on.

'Tom, I think you should think about what Radu is saying,' she said. 'Maybe you need a couple more days to get fully fit again, you were in a really bad way back in the mountains. Plus, you wouldn't mind watching a bit of rugby would you?'

Blimey! Now Jodie was telling me to rest as well. Did nobody realise that I'd already agreed to it? Ah, of course they didn't, I hadn't told them yet. Holding my cards close to my chest, I put on my 'thoughtful and reluctant' expression.

'I suppose it makes sense,' I glanced between the two concerned faces, 'but let me check the schedule to see if we have time.' I had never written down a schedule, so I picked up the map instead and made a slow and seemingly calculated motion with my finger from Bucharest to the end of the page.

'Yes, we have time,' I confirmed, trying not to blow the pretence.

'Good, I'm really happy that you guys are staying!' Radu clapped his hands together to seal the deal. 'We get to watch more rugby together! And Jodie,' he continued, 'you won't have to clean Tom's knee!'

Jodie gave a 'thoughtful and reluctant' expression.

'You little bugger,' I finally realised, 'I knew there was a reason!'

By the weekend I was feeling much better, and even managed a couple of Romanian beers as we watched Namibia win the cup with a third successive victory. Jacques Burger, one of our scroll signatures from Saracens, led the way in both attack and defence, taking a good kicking in the process. After the match we bumped into him outside the ground, as he made his way to an ambulance to get some stitches.

'Hey Jacques!' I said to him, as if we'd known each other for years.

'Hey guys,' he answered, as if he'd never met me before.

'Do you remember us? We came to meet you at Saracens a few weeks ago,' Jodie added.

He now looked down at Jodie and smiled.

'Oh yeah, cool!' he replied, 'Weren't you like walking to the World Cup or something?'

'Close enough!' I answered, impressed with his memory.

'That's so awesome!' he replied, 'So how far have you got?'

CHAPTER 12
KARMA IN VARNA

'I'm sorry about the choice of venue!' Pavel apologised to us a little tongue in cheek, 'I imagine that this is the last place you would have chosen on a rugby journey!'

We had met with Pavel and Stella at the England pub in Varna, by chance at the exact time of an England match at the FIFA World Cup in South Africa. All around us were English holiday makers ordering burgers and chips and drinking pints of lager.

'That's okay!' I replied, 'We appreciate that this is your office.'

Pavel was a leading Bulgarian sports pundit and correspondent for an online betting website. Although he earned from these activities, his main source of income came from following his own recommendations and 'putting his money where his mouth is'. Pavel loved all sports, and it was through his permanent drive to research the sporting world that he had stumbled across our project. Although rugby was a relatively small sport in Bulgaria, he took an interest in the qualification to the Rugby World Cup and to his knowledge, he was the only Bulgarian to write articles on the sport.

A late sliding tackle left an England player rolling round on the floor clutching his ankle, and forgetting that the match was six thousand miles away in South Africa, the crowd began to yell at the referee.

'Nice tackle,' Pavel said quietly.

'It looked pretty late to me,' I answered, as the referee branded a yellow card.

'Yes, I know,' he smiled, 'I've got a bet on the number of bookings!'

Having finished a successful evening at the office, Pavel led us to his brother's empty three story apartment in the heart of town. It didn't come as a big surprise to learn that his brother was a professional poker player, and was currently spending two weeks between Moscow and Las Vegas competing on the professional circuit. Judging by his house he was either a very good player, or had very baggy sleeves.

*   *   *   *   *

Although we enjoyed a relaxing weekend with no commitments, the weather was terrible, and we had heard nothing back from our Bulgarian rugby contacts. On Sunday evening, Pavel invited us round to his for dinner before we headed off the following morning.

'Have you achieved everything you need to here in Bulgaria?' Pavel asked us over dinner.

It was a question that we had tried not to ask of ourselves. Varna was the home of supposed Bulgarian legend, Ivan Ivanov, and had been the destination suggested to us by both Eduard in Prague and Paul in Vienna. Despite this, we had independently made contact with an English speaking Bulgarian called Vassil Varbanov at Murphy's Misfits RFC, in the Bulgarian capital, Sofia.

Vassil had offered to organise everything for our visit to Sofia, but time would not permit us to travel to both, and Varna was by far the shorter journey. Pavel's invite to the coastal town had subsequently won us over, and with plenty of time to chase up on our leads, we opted for a weekend at the beach. Sadly, after several e-mails and text messages, it was becoming clear that we would now fail in our Bulgarian chapter.

We explained the whole situation to Pavel, showing him the scroll of signatures across the world so far. He was very interested by the canvas document and admitted that he was sorry that Bulgaria had let down the project.

'I don't think it's through lack of interest,' I explained, 'I've been reliably informed that this man is the Godfather of Bulgarian rugby. I just get the feeling that he doesn't speak any English.'

'Do you have his phone number on you?' Pavel asked, 'Maybe I could speak to him.'

'Yes, I do actually. His name is Ivan,' I handed Pavel my notebook, 'Ivan Ivanov.'

'Ivan Ivanov?'

'Yes, Ivan Ivanov.' The name was now beginning to lose all meaning, 'Why, do you know him?'

'Ivan Ivanov was my rugby coach when I was a young boy.'

'I didn't know you played rugby! You never mentioned it!'

'We all played rugby here in Varna, Ivan Ivanov made us!' he laughed, 'I haven't seen him for about twenty years.'

Pavel dialled the number and had a long conversation in Bulgarian. Even to my untrained ear it was clear that he first explained how Ivan had known him as a boy, and then proceeded to describe our rugby trip to New Zealand. After a seemingly endless procession of discussion, nodding and grunts of acknowledgement, Pavel placed the phone back down on the table.

'He will see you at breakfast tomorrow.'

'Are you serious?' Jodie replied in disbelief. It was nearly 10 p.m. on Sunday evening and we had already accepted defeat. 'That's brilliant!'

'We'll come along to translate,' he offered, 'Ivan is very excited by your journey and said he would be honoured to meet with you. Did I mention that he will arrange for the national TV channel to come down to film an interview as well?'

'No, you just said we're meeting him for breakfast,' I replied, nearly choking on my chicken.

'Oh, okay. The national TV channel are coming down to film the interview.'

As we sat in the sunshine outside the predetermined café, Pavel leant over and whispered, 'That's Ivan Ivanov coming over now.'

A smartly dressed older man ambled over towards our table. He was quite stocky, with broad shoulders and light grey hair, and was flanked by two further men, also suitably dressed for the occasion. Pavel jumped to his feet and performed the introductions in both Bulgarian and English, starting with Ivan Ivanov. The other two gentlemen turned out to be Plamen Kirov, former national captain, and Dr Nikola Zlatarski, who sits on the Bulgarian Rugby Federation Management Committee. With Pavel's silky translation skills we sat down and talked about Bulgarian rugby.

Despite his current frame, Ivan Ivanov had actually started off his sporting career in the 1950s as a long jumper. At this time, the sports institution in which he trained employed a Romanian coach who, probably becoming homesick, decided to bring his love of rugby to Bulgaria. Using his Romanian contacts, the coach arranged a club fixture between two Romanian sides to be played in Sofia.

The Bulgarian crowd swarmed to witness the historic event, with an attendance quoted as over 70,000 on the day. This was either an early sign for an untapped enthusiasm for rugby or just that there was a big football derby kicking off immediately after. Either way, Ivan Ivanov was converted, and with him at standoff, the first signs of a Bulgarian rugby team began to evolve.

By 1963 a Bulgarian Rugby Federation had taken shape, and at the height of Bulgarian rugby, in the late '80s and early '90s, it was competing regularly in an Eastern European 'Peace and Friendship' competition against teams like Romania and Czechoslovakia. Our new friend Plamen Kirov played his part in this era, leading his team to their greatest victory, defeating the Czech Republic 15-10 in 1990. By the late '90s, the economic climate in Bulgaria had killed off most interest in amateur sports and there was a depleted pool of new players coming through. Even Varna Rugby Club, one of the country's most successful teams, was forced to shut down for many years, before finally being re-launched in 2001.

We asked former captains Ivan and Plamen to sign our scroll, and once our TV interview had been filmed, we made our way upstairs to a Bulgarian food court to eat some lunch before setting off.

'Where would you like to eat?' Pavel asked us, 'They are offering to buy you lunch from anywhere you like.'

We looked around us, everything was in Bulgarian and it was difficult from the pictures to really differentiate.

'Trust me, it's all good with us,' Jodie answered, 'please ask them to choose.'

We sat down at a table and Plamen brought over several trays of kebabs, salads, soups and drinks. Just moments after, an enormous man approached us and stood, casting a shadow over the entire table.

'I hope they paid for the food!' I thought to myself.

Plamen, unaffected, stood up and greeted the new guest with a huge smile. After a quick translation, we learned that the giant was Ruman, a second row from Plamen's national playing days. Ruman was an absolute hench of a man, tall and heavy set, with legs like tree trunks and fists like sledgehammers. He was without doubt the biggest amateur rugby player I had ever seen. He worked on tug boats and had only started playing rugby to help out a friend, but once he had begun he never looked back. My only thought was that if you already employed Ruman, why did you also need the tug boat?

'If you are still thinking of going to Karachi, Ruman can help you,' Pavel explained, 'he works there six months of the year. He said that the rugby family is very big and he can put you in touch with the right people when you land.'

It was yet another bizarre connection in the rugby world, but one that encouraged us further as we waved goodbye and pedalled south along the coastal road towards Turkey.

As if by clockwork, the clouds rolled over and the drizzle started just minutes outside of Varna. The consolation on this occasion was that we wouldn't be camping, not unless we couldn't follow Pavel's directions to his grandmother's house 80 km down the road. After a short five hour cycle, we found it with no problems and the sun had burned through to present us with a beautiful long summer evening.

Pavel's tiny grandmother didn't understand a single word of English, but that didn't prevent her excitement at having two new guests. She was a wonderful lady and certainly wasn't going to let the language problem get in the way of her chatting to us all evening. Before taking herself off for an early bedtime, she brought us two glasses of luke warm curdled milk.

'Yum, curdled milk,' I said, as I swilled the thick lumps around the glass. I would sooner have scavenged crumbs from 'Pants A' than drunk anything from this glass, but with my selective intolerance to dairy products Jodie knew that she would have to take one for the team, or on this occasion, two.

Jodie held her breath as she poured the glupey beverage down her throat watched eagerly by our tiny hostess. She smiled with satisfaction before heading back into the kitchen. The glasses were exchanged and Jodie followed up with a second heroic effort, possibly mixing some regurgitated milk from the first one in the process. I was a little bit sick just watching the performance, and the tears in her eyes indicated that there was a definite imbalance in her current karma. I wasn't sure that Dairy Milk made bars big enough to even out this situation.

We both held out our empty glasses as our little clotted milkmaid returned, this time with an entire jug of the putrid mixture. I turned to Jodie with a sense of urgency, there was still time to agree a plan, and to make it easier we could speak English to each other without fear of discovery.

'Say you don't want any more,' I said, believing that under the circumstances a simple plan would be the best. I took the initiative and shook my head very clearly from side to side before Jodie could interject.

'No more milk for me please.'

I proceeded to pat my stomach indicating that I had already ingested enough poison for one evening, then turned to Jodie to follow my lead. Her face had turned the colour of curdled milk, and as I looked back down at my glass I could see more lumps being poured from the lady's jug, my jaw dropped in bemusement. I looked at Jodie who was now nodding away frantically, looking for all the world as if she wanted to finish the jug.

Pavel's grandmother smiled, and instead of filling her up, returned to the kitchen and placed the jug back in the broken fridge. I handed Jodie her third glass of clotted milk and pondered the situation, the lady was clearly insane.

'It's the other way round here,' she tried to explain, as she fought to keep down the first two glasses.

She took the glass from me and against all her better instincts gulped down the contents.

'You mean you have to nod yes for no?' I asked, a little bit too late in the day for Jodie's stomach.

'I need to go to the bathroom!' she said, handing back the empty glass and running in the other direction, 'If I find that you've ordered rotten fish then you're having mine!'

*　*　*　*　*

As we had often learnt from carrying no detailed maps, no matter how desirable a road may sound in theory, actually cycling along it was another thing entirely. The Bulgarian coastal road fell foul of many of our poor assumptions, first that it might be relatively flat, and second that it might provide us with a nice view of the sea. In reality it was an incredibly hilly experience, and when it didn't present us with views of abandoned half-complete hotel constructions, it took us inland to the rolling Bulgarian hills.

Finding camp spots was often difficult amongst the farmlands, and it was only closer to the Turkish border that we eventually settled down for a comfortable night in the tent at a picnic spot. We had endured a rather unexpected 200 km of tough cycling when we pulled up near to Malko Tornovo, a border crossing with Turkey. About to cross into our first Islamic country the next day, I could see no better time to drink the homebrew gin given to us by Claudiu's father in Romania. I lit a fire in a brick built barbecue area and we sipped the intoxicating fluid, as the fluorescent bottoms of dragon flies sparkled in the fading evening light.

We crossed the border early in the morning, carrying nothing more than a handful of Bulgarian peanuts and a litre of water. The border crossing was painless enough, and apart from finally having to pay a visa fee of $20 each, we were through and left to our own devices on a desolate 50 km road into the hills leading to Kirklareli. We had no local money and were now craving food, water and anything else that could counteract the effects of Romanian gin. Sadly the cycling was tough, and so was our luck that day as there were only dry water fountains until a few kilometres outside the town.

To allow us an opportunity to settle into our four week Turkish schedule, Jodie had prearranged a night with a Turkish 'couch surfer' called Selcuk in Kirklareli. This was great anticipation on her part as we were thoroughly exhausted by the time we arrived mid afternoon. After a Turkish feast of tsaziki, humous, bread and salad, we decided that the best way to start our cycle across Turkey was with a day off, doing nothing at all. Sleeping in a spare bed, we closed our eyes content in the knowledge that for once, we wouldn't have to wake up early the next morning.

CHAPTER 13
THE RISE OF THE OTTOMANS

'Allahuuuu Akbar-allahuu-ee-uu-ee-uuu Akbar!' A crackly loudspeaker erupted just outside of our bedroom window.

'Argh!' I woke with a startle, 'What in hell's bells is *that*!'

I sat bolt upright wide awake, listening out for what had very nearly killed me in my sleep. All was now silent and I collapsed back on the pillow with exhaustion.

'Jodie, did you just hear someone shouting outside?'

'Alla-haaaa-hu-uu-woo-woo-Akbar! Alla-ahh-haaaa-ahh-he-ah-he-ahhhhhhhu Akbar!'

'Oh God! I thought I was dreaming! What on earth is he doing?'

'Ash-hadu al-la ilaha illa llah!'

'Doesn't he know what time it is?'

'I don't know Tom,' came a sleepy response from Jodie, 'just go back to sleep.'

'What time is it?'

'It's 5 a.m... ' replied Jodie, squinting at her watch, then burying her head in the pillow.

'Ash-hadu al-la ilaha illa llah!' came the tinny racket again through the window.

'Jo!' I said, trying to refrain from yelling out of the window, 'I have just one question.'

'What Tom?' she sighed.

'What the fuck!' I pulled my cycling shorts over my head and pressed down hard on my ears, but it was no good.

'It's the Adhān Tom,' she mumbled, 'the Islamic call to prayer. You'd better get used to it because you'll be hearing it quite a bit from now on... '

'But what if I don't want to wake up at 5 a.m.?'

'Then you had better find a way to ignore it.'

The raucous finally ended and peace was restored to the town of Kirklareli. I lay awake for many minutes feeling audibly assaulted as I stared at the sunrise creeping through the window. Slowly I settled back down and slept away the remaining morning hours.

'Did you hear the Adhān this morning?' asked Selcuk, with almost believable innocence.

'Did I hear it?' I answered, 'I thought he was in bed with me! Where does he live? I'm going round to wake *him* up now.'

Crossing into Turkey was one of the defining cultural moments of our long journey. Although we were still technically in Europe, we had clearly left behind the sort of basic standards that came with a western lifestyle. Things like having the choice to get drunk and then lay asleep at 5 a.m. It suddenly felt as if we really had come a long way from home. Travelling through Europe, no matter how diverse the individual customs, had always felt like a journey of small, gradual but continuous changes. Now we had hit big changes overnight, and despite the obvious sacrifices, it was suddenly quite exciting.

Turkish hospitality is often widely talked about by travellers, and potentially causes other countries and cultures to be overlooked. But it is true, the Turkish, by nature or obligation, are incredibly friendly, courteous and hospitable people. They are also proud to be Turkish and maintain this high reputation. Our first day with Selcuk confirmed every single report, and we wondered just how much we would experience throughout our 2,000 km Turkish leg.

*   *   *   *   *

'What shall I get for lunch?' Jodie asked me as I propped the bikes against the shop wall outside. It was day eighty-nine and we had reached Silivri, a town on the Sea of Marmara, perched just outside of Istanbul.

'Just see what they have,' I advised her sensibly, now for the eighty-ninth consecutive lunchtime. Under the usual gaze of local villagers, she strolled into the shop as I waited outside with the bikes. Moments later, a Jodie shaped head reappeared from the doorway.

'They have bread, cheese and some diced monkey bum,' she said, awaiting my decision straight-faced.

Jodie had picked up a little Turkish, but I hoped not enough for her to have identified this meat. It was just another daily amusement that had now become her routine. One day I'd be offered 'spicy donkey scrotum', the next day it would be 'badger cheek butties'. It was Jodie's way of suggesting that we didn't experiment with the meats too much, but just to satisfy my own curiosity, I had tried calling her bluff one day in Bulgaria.

'Mmm... steamed rat lung please,' I said to her, after pretend consideration. She assessed my response in a microsecond and returned into the shop. After a short delay, presumably to allow for the steaming, she emerged from the café holding a small brown bag.

'You still like the film Rat-a-touille?' she asked, as she handed me the warm bag.

I felt the squishy little balls through the paper and remembered the old wives' tale autopsy identifying what had 'killed the cat'. It had become apparent that while I was outside holding the bikes, Jodie was inside clearly holding all the cards, although on that occasion the dumplings did make an agreeable addition to our lunch, whatever the filling.

'Yeah, bread and cheese is good,' I decided, for the eighty-ninth lunchtime.

It was a simple combination that was within our miserly budget and had been available at nearly all shops this far. Jodie would chop up a tomato and combine it with the cheese and bread to form our lunch, calling her creation various derivations on the standard 'cheese and tomato sandwich'.

It might sound a little repetitive, and most of the time it certainly was, but our taste buds were just about being kept on life-support by the subtle variations in cheeses as we travelled. Throughout the trip we had held firm to the cheapest cheese available, throwing our fate into the hands of the dairy gods. In Slovakia this had meant eating curdled wolf milk churned by the writhing larvae of dragonflies, but in Germany, Aldi had run a manager special on Dairylea.

In fairness, the cheeses we encountered across the world could probably warrant its own chapter, with local ingredients varying from country to country, and even unique techniques differing from town to town. It won't get one here though, this is a rugby-cycling book and as you can probably already tell, I'm particularly rigid about sticking to this criteria.

We ate our eight-ninth lunch by the Marmaris as we tapped some free wifi from a local college. I found a website within our daily budget and uploaded my 'Last Will and Testament' online, before we set off the next morning to join the suicidal ten lane highway into Istanbul. I also sent an e-mail to Hakan reminding him that we hadn't yet arranged anywhere to meet in his city.

Getting cold at night was no longer an issue, the sun rose early and the daytime temperatures were high enough to maintain a comfortable climate throughout the clear nights. We quickly began to utilise our urban camping skills and would sleep at petrol station picnic areas, empty building sites and pretty much anywhere not too close to a loudspeaker. The night before our arrival in Istanbul, we had tried to avoid the biting ants by sleeping on top of a picnic bench by the Sea of Marmara. Only when the late evening socialites dispersed around 1 a.m. did we really settle down.

At 3 a.m. I felt a tap on my shoulder. Jodie was still fast asleep on the bench part of the table, and so I rolled over and looked up to identify the sleep assassin. Three young men stood beside the table, staring down at us with curiosity. Perhaps usually I would have been a little concerned in such a situation, but in Turkey, these men were almost guaranteed to be sober and probably wanted nothing more than to say hello.

Jodie woke up with the commotion and between us we made a special effort to explain what we were doing. They seemed happy enough just to learn that we were English, because it became clear that 'English' was undoubtedly the only English word they understood. Nevertheless, after confirming six times that neither of us wanted a cigarette, they waved goodbye and left us alone.

The bright headlights of a car woke us again at 3:30 a.m. and three silhouettes stepped out from the vehicle. As the figures came closer to our table we could tell that they were the same three boys, this time bringing a plastic bag.

'Bloody hell Jo,' I whispered to her, 'I don't have anything left to say.'

The boys had driven off to find a shop open after 3 a.m. and had returned with bottles of water and spongey cakes for us. It was a very random and generous gesture, but we were already craving some well needed sleep to keep up with the daily cycling. We smiled, drank our water, and ate a cake with them as they smoked like chimneys. They were in no hurry, they'd probably sleep throughout the next day while we were negotiating a ten lane motorway pumped with caffeine. When the university campus speaker crackled into life at 5 a.m. we had long given up hope of a good night's rest. We reluctantly pulled ourselves out of our sleeping bags and cranked up the petrol stove - four coffees each that morning.

I thought it would be easy to find a city with a population of 25 million people, but as had happened with Belgium, it emerged that it was Istanbul that found us. After the initial panic caused by thousands of lorries rushing past, inches from our panniers, our concerns were drawn to the road signs for Istanbul, or more worryingly, their disappearance.

Soon, complex road signs appeared, with directions to Bakirköy, Beylikduzu, Besiktas and many other places not marked on our free country map from a biscuit company. It seemed that Istanbul had vanished without a welcome or goodbye. As we cycled past more and more exits, we began to fear that unless we chose one soon, we would end up cycling clear out the other side of the city. It wasn't a very rational fear, a bit like Euphobia - the inexplicable fear of hearing good news, and a little more research would have told us that it takes around three entire days to pedal from west to east.

The new names on the signs were in fact cities, within the encompassing area or megacity of Istanbul, and we had barely scratched the surface when we eventually asked for help just 10 km in.

We asked repeatedly for the 'merkez' (Turkish for centre), but there were hundreds of potential centre points in the city and we didn't even have the sub city, let alone an address. After an entirely disorganised two hour search for free wifi, we managed to download a subsequent e-mail from Hakan, and obtained a specific location to meet. Incredibly, it was still a further 60 km across town from where we were sat. Exhausted, we traipsed the final five hours across Istanbul and collapsed at the feet of Hakan's friend, Zabi, our new Afghan rugby host.

*   *   *   *   *

At 10 p.m. that evening, Hakan came round to Zabi's to collect us and take us into Istanbul. As he rightfully pointed out, although it was quite late for two cyclists, this was the best time to view the city.

Hakan himself was a vibrant and colourful man, with an abundance of energy and enthusiasm, the very personification of the city in which he lived. He was as charming as he was rotund, and having been schooled in South West London as a young boy, spoke with a thick and eloquent Surrey accent. The first stop in our tour was the Istanbul Ottomans pub, of which they normally reserve their very own floor upstairs. We sat together and enjoyed a pint of lager.

'Lager?' I asked, 'I thought this is an Islamic country?'

'Tom, let me tell you one thing!' Hakan replied, 'There are people from Turkey, and there are people from Istanbul. These are two very different things.'

'Do you have to wake up at 5 a.m.?' I asked, with a little hope.

'Okay, not *everything* is different!' he laughed, 'But what I was trying to say is that it is very different from everything else. I've lived in London, the United States, Afghanistan, in many other places, but nothing has ever compared to the diversity here in Istanbul.'

'You lived in Afghanistan?' Jodie asked with enthusiasm, 'One cyclist I read about said it was his favourite country. I looked into it, but it was too difficult to get visas!'

'Haha, yes it's true, but it wasn't getting into the country that was a problem for me, it was getting out again... but that's another story!'

I stared blankly at Jodie as if she'd just slapped me round the face with a passport full of Afghani visas. It was news to me that we'd even considered going there.

'Come on Hakan, tell me about the rugby!' I said, gently reminding Jodie what exactly I had agreed to on this trip.

Hakan took us back to December 1999, when having recently relocated to his home city, he had finally begun to instigate his plan to bring rugby to Istanbul. He managed to communicate with a small group of players with overseas rugby experience, and between them they organised some early training sessions with just five available players. They slowly grew in numbers and recruited through the usual international techniques, namely plying friends with alcohol and compliments until they committed.

Hakan and his disciples kept their eyes out for potential opposition, but still the only club in Turkey, they were forced to seek teams belonging to the Navy or overseas corporates. Eventually they gathered a full fifteen players together and got a fixture against a Nato XV.

The next match was organised against the Athens Spartans Rugby Club from neighbouring country, Greece. They played both a home and away fixture, and despite giving away ten years experience to the Greek side, Hakan's men triumphed in both the fixtures. They now needed a name, and with such little rugby history to reflect on, they decided to look towards their first victims for inspiration. The 'Spartans' had been defeated, and as such, the 'Ottomans' were born.

With a strong rugby background in London, Hakan continued to coach and develop his squad. After a couple of years the Ottomans' numbers were strong enough to release two early apprentices to start their own rugby teams, establishing new sides in Kadiköy and Bakirköy.

'You guys must be hungry,' Hakan guessed correctly, after our second pint of lager, 'let's go out and grab some food!'

It was already midnight and the streets were quite literally heaving with activity. As we strolled over the cobbled stone paths, street vendors displayed their skills tossing pizza dough, or flexing toned muscles as they stretched their legendary thick Turkish ice cream.

'Those potatoes look incredible!' I pointed to a happy customer walking in the other direction.

'You want one of those? I know just the place.'

He certainly did, and I needed both hands just to keep the stack of fillings balanced on top of the huge potato. Hakan took us on a long guided walk of the inner city and we soaked up the carnival atmosphere.

'Honestly, it's like this every night!' he said, 'I sometimes come down here at night just to take a walk, it makes you feel so alive.'

Barely had I finished my potato when the clock hit 2 a.m. and Hakan decided it was time for the next course - rice stuffed mussels with lemon. At 3 a.m. it was fried fish in a baguette, and finally, closer to 4 a.m. we went for our dessert.

'You know how I said you can find anything in Istanbul? Well, some things you might not find anywhere else!'

'Why? What are we having?' I asked, already pretty stuffed.

'Ice cream!' he said.

'I've had that before,' I laughed.

'Made with chicken,' he continued.

He wasn't joking. This really was a city to get everything, and it wasn't as bad as it sounded.

After an extremely short sleep we dragged our weary bodies down to the university sports stadium with our host Zabi. Hakan was already onsite, coaching a small female squad, and a couple of Turkish journalists had come down to do an interview.

'How does he do it?' I muttered, more to myself than my present company.

'Mr Hakan is always doing rugby,' Zabi replied, 'his new challenge is to make a girls rugby team in Istanbul.'

Zabi was a slender little guy in his mid twenties and like Hakan, he was intelligent, sharp and incredibly funny. He had been Hakan's translator back in Afghanistan and after learning Turkish, had come to study in Istanbul, he could now speak and understand five languages.

'It's a nice idea,' I agreed, 'but I don't think he should be distracting these girls away from the national sport.'

Jodie caught me off guard and elbowed me in the ribcage. When first searching for rugby information in Turkey, we had discovered that one of the most traditional national sports was a contest called Yağli güreş, meaning 'oiled wrestling'. In a moment of Eureka!, I realised that I had already encountered this historical sport one late evening on Freeview TV. Although the girls had appeared to be more Scandinavian, the oil was a memorably big part in their wrestling techniques, and without studying the entire Yağli güreş rulebook, I could probably assume that jelly and pillows were also permitted. Either way, if I ever chose to cycle back to the UK, I had already decided what sport I would be trying to explore.

Jodie was called into action and thrown a spare female kit while Zabi and I joined a male training session on the same artificial field. It felt good to be thrown a ball again but twenty minutes into the session, I had to sit out with ugly blisters developing on my bare feet. Jodie seemed to fair much better and thankfully the female section appealed more to the photographer's eye.

Hakan's long time teammate, Ozer Onkal, gave a separate interview to the paper promoting the biggest Istanbul rugby project yet, the upcoming Istanbul International 7s. I listened intently throughout the ten minute piece, finally concluding that, as expected, I didn't understand a single word of Turkish. A little bit of dribble in the corner of my mouth appeared to spell this out to everyone, and so he also explained it to me in English after the journalist had left.

The 2010 tournament, an Istanbul first, was all set with a fantastic line up of German, Libyan and Indian national sides, with clubs from UK, Dubai and other overseas destinations. What a shame we would be missing it by just a few weeks.

'What have you guys got planned after Turkey?' Hakan asked us, back at his Bosphorus apartment.

'Georgia next!' I jumped in, using any opportunity to show off what limited knowledge of geography I had.

He looked at me as if I should continue, but my limited knowledge was already being stretched.

'Then Iran?' I guessed, incorrectly.

'It's probably through Armenia to Iran,' Jodie informed both Hakan and myself at the same time.

'Have you thought about going through Azerbaijan?' said Hakan.

I could say with absolute certainty that I hadn't thought of it, I wasn't entirely sure that I had even heard of it.

'We had looked at it,' Jodie explained on our behalf, 'but we also liked the sound of Armenia and we can't cross the border overland to see both.'

I often wondered whether these conversations were more for my benefit than our hosts, because it was normally the first I had ever heard of our plans. I nodded in complete agreement, recollecting imaginary conversations and wondering why you couldn't cross the border to see both. Whichever decision Jodie made, I would be cycling through yet another country that I couldn't point to on a map.

'We'll certainly give it some more thought,' I offered, not wanting to appear any more useless, if not already too late.

'You really should do guys, I know their rugby president and he is definitely a guy to go and visit.'

'Mmm, okay, that sounds like good advice,' I said in my most thoughtful and ponderous voice, 'Jodie, maybe we should look over it all again?'

'Oh no, don't tell me we have to talk it all through, *again*!' she laughed, blowing my flimsy cover.

Hakan continued to take us all for a day time tour of the Istanbul markets, then a boat cruise under the Bosphorus Bridge, the most spectacular crossing between the European and Asian continents. We were treated to another abundance of Turkish flavours, including coffee, roasted on beds of hot sand, red wine infused shisha pipes and whisky laced ice cream. By evening, we were thoroughly exhausted and decided to return to Zabi's for some quiet preparation time.

'Right Jo,' I said, initiating my very first route planning conversation, 'having thought about what Hakan said, I think we should go through Azerbaijan.'

'Okay, I'm listening,' she waited politely, offering me a chance to share my thoughts.

'Good, okay, so first things first,' I clapped my hands together on a mission. 'Can you tell me where Azerbaijan is?'

*   *   *   *   *

```
From: 'Jodie and Tom'
To: 'Eldegiz Rafibeyli'
```

```
'Hi Eldegiz,
We have just been firming up our route plan and
itinerary etc and wanted to keep everyone in the
loop! Since Hakan said such good things about you
guys, we would love to come to Baku to meet with you
there! You will be the perfect man to tell us about
rugby in Azerbaijan! We will arrive in September
some time!
```

```
Thanks
Tom and Jodie'
```

*   *   *   *   *

Although our next rugby stop was up on the Black Sea coast, we first needed to head inland from Istanbul to the capital city, Ankara.

'I thought Istanbul *was* the capital,' I moaned, as we pushed up the seventeenth consecutive hill.

Cycling inland in Turkey wasn't much fun during the heat of the summer. The terrain was formidable and if the sun wasn't scorching you from above, you were being cooked from beneath on the simmering tarmac.

'Yep, I think it's one of those common mistakes. A bit like when people are asked the capitals of America and Australia.'

'I don't know what you mean Jo,' I explained, quite exhausted already.

'Well, a lot of people would say New York and Sydney wouldn't they?'

I thought about it for a very short while indeed.

'Yes, of course they would,' I agreed, 'but I still don't know what you mean?'

Although Ankara was home to a rugby team, built mostly around the university students, we were in the summer holidays and the English speaking contacts had returned home to spend time with their families. Our only job in Ankara was to collect our pre-arranged Iranian visa, a small task for a 700 km inland journey to get back to the coast.

We visited a photographer in town and Jodie got some portrait photos of herself wrapped in a bed sheet. To my huge relief, the photographer indicated to me that I didn't require such a photo, as I had worried that it might look a bit silly in my passport. As we took ourselves off to the embassy, I wondered why he hadn't told me *before* I'd sat down wrapped in the bed sheet, but I tried to put it out of my mind. Four days later the embarrassment was forgotten, despite Jodie's best efforts to remind me, and we collected our thirty day visas for the Islamic Republic of Iran. It was an exciting visa to have in our passports, and despite the practicalities of Jodie cycling wrapped in a bed sheet, it sounded like it might be an amazing adventure. Our Ankara work was done, and we threw ourselves back into the hills for the journey to the Black Sea.

*   *   *   *   *

```
From: 'Jodie and Tom'
To: 'Khuram Haroon'

'Hi Khuram!

It seems certain there is no way of getting our
Pakistan visa on our way to you, we have checked
with the embassies in Romania and Turkey but no
luck! We have to send our passports back to Tom's
brother in London and he will go to the embassy to
apply for us.

Thanks so much for all your help!  Look forward to
meeting you in Lahore!

Cheers, Jodie and Tom'
```

CHAPTER 14
MUSTAFA RUGBY CLUB

By Turkish standards, with a population of only 500,000, the little city of Samsun would be considered nothing more than a coastal town. Despite this, it has become home to the most isolated rugby team in the country, thanks entirely to a man called Mustafa Sagir. It is in Samsun, that we stumbled upon one of our favourite grassroots rugby stories.

The man who we have since named 'Mustafa Rugby Club' had been introduced to us through Hakan. Mustafa is as Turkish as stodgy sweets, but with a huge appetite for language, culture and sport, his childhood had left him frustrated by the dogged Black Sea pace of life.

He'd been a professional volleyball player for nine years but had grown gradually more tired of the sport as he noticed the camaraderie diminishing between professional players. He wanted to be involved in a more honest game, one where politics were left out of the decisions and any differences he had could be settled and left on the pitch.

As a young boy, he remembered sitting with his cousin, Engin 'The Sailor', now Samsun Shark hooker, and watching rugby highlights from the Pacific Island clashes. At last Mustafa had found a sport to ignite a spark in Samsun. He wanted to grow scruffy dreadlocks and go crashing through tackles, sending bodies in all directions, he loved the intensity of the match, the pace and ambition.

'It was the speed of the attack, the contact - *huge* collisions. Such physicality!' he recalled, quite vividly. 'I didn't even know what it was, but I liked it!'

It appeared that Fiji had planted the seed for Black Sea rugby in the mid 1990s, but it took until 2006 for the real Samsun rugby journey to begin. Mustafa officially stepped away from professional volleyball and began searching the internet for any signs of rugby in his country.

'I was really quite surprised when I found the Istanbul Ottomans because I didn't know that Turkey had any teams. There was definitely no league, and I learned that their only opposition was another Istanbul club that had been created by players from the Ottomans.'

He e-mailed the Ottomans and asked for their advice on setting up a team. By now, Mustafa was a qualified sports lawyer, so he knew about the legalities involved in creating a sports club, but not knowing how to play the game he needed the rugby laws themselves. The Ottomans sent Mustafa the necessary manuals, and after reading them, he got to grips with the basics and tried to recruit some interest.

'I asked my friends if they wanted to start a rugby team with me, but they'd never even heard of it! Then I asked friends of friends, and even their friends. It felt like I'd asked everyone in Samsun! It didn't work though, they all thought it was American football. I was really starting from scratch with this idea, I didn't even have a ball. In the end I decided the only way I could bring this honest sport to Samsun was with dishonesty.'

One weekend, Mustafa spent an entire day walking around the many campuses of the Samsun University, and under every single door he slid a flyer that read:

```
Come and join our new American football team - a
sport for all shapes and sizes. Trials will be held
at Central Sports Park, 3 p.m. next Saturday. No
equipment is necessary and all are welcome.
```

Over fifty students and friends turned out for the trial, eager to be included in the new sport. He hadn't been able to get his hands on a real rugby ball, but as part of his plan, Mustafa had managed to get a real American football.

'A few boys asked me why there wasn't any body armour or helmets, so I told them we didn't have enough money yet. For safety, I explained that we would play the alternative American football rules until we got all the equipment. This is the way that all American football teams start. I let them throw a few long passes during the warm-up, but then explained that in alternative rules all passes must be backwards. This was to stop tackles flying in from all directions.'

Mustafa had no playing experience himself, let alone coaching experience, and decided to split the guys into two teams and let nature take its course.

'I couldn't really referee because guys were just smashing each other everywhere, it was chaos. It didn't look much like I had remembered off the TV. I got a bit worried for a while. Sometimes, if I saw something really dangerous, I would blow the whistle and make up a rule to stop it happening again. Most of these guys were wrestlers or martial artists, and all I had really told them was to get the ball to the other end of the pitch and put it down!'

The more I pictured the scenario in my head, the funnier it seemed to get. It reminded me of the days before football and rugby had gone their separate ways, when whole towns used to fight, tooth and nail, to carry a pigs bladder towards their line.

'My aim was to try and pick twenty guys who could catch, run and tackle,' he explained, 'but after two hours of trials, there were about thirty guys injured in the stands, and only twenty guys left standing. That more or less became my new team!'

Even for Mustafa's own skills, there was a long way to go until it represented rugby. Nevertheless, he worked hard, studying the books and as much footage as he could find, then used each training session to get a new basic skill learnt by his new squad.

'We quickly became good friends,' he said, 'because I insisted they had to train four times a week. Everyone looked forward to the next training session and nobody ever asked about the protective gear again.'

Mustafa ordered some rugby balls from his nearest rugby portal, Georgia, and even had a local Samsun blacksmith weld together a scrum machine from spare parts. Under his dedicated guidance, the Sharks quickly developed from a group of cannonballs into a more refined unit, each player being selected and slowly moulded into a position.

'We had a tiny little player we called Big Mehmet. He was 5'5" tall and weighed only 60 kg so I trained him into our scrum half. Then about a year later I recruited the perfect man for our second row. He's over 6'10" and weighs 120 kg and is also called Mehmet - the boys have to call him Little Mehmet.'

Although his team had no fixtures, he wanted to give them an identity by getting their own rugby strip.

'I looked at the prices online,' he told us, 'but it was going to cost hundreds of euros to get a kit printed and sent out to Turkey. Most of our players were students so we didn't have any money. One day, when we were getting dressed for practice, I went round the changing room and measured my guys dimensions with a tape measure - their top half Jodie,' he said, sensing her lewd comment without breaking stride, 'I had seen the All Blacks beat everybody and they all wore tight jerseys. I thought maybe that was why nobody could tackle them.'

Mustafa himself went away, designed a club badge, and even sketched his own version of the 'tight fit' rugby jersey, then repeated the process for each player based on their dimensions. Finally, he went down to the local market and haggled with a tailor to stitch together his creations, using a lightweight and stretchable sky blue material.

He showed us his own team shirt, number 8, and I tried it on. It was an incredible piece of work. It was light, strong, and it actually fitted a normal person. I had never worn a rugby jersey that fitted before, and I thought back to the hundreds of times I'd been caught by a piece of my billowing parachute.

Meeting Mustafa and the Sharks was a reminder of what could be achieved with a dream, a vision and a lot of hard work. Now six years on from his creation, the Sharks train six nights a week, happily bashing each other to a pulp on the field and participate in both the domestic Turkish rugby competition and the summer Istanbul 7s.

Although I had found Istanbul a difficult city to describe, as we had cycled onwards, I hadn't found Turkey any easier. Ideally, I would have pigeon holed the entire country by saying that all Turkish people are jolly friendly and drink a lot of tea. This may well be true, but making slightly more effort, I wanted to find out what could create such a hospitable environment and worrying addiction to caffeine.

At first glance much of the country seemed to have been preserved from a previous generation, the clean water was still hand fetched from town taps by the roadside, and fields were still largely worked by hand. Many houses lay in desperate states of disrepair, and in many towns 'sanitation' had yet to find a Turkish translation. Yet at a second glance you would notice pristine 'Digiturk' satellite dishes hanging from the crumbling walls, and after risking a thirty second squat with the mosquitos, you'd probably be offered a paper towel from an infra-red dispenser. Even in small towns the local farmers would try to communicate with you in German, despite greeting you in English, and at petrol stations you would be attended to by an immaculately dressed employee, flicking the burning embers of his cigarette inches from the pumps.

I couldn't work them out, so I asked Mustafa what it really meant to be Turkish. He had an answer for most things and he didn't let me down. To him, being Turkish was something all young people were proud of, but in contrast most old people were proud to be Ottoman. At hearing this I didn't know whether to frown thoughtfully in agreement, quizzically with interest, or ask him politely to stop talking to me in Turkish riddles. I was too hot to experiment with my frowning facial muscles so just opted for the latter, at which point we were treated to a Turkish history lesson. In fairness it was genuinely interesting, but not quite interesting enough for me to repeat to you a year down the line, or more honestly, even remember two minutes after the conversation.

If like me, you base all your worldly assumptions on largely inaccurate generic summaries, I can try to explain a little further. Your 'Ottomans at heart' were the colonialists, who remained proud of the way in which the Ottoman Empire had preserved the integrity of individual cultures during their long empire. In over 2,000 years they had often allowed the continuation of both local language and religion, and so when the empire eventually disbanded, these governed countries were again left to revert back to their pre-empire days. These people preserved old Ottoman values such as drinking tea, smoking at petrol stations and allowing toilets to establish their own ecosystems.

The 'Turks' were the new generation, the youngsters that were free minded, forward thinking but who also wanted to preserve Turkey's reputation as genuinely first class people. These people wanted to promote new Turkish values such as drinking tea, smoking low-tar cigarettes at petrol stations and fighting the censorship of Youtube to document the plight of Turkish toilets.

He was evocatively proud to be Turkish, and to be part of a country where no matter what your heritage, you were all part of the same movement. It was inspiring to hear such youthful positivity about his society, and as I opened a packet of dark chocolate Turkish biscuits I admired their indiscriminating attitude.

'Would anyone care for a Negroe?' I asked, offering them around.

*   *   *   *   *

It was early morning as we sat on the fishing hut porch cleaning our dirty wheel rims, when a lone silhouette appeared on the beach to our right. As the figure got closer, we could see that it was our host, Hakan's cousin Ufuk, and he was holding something.

'For you,' he simply said, as he passed us the package.

Ufuk had a gentle and tentative demeanour, and we both suspected he might be a man of few words. Thankfully, he didn't understand much English at all, so could say his own name quite easily without laughing, unlike Jodie.

'No way! Thanks Ufuk!' we replied together as we suspected what the package might contain.

I turned to Jodie who, as expected, was laughing again. It was Friday morning and in our minds, we had already added a further weekend to the growing delay. Had my brother Adam managed to turn the Pakistan visa around in just two weeks?

'Adam, you are a bloody legend!' Jodie said, having already opened the passports. 'Look, it's all done, forty-five days.'

Pakistan was a significant part of our journey, and our relief at getting the visa, not to mention our passports back, was huge. We had already built a solid relationship with Khuram, and despite my initial hesitations, Jodie had now convinced me what a great cultural opportunity this was. I was eager to form my own opinion on the country.

Logistically speaking, our whole tour relied on being able to progress through Pakistan. The alternative would have resulted in much larger visa delays, using the route exiting Iran from the northeast, through Turkmenistan, Uzbekistan and either Tajikistan or Kyrgyzstan before entering West China and rejoining our intended route at Kashgar. Although this path presented its own appeal, we had read that this could involve waiting weeks for visas and frantic peddling across certain areas on limited period transit visas. This option would leave us no time to explore the rugby, and mean we would arrive in West China in the thick of winter.

Whatever route we would now use, another rugby adventure awaited us just 50 km further round the Black Sea coastline.

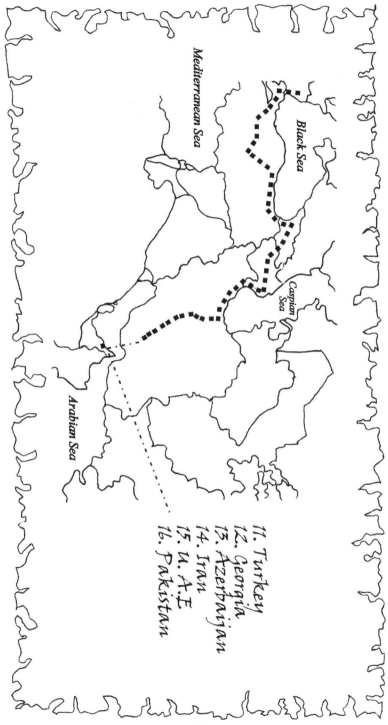

Mediterranean Sea

Black Sea

Caspian Sea

Arabian Sea

11. Turkey
12. Georgia
13. Azerbaijan
14. Iran
15. U.A.E
16. Pakistan

CHAPTER 15
GROWING OLD DISGRACEFULLY

Georgia had not been a definite feature in our original route plan, but after making such strong progress through to Istanbul, we had gained confidence, and more importantly not eaten into our small contingency of two weeks. Taking a small detour of 1,000 km would mean avoiding the mountains of southeastern Turkey, and would allow us to investigate the strongest rugby power in the European Tier 2. We no longer talked these decisions through, if it was another country, and it was possible, the deal was done.

Having watched Georgia compete in the 2003 and 2007 Rugby World Cup, I was already aware that the Georgians had a natural affiliation with the game. By observing their stocky physiques and learning of their strength at wrestling, I had wrongly made assumptions that rugby was their national sport. Much like the rest of the planet, the statistics point to the popularity of soccer, irrespective of their national ranking. Nevertheless, many areas of Georgia have a huge number of rugby followers and I was confident we could find further encouragement of rugby growth, outside of the top ranked sides.

Radu, our Romanian commentator friend, had often talked about the fierce rivalry between themselves and the Georgians, but for the Georgians it appeared that the historical relationship with Russia had, in recent years, created an even bigger interest. In 2001, 65,000 fans had packed into the national stadium in Tbilisi to watch Georgia play Russia in the European Nations Cup. A year later, 44,000 came back to watch Georgia beat Russia 17-13 to qualify for the 2003 Rugby World Cup.

Having already secured a spot at the 2011 Rugby World Cup, their third successive tournament, I tried to look for reasons why it was not considered their national sport. What should define or constitute a national sport? Should it be the ease of which you could follow something on the TV i.e. soccer, or something that brought out the very best in your people, in this case wrestling and rugby?

Having played soccer for a large part of my childhood, I wasn't about to jump on the predictable rugby bandwagon, sulking that soccer stole all the media, cash and fan base. Of course it did, it was easy to follow and had planted irreversible economic and social roots in modern society. I had played in the Queens Park Rangers academy as a teenager, so I could still understand and appreciate many aspects of the game, but what I couldn't ignore any longer was the culture outside and around the sport.

Yesterday I broke the mould and watched a highlights package from the recent Premier League matches. One clip showed a neat ten second build up resulting in a three yard tap in for a goal. This was followed by the opposition players and manager swearing at the referee, while a now half naked goal scorer tried to mimic having sex with the corner flag. It was all too predictable, another dispute over 'offside' - the only real rule in football, and a yellow card to the goal scorer for once again trying to promote his girlfriend's chain of chest waxing salons.

The reality and simplicity of soccer meant that it was easy to play and easy to follow, but once you were in it, there was simply no depth. It was a world of clichés, theatrical injuries, feminine haircuts and advocated an environment where youngsters should ignore and abuse authority figures. Quite simply, it was a sport that didn't bring people together, but divided them. Not that my opinion on world peace has often been sought, but I would think that dividing people into further subgroups was a backward step towards that goal.

So there you go, rugby has officially become a positive step towards world peace, a true 'World in Union' - that is of course until next week, when mid-match, someone sticks their finger up another man's bum hole.

'You do bang on a bit don't you?' said Jodie, as it emerged that my rants had not been confined to paper.

'Sorry,' I muttered back, 'I just can't see why the Georgians follow soccer. They played ten matches to try to qualify for the FIFA World Cup in 2010, and they didn't win a single one!'

'Was Happy Gilmour a hockey player or a golfer?' asked Jodie as we crossed the border into Batumi.

'He was a golfer!' I said, 'Wait... hang on... oh, I see what you did there.'

Even for the very first time, there is something incredibly familiar for an Englishman to step foot in Georgia. The soft curves of Islamic Turkish architecture were instantly replaced by the rigid, angular lines of castles and fortresses, and all around us hung their proud flag bearing the repeated red cross of St George. Although an ancient crumbling church lay to our right, to our left we could see hoards of holiday makers soaking up the rays of sunshine on the beach down below. We had stepped foot into the Georgian equivalent of Blackpool, only instead of having ice creams, the Black Sea had enticed hundreds of Russian women to strip off and sip cocktails by the gentle crashing waves. Good Black Sea.

Having followed the coastline for many kilometres watching suntanned Russians sipping beer with their breakfasts, it dawned on us how different things had been in an Islamic country. We had just spent over three weeks in the sunshine by the Turkish Black Sea coast and we hadn't enjoyed a single drink. More worryingly for our street credibility, we hadn't even thought about one. Aside from a couple of beers in Istanbul, we had literally had five weeks of entirely sober cycling.

In the heaving town of Batumi we managed to get lost several times before eventually locating the road signposted, 'Tblisi 337 km'. It wasn't the road that was implied by the Turkish biscuit map, but it was very hot, and it would have to make do. We were now officially heading off the map, but assuming the road ran continuously to the capital, we wouldn't have to make a turning for three days.

Before leaving the outskirts of Batumi we made a very surprising discovery. Through the lines of palm trees to my right, I had caught sight of the familiar H-frame of rugby posts. Upon closer inspection we could see that it was indeed a rugby pitch. Having cycled in twelve countries, it was the very first time that we had stumbled across a rugby club, rather than going searching for one. I was very, very excited and insisted that we cycled down into the ground to explore.

We pushed into the empty gravel car park and leaned our bicycles against the crumbling outer wall. A rusty chain lay coiled to the side of two large wrought iron gates which were partially open, and you could now see clearly through to the pitch. It didn't look particularly used, other than a herd of cows chomping on the long grass by the twenty-two line. We walked in, surprising a farmer who sat watching his flock of sheep in the cow's opposing half.

'This will be an interesting match,' I laughed to Jodie, 'I think it's the Baa Baa's vs Moo Zealand!'

Jodie cracked a smile, and turned away so as not to encourage me, she was a tough audience. Inside, the changing rooms were littered with sheep droppings and bundles of straw were piled in the corner.

'Do you think it's still used?' I asked her.

On hearing my own question out loud, I realised fairly quickly that I didn't need an answer. She seemed to agree and didn't give me one.

'It would have been used once upon a time!' I pointed out, realising once more that I wasn't massively contributing to the investigation. She looked at me absently, perhaps waiting for a final jaw dropping revelation, but short of picking up a sheep dropping and sniffing it, I had probably already played my detective cards.

'Well, that was interesting!' Jodie announced, wrapping up the Batumi Rugby Club chapter. 'Come on, we've got pedalling to do!'

I didn't know what to make of the situation. Was this rugby club dead and buried, or was it so deeply rooted in the community, that other industries utilised the facilities in the off season?

'There was quite a lot of poo,' I thought to myself, as it dawned on me which of these was the more likely story.

*   *   *   *   *

As fun as it was to enter a new country, we were always thankful to get the first night safely behind us. Although we had wild camped a hundred times before, little nagging doubts would creep into our mind as we'd recall the warnings given to us in the previous country. It was always the same type of concern.

'Please be very careful. We are very kind people here, but over there they are all gypsies. They will attack you, cheat you, steal from you and probably shit all over your bicycles... '

Of course this had never happened, not since our training ride in Wales, but no matter how trusting we had tried to become, it always took us a little longer to find a suitable camp spot. Our first night in Georgia was no different, and we'd covered a full 150 km before eventually conceding that we would not find a hidden spot before dark. We opted to push down a dusty pathway towards a small group of houses. A little way down the track, we found a clear patch of grass large enough to pitch our tent. Happy enough that this was safe, we put the kettle on and waited for the light to disappear.

Before darkness had even settled, quite predictably a lone man passed immediately by our spot on a seemingly random evening walk. You could almost guarantee that this will happen when you are wild camping, and even if you believe you've found the most isolated spot on the planet, some solitary weirdo will still find a way to walk past your tent at midnight. This man spoke not a single word of English, and even after gesturing towards a nearby house many times, it wasn't entirely clear what he was trying to suggest.

Eventually we took the assumption that he was inviting us to camp inside his garden, or perhaps even stay in his house, so we put out the stove, packed up our belongings and followed him to the gate. We waited with our bicycles while the little wanderer ran down to the front door, and moments later he reappeared with an older man. The new face looked very solemn and didn't seem at all excited to have visitors, but he beckoned that we bring our bicycles into his courtyard nevertheless. The first man waved goodbye and disappeared - we never saw him again.

'My uncle would like to propose a toast to the health of our mothers!' said the old man's nephew later that evening.

'Bloody hell, I'm not sure if I can do another one!' Jodie whispered to me, 'That's about the fifth shot already.'

'Now to our fathers!' translated his nephew again, as his uncle refilled the homebrew cha-cha.

Although the old man's grumpy expression hadn't changed, he seemed noticeably more enthusiastic with every shot and toast. Jodie and I assumed that maybe his face had got stuck like that with time. While he seemed in positive spirits I took my chance to ask him about the rugby.

'Could you please ask your uncle who he thinks will win the Rugby World Cup next year?'

The young student translated my question and caused the old man to pause in thought.

'Most people think New Zealand will win,' Jodie explained to his nephew, who nodded in agreement.

'I believe so as well,' he replied, 'I like the All Blacks very much'

For a moment it seemed as if the old man had dropped off to sleep before he finally opened his eyes.

'Georgia!' he said triumphantly, looking up with a smile.

We made another toast...

*   *   *   *   *

We set off early the next morning into the thick dawn mist with a bag full of unshelled hazelnuts in our pannier. Flashy BMWs hurtled passed us on the narrow winding road, disappearing into the clouds as quickly as they had appeared. All morning we cycled, fully expecting to see one of these vehicles wrapped around a lamp post, yet we all progressed without incident. If they weren't behind the wheels of a high powered BMW, the second car of choice appeared to be a rusty old Skoda with a cracked windscreen, equally as dangerous in their own right.

We pulled over at lunchtime and pushed up to a quiet spot on the hill under a tree. I waited for the kettle to boil while I watched Jodie, my neanderthal girlfriend, slowly perfect her nut cracking technique with two large rocks. The more she concentrated, the more her bottom lip protruded, and the more I felt like I was in a scene from the Jungle Book. Again, like clockwork, and quite literally miles from any civilisation, a customary phantom walker appeared from nowhere and came to greet us.

The years had been quite unkind to him, and we could only hope that over those tough years, the tooth fairy had at least given him a fair price. He opened up his bag and pulled out three extremely bruised looking pears, before offering me the clear worst of the three. I paused, staring down at the lump of mush in his filthy little hand. It was so disgusting that I wouldn't have even stepped on it.

'Oh, for me?' I tried to fain interest, 'That's very kind, but I really can't.'

'Don't be ungrateful Tom,' Jodie laughed, 'you don't want to offend him.'

'But Jo!' I tried to protest, 'Look at it, he's just trying to give me his crap fruit!'

The man held out his hand closer. Against all my better instincts, I very reluctantly followed Jodie's advice and transferred the putrid mess into my own outstretched palm.

'Didi Madloba, thank you!' I tried to sound a little bit sarcastic, 'Es lamazia!'

Although completely inaccurate, it was the only Georgian I knew and I said it to everything. I only hoped he would see the irony in me thanking him and describing his gesture as 'very beautiful'. He didn't, and maybe Jodie had been right. These people were incredibly self sufficient, and maybe he would have eaten it himself if we hadn't have been here.

'I know!' I said to Jodie, 'Do we still have those bruised figs in the food pannier?'

'Yes, it didn't seem right to just throw them away, why's that?' she replied.

'Well, we're not going to eat them are we? I'll give them to him!'

'Sure, okay, that sounds like a good idea.'

I grabbed the bag with enthusiasm and insisted in the very same way that he accept our gift. He took the bag from me and with a little curiosity he peeked inside. His disinterest was plain to see as he laid his eyes on the mushy figs, but instead he placed the bag at my feet and pretended to graciously refuse our offering, with his hand on his heart.

'There, I told you!' I said to Jodie, 'He *was* just trying to give me his crap fruit!'

There had been much talk about the apparent poverty of Georgia, but aside from the toothless pear abuser, this wasn't the underlying feeling we experienced in the country as we crossed it. Many perceivably poor communities lived in very grand and ornate rustic houses, with an abundance of outside space. Around these houses you would see chickens pecking at the ground, as goats, cows and pigs ambled about feeding from the fallen spoils of fruit and nut trees. Many would be growing vegetables in the garden patches, and although they often relied on shared water pumps, this seemed a small price to pay for such a self sufficient lifestyle. It seemed that although the Georgian people had very little money, there weren't many basics that they needed to buy, they even brewed most of their own alcohol.

Although a relatively short trip to Tblisi, we encountered a staggering amount of hospitality in these communities along the way. On both subsequent nights we were offered indoors accommodation, and even had to turn down an invitation to a party at 2 a.m. It seemed standard for many houses to have a spare bedroom, no matter how basic the furniture. Road side vendors beckoned us to come and sit with them, feeding us copious amounts of watermelons, figs and hazelnuts as we pretended to understand each other. All things considered, we found the Georgian people great and easy people to share our time with.

'How far have we got left?' I called up to Jodie, as we approached a road sign outside the capital.

'1,340 km!' she replied, laughing.

'That sounds a bit far?' I answered back, 'We should only have about 20 km left to Tblisi!'

'That's to Tehran!' she called back triumphantly, 'Isn't that weird, this one road must go all the way to Iran!'

It was the kind of news to make 'Chief of Directions' very happy indeed.

* * * * *

'Hey Jo,' I asked her, 'how many kisses do I have to go in for?'

Since being introduced to man on man smooching in Belgium, I had felt a great sense of anxiety until I learned the correct greetings in each country. If I just stuck out a hand and kept my distance, this could be taken as quite rude and antisocial, but if I went in for a kiss, or too many kisses, this could give the wrong impression altogether. When you think about it, any jokers out there really do have you over a barrel, knowing that you would pretty much adhere to anything just to prove you are an open minded traveller.

Some countries had been one kiss for boys, two kisses for girls, some seemed to be one or two kisses for both, depending on how familiar or formal the situation was. If the President of Georgian Rugby chose to slap me around the face with his willy, I would probably still smile and say how honoured I was to meet him. The only guarantee I really had was that unless I was told otherwise, it was usually best not to use tongues.

As it turned out, he just shook our hands.

The Georgian Rugby Union office was a very relaxed but clearly passionate environment. We had already met with the new Georgian coach, Richard Dixon, at the Nations Cup in Bucharest, and now waiting in the office with PR girl Maia Chickvaidze, we got to understand what it meant for an everyday Georgian to be involved in their national setup. Although Maia was a full time employee of the union, she was also a part time children's book illustrator, and had been our enthusiastic contact for some time by e-mail.

The rugby structure in Georgia is far smaller than their national abilities would suggest, and having an opportunity to contribute from any angle was clearly an interesting and rare opportunity. It came as no surprise to then meet Richard Dixon's son, Mark, who had taken his chance to follow in his father's coaching footsteps and accept the responsibility of developing the Georgian strength training.

We were shown into the Georgian boardroom where Lasha 'Bacho' Khurtsidze, the Georgian Media Manager presented us with two bottles of Georgian red wine, commemorating fifty years of official Georgian rugby in 2009. Knowing the Georgians, that would have been some party, and we both assumed that for these bottles to have survived, they must have been put somewhere and then forgotten.

'Thanks Lasha!' Jodie said, 'It's Tom's birthday tomorrow, that looks like a good way to celebrate.'

'Do you need a Georgian signature for your World in Union scroll?' Lasha asked us, before we wrapped up our interview.

'We already managed to get our Georgian signature in Bucharest, at the Nations Cup,' I explained.

'Oh, who did you get?'

'We got Tedo Zibzibadze!' Jodie said, looking for any opportunity to say his name. It literally rolled off her tongue.

Lasha nodded in agreement, 'Yes, very good choice,' he said, 'Tedo is one of our most experienced players and a very popular face here in Georgia. He chose to stay and play domestically for most of his life. Most of our top players understandably accept contracts to play in France.'

We left the Georgian office with big smiles, two bottles of wine, and the national television news crew who had been filming us all day long in Tblisi.

'Zibzibadze! Zibzibadze!' Jodie sang theatrically, on our way out of the union office.

'Have you got time for a beer?' the young female presenter asked us.

'Sure, why not?' we both said, happy with another good day at the office. We piled into two cars and they took us down to a place on the river.

'Where is it?' I asked, looking around as we pulled up into a car park. We were surrounded by very drunk, sunburnt men swigging from clear plastic bottles, but there was no sign of a pub. She laughed and pointed to a small hatch in the wall with wooden shutters.

'Don't worry, we'll order these!' she said, 'I know you're on a tight budget.'

The cameraman took a watering can out from the boot of his car and accompanied the girl to the small hatch. Moments later they returned with a stack of plastic cups and a visibly heavier watering can.

'Welcome to Georgia!' they all toasted us in the scorching sunshine.

'Blimey, this is strong!' I said, noticing the effects almost instantly. 'No wonder these guys are struggling so early in the day!'

'You can't buy this one in the shops,' the young presenter laughed again, 'they brew this themselves somewhere behind that wall.'

'Say no more.'

After a chatty hour with the Georgian crew, they dropped us back into town and we strolled through the Tblisi backstreets to see if our host, Uta, had finished work. Uta was a German business consultant, and a friend of Hakan's wife, Esbie, from her time working in Istanbul. She'd been more than happy to have us stay, and as always was looking to wrap things up early on a Friday.

'Hi guys!' Uta said, with her feet on the desk and a glass of wine in her hand, 'I'm almost finished for the day. You should come out with us for a quick drink after work.'

'Sounds great Uta,' I answered, already feeling pretty intoxicated, and looking back out at the sunny Friday afternoon sky.

It didn't sound like such a great idea when I woke the next morning.

'Happy birthday to *you*! Happy birthday to *you*!' Jodie sang to me as I tried to open my eyes.

'Oh God... what time is it?' I asked desperately.

'It's nine-thirty,' she answered, 'time to get up and celebrate your birthday!'

'Urgh... I don't feel well,' I rolled over and closed my eyes in pain, 'I need more sleep.'

'You've had lots of sleep! Don't you remember falling asleep in the nightclub?'

'Nightclub? What nightclub? I thought we just went for a drink by Uta's work?'

'We did!' she explained, 'We had a couple of drinks by Uta's work, then we went to that posh pub on the hill, you remember? Then we went on to Uta's friends' place for a party, and once you'd drunk all their homebrew wine, you said you wanted to follow them to the nightclub.'

'Urgh... I don't feel well,' I mentioned again, the room began to spin even faster. This was all Stefan's fault.

My entire birthday consisted of nothing more than the very short walk between our bed and the toilet, it was a cruel and painful way to grow another year older. When I accidently locked myself inside the toilet I sensed that things wouldn't improve, and I spent the best part of an hour trying to attract Jodie and Uta's attention by yelling out through a small window to the courtyard below. To their credit, the two girls did a very fine job in taking apart the lock and door hinges to rescue me.

*   *   *   *   *

From: 'Khuram Haroon'
To: 'Jodie and Tom'

'Hey guys,

The floods have caused many problems in Pakistan. I strongly recommend you do not cross the border on your bicycles from Iran. This will be very dangerous for you. I know it is against your rules but maybe you could take a ferry or plane? Perhaps you could visit the rugby in Dubai before coming to Pakistan? There are many flights from Dubai to Pakistan. It's not cheating!

Let me know what you plan or if you need any help to organise your schedule. Cheers, K'

CHAPTER 16
ELDEGIZ THE BRAVE

The comedy was lost on the locals, but as we approached the final metres of Georgian soil, an ominous sign above our heads read 'Azerbaijan border - Good Luck'. At passport control the Georgian official thanked me for visiting his country and invited me to come back again. He even hoped that I had enjoyed my birthday in Georgia! I didn't mention the toilet incident, and it was a fine end to what had been the biggest surprise of our journey so far.

Crossing a bridge over a dried river bed, home to a herd of cows grazing on rubble, we stepped onto Azeri territory and the routine started again. We usually crossed borders earlier in the day, but the morning cycle had been slow on the cracked and damaged roads, and it was now already afternoon. Once through, we would only have a few hours to adapt to our new surroundings before seeking a safe place to sleep. Luckily for Jodie, I had taken the liberty of performing some Azeri cultural investigation, by way of a quick search on Wikitravel. The usual information was presented to me, 'They drive on the right, they don't eat bacon etc etc', but with the list came a surprise addition:

'Don't smile at an Azerbaijani in the street, people will regard you either as odd or think that you are mentally handicapped. Smiling at a stranger will be considered offensive, as they will either think that you are making fun of them and there is something wrong with their clothes or hair.'

I didn't know what to believe, and although insanity had helped me along this far, rudeness certainly wasn't required. The old me would have laughed and ignored it, but the new me had already seen a 'werebear' and eaten chicken ice cream. With precaution, I took the advice on board as the last thing I needed was problems with officials at this time of day.

Smiling had been our primary weapon in fighting the language war, perhaps even our only weapon in the absence of actual languages. Throughout the journey most of my responses had been a polite smile, whilst Jodie would build up a vocabulary of essential words. Upon further questioning, I would pull out a bigger smile, a fake laugh, and where necessary, the 'comedy shrug'. It was a Harry Enfield 'Tim, nice but dim' tool, but very universal. It translated in most places as, 'Yep, look at me, I'm an idiot. I've come to your country on a bicycle, I can't even speak your language but I'm probably too stupid to cause any trouble.'

We wheeled our clumsy bicycles towards the border with as little facial expression as possible. Although successful, this did little to lighten the mood with our new rifle wielding company, who matched our blank faces and raised us a stare. I fought the ache in my cheeks and continued as they beckoned us round the queue of Azeris trying to get back home.

'Salam,' the guard said to me. Stricken with panic, I turned to Jodie for language support. She wasn't there, and as I looked back I could see she was already being processed at the next window.

'Ah... salam,' I offered in parrot fashion, my cheek muscles now burning with an intense heat.

'Passport?' I strained weakly, hoping to end this conversation before the cramp in my face caused any long term damage. He pointed me to Jodie's window.

As expected, Jodie was busy chatting with the passport man when I arrived, and he acknowledged me with a polite nod. The 'Chief of Languages' was dutifully collecting the essentials and thankfully his English was passable enough to translate the basic words for us. He stamped our passports and wished us a safe journey through his country. I thanked him, and as I turned away I thought I caught a smile through the nicotine stained glass. I looked again, but whatever it was, it was now gone and his pristine cheek muscles were back on full display, either side of a most tidy moustache.

We cleared the border and cycled down a desolate hill to a T-junction.

'I'm buggered!' I proclaimed, as I leaned my bicycle against a tree.

'Yep, me too, but we're here now so let's get to a village and find some food,' she consoled.

'What? We have no food?' I said, as I tried not to cry, 'I think I've torn a muscle in my face. Do you think it's going to be like that all the way?'

'What are you talking about silly?' she replied, 'The smiling thing was just a joke, the guy at the border was very friendly with us.'

'I know, but did you actually see him smile?' I asked, 'Did you?'

'Yes, I did,' she said, hoping to put an end to my thoughts.

'Ah, well I didn't,' I said, massaging my cheeks, 'I think they are told to grow moustaches and if they aren't straight, they get accused of smiling and thrown in an asylum.'

'Okay, let's get you some food,' she instructed, deciding that my brain was now short on nutrition.

'That way!' I decided, checking the compass and pointing to the road due east. As a formality I also referenced our 'map', which on this occasion was a pencil drawing of the country sketched on a scrap of paper. Conveniently, there was a solitary road drawn across the entire country, from the border crossing to the capital 'Baku', several hundred kilometres away. It was a nice sketch, but I suspected that Jodie had become a little lost in her project, spending longer than necessary drawing the waves of the Caspian Sea, and mountains of the Caucasian range. I haven't read Lord of the Rings, but she has, and all I will say is this, 'You can tell.'

We pedalled on for an hour before finding a small village at the top of a hill. Outside the village shop a handful of locals were sat doing nothing much at all. Although naturally surprised to see such a ridiculous sight, they invited us to sit with them and offered up a couple of their stools for us to take some rest. I tried to thank the first man without smiling, but as we approached I realised that this wouldn't be necessary. He could have been incredibly rude or just a complete nutcase, but more likely it seemed that Jodie's suspicions carried some weight after all. Whatever the case, I think this man had found an excuse to show off his shiny gold teeth. I was overcome with relief and slumped onto the stool as my facial muscles collapsed onto the floor.

Armed with Jodie's pigeon Azeri, we explained our journey to the group in the usual manner. 'Bicycle' we pointed to the bikes as they nodded in acknowledgement, 'Chador' we said to their astonishment as we made a tent shape with our hands, and 'World' as we drew an imaginary circle in the air.

The last rarely invoked more than a glazed look, but they grasped the basics, that we cycled and lived in a tent. Perhaps it was us that learnt more from our interaction. After all, we deduced that the villagers all used the same twenty-four carat dentist, and that the crackdown on unnecessary smiling in public was probably a government initiative to reduce road accidents. With those teeth, maintaining a solemn expression would be the facial equivalent of dipping the headlights.

We exchanged our last Georgian note in the village store, walking away with some bread, melted chocolate, and a handful of Azeri coins for the road. Buoyed with our newfound smiley enthusiasm, we weaved our way through the subsequent towns, now waving and shouting 'Salam!' at the kids with cheeks pinned to our ears.

*   *   *   *   *

Although Georgia and Azerbaijan had previously been part of the same Soviet Bloc, the architecture and religion in each had clearly remained very independent. Azerbaijan reminded us immediately of our time back in Turkey, most notably the numerous water stations present throughout the towns in Muslim countries. Cleanliness is very important in the Muslim faith, and so mosques and these clean water stations often made for much appreciated breaks in the heat of the day. We stopped at our first fountain to cool off and were immediately surrounded by curious men and children.

'Mister mister, what is your name?' they chirped with rehearsed English.

'My name is Tom,' I answered politely, to much laughter.

'Mister Tom,' the confident ones would continue, 'where are you from?'

'We are English!' I replied again, naturally in English.

'English!' they exclaimed, rather pleased with their discovery.

'From Italia?' one boy asked hopefully, wearing a Chelsea shirt.

'What? No, not Italia. English from England,' I explained, a little confused, 'you know, London?'

When their faces registered nothing, I pointed to the boy's shirt badge, but still with no success.

'David Beckham!' Jodie chipped in.

'David Beckham!' the boys cheered with excitement, 'Michael Owen!'

'Hey,' I turned to her, 'that's not exactly promoting rugby to the world is it?'

'Sorry,' she said, 'but if they haven't heard of London, then they probably haven't heard of London Wasps.'

She had a point.

As we headed east, Ladas with cracked windscreens chugged passed, honking to us at every opportunity. Many cars even slowed and attempted a conversation, the drivers leaning into the passenger seats as they nearly ran us off the road. The roads themselves were constantly testing our tyres, brakes, and more often than not, our patience. Some were surprisingly immaculate with pristine flat tarmac, others bore huge craters, but most parts looked as though they had just dropped tarmac over a camel graveyard.

Finding camp took a little adjusting, but we soon identified that farmers' huts made good spots after dark. One night, without such luck, we had continued into the early evening to escape unwanted attention before putting up our tent. As we finally gave up hope on the main road, we pulled off into a small village and waited for the usual divine intervention.

Moments later, a man chugged past in a Lada full to the roof with watermelons. He jumped out of the car and thrust one into my arms before driving off. Getting free food on our budget was a welcome bonus, only the bulbous fruit was now preventing me from pushing my bike to a quiet area.

Leaning the bikes against a wall, we took the sun-warmed melon and cooled it in the village fountain. It was here that the adjacent café owner spotted our activity and beckoned us to sit with him and his brother. For such a rural area, this man had an impressive grasp of English, and we explained our predicament. With no such language skills, his brother had to settle on drinking beer laced with salt as our café owner drank tea and listened to our plans, sucking a new sugar cube with every sip.

'You can camp here,' he offered, 'behind our café.'

'Oh, that's great! Thank you!' Jodie replied, quickly taking up the offer.

The larger of the brothers took our melon from the table and his two empty beer bottles, before disappearing into the kitchen. Moments later, he returned with two fresh bottles and a platter of our melon pieces. We had explained our story already, but with nothing much happening in the area to talk about, it was difficult to keep any conversation alive. As a last resort, there were always two standard questions on offer, and Jodie jumped in with our first one.

'So, you and your brother live here then?' she asked.

'Yes,' our man replied, 'we both live in this village. I live down the road with my family. My brother lives here, he doesn't have a family, he is fat.'

We all looked at his fat brother with a little sympathy before the thin brother pulled out his mobile phone and showed us photos of his wife and three daughters. It was nice to see such happiness in his face and we smiled as he showed off the pride of his life. It was also killing some time and delaying my daft question, but by the third video of him and his dog, I realised that he might have a very large memory card, much larger than my interest in his pets.

I turned to the two men, wearing café aprons and sitting outside their café, before reluctantly asking, 'So, what do you do for work?'

As it turned out, the thin brother was a dentist, and judging by his own set of golden teeth, presumably studied at the same School of Alchemy as all the other Azeri dentists. Occasionally, he explained, he would help his brother at the café, who was now gesturing the spare beer to me.

'My brother is unhealthy,' he said, as he lit himself another cigarette, 'he drinks too much beer and he is very fat. I don't drink beer because I am a dentist and I understand that it is unhealthy!'

The slim dentist inhaled from his cigarette, then finished the bowl of sugar cubes with a final slurp of tea.

'You are very healthy because you ride bicycle,' he said, before I could accept the beer from his brother.

Despite the roads, our route guided us through some of the more attractive regions of northern Azerbaijan, and over one memorable pass in particular. The path was windy, weaving around enough hairpins to give Rapunzel a nice tidy bun, before levelling off at a pass littered with cafés and çay parks. We sought a well earned rest in the shade, but even before dismounting, the café workers had circled us like chimpanzees, prodding and poking at the bikes and everything on them, barely excluding us.

In seemingly reversed roles, we managed to lure the chimps away from the bikes to one of their own tables, and once they had calmed down, we sat and drank some free tea. The usual conversation process began, a question asked in Azeri, an answer in English, shrugs from both camps and then laughter from all. It was a simple formula but a proven method for success. With absolutely no language barrier broken at all, I took my chance to enter the slapstick Azeri comedy circle. These country folk seemed to find most things genuinely hysterical, and I had an absolute winner up my sleeve.

One of the most surprising elements on our trip had been the international inability to pronounce the name 'Jodie'. Over time, she had been forced to adopt local versions of the name, or just settle for the closest audible noise, 'JoJee', 'Gugee', 'Guly', 'Jada' the list went on. This time, I was determined to cut out the middle man.

'My name is Tom,' I punctuated clearly as I pointed to myself with even more clarity, just to be sure.

'Tom,' I repeated again, in case there had been any confusion either surrounding the name, or the pointing.

'Ah, Tom,' they would say in unison, pausing to absorb this information. This was big news on the mountain. 'Tom' was here, the English guy, from Italy.

'And this,' I continued, as I changed the angle of my hand and extended my finger towards the smaller cyclist, 'is Jerry.'

'Jerry,' they replied together, quite delighted at receiving so much news in just one day. As their minds ticked away, there was another pause, and a few seconds later the Azeri 'Manat' dropped.

'Tom and Jerry!' they roared with laughter. This was the funniest thing ever to happen on the mountain. If I'm honest, I think they realised it was just a joke but they were too busy enjoying themselves to dig any further - I had cracked the market.

Sadly, my comedy career was quickly put into perspective, when one of the tea boys discovered the teapot bell on Jodie's bike. Now into the fourth minute of bell ringing, interrupted only by eruptuous laughter, and the occasional clash of hands as several Azeris clasped at the yellow bell, I was reminded of the 'Infinite Monkey Theorem'. I don't know how monkeys became involved in such a theorem, but the concept is that if you sat enough of them down with typewriters for an infinite amount of time, they would eventually randomly tap out the complete works of William Shakespeare.

Conveniently for the 'Infinite Monkey Theorem' scientist, this is a long time to wait to prove his theorem absolute garbage. One obvious hurdle is trying to stop the monkeys from urinating on the typewriters and rusting the carriage, not to mention the ever increasing difficulty of finding replacement ribbons for older models.

It's a flawed theorem on many levels, again confirming that if theorems had any value, they would be used in real life. Despite this, I suppose there could be a slim chance for the monkeys, which can't be said for the Azeris who, at the point the universe imploded, would still be ringing Jodie's bell.

Now only a day outside the capital we had found the real Azerbaijan to be an interesting experience. Most towns outside of Baku contained extremely poor but seemingly self sufficient farming communities, in stark contrast to the multi-million pound oil industry we had heard was flowing from the Caspian Sea via the capital. Life out in rural regions was often tough and uninspiring and, as it had done to many farming areas, led to the fatigue of men and the repression of women. In previous generations, men and boys would have been seen slaving away in the fields while women wouldn't have been seen at all. Times however had changed.

Saviour seems to have arrived in the form of the 'Azeri Plastic Chair Company Inc.', which clearly provided new and exciting work opportunities to the Azeri people. From our observations of the rural male population, it is guessed that 98% had been able to cease farming jobs and take on full time roles as 'durability consultants'.

Although out of the fields, the Azeri males continued to work long hours, and were seen sitting and testing their chairs from breakfast through to dinner, often without a break.

As the new company had eased the farming expectations of the male population, the 'Azeri Plastic Chair Company Inc.' had also been a blessing to the Azeri women. Having been previously confined to the home, with only domestic obligations to fulfil their career aspirations, women were now liberated to take on outdoors work, and labour in the fields for as long as daylight would permit. These women had seized their opportunity and seemed keen to prove themselves. We witnessed entire teams of women on their knees digging, planting and attending to the fields, desperate to impress the remaining 2% of males, who now stood motionless watching over them in 'field supervisor' roles.

The 'Azeri Plastic Chair Company Inc.' had clearly found a very committed workforce, and no matter how much their wives might have struggled in the fields, we doubted whether their employees would ever have been distracted from their duty.

'You know, I never thought I'd say this,' Jodie looked across at me, 'but those men are ten times lazier than you!'

'Thanks honey!' I smiled, taking anything as a compliment at this stage, 'You know what, I think that 'Azeri male' might actually be an anagram of 'A lazier me'!'

*   *   *   *   *

'How ye doin?' came a voice from behind us, as we stood outside a Baku Mosque. A rather buff looking guy walked up to us and shook my hand.

'Good thanks,' I said, 'and you?'

'Aye, I'm gud,' he laughed, 'so wha' took ye so long?'

'Er, I don't know,' I answered again, 'we just got here from London.'

'I know that!' the Scotsman laughed, 'I'm Eldegiz!'

'Eldegiz!' I admitted my surprise, 'How are you doing?'

'Diddinee just tell ye?' he looked at me very seriously. 'Oh arm just messin with ye!' he laughed, breaking a huge smile, 'Come, follow me an' I'll show ye to yer hotel.'

We cycled behind Eldegiz's Skoda as he wove through the back streets of Baku. A few more steep hills conquered and just minutes later we arrived at a sports hotel, normally used to host touring teams.

'We've booked yuz in fur four nights as ye said, but ye ken stay for as long as ye like,' he said.

'Hey Eldegiz, we can't stay in a hotel,' I said, 'we've got no money. Honestly, we're happy just to crash in a spare room somewhere.'

'Leuk ye guys, don't be so daft, this is OUR pleasure tae host ye!' he said as he personally showed us to our room. 'We're paying fur ye room! Please mak' yerselves at home 'n' ah wull come back 'n' collect ye fur lunch, ye kin meet some o' me boys. Ah huv a break at 1 p.m. Hoo diz 'at soond?'

'That sounds great, thank you Eldegiz!' I said, as he pulled the door shut behind him.

'Bloody weird isn't it sometimes!'

'What is?' Jodie replied.

'This trip!' I said, 'One minute you're sleeping in a desert, the next minute you're being shown to a hotel room by a Scottish speaking Azeri!'

'I wonder how long he's spent in Scotland?' Jodie called out from the shower.

'I have no idea!' I called back, 'I guess people get everywhere nowadays.'

'And you didn't pick it up from any of the e-mails?'

'No, come to think of it, I didn't! That's weird.'

I sat wondering how I could have overlooked such an obvious accent. Then I heard laughing from the shower.

'Stupid girl,' I said, realising who she was laughing at. I collapsed on the bed and rested my tired head.

Eldegiz introduced us to the Azeri Rugby Federation (ARF) General Manager, the ARF Secretary, and the national hooker - also his best friend. Everyone on the table was excited by our visit and we felt very at home in our new company.

'Wot wud ye like fur lunch?' Eldegiz put to us.

The menu had an English translation making our decision harder than normal, compared to two-minute noodles it all looked so good.

'What are you having?' I asked Eldegiz.

'Aye'd normally go fur th' Azeri food, th' lamb kebab wi' a combination ay spices an' dips.'

'Mmm, great stuff, I'll have that then please.'

He looked very happy that I was going with his suggestion, 'An' what aboot ye Jodie?'

'Could I please have the same, but with chicken instead of lamb?'

'Ay coorse ye can,' he sat in thought, 'ye knaw, th' food here is really very gud.'

The other three Azeri boys gave their order to a waitress, and Eldegiz did so for us.

'Did you order for yourself?' Jodie asked, concentrating on his translations.

'Ah actually nae,' he said, 'it's Ramadam, so aam fastin' at th' moment.'

'But you've taken us out for lunch? That's not fair on you to watch us eat!'

'It's nae a problem, that's whit happens when ye fast! It's mah choice. Noo, whit soup would ye like?'

'Soup?' I said, 'We've just ordered kebabs!'

'Aye, but ye shoods definitely hae a soup first. Th' soup here is really very gud.'

'But you're not eating *anything* at all?' I reminded him, despite the fact that the soup did actually sound pretty good.

'Aye, ah knaw, but if ah wasnae eatin' nothing, Eh'd definitely have soup as well!'

'Mushroom.' I said, without hesitation.

'Gud choice,' he emphasized.

I wasn't sure how comfortable I would be eating in front of a fasting Eldegiz. The poor guy was clearly passionate about his food, was paying for our lunch, and he couldn't even order a glass of water. Still, as he had said, it was all part of the deal, and his mates clearly weren't fasting. I put to rest my worries by demolishing a bowl of hot mushroom soup.

'Wow, that was good,' I nodded in agreement to everyone.

Two huge kebabs came out and were placed in front of us, complete with all the trimmings, dips and salads. Jodie took one look at the plate, made her infamous pregnant impression, and unleashed her favourite 'Austin Powers' party piece.

'Gitt'in ma *belly*!' she bellowed in the voice of Fat Bastard.

The Azeri boys looked at her, then collapsed in fits of laughter. Who said that Azeri humour wasn't sophisticated? As Fat Bastard and I began to tuck into our kebabs, it reminded me of something I had been meaning to ask.

'So how long did you spend in Scotland then Eldegiz?'

He gave me a little look of suspicion, 'Ah've nae been to Scotland,' he replied quite simply.

'England then?'

'Nae.'

'Ireland?'

'Nae! Ah've nae really been past Eastern Europe,' he said.

'Oh, I just thought? Never mind,' I said, wondering what part of the puzzle I was missing. Maybe I should leave the matter alone.

'But has anyone ever told you that you sound a little Scottish?' I continued, unable to take my own advice.

'Aye, sometimes,' he replied, almost deliberately creating an air of unfinished business.

We both stared at him, waiting for a forthcoming explanation that didn't come. He was now onto us and I suspect also enjoying the moment for what it was worth.

'So, ye have come a long way already,' he said, trying to make small talk.

'No, hang on, was that it?' I said laughing, because now I really needed to know.

At first I had been a little hesitant, worried that the true mystery might unearth something deep and personal. Perhaps he had been adopted by Billy Connolly as a young boy, or maybe he had been moonlighting as a Scottish cleaning lady to get access to his kids. Either way, I had to know how he had picked up such an accent.

'Okay,' he said, almost a little embarrassed, 'Ah've been workin' fur BP as a contract's engineer fur many years noo, an' by coincidence, mah entire team ur Scottish. So mah accent may have changed a wee bit.'

'Ah, so that's why then!' I said, with a sense of relief, 'And that explains how you got interested in rugby!'

I sat back with a smile and enjoyed my kebab, it felt good to finally nail the connection with the sport.

'Nae, actually, they all like soccer,' he said, bursting my bubble of satisfaction. I finally admitted defeat, I was going round in circles and nothing in Azerbaijan had made any sense at all.

'I think it might be easier if you explain things from here.'

'Eldegiz the Brave', as he became known to us, sat and watched us eat our meal while he gave us an overview of the history of Azeri rugby. In earlier e-mail correspondence, he had told us that Azeri rugby was 'fairly young', and that he was part of the 'third generation of players'. I had taken this literally, thinking that rugby was probably in its third decade or so, but as it happened he was quite literally part of a third independent generation of the sport. Rugby had first come to the country in the 1930s, when a group of British sailors organised some matches amongst themselves in Baku.

'It's kind of a funny story wouldnae ye say?' Eldegiz laughed.

'Unbelievable!' I giggled, trying to work out why this was funny. It wasn't a particularly unusual situation as rugby had been introduced to many places around the world by the British or French forces based overseas. After further thought, having seen the Azeri reception to Jodie's yellow teapot bell, I had to assume I was looking too deep for the comedy.

'When ye get back tae th' hotel, look at th' Caspian Sea on a map,' Eldegiz smiled, sensing I was lost.

'Tom, just to let you know, the Caspian Sea is a lake, *not* a sea,' Jodie piped up, as they both started to laugh. 'It is quite funny.'

I looked slowly back between the two sets of raised eyebrows. What were they waiting for?

'Okay, where are we?' Jodie asked me.

'On the Caspian Sea!'

'And where do you normally find the Navy?'

'In the water? Oh! Is the Caspian Sea not made from water?' My mind wandered as I began to picture ludicrous scenes of surfers riding waves of marmalade and caramel lattes.

'It's a lake, Tom!' Jodie burst my entertaining bubble, 'How do you think they even got here with their ships?'

'You know, it's not so funny if you have to explain it,' I said, as I finished off my kebab.

Apparently, rugby in the 1930s had caught on even slower than myself, and suffered a similar fate when the game briefly re-emerged in the 1960s. It wasn't until Eldegiz and his companions put together a side that things started to progress. Soon, they had established an organised rugby federation and had several local teams ready to form a small league. More importantly, on a social level, the national players worked with three local orphanages to bring rugby into the children's lives. Eldegiz in particular believed that if he could bring these children into a rugby family, it would present them with their own opportunities, as well as nurture a pool of individuals who would truly understand and advocate the off-field values of the sport.

Most of the older children were on and off the streets and often couldn't afford to travel to training. When this happened, Eldegiz and the national players always ensured they had enough money to continue playing, but with no funding it always had to come entirely from their own pockets.

These children are the first genuine youth in the country to receive rugby coaching, and many look destined to soon represent their national side. As a pleasant twist, the primary coach, Vagif Saadatkhan, was actually a local born scrum half from the Baku second generation in the 1960s. As Eldegiz now prepares to retire, he hopes the new captain won't need to 'bribe' his own mates to play an away fixture in Bosnia.

*   *   *   *   *

Soon Iran beckoned us, and with our short Baku break over, we knew it was finally time to get back out there and face the chimpanzees. As we pedalled towards the Iranian border, we rested by a small roadside café. No sooner were our bikes leaning against a tree when a young lad emerged, no older than twelve, and enticed us over to sit at his establishment. Amusingly, the little lad snapped his fingers and ordered a much older boy to fetch us some treats from the kitchen. Despite the young boss sporting a very premature moustache, the boy listened to the list of demands, presumably too afraid to question his master, and proceeded to bring us a platter of melon, cheese and ants.

The live ant colony was an unexpected addition to the feast, and on reflection, didn't really add value to the meal. If I was to be a little critical, I'd say that perhaps they were even reducing the amount of melon and cheese we could stomach. Harder to stomach though, was the bill he then tried to give us.

'How much?' I said staring at him, we hadn't even ordered anything so had assumed it was a gift.

'That's a day's budget,' Jodie said, 'we can't pay that!'

'We should have asked for cheaper ants?' I said back to her.

He was only a child, and one of the very few people to try to take advantage of us, as foreigners, on our entire trip. We'd travelled the entire width of the country and had been treated to roadside tea and snacks by generous and interested owners. We decided to pay nothing and I performed the self-explanatory 'my cycling shorts have no pockets' routine. Eventually, he conceded defeat and sloped off to collect some more ants.

As happy as I am to joke about aspects of any country, I must ensure there is no misinterpretation of the Azeri people. It would be a disservice to the gracious and warm hospitality that we received throughout the country. Many people, although often poor and without much to give, saw no limit on what they would do to help us out. Some Azeris were so generous that they would have willingly dismantled their own homes if they had felt we were looking for firewood.

We want to say a special thank you to everyone there, from 'Eldegiz the Brave' for being such a Baku gentlemen, to the unsung farmer boys who slept an entire night outside in the cold, whilst we slept inside their house with all their lovely warm blankets. Perhaps that is the real story.

CHAPTER 17
THE KING OF CONES

'That way!' the man pointed right.

'Thanks,' I replied automatically, 'come on Jo, this way!'

'Why are we turning right?' Jodie asked me.

'That man, he said... ' I tried to explain.

'Yes, I know what he said,' she persisted, 'but did you tell him where we were going?'

'Well, now that you mention it... no, not really,' I realised, 'I see what you're saying now.'

Eventually we made our way through the border town of Astara only to find the road stop dead at a large group of people. Behind the mob were several sets of huge wooden doors, all closed shut.

As we walked our bikes towards some shade, an extremely drunk Iranian man tapped me on the shoulder and told us to wait outside door number three. I looked at the blank door, it was no different to any of the others. He noticed my hesitation, and assured me once more that we should wait at that gate, he even came with us.

Door number two was thrown open and a few exhausted looking faces spilled out onto the street. The doors were pulled shut again behind them as guards held back members of our group who tried to force their way through. With our large clumsy loads we anticipated a struggle to get through the disorganised border control.

Our unsteady little stranger had plenty to say and seemed to chatter away quite freely, mostly about Bob Dylan and his other favourite singers. He babbled on in the scorching sun for so long that we wondered whether perhaps he had left Iranian soil just to get drunk and listen to 'Blowin in the Wind'. He was right about door number three though, it did turn out to be our gateway into Iran.

As the door swung open and the carnage continued, Jodie and I used our standard tactics and stayed well clear from the action. Although this left us at the back of the queue, we knew that pushing was not a game we could win. From a little experience, we had learnt that the best method was just to stand tall, smile, look western and get noticed. A guard through the doorway caught my eye and quickly barked a few instructions to the mob, who obediently parted like the Red Sea.

'Easy as that,' I laughed to Jodie as we pushed through at our leisure.

'I wouldn't hold your breath!' Jodie replied.

'Oh bugger!'

We had walked directly into a huge cage already containing around fifty faces. Once we were through, our group piled in behind us and the cage door was slammed shut. Our little man was still at our side, looking perfectly at ease with the process and babbling on about the Beatles.

'At least we're in the shade!' I offered, trying to stay positive.

Several people tried to climb up over the caged walls, but only succeeded in dropping down into a parallel cage and being wrestled back to the door by the angry border guards. There was a lot of shouting all round, and rather than any organised queuing system, the border guards seemingly fetched small groups of people from the cage at random.

Soon it was our turn, and we pushed our bicycles across a derelict building site towards a wooden hut. At the counter, there were more guards and a lady crying in hysterics. We had no idea what it was all about, but this was clearly a particularly fragile environment. This area of no man's land was paraded by men trying to sell batteries out of suitcases, and women dressing as much like prostitutes as any Islamic customs could tolerate. By now Jodie had fully covered her skin, wearing a headscarf and a long baggy tunic over the top of her full length black leggings.

Surprisingly our exit stamp took no time at all and we were soon pushing across a bridge leading to Iranian soil. One man, travelling back to Iran himself, took enough offense at Jodie's appearance to start pointing towards her legs. He was getting much more excited than I could understand and I looked at Jodie with a mixture of confusion and despair.

'I think he wants me to cover up my knees,' Jodie said, snatching at her pannier to try to retrieve a spare scarf.

'But you can't see your knees? They're somewhere underneath all those clothes!' I explained, wondering whether the man had accidently walked out the house with his x-ray spectacles.

'I know, but it's not just about covering the skin,' Jodie explained, 'you have to cover most of the female form too.'

'Trust me Jodie, I'm looking at you and I promise I see absolutely nothing feminine.'

'Thanks honey. That's very reassuring,' she said wrapping the scarf round her waist to form a makeshift skirt.

'My pleasure!'

With a third layer now over her upper legs, the knee nazi seemed suitably appeased and stomped off to take his miserable face over the border.

Now inside a more organised terminal building, a man entered our passport information into his computer.

'Ireland! You?' I believe was what he said to us.

He placed our passport on the desk and pointed to the final word: United Kingdom of Great Britain and Northern Ireland.

'No, we're from England,' we answered him, not wanting to give any false information on our entry to Iran.

'Country, Ireland? You?' he replied again, pointing to our passport.

'No, listen, we are from England! In the United Kingdom,' I tried to explain.

'Ireland!' he pointed at the word again on our passport, it was clearly the only word he had been able to understand.

'Oh, why can't they write England on our passports?' Jodie asked me.

The confusion was enough for him to pick up the phone, and before long we were being escorted into an interview room up two flights of stairs. Told to bring our bicycles along with us, we struggled up the steps, heaving the heavy loads one at a time.

Although we were only asked a few questions, who we were, where we wanted to go, what we did for a profession and abstractly what our fathers had done for a profession, the process took nearly two hours with many people in and out of the room performing different duties. One man brought in a pad of thick ink and took our finger prints, another even followed us to the toilets to watch us wash off the ink. Suddenly, with all the curiosity satisfied we were free to go.

The border experience aside, the country of Iran was another story entirely. In 2010, Iran had been all over the news with apparent international concerns over an application to build a nuclear power station. Almost all of our family and friends voiced fears for our safety, asking us to stay clear of war zones and areas associated with terrorists. Luckily for us, none of these people had ever been anywhere near Iran, and it was a forgivable mistake to have made.

Iran as a country seems to draw many common misconceptions, but it hasn't invaded another country in over 2,000 years. Considering that they are recognised as one of the world's economic super powers, this is quite a staggering accomplishment. Thought to have been one of the very first significant societies on the planet, the rich 5,000 years of history has left a quiet and peaceful, if not extremely bored, society behind. It is the home of polo for heaven's sake.

In many western eyes, the Islamic regime in some countries is too repressive on society, but that didn't correspond into it becoming a 'dangerous' place to travel through, quite the opposite in fact. When the Armenians were massacred by the Turks in one of the more 'swept under the carpet' genocides in modern history, it was Iran that provided them with a home and the opportunity to continue their customs. How many of you thought you'd find a Christian church around the corner from a pig butcher and bottle store in Iran?

'Hello there!' A voice came from over the little wall.

'Shit!' I said, trying to scoff down my sandwich, 'Do you think we're in trouble?'

'Don't worry guys, it's okay for you to eat your lunch!' the stranger replied, 'I just came down to meet you.'

'Oh hello,' I said, standing up. Admittedly, it hadn't been that pleasant eating so close to a pile of discarded nappies.

'Would you like a cheese sandwich?' I offered him, before remembering why we had been hiding by a pile of discarded nappies. We were still in the middle of Ramadan, and whereas Azerbaijan had been quite a relaxed Islamic environment, the Republic of Iran was governed by Sharia law, and eating at this time of day was forbidden.

'No, thankyou,' he replied. 'I had my lunch before I came to find you.'

'Oh, I see!' I said, not expecting to hear that, 'So, do you live near to here then?'

'I come from just down the road,' he answered, 'I heard about you when you crossed the border town.'

'Blimey, word really *does* travel fast here,' I laughed, 'that was 15 km back! So where do you live?'

'About another 20 km down the road,' he said, 'I imagine that half of Iran knows about you already!'

I began to wonder how many other people had seen us crouch behind the wall to eat our lunch. We thought we'd been the epitome of stealth.

'If you would like a place to stay tonight, I'd like to invite you to my house. My name is Mike.'

We followed Mike to his house, then stowed our gear in an open room and sat down, not on the sofa or chairs that decorated the living room, but on the hard porch floor. This was to become a common theme throughout our Iranian experience. So many houses were filled with comfortable furniture, as the inhabitants sat with sore bums, cross legged on the bare floor. I studied this behaviour from family to family, rich to poor and came to no real conclusions. The only theory I decided on was that the furniture was saved for 'best', similar to the cutlery set my parents kept in a velvet lined box in their glass cabinet. Jodie agreed that she had also spent her younger years eating yoghurts with rusty old tea spoons while sterling silver utensils sat glimmering, out of bounds, only metres away. One family invited us to sit on these chairs and watched on eagerly as we lowered our still un-toned butt cheeks onto their plump soft cushions. Yet, even with the special English guests gracing their home and using their 'best' chairs, most of the family remained sat with their backs against the wall on the floor.

'Mike', who's real name was unpronounceable without looking like we had a serious twitch, was a self taught English teacher. He ran a small class in a small town with a small budget, and to our amusement had an even smaller dress sense. Although pristinely smart, he would have looked more suited to exploring jungles on an elephant than teaching in a classroom.

Mike talked about his desire to travel and see the world, and hoped that one day he would meet a beautiful blonde girl who he could take to be his wife. He had clearly given the whole situation a lot of thought and explained that his dreams were *only* hampered by the difficulty of gaining travel visas as an Iranian. It was attracting a beautiful blonde wife with his taste in clothes that seemed the bigger obstacle, but I did sympathise with his situation.

'Well, hopefully you'll get the chance to travel one day,' I said in encouragement, 'but what does your wife make of all your plans?'

Mike's brown haired wife shyly brought us more grapes and some surprisingly satisfying alcohol free beer.

'She doesn't speak English does she?' Jodie whispered to Mike with embarrassed concern over the topic of conversation.

'Not very well,' Mike assured her.

*   *   *   *   *

I was wrong about the address system back in the Czech Republic as I had never been to Tehran before. Their address system was so confusing that our hosts, Rahim and Farideh, had arranged to meet us by a nearby landmark.

'It's more a set of directions than an address,' Rahim explained to us after our hellos.

'What do we have here then?' I asked, showing him the Farsi e-mail he had sent us in case we got lost.

'That's our address, but it literally means second turning off the main road, third alley on the right, next alley on the left, follow round to the left again and we are on the second floor, number 21D.'

'Stuff being a postman!' Jodie chipped in, 'I'd give myself the sack!'

'You bugger! I was going to say that!'

I glanced back at the address but the squiggles were indecipherable. Although basic 'Farsi' words were easy enough to grasp, conquering the written language was a whole different challenge. Learning a new alphabet was combined with having to read in reverse, in several different written styles, and having to mentally replace many omitted vowels. Everyday words were often written incompletely, on the basis that you learned the sounds between the consonants when you were a child. Even more bizarrely, they sometimes used the same written word for many different meanings. The same Farsi word for 'milk' was also used for 'tap' and for 'lion'. Without criticising a language I can't even speak, if you called me to help with a leaky tap, I would have to turn up with a straw, a spanner and a tranquiliser dart just to make sure I could help.

Back at flat 21D, our fantastic Iranian couple fixed us some lunch and more alcohol free beer.

'Farideh,' Jodie asked her, 'why do so many girls have plasters on their noses?'

'Ha, you've noticed that have you? They are covering up their new scars from their nose jobs.'

'Nose jobs?' I interrupted.

'A girl's nose is one of the only things that the boys can see here, so having the perfect nose is a bit of a status symbol.'

'Really?' Jodie pondered, 'But everyone seems to be wearing them, even the boys!'

Farideh rolled her eyes and shook her head in disapproval.

'The funny thing is that half of them can't even afford the operation. They just wear the plasters to make it look like they have.'

'That's ridiculous! Have you had yours done Rahim?' I asked him. He shook his head a little embarrassed.

'Poor Rahim!' Farideh laughed.

'Oh, there is one thing I should tell you about Iranian people,' she continued, 'they'll be extremely nice to you, but be careful what you believe. There are no better liars than Iranians.'

'Okay! Well, thanks for the advice!'

'Seriously guys, I mean it!' Farideh laughed again. 'They are very clever! They can look you straight in the eye and tell you that the sky is green.'

The following day we cycled through Tehran to the rugby union office, under the constant gaze of two bearded religious leaders on huge posters. Inside, we were warmly received by Minoo, the International Relations representative for the Iranian Rugby & Cricket Federation.

Minoo was every bit the professional, a small and delicate girl, with a beautifully relaxed ability to speak in English. She had a sharp and cutting wit and one could easily be misled by the innocent appearance of her smart and formal hijab. She was also very protective and affectionate towards Jodie.

'Tom! I hope you will take good care of Jodie,' she insisted to me, 'she is so brave to be doing this with you!'

'Hey!! This is all *her* idea!' I kept reminding her.

Minoo conducted a meeting, translating for the new President of Iranian rugby, Mr Sadeghi, and the Rugby Development Manager, Alireza Aerabi. We started to learn about the history of Iranian rugby, chatting about their recent promotions through the Asian lower divisions, but we soon gathered that we were simultaneously being interviewed to satisfy their own curiosities.

Chatting to locals on the way to Tehran, we had noticed that Iranians were full of questions about the outside world. As we asked our questions on school rugby plans, Minoo translated questions on world politics and the English media. As fast as I could jot down broken notes on their rugby programmes, a silent female rugby player to our left scribbled down our every comment in Farsi. Midway through our meeting, the two men disappeared together.

'They've gone to pray,' Minoo explained, 'I'm sorry that we have no tea and biscuits for you.'

We all stared at the empty table and it suddenly dawned on us what had been missing all along. Back in London, most meetings wouldn't have even started without a tray of biscuits acting as an edible agenda timer. The presence of a solitary remaining Jammy Dodger was usually a sign for the chairman to move swiftly onto 'Any other items'.

On the men's return we learned about the surprising success of the female rugby programme and watched a video showing their recent performance at the Cortina 7s in Italy. The female national team played in skin-tight hijabs, and although they still concealed their appearance in the required Islamic way, it was clear that they had thrown off many social shackles in the process of playing. They eventually finished in second place, losing only to the Italian national side in the final.

Alireza ran off to grab a couple of fake Nike training shirts for us, and not wanting to be outdone, the president reached blindly back to his desk and handed me a small blue box. I opened it in excitement for my new rugby gift, but inside was instead a rather thick and heavy wrestling medal.

'Oh, thank you,' I tried to say, without displaying my confusion.

'He was given that last week as a gift,' Minoo explained, 'he would like to give it to you.'

Mr Adeghi spoke again to Minoo.

'We will book your ferry ticket for your journey to Dubai,' she explained.

'Oh really? Thank you,' Jodie replied, 'that would be a great help!'

'It is no problem at all! And we will also arrange some accommodation for your visit to Shiraz Rugby Club.'

'Are you sure?'

'Yes, don't worry. No problems.'

*   *   *   *   *

There was a solitary main road dissecting the desert through to Esfahan and Shiraz, but yet for days as we travelled south, sleeping only on a rolled out groundsheet, nobody seemed able to refrain from asking the same obvious question.

'Where are you going?' they asked, pulling over in front of us on the road to Esfahan and Shiraz.

'Esfahan and Shiraz!' we always answered, displaying varying degrees of patience. Unless you were cycling into the desert to perform a U-turn and head back, there was absolutely nowhere else you could be going.

The midday temperatures were stifling and taking on fluids felt like we were drinking bath water. Jodie was still wrapped up from head to toe, and with so little shade, we spent most of the daylight hours trying to progress on the bicycles. The evenings were pleasant though, with long colourful sunsets and clear nights with a staggering view of a billion stars.

Halfway to Esfahan we treated ourselves to an afternoon off at a small traditional town called Kashan. We had pre-arranged to stay with a friend of Rahim overnight and so we dropped our things and took the bus to a local attraction called 'Fin Gardens'. We stepped onto the rear entrance together, and as the doors closed behind us I immediately noticed that something was wrong. Midway down the bus was a dividing barrier preventing movement between the front and back, and it quickly became obvious that it was separating the men from the women - or at least had done until my clumsy arrival. Suitably embarrassed, I lifted myself up and over the barrier mid-journey and took my seat.

At the next stop, the doors opened again and in poured a swirling cloud of black cloth. I looked round at Jodie, dressed in her bright green tunic, as a scene not dissimilar to a Harry Potter movie began to take shape. The 'dementor-like' women swirled around her, closing off her escape, before clasping around her head for a handle to hold onto. Soon, all I could see of Jodie was a faint glimpse of her green tunic, and then she was gone.

Several stops later the dementors swirled back out the doors and we realised we had come to the end of the route. As we disembarked at Fin Gardens Jodie spotted a most unexpected sight.

'Look over there!' Jodie pointed, 'It's *you*!'

'What?' I turned to follow her outstretched finger. Across the street was a slim bearded young man pushing a heavily laden bicycle, he was clearly western.

'Let's go and say hello,' she insisted.

The young man was from Switzerland and was called Remo. When he had suggested to his father that he would take a long bicycle trip, his dad had bought him a bicycle from eBay. It wasn't quite the same spec that we had picked up in London, but it only cost $50 and had served someone very reliably through World War II. It was an incredibly heavy unit, with only a solitary gear, and he hadn't even connected it to a basic bicycle computer. Remo had pedalled the relic from his front door to Iran without even a firm plan of where he wanted to go.

'When I have spent half of my budget, I will turn around and go home,' he explained.

Remo was very amusing company and his carefree attitude shamed us at being so controlling over our own schedule. Sometimes looking at the amassed kilometres on our own bicycle computer was the only thing that kept us going.

'What do you do when you get to a steep hill?' I asked him, pointing to his single gear.

'I usually just get off and push,' he shrugged.

'Bloody hell,' I said out loud, 'we've got 27 gears and that's exactly what we do!'

Leaving Remo with our Iranian hosts the next morning, we continued towards Esfahan. On the final day we took our lunch break down by a river in the cool shade of some trees. After a short time, a car pulled up behind us and a man approached carrying something from a nearby bakery. To our surprise he sat down and started to chat to us in English.

'Welcome to Iran!' he greeted us, although we had clearly been there for some time.

'Thanks very much,' I replied on autopilot but with a smile.

'Are you from around here?' Jodie asked her favourite question, but guessing that he was probably too clean and smart to be living in such a barren place.

'No, actually I'm from Esfahan,' the man replied, 'and it's not true what they say.'

'What do they say?' I asked.

'People always say such bad things about their neighbours in Iran, but it's mostly just made up. People are a bit bored.'

'Oh right, but what do they say?' I asked again.

'Well, if you come from Yadz, they say you are a bit flirty. If you come from Tabriz, then you are a bit punchy, and if you come from Esfahan, they say we are very tight. It's utter rubbish.'

He opened his bag of treats, 'Here, would you like a day old cookie?'

'Oh, yes please!' I replied gratefully.

'Okay, good then come back tomorrow!' he laughed, closing up the bag.

After we had finished his cookies I took my foot off the man's head and helped Jodie pack up the panniers. With our stomachs full, we finally tackled the last 60 km into Esfahan.

*　　*　　*　　*　　*

'Wow, look at that photo!' I pointed out to Jodie, 'It looks like you're holding a light saber!'

'Does it?' she replied absently, 'Never mind, I guess that sometimes happens when there's bright sunlight.'

'Are you sure you're not a Jedi?'

'I doubt it Tom, I can't get you to do *anything* I want, can I?'

I thought about it carefully, and then decided to check back on the Hungarian photos with Pal Turi. If I found a light saber in any *those* photos that would really make my day.

'We haven't heard anything about Shiraz?' Jodie mentioned as she downloaded our e-mails.

'Don't worry!' I put on my best Iranian accent, 'No problems!'

'Why do all your accents sound like the Godfather?'

'They don't!'

'Well, once we get on the road we won't be able to get any internet.'

With that, Jodie sent another e-mail to Minoo in Tehran chasing on the ferry and Shiraz address, as I sadly found that not a single photo of Pal showed any signs of a light saber.

'Come on, let's go and explore the bazaars!' Jodie said, indicating that our afternoon activity was already planned.

We strolled on foot around one of the most spectacular cities on our journey, walking across the Khaju Bridge and exploring the Shah mosque at Naghsh-e Jahan Square. At one point in time, Esfahan was the capital of the Persian empire, and one of the largest cities in the world. Many of the buildings were highly ornate with grand architectural reminders of Iran's former glory, but although still charming and vibrant, it was now in many ways a calm and relaxed place to wander. Jodie clicked away on her SLR, fascinated by the deep and rich colours in the spice bazaar, but eventually I dragged her away to come and see the Persian carpets.

'Feel this one Jo!' I called to her, 'It's actually softer than a Mr Whippy!'

'How much is it?' she asked me.

'£25,000,' I replied, 'it won't fit on the bike though.'

We finally moved on to a clothes market to find Jodie some more Islamic dress. Knowing that we would be in Pakistan for even longer, we decided it was best for everyone if she increased her options. Her only green tunic was now quite stinky, and buying another one would at least give her something to wear while she gave it a first wash.

'Jo? There's one thing that still confuses me,' I said.

'Are you sure it's just one thing?' she replied trying on a cotton cream number. 'Go on, what is it?'

'You always said my Godfather impression sounded nothing like him!'

We finally got hold of a telephone number for the Iranian national coach, based down in Shiraz.

'Wayne Marsters?' I read out the name, 'Doesn't sound very Persian to me!'

I gave him a call to try to help us arrange things. Wayne was in fact a New Zealander, with almost an entire lifetime in the game in various countries across the globe.

After finally hanging up the phone I'd almost forgotten whether I'd even mentioned anything about Shiraz.

'What did he say?' Jodie asked.

'He sounds like a really amazing guy to meet,' I replied, still shaking my head and rattling through his vast experiences.

'Excellent!'

'But we're not going to meet him.'

In typical Iranian form, Wayne had been transferred at extremely short notice and sent up to the Iraqi border. He had been placed with the responsibility of outlaying a school's development programme while simultaneously running a national training camp for the upcoming Asian games.

'He's in Tehran meeting with the squad now,' I said, 'but he's given me the phone number of his translator down in Shiraz if we need any help.'

'Okay, look we've done everything we can, let's just go down there and see.'

After being rear ended by a careless taxi driver, we crawled up the huge hill out of Esfahan and found our rhythm on the long road south. It took many more oven baked afternoons and hilly desert stretches before we finally pulled ourselves to within reach of Shiraz, but still 60 km short of our target, we were distracted by a turning to our left indicating the road to 'Persepolis'.

'It doesn't say how far,' Jodie complained, 'what do you think?'

Some people like to spend their holidays running around cities and taking photos of every tourist attraction, others like to sit in a quiet café, watch the world rush around them and soak up the atmosphere. I have always been drawn to activities that involve sitting down for long periods of time, but Jodie is typically neither. She is a tourist dodging fidget bum. Most of our holidays usually left me scoffing down street food in a dark alley, then chasing Jodie around a city avoiding anything in the slightest bit 'picture postcard'. I was being worked so hard that on one long weekend city break to Europe, I took along a pedometer, and secretly measured our average daily walking distance. It was 20 km! Someone please tell her that *isn't* a holiday.

Despite this, we had read many fantastic things about the ancient site of Persepolis. The magnificent ruins, left behind by the former capital of the Persian empire, had been recommended as one of the primary 'things to see' in Iran. Some dating back to over 500 B.C. the terrace, temples and palaces were of such a unique quality that it had been labelled a UNESCO World Heritage site. It sounded like an incredible location to visit, but we still had four more hours of pedalling before even beginning to try to locate Wayne's translator. We stood for many minutes on the corner deliberating.

'Nah, it's too hot,' we both decided.

Once again we had been left regretting our sluggish method of transport. It wasn't the first time that we had felt like bad tourists, and in this example it hadn't been through lack of interest. We already had to cycle 100 km a day to make the 28,000 km journey and when a sign said 'Turn right - Super Duper Amazing Special Thing - 13 km', we only read it as 'Two hours and 26 km of cycling to get back to where we are right now'.

On really tough days even a single kilometre detour would be enough to ignore, consoling ourselves by saying it was probably just like all the others. You honestly wouldn't believe the things we *didn't* see on our trip, we even started sending postcards back home titled, 'Wish *we* were here!'

It was getting particularly warm, and by the time we finally freewheeled down into Shiraz we were grateful for our decision. We found a phone box and dialled Wayne's translator, Askin.

Comically, the very next morning we found ourselves stepping out of a taxi at the entry booth to 'Persepolis'. Askin had rounded up three of his friends and decided to take us on a guided tour of the Shiraz region. It was worth the journey.

On the return cab ride, our driver stopped to smoke a cigarette with a man from a roadside checkpoint.

'What is he doing?' I asked Askin, wondering if his cigarette break was going to feature in our fare.

Askin called out the window to the man, who replied but continued to chat away.

'He has to wait for five minutes,' Askin explained, 'he's been speeding.'

As a very primitive speed check, all taxis were required to stamp in and stamp out at a booth either end of the highway. Our driver had clearly arrived too early and was now killing time by smoking a cigarette with the man responsible for time stamping the exiting taxis from the road. By now, we were well drilled in dealing with such unorthodox practices and we began to joke about the differences in our cultures.

In Iran, very few procedures seemed to work as they were intended, but thanks to a small but important instruction in the Qu'ran, Muslims must never promise to undertake a task without adding the phrase 'Insha'Allah'. This small but important caveat, meaning 'If it be God's will' or 'If I feel like it', allows for literally everything to be promised and absolutely nothing to be delivered. For example, 'I promise to adhere to the laws of the road... Insha'Allah,' or 'I will book your ferry ticket to Dubai... Insha'Allah.'

While Jodie and Askin phoned the ferry company, I sat down and chatted with Mahiar 'King of Cones' Askari. Mahiar was the town's finest ice cream maker, and in addition to serving up the best sugary icy treats, was also a leading Iranian coach and former national team prop. He was a member of the very first Iranian national side and retired with seven tests and seven victories to his name. At 31 years of age he showed little sign of slowing down, continuing in his role as player and coach of Shiraz RFC. With an empowering smile and a fit, chiselled body, I found it hard to better Jodie's innovative description - 'well buff'. You can take the girl out of Essex.

'What's the *scoop* Jo?' I asked, waiting for a rapturous applause.

'It's not good Tom, we can't book over the phone and they seem to change their answer every time we ask them a question.'

I tried again, I didn't care about the ferry, I was high on sugar.

'Okay, just don't *flake* out on me, we'll figure something out.'

She appeared deep in thought and wasn't really paying enough attention.

'Isn't there a ferry before *Sundae*?' I tried to add casually, now just entertaining myself.

'That's enough ice cream jokes for today please,' she said without even looking at me.

'Hey! You *did* hear my jokes!'

'Tom, I think we need to book a flight.'

'You can definitely bring your bicycles!' Askin announced proudly, as he liaised with the travel company in the office.

'Askin,' Jodie asked, 'is that 'We can definitely bring our bicycles' or is that 'We can definitely bring our bicycles Insh'Allah'?'

'No, they said you can definitely bring your bicycles,' he confirmed confidently.

'Okay, please ask them if we need to box up the bicycles?' Jodie then asked.

Askin turned back to the smart lady behind the desk, who picked up the phone.

'She's phoning the airport again,' he explained.

After a more lengthy discussion she recalled the conversation to Askin, who nodded repeatedly and finally relayed the information to us.

'No!' he said.

Jodie stared at him with clear implication she expected a more detailed explanation.

'They said no!' Askin replied defensively, 'You don't need to box your bicycles, they will do it at check in. No problem!'

We booked two flights from Shiraz to Dubai and behind Askin's back, asked his friend to independently phone the airport to double check.

'They confirmed you don't need to box up your bicycles,' he whispered to us, 'they said they will do it at check in.'

We allowed two extra hours before our check in time to ensure there were no problems. We only had a day remaining on our visa and we were determined not to deal with the situation of overstaying. We handed over our passports and tickets to the lady behind the glass screen, while Askin listened and translated for us.

'Erm, she said that you can't take your bicycles through like this.'

'Askin, they said to bring them un-boxed because they would do it here?' Jodie said, as if she had expected this situation.

He spoke to the lady again, but we didn't need Farsi to understand her gestures. I crossed my fingers and hoped that she was Bulgarian.

'She says you need to go to the other airport building and leave them with the freight people.'

'Fine,' Jodie said, already frustrated with the disorganisation, 'which way do we have to go?'

'Erm,' Askin hesitated again, 'it's a short taxi ride.'

Over at the other terminal the men stared at us as if we were asking them to box up their elderly grandmothers. They shook their head as they sat on the steps outside smoking cigarettes.

'They can't take bicycles here,' Askin translated for us, 'they say you have to take them back to the airport.'

'Oh for heaven's sake Askin. Tell them that they just sent us here!'

Askin's face was like a rabbit caught in the headlights, and he turned slowly and obeyed the orders. One of the men stepped inside the small office and picked up the phone, seconds later and he was yelling at someone on the other end. He put down the handset and came back outside.

'He said they still can't take it,' Askin explained, 'the only way is if you pay for it to be put on plane as a private delivery. He says it will be about one thousand dollars.'

We pleaded with the men but after a full twenty minutes it became clear that they weren't able to help. Eventually they suggested that we box the bicycles at a nearby store and take them back to the main terminal. Time was running out, and we hurried to follow their advice.

The shop owners responded to the situation well and using a number of broken banana boxes, bound together a protective shield of cardboard, with some strong nylon cord. In the circumstances, twenty dollars seemed a significant sum to hand over, but the results were very impressive under such stressful conditions.

In two separate taxis, we hurried back to the main terminal, handed our passports back to the front desk lady, and finally joined the queue for the X-ray machine. When confronted by the policeman on duty I finally found a man I disliked more than Louis Theroux.

We patiently dragged the bicycles to one side, but before we even had chance to explain he yelled at us to lift our bicycles onto the small conveyor belt. I looked ahead to the machine and gestured to say they would not fit through. Unless the tiny door frame to the X-ray machine was a deceptively long way away, it should have been clear that these boxes were too large. He shouted again, this time grabbing the boxes and trying to force them into the tiny frame.

'Hey! Careful!' we both cried, grabbing at the boxes to prevent any damage.

There was a commotion as more and more queuing passengers banked up behind us and Askin ran to fetch assistance. Out stepped the General Manager of the airport who patiently and politely introduced himself and spoke to the police man. He turned to us and explained with enough English, that the police official had overriding jurisdiction, even above him. We would have to comply.

'Okay, but the boxes won't fit through this X-ray machine!' we replied, keeping our cool.

He turned to the police man, possibly trying to talk sense into him, we will never know.

'You must open up your bicycles so that he can see them.'

Despite having been just told to box them, we now took a knife and cut away the carefully bound cord, leaving a pile of useless cardboard banana boxes on the floor. Overseen by the airport manager, the police man prodded and poked at the disassembled bike pieces. Finally satisfied that there was nothing untoward, he left them on the floor.

'Okay?' I asked the police man. He grumbled something and pointed again to the X-ray machine.

'I'm afraid you will still have to put them through the X-ray machine,' the manager apologised.

'Is this what you do every time someone wants to fly with a bicycle?' I asked him calmly.

I was determined not to lose my cool after getting this far. He didn't have to answer for us to see that this wasn't an every day event in Iran. Reluctantly we picked up each piece of bicycle and guided it through one by one, X-raying most of our arms in the process. Jodie rushed to the other side just in time to stop our equipment spilling onto the floor. The manager followed us round and explained that we would need to box the bicycles if we wanted to check them onto the plane. We both stared at him.

'You can pay that boy over there,' he pointed to the in-house shrink wrapping service.

We didn't even argue, and between us dragged what was left of the banana boxes over to the boy. After successfully shrink wrapping back some of the cardboard, Jodie loaded a trolley and wheeled our equipment to the final check-in desk. I reached into the usual pocket and tried to settle the bill, I had about twelve dollars in Rials left, the boy asked for twenty. I made it very clear we had no more money and he didn't seem all that concerned about the missing cost, so thanking him I ran back to join Jodie.

'You seem to have too much weight?' the manager explained to us at the desk.

'We were told there was no charge for bicycles on the phone?' we lied to him, now realising that this whole process was one big scam.

'Oh? Well, that doesn't sound right,' he said, and spoke in Farsi to the girl at the counter.

She pulled out a calculator, looked at our bags and bashed in a series of completely incidental numbers, before turning the screen around to face us.

'You have to pay 420,000 Rials,' he explained, although I could read the number quite clearly.

'Sorry, you have just taken all our remaining money by charging us twice to box up our bicycles?'

He seemed to accept this situation without argument but tried a different line of enquiry. 'No problems,' he said, 'how many dollars do you have with you?'

Jodie kept our $250 safely in the pannier and shrugged her shoulders. 'Sorry, we don't have any US dollars. We have our debit cards though!'

Jodie pulled out our two debit cards and a Mastercard offering him the choice. It was a smart play, knowing full well that the Iranian banking system is closed to all these methods of international payment.

'We can't accept these methods of payment,' he explained, glancing at his watch, 'maybe you could take a few things on as hand luggage?'

Our hand luggage panniers were practically tearing our shoulders from their sockets, but we followed his advice and made a small token exchange of items. He spoke again to the lady behind the till, who re-tapped into her annoying little calculator.

'Ah, good!' the manager exclaimed with a smile. 'Everything now appears to be in order.'

With nothing better to do, he followed us to the final passport control and tapped me on the shoulder.

'You were both very calm,' he said, without explanation, 'I hope you had a pleasant stay in Iran.'

CHAPTER 18
IN BED WITH JOHN BENTLEY

From: 'Maggie Dillon'
To: 'Jodie and Tom'

'Dear Jodie and Tom,

I just read an article about your ride to the RWC.
It sounds incredible, and it's fantastic what you're
doing to raise awareness for your charities and
rugby in general. I saw on your site that you plan
on coming through Laos. Lao Rugby would love to show
you around - we have school and community
development projects, four domestic teams, and
men's, women's, and U20s national teams.

I hope we have the chance to welcome you to
Vientiane! Until then, sok dee der! (best of luck)
and take care, Maggie'

*   *   *   *   *

We were in Dubai at a particularly good time, for a start the Arabian Gulf Rugby Union was going through an interesting and significant transition, but also because Jodie's old work mate, Rob, was just moving into a lovely big house with his family.

We had our very own bedroom and helping them move a few bits of furniture was a small price to pay to escape the 50 degree heat outside.

As if they needed to thank us, they took us out for some western food. Jodie had the grilled chicken breast with salad, chips and a chilled glass of white wine. I had a bacon double cheeseburger with chips, an extra portion of chips and most of Jodie's chips. While I shovelled down my calories, Rob thoughtfully ordered me a cold pint of beer to help wash down the chips. Rob was from Norfolk, and by design was a big strong 'country lad'. His wife, Kate, quite liked rugby too and she proudly revealed that she never missed any of Rob's rugby dinners.

'That's amazing commitment Kate!' I congratulated her, turning to Jodie to learn from her diligent example.

'Jodie, the last time I let Rob go on his own, I woke up next to a kebab and a signed photo of John Bentley!'

The girls exchanged a knowing nod, followed by the infuriating laugh of agreement whenever a man has put a foot wrong.

'£500 it cost us!'

'Blimey Rob, I hope you got chips with it!' I laughed, as we exchanged our own nods. I could tell he was still in trouble.

'That's ridiculous!' I said, as we stood staring up at the kilometre tall tower. We had seen this building wherever we went, but up close it just seemed even more absurd. You needed reminding that it was indeed a building, and not a mountain. It was enormous and I began to feel a little daft, realizing that I had been staring blankly at the building for too long already.

'It's taller than Freeway!' I said, concluding that this would be an accurate assessment. Our friend 'Freeway' was nowhere near a kilometre tall.

In 2001, Ricky Gervais had written and performed a song titled 'Freelove Freeway' in his hit sitcom 'The Office'. The series had struck an instant chord with most office workers in London and many of the us introduced 'Office-isms' into our day-to-day speak, if only to help pass the tediously long working hours. One memorably funny line went, 'The love is free and the freeway's long'.

By coincidence, one of my friends at work was a very tall guy called Paul Highway, and he was single. Tragically, having had any sign of creativity stamped out of us, I recall it took a little time before our team pieced together the puzzle.

'Hey you know what! Highway's pretty long, he's single. That would make him a Freelove Freeway!'

'Hey Highway! Guess what! We've got a new name for you!'

'Boys, the other team have been calling me that for two years,' he replied, 'what took you so long?'

Despite the delay, his new nickname stuck for many years, both in and out of work, before finally all traces to his former life as 'Paul Highway' had vanished into thin air.

Inside the office, new staff would come and go, no doubt wondering why they had never found the leggy phantom anywhere on the e-mail system. Years later, when he eventually settled down with a beautiful blonde Australian called Kristy, we called an emergency meeting. After much deliberation, it was decided to officially drop the 'Freelove' part in her honour, and as a result our 6'6" friend is now simply known as 'Freeway'.

'I feel like I should do something,' I said, as I stood with my head hung back and chin to the sky.

'You could start by closing your mouth,' Jodie suggested, looking at me with partially disguised disappointment.

'I'll take a photo,' I declared, triumphantly breaking the trance. I reached for my little digital camera. 'Hold still.'

'Why are you laying on the floor?' Jodie asked, 'Get up, people are staring!'

'I can't fit you both in,' I said, 'I'll just have to work with a few angles.'

I shifted around the decking like a highly trained marine to work the shot. Many moments later I stood proudly displaying my artistic efforts on the footbridge.

'Tom, you were moving around the floor like an elephant seal, it was quite embarrassing, that man nearly threw you a fish!'

I turned to see the man in question, he didn't even have any fish. 'Hey! That's how the marines move!' I tried to argue.

Jodie took the camera and browsed through the photos on the digital screen.

'Didn't you want one of me *and* the building?' she kindly reminded me, as I waited hoping that she had forgotten.

'I never actually found that angle,' I explained with limited conviction, 'but look at this one, this is in black and white.'

The previous day, I had found a new setting, 'Press *yes* to take photos in black and white' it said. There were no further instructions, nor any suggestions when I should use it, but silently I hoped that this discovery would propel me to new photographic heights.

Jodie looked at it and pondered, she was clearly most impressed with my work.

'I don't like black and white as much as I used to,' she said frankly, 'I find it takes a lot of the colour away.'

Such a damning response left me a little deflated. Sadly, after giving her words some serious consideration, I became inclined to agree with her. The setting had indeed removed a lot of the colour, and with such a flawless argument my one-button photography lesson seemed a pretty flimsy defense. As we walked back to the bus stop I pushed the menu again 'Press *yes* to take photos in colour.'

Much better, I thought.

*   *   *   *   *

On Saturday morning, Ghaith Jalajel collected us from Dubai and drove us two hours into the desert for a pre-season development tournament at Al Ain RFC. Ghaith worked for the brand new United Arab Emirates Rugby Association (UAERA), having successfully applied from the previous umbrella union, the recently disbanded Arabian Gulf Rugby Football Union (AGRFU). In 2010, the AGRFU had been responsible for the combined development of rugby in Bahrain, Kuwait, Oman, Qatar, Saudi Arabia, the UAE, Lebanon and Jordan.

Ghaith was a former Jordanian national player and was also due to be playing in the tournament. On the drive over, he explained that the main reason for creating independent unions, was that the money currently spent on long distance travel would be better spent on developing the domestic programmes. The AGRFU had served a specific purpose to bring rugby up to a certain level in the Gulf region, but it couldn't afford to take it any higher.

The UAE representative side is still mainly formed from ex-pats working in Dubai, and finding solutions to some of the cultural obstacles may be a big challenge. Although alcohol licenses can be bought by rugby clubs in the Emirates, it can only be granted if the club adheres to prohibiting locals i.e. Muslims, from joining.

We finally pulled up in the Al Ain RFC car park.

'Geez! Look at the size of him!' I pointed enthusiastically to a Samoan looking human tank, 'He looks like an overweight Trevor Leota!'

'Shh!!' hushed Ghaith, 'That *is* Trevor Leota!'

Trevor Leota was in Dubai not only as a player and coach to his own club Dubai Wasps, but he was also employed to develop the rugby programmes at a local talent development centre - The Elite Sports Academy. He was even larger than I had remembered him from his London days.

'Will he play today?' I asked Ghaith.

'If he does, I won't be!' he laughed, as he hurried off to the changing room.

*   *   *   *   *

'Tom Hudson!' I looked up as a familiar figure strolled into the bar.

'Hamza Girach!' I said, feeling now that only a full name would do. Hamza Girach was my old friend and fellow teammate, the hooker in our school 'B' team. Facially he hadn't changed one bit, but if he was still playing he'd more likely be out on the wing than in the front row. Although a scheduled reunion, we hadn't seen each other in years, and to catch up with any familiar face after so many months of cycling was a great relief.

'You crazy guys! I can't believe what you are doing. You must have so many stories! I'm sorry I'm late, I've been running around in meetings all day and I've got to be on a flight back to London in 5 hours!'

'Hey, don't mind us, the World Cup doesn't kick off for another year, we've got plenty of time.'

'Right guys, seeing as you are cycling across the entire world, the least I could do is buy you dinner!'

'Do you they do chips?' I asked.

'Yes Tom, I suspect they do,' he said, 'you could probably order something with them too!'

As I chomped down on my bacon double cheeseburger I eyed up Jodie's chips.

'You know, I hope you don't mind me saying this, but I don't remember you being much of a rugby person back at school.'

'Well, I don't remember you being much of a Muslim!' I laughed, as Hamza sipped on his Diet Coke.

'Haha, nobody does!' he smiled, 'Very few people at school noticed, even when I didn't eat or drink for four weeks!'

'You fasted at school? Crikey! I used to eat half my packed lunch in morning assembly! Do you still play rugby?'

'Oh no way! Not any more!'

'But you come out here regularly for work?'

'Fairly regularly, why?'

'Haha, I'm giving Trevor Leota your phone number.'

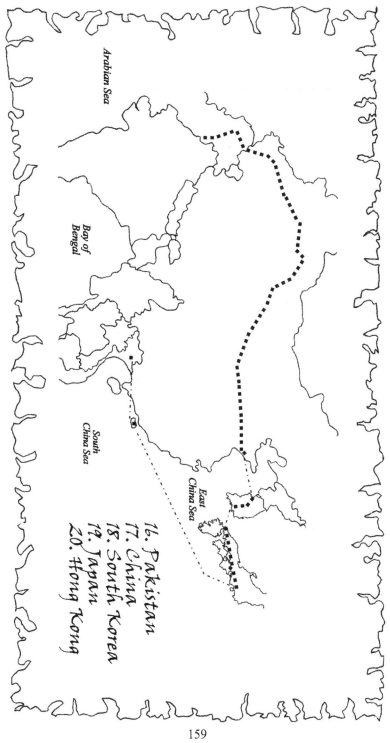

Arabian Sea

Bay of Bengal

South China Sea

East China Sea

16. Pakistan
17. China
18. South Korea
19. Japan
20. Hong Kong

CHAPTER 19
SPECIAL K

In all her wisdom, while safe in our London flat, the 'Chief of Route Planning' had decided that cycling across the Himalayas would be a satisfying and rewarding experience for us. Reviewing the 15,000 foot high road on the map, I considered how different our personal ambitions might be.

I'm a strong believer in chasing satisfaction, but I could achieve enough of it simply by watching back-to-back episodes of 'Scrubs' on a Sunday morning. Cycling the Himalayas would be a notch more intense, and would at least involve me putting on more than just my Sunday pants.

'Okay fine, we'll give it a go,' I had said, unrealistically defiant, 'so we're going to India then? To get to Nepal?'

I knew from a previous holiday that Mount Everest was in Nepal, and therefore by default, most of the other Himalayan mountains must be close at hand.

When you are living with a very substandard knowledge of the world, it's often best to display what little you do know whenever you get the chance. Like at school when you've only done 10% of your homework, you make sure the teacher only catches your eye in the first 10% of the class. If you get a couple of answers in early doors, it'll probably see you through the rest of the lesson.

'So you were paying attention on our trek?' Jodie had offered in return, clearly impressed, 'Although sadly no, we can't cross from India or Nepal. If we take that route we'll arrive too late in the year and the roads will all be closed off for winter.'

'So from where then?' I had no more mountain cards to play.

'We'll go straight from Pakistan to China over the Karakoram Highway.'

She had said it with such authority, you'd think she'd done it a few times that week already.

'Pakistan!' I'd tried not to shout, 'I mean, come on, Pakistan?' I didn't actually know anything about Pakistan, but it sounded like a ropey idea, and I thought my chances of survival were already pretty low.

'How else did you think you were cycling to India?' Jodie had queried with genuine interest.

'The way everyone else does I expect?' I'd despaired, 'How does everyone else get there?'

'By plane, or from Nepal I suppose.'

'Well, what's wrong with that?'

'I checked before we left, there was already someone flying to the Rugby World Cup!' she'd smiled, quite pleased with her answer, 'And if you're already in Nepal, there isn't much need to come back south over the Himalayas to India.'

I'd been lost enough already and didn't want to think about anything further than Gravesend, in my mind, this was still a point at which I could turn around and give up.

'Okay fine, but I'm turning the news off now, most of those bomb reports were in Pakistan. I assume that your bike is bomb proof?'

'Isn't yours?' Jodie had replied, as she brought my ramblings to an abrupt and nervous conclusion.

'I'm still bidding,' I had lied, knowing that eBay wasn't bringing any joy.

Once the Pakistan route had been decided, I proudly informed my friends, who decided this was good enough reason to celebrate my demise. In particular Scott, the occasional plumber from Newport, had endlessly teased me about being chained to a radiator by the Taliban. As a foolhardy adventure cyclist, I had laughed off the taunts, but after some time I began to think to myself 'Could this actually happen?'

My only education on the world of terrorism had come from reading free copies of The Daily Mail in the gym sauna. From this it was clear to me that the world was indeed an incredibly dangerous place. I wanted to be a little brave, but not so brave that actual bravery would ever be required. I decided that it would be best to conduct some real research on the matter, but working for a large American bank, I chose not to google 'Taliban' or 'Terrorists' until I got home that evening.

Before I'd even sat down for dinner, I logged on and tried to explore his warnings. Could Scott be onto something? And how was the internet going to give me any reassurance?

'Taliban domestic heating systems,' I typed carefully. The screen flickered as it processed the search.

I had meant to get the flickering problem fixed months before, but with only a few weeks remaining it just didn't seem worthwhile anymore.

References to opium, bombs, and randomly a Tesla Roadster sports car filled my results screen. Interesting nonetheless, this wasn't helping to fulfill my requirements. I tried once more, 'Domestic heating systems used in Pakistan?' glancing over my shoulder for anti-terrorist police at the window. Still nothing.

I broadened my criteria and finally, after a more thorough investigation into West Asian central heating systems, I discovered that most areas of Asia were simply heated by fires or wood burning air ducts. Radiators were very much a western device, and so for now this logic would have to suffice, and I concluded that we should be okay. The chances of finding a terrorist with wall mounted panel radiators seemed remote, this would be a very risky heating strategy, and would surely raise suspicions in the local community. After my initial panic, it now appeared the 'chained to a radiator' scenario was just a hoax. Of course, Scott would have known that, after all, he was a fully trained occasional plumber.

'I'll get that little rascal back!' I told myself, cackling wickedly before realising that no, in truth I had no chance of ever getting him back.

*   *   *   *   *

From: 'Khuram Haroon'
To: 'Jodie and Tom'

'Hi guys

I will pick you up at the airport at 8pm. When you come out of customs go left and towards the car park. I will be standing with a PRU green rugby jersey. I am sure you won't miss me.

Thanks
Khuram'

*   *   *   *   *

Living in Lahore, Khuram Haroon had long been our voice in Pakistan, keeping us posted with the devastation caused by the recent floods. As we had progressed through Turkey, Georgia and Azerbaijan, the waters had continued to spread across more and more areas of our planned route, until 85% of the country had been affected.

While volunteering as the webmaster for the Asian Rugby Football Union (ARFU) website, he was also a volunteer Utility Manager for the Pakistan Rugby Union (PRU), a father to two young children and ran a handmade carpet business in any spare hours he could find. Despite these commitments, he hadn't hesitated to assist a privately organised relief effort involving individuals from the Lahore rugby community, and notably his younger brother Jawad.

We scouted the arrivals lounge for our new host, who to his friends was known simply as 'K'.

'He'll be wearing a green Pakistan rugby jersey,' I reminded her looking at the sea of beige 'salwar kameez', the long shirts commonly worn by Pakistani men.

'Haha, there he is!' Jodie laughed, as K stood blocking the doorway with a huge smile.

'I am sure you won't miss me,' K had written to us, and even in the airport bedlam, we were in no danger of that.

At 6 feet tall and weighing in at over 180 kg, K was not merely a man-mountain but the entire man-mountain range. True to his word, K had waited for us in his green rugby jersey, despite the sweaty 30 degree heat outside. This proved to be as necessary as King Kong wearing a carnation, and if all 175 million Pakistanis had stood waiting in green rugby jerseys, I'm still quite sure we'd have picked him. If this hadn't been enough on its own, we were the only two white people to get off the plane and were pushing a trolley with two enormous bicycle boxes and ten fluorescent bags.

The former Pakistan national prop had in fact been born in Barking, Essex, and had gone through an education in England before moving to study a degree in the US. It was at trials for the college American football team that K had been spotted and snatched by the rugby fraternity, and what an impact he would have made too. The more astute rugby fans might note that Barking had already produced a rather large front row legend, the most capped forward ever, Jason Leonard. Jason's attitude both in and out of rugby had earned him the nickname 'fun-bus', but despite having piled on some pounds after retirement, this may yet come under threat from our new friend, the 'double-decker' legend with the carpets.

We got outside and loaded our gear into K's minibus, which later became known as 'Jason', and we were transported to our Lahore HQ, an area also referred to as K's spare room. We were pleased to have finally arrived in Pakistan, not only to witness the remarkable unification of their society, but because a very special guest had also just arrived in Lahore.

Ismail Kadir, known to nearly every developing rugby community in Asia as 'Izzy', is a former Singapore national player, and now IRB Asian Development Officer. His primary role is to assist with their development plans by providing a range of coaching certificate courses to nurture the local development of the sport. Due to the usual security concerns, Pakistan had waited a particularly long time for an official visit from the IRB, so Izzy's arrival was met with great interest from the community and national media.

There was a spare day before the IRB course began, so we all decided to go for a tour of the city. We squeezed into 'Jason' and headed over to collect Izzy, who was being hosted by PRU President, Fawzi Khawaja.

'Morning,' Fawzi said to us, 'sorry I can't chat now, but I'll see you at lunch! Oh, and K,' he continued, 'you know the location don't you?'

'Yes Fawzi!' K said, rolling his eyes.

'And you know it's 1 p.m.?'

'Yes Fawzi!'

'K, that's 1 p.m. *real* time, not 1 p.m. Pakistani whenever I feel like it time.'

We all burst out laughing.

'Have fun guys,' he said as he waved us goodbye.

The city of Lahore is ideally situated on one of the six primary Indus water flows, the Ravi river, and is only 25 km from one of the primary trade crossings into India at the Wagga border. The history of the city has been traced back at least two thousand years, and it has been an integral part of many empires and eras in the Subcontinent. Originally known as the 'City of Lava', it later became known by many names, 'The Paris of the East', 'The Pearl of Punjab', and most recently, 'K's Food Court'.

'Fried chicken?' K asked, 'Izzy? Tom?'

'It's ten in the morning!' I reminded him.

'Don't worry, they open at nine!' he replied, with a twinkle in his eye, 'They have every food you could ever want here in Lahore!'

He was right about that. Over time, Lahore had become a melting pot for traditional and modern restaurants, showcasing menus and flavours from all around the world. In more recent years, the list of western fast food chains had also infiltrated the Lahori eating habits, with 24 hour McDonald's, Pizza Huts and Dunkin Donuts.

'I know what KFC stands for,' said Izzy laughing, the two of them had met before at a rugby tournament in Bali.

'So do I,' K giggled in agreement, 'it's *my* fried chicken!'

As we drove slowly through the daily carnage, dodging thousands of motorised rickshaws, we arrived at the heart of the city outside the grand colonial building of the Lahore Museum. Inside was an array of artefacts, stories and images detailing the history of the country as far back as several thousand years B.C. We walked through the themed rooms, from cave men to colonial treasures, and finally to a glorious room filled with artillery from floor to ceiling. A full armoury of cannons, fixed bayonets, grenades and evil looking clubs encircled us, but by far the most jaw dropping was a collection of finely crafted ornate swords.

'This is what we used to kick you lot out,' K pointed and laughed.

'No way! You made all this stuff just for us?' I said in surprise.

'Well, no, not just for you. Most of it is much older, but it would have done the job right?'

In truth I had felt a little nervous even entering the room, so one could assume I would have crapped myself on the battlefield.

'I'm quite sad that you guys left,' K added in reflection.

'Why's that?'

'The British brought lots of good things to Pakistan, you've only got to look at this building to see that. Don't forget that you also brought us rugby.'

'Good point!' I agreed.

'The revolution gave us independence but in many ways this didn't serve to improve the country.'

I stood in silence staring at the range of weaponry, I couldn't add much to the discussion, after all I had no idea what life was like before, or after, the rule of the British Raj.

While Jodie and Izzy continued around the museum, K and I sat down, fatigued from the 45 minutes entertainment on foot. It was hard to tell we had once played rugby.

'We came to Pakistan at a good time,' I said, 'in terms of rugby I mean, I wasn't referring to the floods!'

'Yes, you did actually!' K's eyes lit up with an undisguised passion for his sport. 'There are so many things happening here right now on the rugby agenda. Izzy being here is a huge stepping stone for us because now we can get trained coaches out to develop the existing clubs, then lay platforms in other areas.'

'Do you mean other parts of Pakistan?' I asked, trying to work out how big the Pakistan rugby plans really were.

'Well, yes and no,' K replied, quite mystically. 'We already have many regional rugby associations in Pakistan, they run the local competitions between the schools, but now we are looking to strengthen our player base by developing an inter-services rugby tournament. This means the army, navy, police, railways and the energy sector.'

As K went on to explain, rugby in Pakistan was already far bigger than I was aware. It was first introduced in 1926, when a group of ex-pats working in the huge port city of Karachi, had decided to create a union. Originally they provided opposition to established Indian clubs on the All-India circuit, then to visiting British Navy ships. The side was built mostly around ex-pats until 1968 when a small handful of local Pakistani boys became regulars at the club.

As travel between India and Pakistan became more restricted they relied heavily on the British Navy for opposition, but by the 1970s the British had already begun to reduce their presence in the Indian Ocean. By the 1980s rugby had almost ceased to exist in Pakistan, and although the Karachi side continued to play whenever possible, they had no funds to travel, and only manufactured opposition that they could arrange themselves.

The modern day resurgence came in the 1990s when the same small group of local Pakistanis from the 1960s, teamed up with some new ex-pat blood to spread rugby across the country. The local based Pakistanis created modern day clubs in both Karachi and Lahore, while the ex-pats in Islamabad created a team in the north. Not long after, the modern day Islamabad Rugby Club, consisting mainly of locals, was also created and today these three sides form the pillars of Pakistan rugby.

'That sounds like a good plan,' I said, 'I've heard that India and China built most of their rugby around the army. It's an easy way of getting professionally trained athletes into the sport.'

'I've got some very good friends in Indian rugby,' K laughed, bringing back some memories. 'We've toured there quite a few times now. Those guys are doing a fantastic job, I just hope they continue to show us the way forward.'

'I thought that you would have a big rivalry with India?' I asked, knowing how fiercely they contested the international cricket fixtures.

'The situation with India isn't really as you'd think. The rugby clubs in Lahore and Delhi actually have a very strong relationship, and until quite recently we've relied heavily on each other to develop at a club and national level.'

'So what happened recently?' I asked.

'They've had some good high level funding over the last few seasons and they've left us behind... for the moment,' he added. 'Even in the Commonwealth Games last week we could see they've made huge steps forward. We're doing everything we can right now. We already have nearly four thousand players nationwide, we have the media's attention and we have hundreds of programmes now operating in schools and clubs. The biggest challenge we have is to fund a structure that can develop the best players to emerge from these schemes.'

'Where are we having lunch then K?' Izzy said, as he popped out from behind a giant clay pot.

'Right okay, yes, it's probably about time we left,' K glanced at his watch. 'Let's grab Jodie and we'll head off!'

On the drive back we were delayed by a large crowd of people rallying in the streets. They were appealing for more of something, and less of something else, and although we couldn't work out exactly what it was, we were quite sure they wanted it now.

'That's Lahore Zoo on the right,' K continued his tour guiding duties as we drove past yet another heavily armoured gate. We all stared beyond the rifles, searching for animals as we sat waiting by the procession. I heard a light tap on my passenger window and turned to see a man pointing at his feet, so I pushed my face to the glass to get a better angle. He wasn't pointing to his feet after all, it was to his pet monkey begging on his behalf in a tiny pink tutu.

'Think I'll give the zoo a miss!' I muttered to myself.

Armed police guided us through the chaos, and soon we were back on track for a surprise lunch arrangement with some very distinguished guests.

'So great to have you here!' said Arif, the Secretary of the PRU. He was very smartly dressed, as was everyone at the prestigious Lahore Golf Club. The sign at the front door had indicated a dress code in both Urdu and English.

'Patrons are kindly requested to maintain the Club dress code at all times. Men should wear a shirt with a collar, and cover the full extent of their legs and feet. Please no jeans or trainers.'

He tried hard not to stare at my trousers, as had the girl at reception, but technically I wasn't breaking any rules so we took our places at the large table, overlooking the immaculate eighteenth green. A minute later, Fawzi arrived and we ordered a round of soft drinks.

'They have beer,' Arif offered us.

'Oh no, Coke is good,' I lied, 'but how do they get a license to serve beer in an Islamic country?'

'Alcohol consumption is considered a social disorder,' he replied, 'so if you sign to say you are an alcoholic, they are allowed to prescribe you what you need!'

'There you go Jo, post-alcohol self loathing isn't so bad! Here you'd have it before *and* after!'

Fawzi, Arif and K got to their feet as two older men approached the table. We followed suit and were introduced one at a time. The new guests were Syed Shahid Ali and the retired Major General M. Ashraf Chaudhry (peculiarly known as the 'Colonel'). The Colonel was widely respected and had been supporting rugby development wherever he could for many years, including his own rugby programme at a college he oversaw. Syed Shahid Ali was Pakistan's representative on the International Olympic Committee, and had become a strong ally since the introduction of rugby 7s in the 2009 Copenhagen meeting.

Although retired, Arif, Fawzi and K had many fond memories from their playing days together, and as the freshly squeezed fruit juice flowed, the conversations degenerated into tales of rugby tours and jokes about their own culture.

'You will really enjoy parts of Northern Pakistan,' Arif explained, 'we have gone on many hunting trips up in the mountains there.'

'What areas do you hunt in?' I asked, wondering whether we'd end up cycling through any recreational cross fire.

'Sometimes we go pig hunting close to the Indian border,' he laughed, 'we try to shoot wild pigs just on the Indian side so we can leave it for the villagers. 'There you go guys!' we call over. It's not much use to us!'

Having spent a supposed business lunch with the rugby boys, we were already getting a sense of how much fun it could be to play in a Pakistani rugby team.

'Before we go, we should get a photo of us all,' suggested K.

'Good idea,' barked the Colonel.

'Oh no,' I whispered to Jodie, 'now I really *do* feel stupid.'

'Stand at the back,' she whispered as we stood up, 'that way nobody can see you're wearing pyjamas!'

*   *   *   *   *

Two days later, I now found myself sitting beside the Lahore Rugby Club pitch under the shade of palm leaves. The second morning of Izzy's course had been outdoors, a practical based assessment on what we had learnt previously in the dingy and humid classroom. Despite the relentless squeaking of the overhead fan, and at least two scheduled daily power cuts, the course had been well presented and of huge benefit to those with little playing or coaching experience. Some basics in particular had never even been explained to me. The art of creating space was a memorable example.

'Space isn't something you can create in front of you,' Izzy explained, 'it's something that you leave behind when you move.'

Before I even had time to mull this over he had continued, 'So if a player makes a run like so,' he pointed to a diagram, 'he leaves a space from where he has just come.'

We all nodded in agreement, trying our best to keep up.

'And if the defence is moving in the same way, there will naturally be a gap opposite this space. If you turn the page you will now see a selection of drills used to teach players running lines.'

I turned the page and browsed through the drill diagrams - this was great. One of the drills I even recognised, we had been running it every week back at home and nobody knew why. For many seasons it had been perfectly acceptable to practice running straight, up and down the pitch, then suddenly one session there were cones everywhere, and we started running angles. Our coach tried talking about 'predictability' and 'new game plans', but we later discovered the grounds man had just asked him to stop wearing out the same patches of grass.

The thirty student coaches had long since disappeared for a generous one hour lunch break and were already forty five minutes late. K, Izzy, myself and the PRU team manager 'Grouse' had picked up a 'footlong' from Subway, and were eager to complete the course, get home, and maybe watch a DVD. Grouse was a little younger than the other PRU members and was still an active player. He had earned his nickname from an experience with the 'Famous Grouse' on one of their overseas tours. Izzy looked at his watch.

'Is this what Fawzi meant about Pakistan time?'

'It's always like this,' Grouse replied, 'I have to lie about the kick-off time and make it an hour earlier. It's the only way.'

It was getting very hot and so we relaxed, spread out on the grass, using tackle bags as cushions.

'When did you say you were going to Bali, Izzy?' K asked, 'I love Bali!'

'I'm going to Malaysia for three days next week,' Izzy replied, 'then I go to Bali on Friday for the weekend. After that I have to go to Laos.'

'God Izzy, you have a great job. If there are *ever* any jobs going at ARFU, please tell me!'

'Wow, that sounds great!' Grouse spoke up, 'K, I could be your assistant! Would you need an assistant K?'

'Grouse, you don't assist me now, and we *already* work together!'

A handful of boys slowly filtered back onto the pitch and we started the assessments. Three sweaty hours later and I had completed my IRB Level II Coaching course.

*   *   *   *   *

With the regular and frustrating power cuts in Pakistan, getting anything achieved online was a painful, dogged affair, and I almost developed bedsores just trying to upload our videos to 'Youtube'. We were now holding on in Lahore for a further week so that we could join K's brother Jawad, known as 'Jay', in a voluntary distribution effort to the destroyed village of Sandeela. Following the devastating floods, K and Jay had joined forces with a team of students at the university, where Jay lectured on English Literature and ran a rugby side.

With the protection of some rugby muscle and army support, they had already run operations to transport supplies to some of the worst hit areas, whilst simultaneously labouring over plans to regenerate the villages with a view that the communities could emerge stronger. Indeed, one night over a homemade curry, they made no secret that these floods, however devastating, may one day prove to be a blessing in disguise, directing attention and support to areas of rural Pakistan which had been a forgotten anomaly for many generations.

The devastation had been so complete that the young architects in the group were quite literally working with a blank canvas with which to build. The team arranged a private presentation for us, and having listened to the extent of the damage, we were staggered by how they had approached the complex issues at hand, from cultural sensitivity, to the legacy of the regeneration.

The project aimed to source, distribute, and even build small machines that could produce bricks made almost entirely from local materials such as mud and straw, with a small amount of cement to bind the earthy compound together. Bamboo construction technologies would then be implemented to complete the roof, creating a house that was elegant, easy to maintain and safe from the elements. With many thousands of individuals left stranded and homeless, labour was already waiting onsite, and the simple but functional town and house plans were only waiting for final approval from the local officials.

Unfortunately the flood had also revealed some of the darker sides of Pakistan. Many previous aid efforts had been plighted by looters, terrorists or landowners not wishing to lose their grip on power. Even one of Jay's previous ventures had been met with danger, requiring more than just strong words to free them from the situation. An armed security officer had since become a prerequisite of journeying out into these parts again.

As happy as Jay was to be able to show us their operations, he had also created himself an extra series of headaches. Now needing to guarantee the safety of two white tourists, he was having to use all the contacts he had made, both trusted locals in the area and with the army unit who were independently supporting the effort. He arranged a secret location where all eighteen volunteers could sleep for two nights while we worked the weekend.

To reach Sandeela we first needed to endure a nine hour bus ride from Lahore, whilst our diligent team of students became chain smokers, puffing relentlessly away on various tobacco blends. The ride was choking and uncomfortable, and suddenly we felt a whole world away from the freedom and choice that we enjoyed while cycling. Our safe house was a primary school situated an hour from the flood areas, very safe, and a comfortable place to rest for a few hours before our final launch. We arrived around 4 a.m. and slept in separate rooms before our 7 a.m. departure. It was only then that it occurred to me that in over five months, Jodie had not been out of my sight for more than a bathroom break, and for too many of those, I had *still* been able to see her.

We arrived at the fields, setting up two camps around 2 km apart. The first was an entertainment camp in a nearby village, where games would be designed as a method of distributing toys, clothes and books to the children and families. The other camp would be closer to the seriously affected area, and would be a protected and more heavily supervised medical distribution with collaboration from the military.

Pods of architects assessed construction needs in the village, whilst psychiatrists conducted interviews with queuing patients. By chance, the team included Dr Omer, a young qualified doctor who had been visiting family in Pakistan. He worked relentlessly through the remaining daylight hours to treat patients, assisted by his two foreign pharmaceutical sidekicks, who not only required the name of the drugs required, but the colour of the box they were contained within. Despite his two amateur assistants, the camp provided much needed medical attention to a segment of rural Pakistan that has long since been forgotten. Many afflictions were not caused by the flood, but were conditions that locals had been living with for much of their lives, some cases tragic and now far beyond any cure. We would have helped for days given the chance.

As drugs were prescribed to the sick, children down the road screamed with excitement as our toy distributors ran rugby and other ball games in a circus-like marquee. Most queued orderly, at least until they discovered ways of creeping under the canvas, and by the end of the day the volunteers were left defeated by the innovative ways the children infiltrated the camp.

We joined the fun at the end of what had been a fantastic afternoon, making a huge short term impact on many lives, not to mention our own. As the day concluded and the military retreated to base, our team prepared for the following day. Toys, clothes and drugs were locked down in a local secure house, and we returned to the school awaiting an early start and a full day in the field. There had been many patients turned away at sunset, and many more with serious conditions that required further examination, so with the wake up call set for 5 a.m. we bedded down on the floor and grabbed a few hours rest.

Morning came, and as I stepped outside to light the stove, one of the students broke the devastating news to me. In the night, there had been a high level security threat, the military had not only informed all relief projects to leave the area, but were evacuating themselves too. I didn't want to believe it, the previous day had been so inspiring, and in just a few hours we had begun to sense what could be achieved with a little more time. Now, there was to be no opportunity and we would have to withdraw with immediate effect. In a single moment the whole project had been put on ice, and we had no choice but to re-board the bus for the long and frustrating return.

Today's international news focuses on terrorism and controversy, and so part of our mission had been to feed back more inspiring stories - stories of courage and sacrifice in adversity. Ironically, our trip to Sandeela had served to further highlight these problems. So much effort and coordination had gone into getting aid to the many suffering, and although the experience hadn't been overshadowed, it had certainly been tarnished. As we prepared to leave Lahore, we hoped that the team were able to get back to the field soon and continue with their invaluable mission.

*   *   *   *   *

As it was our final night in Lahore, K and Grouse wanted to take us for a night on the town.

'Where are we going?' we asked them excitedly.

'We'll take you to a really good traditional Pakistani restaurant and get you some Tak-a-tak,' K explained.

'Cool! What's Tak-a-tak?' I asked again.

'You'll see!' he laughed.

'K, can we smoke some hubbly bubbly?'

'Yes, Grouse. We can smoke some hubbly bubbly, but I'm not carrying you home again.'

We jumped out of 'Jason' and occupied a low level seating area in the busy outdoors restaurant. Sunset had long since passed and the evening temperature was now perfect. The restaurant was one single business but around the edges were numerous BBQ stalls and kitchen areas to cater for the various orders. We reserved our table and took a short walk around the areas to view the menu at source. Chickens were rotated slowly over hot coals, while huge pots of curry simmered on portable gas stoves. Soon we got to the restaurant's speciality.

'Tak-a-tak...Tak-a-tak...Tak-a-tak-a-tak-a-tak-a-tak-a-tak...'

A big man was wielding a giant pair of sword-like cleavers, beating down on a huge mincey looking mixture in a giant frying pan.

'Can you hear that sound?' K asked us, 'That's why it's called Tak-a-tak!'

'What is it?' Jodie asked.

'Do you want to try some?' K asked, 'It's a traditional Lahore dish, it's very good.'

'Yeah! Let's have some Tak-a-tak!' I decided, on both of our behalf. Our table was soon filled with exotic looking dishes, bowls of rice, and thick, meaty breads. I couldn't decide what to pile onto my plate first.

'That's the one,' K pointed to the bowl nearest me and I dived right in.

'It's pretty good!' I explained to everyone, still chewing on the peppery but quite gristly concoction.

'What is it?' Jodie asked again, as Grouse began to smile.

'It's camel balls!' he broke into a laugh, 'Mixed with their brains, heart and kidneys!'

'Mmmm!' I said with my mouth full. I didn't know whether to spit or swallow.

We finished our meal by ordering an apple flavoured shisha pipe which we passed around, each trying to blow vapour rings into the late evening air. Grouse had slowly sunk further into his chair the more he became intoxicated by the pipe, and when he reached an almost horizontal angle, we all agreed it was time to head off for a coffee. With a shot of caffeine back in his veins, he perked up and insisted on more entertainment.

'Hey, let's go to the red light district!' he suggested with a childish little dance.

'Ah, I don't know,' I said out of courtesy for Jodie, 'unless we could drop her off first?'

'Who said I want to go home?' Jodie pointed out.

'Don't worry,' K stepped in, 'it isn't quite what you think.'

K was certainly right. As we crawled around the red light district in our minibus, we looked from side to side expecting the lid on the Islamic world to be blown open. In each window, the bare ankles of the shameless ladies in glittering shoes protruded from beneath a partially raised curtain.

'Is that it?' I asked, as Grouse was drooling on his window.

'Brilliant isn't it!' he said, 'You can go inside and get a dance if you pay for it.'

'What? A tap dance?' Jodie laughed.

'See Jo! This is all that really happens when boys go to red light districts. You girls have such a low impression of us!'

*   *   *   *   *

To cycle to Islamabad we had to join an integral sub-continental trade route called the Grand Trunk Road. From it's origins at Chittagong in Bangladesh, it stretches out on a 2,500 km journey, finishing at Kabul in Afghanistan, via the Khyber pass. Our journey would only take us three days, before exiting at Rawalpindi, a joining city of Islamabad.

Judging by the volume of traffic coming out of Lahore, the road is still heavily used as a main artery for the north of the country. For hours we switched to full time alertness, watching out for the thousands of motorised tuk-tuks that swung out blindly from alleyways, desperately trying to accelerate away on their spluttering two-stroke engines. There was no silence for two entire days, not at any time of day or night, but by the third day the road had narrowed and began to weave through the undulating hills. The respite was short lived as we passed through the range and descended towards the Pakistani capital city.

En route I saw an entire school hanging off a single bus, clinging on wherever they could, following a sign indicating an education centre - 'AIOU'.

'Look Jo! They missed the E!' I pointed out.

'I don't think they are just trying to list vowels Tom! That's the name of the university.'

Our first job in Islamabad was to get our visa for China. The visa should be no more than a formality, providing we didn't mention Tibet, or our method of transport. At the Chinese embassy, a long line of Pakistanis queued patiently outside clutching wads of paperwork. At the front, was a security guard positioned by the main gate with a table and some forms. We had nothing so bypassed the queue and approached the man, who politely checked our passports and handed us an application form. We filled out the small form, attached some spare photographs, and handed it back to the man who passed it through the gate to another.

'That was easy!' I said, 'I thought it would take longer!'

'We've still got our passports Tom, I don't think that's it.'

Shortly after, the second man returned and handed us back our paperwork, before pointing to the end of the line. I looked to the long queue of people and an unexpected thought ran through my mind. Did he really expect us to stand and queue with everyone else? I expected the VIP treatment, I was English! My bubble had been burst and my arse had come crashing down on terra firma. When we had set out, my only wish was not to die somewhere on a hard shoulder, but only a third into the trip and apparently nothing less than the red carpet treatment would suffice. My charming smile had clearly lost it's power and we were about to get our first taste of Chinese bureaucracy.

'We've ticked the box for a three month visa,' I smiled to the Chinese man behind the glass, 'but we'll also pay the extra charge listed here and order the express visa please.' It wasn't so much a question, but a polite confirmation of the service that we required.

'You can have a 30 day visa and you can collect it next Thursday.'

The man barely looked up from his desk, and handed back the extra money. It wasn't so much a discussion but a dismissal. The only positive to come from another week sat rooted in a city was the chance to hang out with the current Pakistan club champions, the Islamabad Jinns RFC.

We arranged to meet with the Jinns down at their pitch for a Sunday inter-club tournament. Whereas we had possibly met the largest rugby player in K, meeting the captain Bilal Butt, we had now almost certainly met the smallest. What he lacked in stature, he certainly made up for in cunning, and at one scrum I was left wiping my eyes as the little hooker ran back out of the tunnel with the ball in his hands. Again, the dry Pakistani humour proved great entertainment as they treated us to some local cuisine, where 'local' simply meant a short drive to the nearby McDonalds.

Bilal bade us farewell by shaking my hand and then standing on tiptoes to pat Jodie on the head. Jodie's face was a picture of surprise and bewilderment as Bilal insisted that, in his culture, it was a very polite and respectful way to part company with women. Not doubting Bilal's integrity for one second, we didn't experience this custom anywhere again, and personally I reckon Bilal just saw his chance to feel tall.

'Don't you dare say it!' Jodie warned me with a smirk as we walked back.

I couldn't contain myself any longer.

'Fetch!' I cried in laughter.

CHAPTER 20
THE LONG, WINDING PAIN IN THE ARSE

Having taken some stern advice from locals, we opted for the longer, quieter roads weaving up into the hills. Too many people had warned us about Taliban presence in many of the areas around Abbotobad and Besham, and the less time we spent on the southerly Karakoram Highway (or 'KKH'), the more unnoticed we would pass. The long winding road to Murree, however steep, made for some idyllic viewpoints and we were initially pleased with our choice of route. We knew that the detour rejoined the KKH before Abbotobad though, and keeping the previous advice in mind, we progressed directly through the busy town only stopping for a quick water refill.

A few kilometres outside the town, we hid behind a small school and set up camp next to a herd of grazing goats. In Pakistan, this was as quiet as it could possibly get so close to civilisation. Our presence attracted a little bit of interest, but nothing out of the ordinary, and we lit a small fire to keep us company. A few children enjoyed the entertainment so much that they ran to search for more firewood, returning and throwing their findings onto the leaping flames.

Having been cycling north and simultaneously approaching winter, the sunsets were now both early and rapid. As we prepared to boil our evening pasta, three guys in their early twenties came and sat next to us. They spoke proficient English and explained that they had travelled down from a nearby medical college on a phone call from a relative.

'I don't think it is so safe for you to sleep here,' one boy said to us, 'maybe you could sleep at our college?'

Although it was a kind offer, the college was 15 km back in the wrong direction, it was already dark, and we'd regularly been warned how dangerous it was to sleep in such circumstances by concerned locals. Often, as genuinely kind as many people can be, they were as much interested in their own entertainment as they were in our welfare. They would do their best to stop you from sleeping and look hurt if you tried to leave early the following morning. As such, in many areas we preferred to camp late and depart early, avoiding these situations and covering large distances in just a few days.

We kindly refused the offer and made it clear that we were all set up. No sooner had we explained this when a large vehicle turned up shining their large spotlights directly at our group.

'Somebody has phoned for the police,' the boy said to us, 'many people know that you are here.'

'Oh for God's sake,' I complained, 'look we are fine, please tell everyone to go home.'

We had already been on the road for three days and this unnecessary disturbance was now cutting into our sleep cycle. The armed police men approached us politely before passing me a mobile phone.

'Hello?' I spoke into the handset.

'Yes, hello,' came the hesitant reply, 'are you okay?'

I explained the situation to him, that we were two New Zealanders cycling back home for the Rugby World Cup. We told everyone the same story, after all, what had the Kiwis ever done to upset the world.

'I'm sorry but I would very much like you to return to our station with my officers,' he explained. 'I can provide a safe place for you to sleep here.'

Realising that we wouldn't have much choice, and that half of the town had now gathered round to watch the activity, we agreed to load our equipment into their vehicle and accept a ride back to the station in Abbotobad. We arrived and passed through some heavy gates before being led to a permanent tent fixture behind a protected wall of sand bags.

'You can sleep here safe tonight,' the chief of the station insisted. 'My men will be on watch all night.'

By now our frustration had long since washed away and we could enjoy the comfort of a good night's sleep. First though, the night force sat with us in a separate tent, and an older official with a bright red beard brought us all a takeaway curry.

As we turned off the KKH again the following day, we hoped for a similarly quiet route to the one from Islamabad. This time we gained significantly more altitude, and the slow average ascent was disguised by sharp climbs and steep descents in the process. After an exhausting day taking us up into the mountains, we eventually attempted sleeping on the doorstep of a temporary school, established after the 2006 earthquakes. Again we were found, this time by the local teacher and after returning to his small home for the evening, we learned more troublesome news.

Reports from travellers returning down the mountains on foot had indicated that heavy snowfall and avalanches further ahead had blocked the path. From our teacher's friends, it sounded like the blockage was a further two days into the mountains on bicycle, and that it was un-passable. Even at the best times of the year, a four-wheel drive vehicle was needed for the pass, but stranded the other side of the blockage they weren't able to refuel for the dangerous journey.

'I don't know Jo, what do you think?'

'Well, we either back track for one day, or risk turning a two day return journey into a six day one.'

She was absolutely right, and if she had phrased it in any other way, I would have searched for reasons to carry on and try. A two day journey, as painful as it felt, was something we could process, especially with one day already behind us, but a six day one would put serious strains on us reaching the border before our visa expired. After a good night's rest, we rose early in the freezing mountain air, and reluctantly retraced a day on the bikes.

Back on the KKH, things didn't get much better. The road was only sealed up to a certain point, and after that it quickly became a trail of rubble, stretching for hundreds of kilometres towards the highest border crossing on the planet. Due to the gradual degeneration on the Pakistan side, the Chinese government had signed an agreement to help the Pakistan Army's engineering arm widen and toughen the road surface. In a moment of now questionable genius, their method was to dig up the entire road, then begin to relay it.

The Chinese had already laid a beautiful tarmac surface on their side, and it would benefit them equally to have a smooth trade route down into Pakistan. After destroying much of what was left of the road, they began to send over supplies to build a new one.

Unfortunately, in January 2010, a series of avalanches blocked off the Hunza river and the KKH, removing all road access to Pakistan from China. The huge avalanche formed a natural dam, behind which a 15 km long glacial lake quickly collected, submerging the road and an integral bridge crossing at Shishkat. Needless to say, that by the time we had arrived, there was little progress being made on the highway.

Failing to complete the necessary 80 km each day, and being detained for lengthy periods at strategic military check points, crossing the Khunjerab Pass was quickly becoming an unlikely target before our visa expired. When we were forced onto a police escort vehicle for part of the road, our instincts told us to argue, but our common sense told us to shut up and make up some distance.

Although the road was often no better, we had recouped some lost time, and found ourselves cycling into the town of Karimabad a few days later. A delightful old man ambled down the hill as we pushed our bikes slowly up towards him. Jodie performed the most extraordinary haggle as we walked and talked, refusing to pay two dollars fifty for a room, and getting him down to two dollars before we had even arrived. The old man, with an empty hotel, was only too happy to earn himself four dollars for two nights accommodation, while we prepared ourselves for the ordeal across the landslide.

As he unlocked our room, we turned around and gazed over our balcony to a spectacular view of the Hunza valley. It was certainly not a two dollar view, and we later found out that the larger international hotels immediately behind us were charging over one hundred dollars a night.

'This is perfect Homer,' I said, forgetting his name was Heider. Inside, there were three identical looking single beds, each with duvets pulled back revealing surprisingly clean sheets beneath. I threw down my bag onto the first bed and leapt towards the last duvet.

'Sorry, only *those* two have real mattresses,' he pointed out, a little too late, as I thumped down onto a disguised sheet of plywood.

Only in Pakistan.

Crossing the landslide was the single most difficult task of our entire trip. We faced a mound of rock and dust, seemingly hundreds of metres into the sky, covered in at least a foot of fine, grey ash. The only method of transport was a chain of huge tractors pulling trailers of cargo. We were not in a position to get into a bidding war with the local merchants, but the alternative was an extremely daunting task.

I put my entire body weight behind my 60 kg bike, and one small step at a time, I heaved my load thirty metres into the mound. Jodie followed behind, screaming with frustration, but refusing to give in. After ten minutes, we both stood exhausted and we had only climbed a handful of metres off the ground. The fine grey dust had already filled our socks, shoes, coated our bikes, and even the headscarves tied around our faces did little to prevent the inhalation of the bitter tasting clouds. I pushed on ahead to a flag mark at the first bend manned by a tractor traffic controller. He looked at me with an expression of temporary amusement, before looking over his head towards the top and turning up his nose.

'Sir,' he said to me, 'no chance... and Madam... ' he pointed dismissively to Jodie, 'definitely no chance.' With that, he turned his back and very slowly waded his way back to work around the corner.

I waited for Jodie to slowly catch up to my position, 'Hey Jo!' I said, seeing the pain in her eyes and armed with the perfect motivation, 'You'll never guess what he just said!'

Two hours later we had conquered the mound and looked down on the chaos of tractors, boats and cargo below. We were charged four times the local rate to hitch a ride across the lake on one of the heaving motor boats, but after our ordeal in the ash, it was still twelve dollars well spent. The lake, locked by surrounding rock and filled entirely from glacial water was a magnificent turquoise mirror.

As our boat cut slowly through the still waters, the reflections of towering mountains rippled in our wake. When we reached the designated section of lake, the boat finally docked up and we lifted our equipment onto dry land. Around us, were a group of displaced villagers, struggling with life in the mountains, and living under what looked like makeshift shelters, their homes destroyed by the rising waters. The weather was already getting below freezing at night and this was quickly becoming a harsh environment.

After an incredible six weeks in Pakistan, our final day's cycle took us to the border town of Sost where we met with one final frustration - there was no more cycling allowed.

'For fuck's sake!' we laughed, as we collapsed on the doorstep of the exit post, 'This is all Stefan's fault!'

CHAPTER 21
THE DEEP FREEZE

'Don't worry Jo! We did our best!' I tried to console Jodie who was distraught at our failure to cycle over the Khunjerab Pass.

'You didn't *fail*!' I explained, in response to her silence, 'You're just not allowed to do it.'

'We came all this way Tom! We chose this specific route, just for this one challenge.'

'I know, I know, I feel the same,' I lied to her. I didn't at all, I bloody hated heights, nearly as much as I hated being at high altitude. This was the worst of both worlds. I was stuck at high altitude, spending most of my day staring over the road's edge, from a bloody big height. I was glad for the bus.

'I tell you what, you've had this dream taken away, why don't we replace this dream with another one?'

Jodie seemed to contemplate my suggestion. Had I finally managed to say the right thing to my girl, at the right time?

'Okay! Can we cycle to Mount Fuji?'

In reality I was thinking more along the lines of a week scuba diving somewhere, but then I recalled what trouble that had landed me in last time.

'Of course we can Jo, great idea. Which way is it?'

'It's in Japan.'

'Japan!' I repeated, realising that I hadn't said the right thing after all, I'd just made my life even more complicated.

At the end of a rocky and turbulent government bus ride, we were perched at the highest border crossing in the world, not much below 5 km in the air. It appeared that the Chinese officials at the top post had clearly forgotten to pack their sense of humour before setting off up the mountain. Under such non threatening circumstances, the patrol of seven armed soldiers unnecessarily screamed and barked orders, irrespective of the fact that nobody spoke Chinese. At one point, struggling with the altitude, I risked being shot down as I ran to the outdoors toilet, squatted on a converted pig trough, and emptied five pints of slushy bottom deposits into the thin, freezing air. It wasn't my finest moment, and the soldier who stood watching me, did nothing to improve my mood as my stomach performed gymnastic routines inside me.

With several hours of rigorous searching performed, passengers and equipment were finally boarded back onto the bus, and we were escorted by armed vehicle, to the Chinese entry post four hours further down the mountain. With another identical equipment search completed, the office closed and we were deposited out into the cold Tashkurgen night. It was 10 p.m., the air was bitter and we could barely push the tent pegs into the frozen soil. Our winter had just set in.

The following morning we wasted no time in taking on the three day cycle to Kashgar. We loaded up our food pannier with an assortment of sugary Chinese snacks and a bag of steaming hot flat bread, it wouldn't stay warm for long. Having been previously advised of the road ahead, we were especially nervous about the next 300 km. Although we had descended from the Khunjerab Pass into Tashkurgen on bus, we now had to climb over 2 km back to a similar height, and tackle an even more desolate crossing. The air was incredibly cold already and I wondered where we would find to sleep at over 4,000 metres, let alone how I would deal with the altitude.

The ascent was every bit as tough as I had feared. A gradual 90 km climb, while nothing of the hairpins we had been dealt in Romania and Pakistan, slowly and gradually began to wear down at my energy reserves. Never knowing quite when we had reached the crossing, we experienced many disappointments as every hidden corner would reveal nothing more than another hefty climb ahead.

The ascent took a full day, from morning until an early sunset, and as we sensed the summit was near, a thick snow storm began to envelop us. My health had long since deteriorated, and Jodie's face of concern worsened with every desperate wheezing of my chest. My organs ached as we pushed ahead, one small step behind the other, forcing in nothing more than a painfully shallow breath at a time. Our situation was becoming increasingly desperate, and for my own safety I knew we had to descend very soon. The simplest solution would be to turn around and descend back to where we had started. Knowing that this would leave us the same climb tomorrow and risk exhausting our food supply before Kashgar, against our better instincts, we pressed on hoping that we could quickly descend to a safer level on the other side.

Eventually the road levelled out and we stared ahead to the summits of far away mountains - we had made it. We stood, side by side, for a handful of seconds as a faint pink sunset tried desperately to burn through the thick grey clouds. I had lost all feeling in my hands and feet, despite the winter gloves, and not being able to take on food because of the altitude sickness, my body was now beginning to shiver uncontrollably. The snowfall was already settling on the other side, and freewheeling down into the freezing wind only heightened my problem. We both struggled, trying to force down our brakes with numb fingers, and could only hope that we would find some shelter very quickly.

Several hundred metres down the winding road, the small silhouette of a building appeared in the distance to our right. The empty rocky valley was otherwise desolate, and I had to take a second glance to believe that it was real. Shouting to each other, we agreed to pull over and dragged our bicycles down the slope towards the ramshackle structure.

I couldn't believe that anyone would live alone in such conditions, and as we neared the small house, we could see that it had been deserted for quite some time. The door frames and windows had long since been removed, and many areas of the roof had collapsed into the floor below. The solid brick and stone structure still remained mostly intact however, and we were able to identify several rooms inside the building, one with a large domelike oven.

Jodie put up the tent inside the most central room, hoping that this would be the most protected, despite the snow storm piling in through the missing window. I scavenged enough wood from the shattered foundations to start a small fire, but to my despair the air was too thin for even a match to burn down. I poured on a small amount of petrol from our camping stove, but it became clear that it was a battle I couldn't win. I crawled inside the tent and passed out.

Surviving our night in the mountains we woke to a much clearer morning. Our view now extended across the mountain plains and we could trace our weaving road many miles into the distance. The snow had settled to form a thick white carpet outside the house, and as I took a final opportunity to investigate the life saving accommodation, a peculiar sight caught my eye. Leading to the front door was a set of small paw prints in the fresh snow. I looked around at the terrain but there wasn't a visible living thing for as far as the eye could see. What sort of animal would be living up here, so far from any plants or other life? Had we slept in his home only to scare him off?

A day's ride later and the physical effects of the mountain had worn off. We had descended dramatically into valleys to the northeast, and our views were now that of sunshine and stunning lakes.

'You know, I had some really strange dreams last night,' Jodie brought up without prompting, 'I kept dreaming things about that house.'

'Go on!' I replied, in curiosity.

'Well, I dreamt that the house was as it once used to be, and although we were still there, a family was also there, and there was this young boy. It was quite scary.'

'Are you serious?' I asked her, knowing that she was.

'I promise you, why?'

I felt a little shudder run down my spine, 'Because I had the exact same dream!'

Laughing out nervously we began to pedal a little bit faster.

*   *   *   *   *

The winter mornings in the mountains had been well below freezing, so cold that I wanted to cry, and would have, if my tear ducts had not frozen. We reached Kashgar and it was time for us to review our 'winter gear' - a second hand coat each and some extra socks. We searched the city and eventually found a faux army store selling gear emblazoned with camouflage patterns. Two old men sat behind a desk watching a film on a computer, the soundtrack sounded like Celine Dion. In the shop we found some fur lined boots, these would certainly do the trick, and they even had my size.

We asked for the price by miming a scribble with our imaginary notepad and pencil. It seemed to work in China where no other method of communication would do. Even basic finger counting was met with confusion, as the Chinese used their own set of finger combinations.

One man broke his attention from the film and got up, smiling as we approached with our boots.

'180 RMB.' The little man displayed after his calculation.

'Ninety times two,' I stated, first with pride, then with embarrassment as I considered the weight of my achievement.

'Should we haggle?' Jodie suggested, '£18 is quite a lot here right?'

'Yeah, go on, let's haggle!' I cheered her on.

Jodie took the calculator and typed '150'. The man squinted at the number before slowly shaking his head. He took the calculator and performed a slow thoughtful calculation as we both looked on in anticipation.

'180,' the screen read, as he showed us again. Had he mistyped? This was the same number as before. He might well be very old, but maybe he hadn't caught onto this game yet. We stood firm and played hardball once again.

'160,' we typed and showed him. He turned to his boss, presumably muttered some Chinese proverbs about English people and shoes, and performed a further calculation - '180'.

I was confused, so I gratefully handed over my money, thankful that the price hadn't inflated to '200' in the process. I had cold feet, this was the only shop, and it appeared that I had the haggling problem, not him. I clearly hadn't grasped the rules.

Maybe it was a bit like the Black-Black-White game our team would play on the rugby bus home. Some of you will know what I'm talking about, others will say, 'Yeah, what *are* the rules for the Black-Black-White game? Why do I always end up drinking?'. For those people, I'm certainly not going to spoil the fun, but I should add that if you find yourself with frequent drinking forfeits, it might be time to change clubs.

'I can't believe that man wouldn't come down on the price!' Jodie complained, 'I must have lost my touch!'

'I think it's just the way that things are here,' I tried to rationalise. 'We're a long, long way from anywhere and he didn't really need to offer us a discount.'

Jodie seemed to roll it over in her mind, reluctantly accepting the situation in the process, as she looked down at her new furry feet.

'You know Jo, it reminds me of a famous Chinese proverb,' I said, remembering the words of wisdom.

'What Chinese proverb?'

'Before you criticise someone, you should walk a mile in their shoes. That way, if they get angry, you're a mile away, and you have their shoes.'

*   *   *   *   *

After two days of cycling from Kashgar, we finally arrived at civilisation. The civilisation's name was Peng and he worked, on his own, in a solitary petrol station. Considering we were cycling towards the furthest inland city in the world, we were quite thrilled to see Peng and his little electric heater.

After a brief conversation, using the art of mime, we both made our way to the joint toilet facilities where we found a single basin. I turned on the tap to let the water flush out whatever deposits had collected since its last unlikely use. It looked like Fanta. We put the plug into the basin and filled it up.

'Should we start using the water filter?' Jodie questioned after we lost visibility of the plug.

'What is it?' I said, 'Do you think a filter is going to help with that?'

We stared again in the faint hope that it would dissipate. It didn't.

'I've heard of taps connected to the water that goes *into* the toilets, but not coming *out* of it!'

We both laughed, what else could we do? It was probably the only tap for another two days and we were out of water. Collecting water outside was not going to happen. The hot dry summer had left the Taklamakan a very barren area, and although there was clear evidence of water channels passing under the Old Silk Road, there wouldn't even be a trickle until the winter build up of snow began to melt in the mountains next spring.

The Taklamakan Desert region is predominantly a cold climate desert, situated close to the air flows from Siberia. It covers an area over 25% larger than the entire land mass of New Zealand, and is literally thousands of kilometres from the nearest body of water. Within the desert there is a huge depression called the Tarim Basin, 1,000 km in length and 400 km wide, which we would follow into a further descent, the Turpan depression, sinking as low as 940 feet below sea level.

In short, we were on a two week 'mini mission' to get ourselves into a very deep, cold hole. It is virtually the epicentre of Asia and as such, many speculating historians have suggested it was the very last place in Asia to have been inhabited. The name Taklamakan is thought to have descended from an Arabic description, 'the place you leave alone'. Those Arabs were right, but further speculation suggests it wasn't always that way.

Most of us have grown up with some awareness of the Old Testament, and in particular the Garden of Eden - not to be confused with Eden Park, which was still 17,000 km away in Auckland. In fairness, my knowledge of the Old Testament didn't go much further than Adam and Eve, Noah's ark, an apple and a snake, but the writings of a group from London called the 'Ensign Trust' had me a little captivated.

A staggering amount of literary research, compiled with enough scientific evidence to make it discussable, has pointed to the Taklamakan Desert as being the exact location of the lost Garden of Eden. Judging by the look on Peng's face, he was either unaware of this story, or just too cold to care.

'I guess we should use the filter,' I finally agreed.

'Good, at last,' Jodie replied, 'I don't know why you are always so hesitant to use our equipment.'

'I'm not hesitant,' I argued, trying not to sound defensive, but more importantly not hesitant.

'Yes you are. You didn't want to use our water bags until Turkey.'

'I had a ten litre bottle instead!' I answered.

'Yep, I remember. You carried a giant ten litre plastic bottle when we had two empty ten litre water sacks folded up in our panniers.'

'Okay, okay, fine, I know we should have used the water bags earlier. But that's the *only* example.'

'Can you remember what we ate on the first night in France?'

'Yes, we ate cold beans straight out of the tin, no washing up.'

'Why didn't we get the cooker out that night?'

'That was *one* night, I hadn't settled into my routine that early!'

'What about the compass?'

'I didn't need a compass!' I lied, having already got us lost on a couple of occasions, 'I had the sun!'

'Okay, so why don't you want to use the water filter?'

This time I did hesitate, 'I looked at the instruction book a few months ago.'

'Odd, but go on.'

'*and...* ' I emphasised to imply I hadn't previously finished, '... it looks like quite a drama to keep it clean. You have to take bits apart every five days and scrub bits, then boil other bits... there's just a lot of bits.'

'So *all* this time we've avoided using it,' Jodie appeared shocked by this revelation, 'because you were worried about cleaning it?'

'I'm just saying it looks like a lot of hassle, and once you start, there's no going back.'

'I'm just surprised that's all!' Jodie added, 'Why would you be worried about cleaning something when we *both* know you'll never do it!'

I started to pump the orange liquid into our water sacks, mulling over the situation as I did. She was right. Why had I suddenly been put off by the maintenance instructions? I had never taken notice of any before. I'd only changed the oil in my car once, and technically speaking it was a joint effort - dad having changed the oil and me having made him a cup of tea.

Similarly, in the two years that Jodie and I had shared a bathroom, it had quickly become apparent which of us had the highest dirt threshold. If this unit required regular cleaning, it would probably take care of itself behind my back. Having relinquished all responsibility I pumped away until twenty litres of copper liquid filled the sacks, enough for two more days.

We were soon back on the quiet desert road, kept company only by remnants of scattered road-worker campsites, and hundreds of discarded drug bottles. It compounded many rumours that Chinese workers were fuelled by Methamphetamine, a highly damaging drug used to increase alertness, and help them work unnaturally long hours in very tough climates.

Our first enforced pit stop was in the city of Turpan, where we had to visit the Public Security Bureau (PSB) to apply for a visa extension. Again we tried our luck by ticking the 'three months' option, but a sneer and a shake of the head later, we figured out we'd be lucky just to get our passports back at all.

Oddly, having cycled without a break for fifteen days, we now had to wait a full seven days to pick up our new visas. Not only that, but we had to pay for seven nights in one of the few pre-approved hotels allowing the Chinese authorities to keep a track on tourists.

We had been given a free breakfast voucher for our first morning, and I was determined not to miss out. Dragging myself away from the bedroom heater, we made ourselves at home on a large empty table inside the large empty dining room. At the far end of the room sat three Chinese business men, quietly finishing breakfast and preparing to leave - there were only ten minutes of self service left.

I loaded my plate with noodles, toast, something with rice and three boiled eggs, then sat back with Jodie.

'It's a bit random, isn't it?' I pointed out as I stared at my rice on toast, 'Is this what the Chinese eat?'

To speed things up and help make my eating process more efficient, Jodie started to peel my egg as I ate. We were on a tight timeframe and we knew from experience the Chinese took no prisoners when it came to procedures.

As she reached for the second egg, the solitary assistant dashed across to our table and placed his hand over my eggs. We stared at each other in confusion, but allowing nature to take its course, we let the man continue with whatever he was doing. To my horror, he picked up my two remaining eggs and returned them back to the huge basket of eggs sat at the buffet.

'Did he just steal my eggs?' I asked Jodie, in case I had passed out at the bedroom heater and this was all a dream.

'Look, he's trying to point at a sign! It must mean only one egg each!'

'There's a whole basket of hot boiled eggs, and the breakfast buffet closes in three minutes.'

'Why don't you have some more rice on toast?' Jodie suggested, but I was busy trying to solve the mystery.

'Hang on a minute! You know that women are only allowed one child. Maybe this is all part of their one-egg policy?'

We spent days walking around the small city of Turpan, but there was very little to do other than make regular trips between the sweet potato man and the BBQ chicken section of the local supermarket. Our only entertainment was trying not to die every time we crossed at a set of traffic lights. China had a slightly different take on the three colour system, from red meaning quite certain suicide, through to green, far from being safe, just indicating a reduced risk of death. China was not a country to mess about in, you were just one in one point two billion people, and you would *not* be missed.

With a huge sense of relief, we finally collected our passports, and in them were our fresh thirty day visas. Perhaps not surprisingly, having applied for it seven days ago, they had backdated the issue and there were only twenty-three days remaining on it. Still, there were no complaints, there was another PSB 2,000 km down the road, and it wasn't as if we had much else to do with our time.

After an arduous morning's work we finally rolled into the small town of Shanshan, around 80 km east of Turpan. Struggling out of the Turpan basin, we now felt like two spiders trying to climb out of a bathtub.

'Let's stock up on a few things,' said Jodie.

'Yep, sounds like a plan,' I replied.

'Which store do you fancy?' she asked, 'They all look the same to me.'

'This one here will do,' I pointed to the first store, 'look, there's a dead rat on the door step!'

Without prior research I would have naively passed to the next store, but some light reading had prepared me for such a situation. In fact, according to the local traditions in the Taklamakan Desert area, your store 'rat-o-meter status' should be clearly displayed to ensure complete customer satisfaction. Under the 'Rat Transparency Act of 1901', all stores were forced into complying, and you could now be sure that if there was a rat on the doorstep, the owners had at least achieved Level 1 on the 'Ratcker Scale'. A full explanation can be found at the back of 'Whittington Weekly', a local magazine for Chinese store owners.

Official Ratcker Scale

Level 0: Clean swept doorstep (no rats) - Of course we have a rat problem, all Chinese stores have rats, but we can't catch them. Right now they are urinating over our tomatoes.

Level 1: Display 1 rat - We have identified a rat problem and are taking steps towards resolution.

Level 2: Display 2 rats - Not only have we identified our rat problem, you can be assured that the first dead rat was not just a fluke.

Level 3:   Display 3 rats - We kill most rats that live in this shop.

Level 4:   Display 4 rats - We kill most rats that live in this shop and we stole an extra dead rat from Chop-Chop the butcher's doorstep this morning.

Level 5: Display 5 or more rats - We have been feeding our cat Methamphetamine, and we are now offering customers a free dead rat with every purchase.

'Eeeugh, that's a little bit gross,' Jodie grimaced, 'look, the intestines didn't even make it fully out of the store!'

It was true, and if the Ruthless Oriental Department Engineering Natural Termination had visited, they would certainly have deducted half a rat point, leaving the store in potential no man's land. Incidentally, after a lengthy campaign headed by officers angry at the length of their name badges, the department had later been shortened to R.O.D.E.N.T. In any case, the trail of rat offal ran inside to an area not far from a box of tomatoes and cabbages.

'The cucumbers look pretty good,' I suggested, 'and perhaps something that has been shrink wrapped outside of China,' I added as I pointed higher to the biscuit shelf.

*   *   *   *   *

After the social intensity of Pakistan, the remote stretches of the Chinese desert brought fresh challenges, mostly inventing new games to pass the time. Sometimes I would try to remember theme tunes from '80s cartoons, or guess the distance to the next living person, but if the opportunity presented itself, I would *definitely* play 'One Hump or Two?'

'One Hump or Two?' was a game inspired by the new unexpected wildlife. The probabilities of winning were similar to that of 'Heads or Tails?', and although both were present, there were no coin requirements or tossing of any kind. You simply took a punt on the next camel. Sadly, all the camels in this region were Bactarian camels, a breed with two humps, and so naturally I scored fairly highly at the game, sometimes up at 80% or 90%. The lifespan of such games was fairly short, and so on one particularly flat stretch of tarmac I decided to rate my friends. At last I had engaged my brain and if I performed the task properly, I could kill an entire day.

'Jo!' I exclaimed, louder than necessary. She was only next to me and there wasn't a soul in sight.

'Yes, my darling?' she replied, teasingly.

'I've got a new game,' I declared, 'it's called 'Rate Your Mates'!'

'I'm listening,' she added, 'so what's the criteria?'

'Criteria, yes. Um... ' I stumbled, 'I was just at the name stage really.'

'Okay - well you could judge them on whether they are good fun to hang out with?' Jodie suggested, 'Or useful things like if they are there for you when you are feeling down?'

'Well yes, there is that,' I replied, 'but what about really good stuff, like if they are really tall or ginger, or have special skills? It's a bit like friends 'Top Trumps'. It's only cool to be fat, if you are the 'fattest' person I know. Otherwise you are just quite fat and probably a little unhealthy.'

Jodie's despair was plain to see but we had little else to pass the time, and were only just over a month into the country.

'So, are you really trying to rate your mates, or are you deciding who is going to be in your superhero group?' she enquired.

'Oh hang on,' I said, overcome with excitement. It seemed that Jo was way ahead of me. This was *so* much better than my game.

'Oh my God!' I said, 'I'm putting Freeway in, he's really tall. We could use him as a ladder for special manoeuvres that needed a ladder... if we didn't have an actual ladder available,' I paused to think.

'And Ben, because he's got a PhD, he will be in charge of the group,' I added, as it all began to fall into place.

Scott would bring his occasional plumbing skills to the party, and of course there was Layth, he *had* to be in. I couldn't risk being replaced, there was a big waiting list already. I had covered all bases.

I continued with my selections, and before long the theoretical team was ready. It was a fine outfit indeed, certainly capable of resolving many day to day problems. Perhaps with larger issues we would refer you to the real emergency services, but it would be done in a most timely manner, with Ben ensuring that all calls were answered and dealt with punctually.

'I feel a bit like Billy Ocean in Ocean's Eleven!' I exclaimed, 'All I need is a small Chinese man I can fit into a box!'

'Well, you've come to the right country,' she chuckled, 'and it's Danny, not Billy. Danny stole from casinos, Billy sang 'When the going gets tough, the tough get going'!'

'I love that song! Remind me to put that on my iPod.'

I loved being reminded of songs I had forgotten. I pedalled on as I hummed the verse, only knowing the words to the chorus.

'It's all good,' Jodie spoke after a little time, 'but you haven't really chosen friends for your team, you've just kind of put them all in.'

Alas, she was right. I hadn't actually emitted anyone. All six of my friends were there, except for Laura, but she was a girl and it would bring unnecessary complications to the group. There would be arguments over superhero outfits, dental plans, all sorts of politics. I was keen to keep the team tidy and focused on the tasks ahead. It would have to remain a team of valiant males, ever present, awaiting the call of duty 24/7, excluding evenings, weekends and bank holidays.

'Jo?' I asked, 'I've just had a really spooky thought. Do you think that I've subconsciously selected these people as my friends *because* of their abilities?'

'Not really, no,' Jo responded quite dismissively. 'You put Freeway in because he's really tall. He's only 6'6", if you wanted a really tall person you could have found someone taller. Admittedly Aussie Chris is super fit, but technically speaking, being ginger isn't a skill... '

'Ben does have a PhD though,' I retorted, defending my team.

'Yeah, I'd have Ben in my team too,' she smiled.

'Now Freeway would make a good second row wouldn't he?' Jodie offered unexpectedly, perhaps using the desert forum to test out her new rugby knowledge. 'Does he play rugby? He's a kiwi, I thought they all played rugby?'

'I think he used to play *back* row, but long before I knew him,' I pondered, 'but did you know he's not a real kiwi, he was born in Derby.'

'Ah, I see,' Jo nodded, pretending not to be lost.

With the super team idea put to rest, I thought about my friends. In the remoteness of Western China, I realised that I was blessed knowing some really good people, some of whom I might not see again for many years. It was a difficult reality to accept, and as I recollected the good times, in the same breath I felt a tinge of sadness. With my short moment of feminine sentiment pushed aside, I systematically proceeded to rate them out of ten - I needed something else to do.

One by one I scored them and read out the results. Again, most of the criteria was flimsy at best, points being awarded for having big arms, or deducted for being Welsh. Ben emerged triumphant as you might expect a friend with a PhD to do. It was just so damn grown up, ironically the sole deduction that cost him a perfect ten.

'Great job, so what am I then?' Jodie served me, without warning.

'Oh, I hadn't given you a score,' I stumbled, 'you're my girlfriend Jo. You don't need a score do you?'

'Maybe not, but what would I get if you evaluated me?' she pressed.

'Err... I'm not sure, should I really answer that?' I looked to change the subject, maybe I'd teach her 'One Hump or Two?'.

'That's up to you isn't it?' she tested again.

The ball was back in my court and I didn't want it. I searched my head for an acceptable answer with no result. Should I give her an appraisal, if only for her own purposes? Perhaps this was a chance to give her areas for improvement. Maybe this is what she was looking for. On reflection, I reminded myself that I didn't understand females, and she was probably just searching for reassurance. I was a little stuck.

In my world, the situation was quite simple, there was only space for one girlfriend and until ten seconds ago I hadn't considered reviewing the situation. But what if relationships were like mortgages? If you stayed with the same one for too long, it might cease to represent good value. New policies often offered better rates, and sometimes even a free introductory gift. Jodie had bought me a hoodie from FatFace when we first got together, and I had contributed a discounted rent in the early months too. Openly evaluating your girlfriend to her face might actually prove to be a step towards understanding girls.

'Mmm okay, I'll have a think!' I said out loud.

I didn't want to sound false and throw her a perfect ten and I decided that a girl wouldn't just want to hear 'Honey, I am the luckiest man alive, there is absolutely nothing that I would *ever* change about you.'.

I gave the matter some brief consideration, tallied a few numbers in my head, added them, deducted a point and then re-added it again. Under the circumstances it wasn't fair to deduct for poor hygiene. She was normally a very clean person and we'd been in the desert for days.

'8.5!' I said, revealing the results without theatrics.

'8.5?' she said, a little surprised, 'But Ben got a 9?'

8.5 had been a much higher score than most, and I felt she was now looking too much at people around her rather than at herself.

'Ben's bought me a lot of drinks over the years. It's worth half a point,' I tried to justify my system to her.

'But I've cooked you more dinners?' she rallied. It was a decent play and deserved consideration.

'Sorry, you're right!' I said, 'You should both be equal.'

'Thank you!' she punctuated with clarity.

'I'll take Ben down to an 8.5, he could have cooked more,' I said, as I thought back to all the lazy cheese sandwiches.

Silence filled the desert once again, and a tumbleweed got caught in my rear derailleur.

'I should have given her a 9!' I thought to myself, but it was too late. It seemed like girlfriends really were like mortgages - just half a point could make all the difference.

*   *   *   *   *

'Film or Fire?' I'd call out to Jodie as we pedalled towards the sunset. It was only 4:30 in the afternoon but the December sun was beginning to set a little earlier with each passing day.

'Oh I don't know!' Jodie would reply with a bit of excitement, 'Maybe a film?'

It was getting below zero at night, but the evenings were just warm enough to boil up and eat noodles inside the tent entrance. Already in our sleeping bags, we then had the option of watching a film on one of our iPods. Of all the devices we carried, bizarrely these had proven to be one of the most useful. We would never have considered buying them, but they had been a free gift for taking an online personal training qualification just prior to setting off. Despite having never used them before, they were very light, and we agreed that they could act as a backup in case our laptop failed. It allowed us to send and view e-mails outside hundreds of European McDonalds, and now in China, it was providing temporary respite from the harsh reality of the chilly desert.

Fire nights were nice because we could eat our noodles outside of the tent, watching the sunset and the flickering flames. But film nights were good too, because for nearly two hours, we could be transported away to a life much more comforting and familiar. Sadly, film nights had to be rationed as we had just enough battery to watch four films on any leg of the journey. Some sections would take fifteen days to cross on bicycle, so often the only thing that could keep you going was knowing you could watch 'Austin Powers - The Spy Who Shagged Me' in another three days time. It's fair to say, that despite the staggering isolation, we got through those early weeks in China in good spirits, but I'd often joke with Jodie as we sat there shivering - 'You just wait for *winter*!'.

Winter did come, and I quickly stopped joking. We'd never experienced anything like it before, and with only clothing bought from a second hand store in Pakistan, we found it increasingly difficult to handle the relentless biting cold.

By mid December, the harsh winter had engulfed the entire country, bringing many parts to a complete standstill. Huddled over a bowl of steaming noodles, we stared up at the café television and watched the scattered news broadcasts. Many towns had become isolated by huge snow storms, and visibility was down to a handful of metres. A weather report indicated that parts just northeast of us were suffering lows of minus 45 degrees. We weren't faring much better, and early signs of frostbite were already noticeable in our feet and hands.

'Jo, this is bordering on stupid,' I said, 'no wonder we're struggling so much, we've been sleeping in minus 25 degrees at night!'

The evenings had quickly become another military operation. We were so cold by late afternoon that sitting and cooking dinner was simply not an option. Fire had now become a necessity, so the minute we had stopped cycling for the day, Jodie set up camp, tucked away all the panniers, before preparing dinner huddled inside the tent porch.

While she worked hard to keep warm, I ran scouting missions around whatever derelict building site we had found to make camp. Although most of it had usually been removed, I would often find small scraps of wood, broken timber buried in piles of rubble or cemented into the concrete foundations.

On the really good days, we would find larger bits of wood by the road, old crates having fallen and broken from the haulage trucks. On the poor days, our only hope was to start a fire with discarded toilet tissue used by workers to wipe their arses. It was grim stuff, but in such an absolute survival situation there were *no* boundaries, and if Jodie had had a wooden leg, I would have burnt it without hesitation.

With heavily diminished daylight hours we had now reduced our daily targets to 80 km, adding days to our interim distances of 2,000 km between visa runs. Knowing how painful that next night was going to be, we became all the more aware how important it was to make a decent fire, defrost some water, and even warm the fingers. We soon developed a phenomenon that we called 'Wood Porn'.

'Aw! Jo, look at that bit of wood!' I'd say, slamming on my brakes.

'Ah, yeah! That's a nice slow burner that one!' she'd respond with excitement.

Some days we barely found a rhythm, stopping for little bits of kindling every kilometre or so, but knowing you had a bag of wood tied onto your bike, psychologically made you *feel* warmer. The deserted landscape was still barren of all living things, so even the tiniest pieces of wood grabbed your attention like a pert pair of boobs did on the beach.

Miraculously, we were even able to start a fire in the snow, but the temperatures were now so low that it was more a placebo than anything else. Our hands and feet were becoming damaged by the cold, and as we daren't take off our shoes or gloves outside the tent, the only way we could feel the heat was to get so close that our clothing smouldered and melted.

Every morning I'd lay there frozen, and Jodie would have to get her smaller body moving so that we could have coffee. Sometimes I'd watch her through my frozen eyelashes, performing her morning routine by unzipping the tent and testing the air temperature with her little finger.

'Cold *Fin-ger!*' she'd start singing, in the style of Shirley Bassey. She did it every day, but it always made me laugh.

One morning, I could sense she was awake, but when the usual rendition didn't occur I opened my eyes.

'Hey Jo! Isn't it cold outside?' I tried to prompt her.

'I can't tell yet,' she said, 'the tent zip is frozen solid.'

It's hard to describe such a cold because there's so little to compare it to, after all, your fridge is 'cold', and that is set about four degrees *above* zero. 'Freezing' itself only describes what happens at zero degrees, and a 'freezer' which turns everything into solid ice, is only set at minus 15 degrees.

We once stopped in a gas station where the manager kept all the cigarettes *inside* the fridge, just to try to keep them from freezing. He couldn't tell me if it had worked, firstly because he was Chinese, and secondly because the door had frozen shut.

From my personal experience I can tell you that at minus 25 degrees, your penis disappears so far inside your body that many people would consider it a successful sex change routine. We woke up every morning with snow *inside* our tent, and despite winter sleeping bags and all our clothes, we couldn't lay down on the same side for more than twenty minutes at a time. It was just too painful.

Possibly the hardest thing in such temperatures is choosing the right moment for your various toilet breaks. At points of the trip I would try and hold on for over a week at a time, but at other moments I found the pressure up from the hard saddle had become unimaginably uncomfortable.

Squatting for a poo in minus 25 is something that needs to be timed with absolute military precision. Unravelled toilet tissue needs to be at hand, and once you have removed a single glove with your teeth, you have approximately six seconds of wipe time before losing your fingers for good. In such conditions, it is of unparalleled importance that your bowels follow strict orders. Too often, I found myself ordering sky diving marines, only to find that once my trousers were round my ankles, I became a training ground for nervous abseilers. On more than one occasion I was forced into 'cutting the rope' and returning back to base with half my troopers still in the plane.

That's probably enough said about freezing nights in the tent, I'm getting cold toes just writing about it. Thankfully, a much warmer prospect awaited us during our week spent relaxing in a Xi'an hostel, to rest and renew our visa over Christmas.

CHAPTER 22
FINDING REMO

Despite our anxieties about spending Christmas in China, it certainly proved an entertaining place to be. Not only did 1.2 billion people appear to celebrate it, but they had 1.2 billion different ideas about *how* to celebrate it. This appeared to be affected by their generation, gender, religion or what tat the local 'one yuan store' was trying to clear out that week. Walking around the streets of Xi'an on Christmas Eve, was a like a party combining the best and worst parts of Halloween, Easter, Valentines Day and a day at Disneyland. They didn't care what they were celebrating, the point was, they *were* celebrating.

On Christmas Day itself, we chose to wander the backstreets of Xi'an and pick up some lunch on the way to a wine-run at the supermarket. As Jodie followed the scent of a sweet potato stall, we disappeared into a small alley off the tourist trail. As we located the stall, a familiar figure stood munching on his own lunch besides the vendor.

'I don't believe it!' Jodie said in an appropriately disbelieving voice, 'It's Remo!'

Despite bumping into the World War II cyclist again by chance, e-mails updating us on his progress had indicated that he had crossed the Taklamakan Desert on a bus heading towards Xi'an. To have found him on Christmas Day was a bizarre coincidence in the most populated country on the planet, and seeing a familiar face was a great present to both of us. Jodie joined him in a sweet potato, and once they had finished their tediously healthy lunch, I made them watch me work through two plates of fried dumplings.

'Haha!' I turned to face Jodie, 'Our Christmas present was 'Finding Remo!''

'Hey Jo!' I called excitedly from the bathroom, 'We've got a response from Hong Kong!'

'Oi, are you downloading our e-mails on the toilet again?' she called back from the bed.

'I'm multitasking,' I replied, 'I thought that's what girls always complain about?'

'That's not multitasking, you're just having a poo, then touching our laptop! It's disgusting.'

I put the laptop back down on the bed, and waited until she had picked it up.

'I'm just going to head back and wash my hands,' I said, entertaining myself, but she didn't bite.

'He certainly seems to know a lot of English words,' Jodie pointed out after reading the message, 'even if they're not in the right order.'

```
From: 'Rambo'
To: 'Jodie and Tom'


'Hi Tom & Jodie: welcome to china, hope u all well,
last hold november running asia game, so as not
reply. u both must very very hard for cycling under
-45, pls take care.
I am in HK at the moment, we would like know more
your planing around in china. That should be easy us
organize to meet u in HK.


Rambo'
```

*   *   *   *   *

The winter weather had eased a little, and although still below zero degrees, the sun was shining brightly as we cycled east out of Xi'an. With a week's rest behind us we were brimming with confidence, so despite the frosty road surface and heavy traffic, we both felt positive we were going to make it across China with a final three week effort.

Out of a little laziness, I hadn't performed any map duties during the week off, not even before leaving the hostel, but with my natural sense of direction and a compass, we were soon clear from the city and slowly climbing into a valley to the east. We made good progress, and with 20 km already negotiated, the road narrowed and the traffic evaporated. It was a beautiful morning, and for the first time we were almost beginning to enjoy the challenge of the Chinese winter. The needle straight motorway dissected farmland to the left, while our quiet country road meandered peacefully through the bordering villages, children dashing across their school playgrounds to wave at the unusual visitors. Bicycle touring rarely got better.

Jodie's usual twitchy mind had clearly not settled into the relaxed pattern I had laid out for us that day. Whereas I was content to pedal for hours, chatting about old times on the bike, what we would treat ourselves to in Quingdao, and about the fact that I could even feel most of my fingers, it soon became apparent that she was going to remain on 'sniffer-dog' alert until further notice.

'Can you check for that town? I haven't seen that symbol before,' she'd ask me, at every new sign. 'Is it worth checking the map quickly?'

Over and over again Jodie would question the directions, apparently oblivious to the fact that we had remained on the same road for 20 km and there had been no choices to make on the way. I decided to pull over, perform my gentlemanly duties and seek to ease her concerns.

'There's really nothing to worry about my littlest Jobo. Look here,' I pointed to the map, 'the only reason those town names aren't on our map is because our map represents the view of China from the moon.'

I laughed, proud of my own analogy, and looked up so I could share my moment of wit with a familiar face. It was a familiar face alright, but sadly for me, one that normally resulted in me buying her flowers further down the line.

'I haven't seen the 'dancing man who needs a wee' yet,' she said, matter of factly.

Jodie wasn't referring to a specific man, and we had only assumed he was a man for ease of communication. 'Dancing man who needs a wee' was just one of a large list of our descriptions for Chinese characters, helping us to remember what we were looking for at junctions. She was however correct, we'd seen 'camp Mexican man', 'spitty Chinese man on house', and several derivatives of telegraph poles, but not our little man at dance class, waiting for the loo.

'We won't reach the next town on our map for another three or four days,' I tried to assure her, 'I'm sure we'll see it later today.'

She seemed unconvinced but agreed to continue. At the very next village Jodie spotted a turnoff with a route down to the main motorway.

'Please can we check out the signs down at the motorway,' she pointed, 'it will only take 30 seconds to get down there and then we'll know for sure.'

'You mean you'll know for sure. Fine okay, let's go and check it out, but *only* if you promise not to question anything else today. We agreed that you are only allowed two questions per day didn't we, you've definitely already used this whole week's allowance.'

We rolled down to the motorway junction where a toll guard held out a hand gesturing no bicycles. We pulled over to one side and looked ahead at the signs. To the left was the motorway back to Xi'an, to the right - Shangluo.

'Oh shitbox!' I said, 'How did that happen? I don't understand!'

'I thought that might be the case,' she replied, she was right... *again*.

'This road is going the wrong way!' I said, unnecessarily stating the obvious, but trying to process the horrible new discovery.

'This is the main road running to the southeast towards Shanghai, and we need to follow the road to the northeast instead,' Jodie recalled, to my surprise.

'I thought there was only one road? If you knew that, why didn't you tell me?' I despaired. We had pedalled over 20 km, one quarter of our daily target in China, and by the time we retraced our steps, we'd be halfway through our day and right back at where we had started.

'I don't have the map, you have the map!' she delivered calmly.

It was a fairly strong argument I had to admit, and from my point of view, one that certainly didn't need expanding on.

'And I thought that *you* were Chief of Directions?' she said, proceeding to expand on it anyway.

'I am!' I had to concede, realising that I was not just digging my own grave, nailing down the coffin, but probably chiselling the headstone to seal the job.

'Perhaps getting us onto the right road would be one of those responsibilities?'

'Er, well... of course... but I didn't check the map before leaving, I thought we just had to follow the city out east and we'd find it.' I was officially broken on day one.

'Look it doesn't matter, we'll just head back to Xi'an and find the correct road out.'

'No way! We're not undoing all that hard work, we'll cut through somehow. If we head northeast from here, we'll eventually join up with the correct road and we'll be back on track.'

I was almost convincing myself, until I was reminded of how ineffective that ploy had proven throughout our journey. I looked past the motorway, over to the north. Not only was there no road in sight, but there stood a rather large mountain range, of which we appeared to be on the wrong side of. I looked back down at the map and waited for some divine intervention.

After a few minutes, I started to lose feeling in my fingers and I realised it might not happen on this occasion. A little hopefully, I looked back over the motorway, but the mountains were still there, although maybe, just maybe, they were a *tad* smaller... Could we?

'Come on, let's just turn back, it's mostly downhill. We'll be back there in 45 minutes,' Jodie broke the silence.

Although it appeared that she had presented a solution, I struggled to accept that undoing all our hard work was the best decision in the circumstances.

'We only have to retrace to the outskirts and we can take one of the ring roads round to the right junction,' she added, making it all the more difficult for me to contribute anything to the debate.

'Fine, okay, you're right,' I eventually agreed. There was clearly no route otherwise, and after all, we were just 20 km into a 500 km stretch that would take us to within a single week of the coast. To continue heading in the wrong direction and waiting for an alternative turnoff not only sounded like patchy logic, but the laws of trigonometry were clearly against us. Bad decisions in a country the size of Europe could mean entire extra days of cycling in sub-zero temperatures.

As we headed back, or rather free-wheeled, as Jodie smugly pointed out by hanging her legs out at 45 degrees to the bicycle, I considered why I'd wasted 30 minutes deliberating over a 45 minute correction. If I had accepted the situation, fixed it, then moved on, we'd now be only 15 minutes from our turnoff. What was wrong with me? Now that the decision had been made, the maths spoke common sense, yet a few minutes before I would have contemplated hauling the bikes over an unquantifiable mountain range, with no road.

A strange vision suddenly filtered into my thoughts. Of all the images I could have had, it was a computer desk, a very specific computer desk, and one that irritated me with a long and nagging memory.

Almost seven years before pedalling away on our adventure, I had furnished my first rental flat with a single trip to Ikea. The downside of course was that everything came flat-packed, and although I was handy enough with a simple set of tools, I had somehow strayed into the philosophy 'when all else fails, refer to the instructions'.

Due to a series of unfortunate, but completely unpreventable circumstances, I had managed to affix the desk top on back to front, with the unsealed edge of the wood facing outwards into the room. For a seasoned DIY specialist like myself, I had of course cursed my bad luck, before assuring myself that the desk was still 100% functional. Within seconds I had convinced myself that it was too late to resolve the situation, then drank beer as I waited two hours for the wet glue to set.

That desk had followed me through four further accommodations, resulting in so many comments from guests that I began to contrive stories of why it *appeared* to be back to front.

Depending on the critic, I would tailor a story that best satisfied their curiosity - 'I had to shave off 2 mm to fit it through the door, I'm varnishing it tomorrow', 'I bought it from a blind man', even 'The local school was selling old desks to raise money for new books'.

I had to prevent this type of problem happening again. As usual, in such circumstances on the road, I searched for a moral or a positive I could take from the situation. The world was too big to be wasting time or energy, if we were to successfully negotiate the mazes of South East Asia, we would have to be a little better prepared. Maybe my lesson should be to step back from future problems and take the simplest steps to resolution, even if that meant unwinding some bad work. Although possibly laden with truth, it sounded too close to the cliché, 'sometimes the only way to move forward is to take a step back'. Instead, I decided that next time I had a week off, I'd be a little less lazy and take a minute to look over the local maps.

After the gruelling cycle across Western and Central China, the East offered us many comforts, namely cities and people. No longer did we need to carry 20 litres of water and stock food for a week, we could now find hot steaming bread, noodles or dumplings along hundreds of main streets and stock up on sugary biscuits and cakes at the ample supermarkets. Those dumpling vendors became our very best of friends, and nowhere on the planet did we ever enjoy tucking into our morning breakfasts and hot lunches more. The only drawback to cycling through cities in China was the Chinese drivers, of which there are quite literally millions on the road at any one point in time.

Do you know that feeling when you wake up in the morning and you've been sleeping on your arm? You try to pick up the dead limb with your other hand only to lose your grip and then slap yourself embarrassingly in the face as a result. No? It must be just Jodie then, I saw her do that this morning. Either way, please try to imagine that feeling, but in your entire body, and then combine that with the fuzziness that might occur if you downed a litre of Chinese homebrew liquor for breakfast. It isn't a combination conducive to driving a vehicle successfully, but it *is* one that the Chinese population appears to struggle with every day.

On countless occasions we became despairing witnesses, often unbearably close ones too, watching locals struggle with the essential basics of moving, steering or stopping their vehicles, whatever was required to rectify their current uncontrollable predicament. I regularly argued that abandoning their vehicles with the engines still running was the safest resolution, but despite my encouragement they remained in their cars and persisted with their experiments.

The theory of using mirrors and indicators was considered too risky due to the already complicated nature of combining wheels, pedals and possibly gears at the same time. When added to the relentless symphony of truck and bus horns, any given hour could be like a grand day out to the Chinese State circus.

Having recognised their driving inabilities, many cars now refused to drive through gaps smaller than 18 foot wide, but for the ones that still shunted you from behind, 18 foot was still not quite enough. For the real liabilities, the ones sitting motionless and sideways across three lanes, we were able to avoid collision by maintaining our average speed of 17 k.p.h, or five times the speed that most Chinese drivers could roll away with their hand brakes on, still fumbling around in neutral.

As confused as we were at the Chinese driving abilities, we were even more bemused at the scene of the inevitable accidents. Men and women would stand in the middle of traffic, yelling at the accused, and gesturing to their back bumper to clarify for all where the misdemeanour had occurred. Despite pointing to an apparently fresh scratch amongst seventy-four older scratches, it was usually difficult to attribute genuine blame, especially when *both* drivers had been trying to purchase roadside dumplings, while steering with their knees, on the wrong side of the road.

We had not seen the sea since leaving Dubai, and after three long months in China, just reaching the East Coast was enough reward in itself. A welcome bonus however, was finally managing to establish communication with an English speaking contact called Luna from the Quingdao Sharks. With a single day left on our final Chinese visa, our visit fortunately coincided with the Sharks' winter holiday rugby camp, and we would therefore get the chance to meet a living Chinese rugby legend - Mr Mu.

The Qingdao Sharks were formed in 1998, and unlike many city based clubs, were made up entirely of local born Chinese players. Their head coach, Mr Mu, was a former Chinese national prop, one of the earliest registered players, and a member of the first *ever* Chinese national XV in 1991.

Given that the population of China in the early 90s was around one billion, finding one of the original fifteen players felt like a huge and extremely fortunate achievement. Thanks to Luna, he at least understood what he was adding his autograph to, and we didn't need her assistance to translate such a huge smile.

As we waited contently for our ferry at the German port of Quingdao, we realised that our trip was about to pick up pace. In the previous five months we had only passed through Pakistan and China, but in the next five, we would be visiting ten more countries. It was clear that serious coordination would be required once again.

*   *   *   *   *

From: 'Seoul Survivors'
To: 'Jodie and Tom'

'Hey Jodie & Tom,

Our contact emailed the KRU - so hopefully we should be able to find the right person to sign your scroll.

We have a place you can stay, addresses aren't too helpful here - so you should try to get to Samgakji subway station and we can have someone come and meet you.

Look forward to meeting you guys soon!

Cheers,
Richard'

CHAPTER 23
THE SEOUL SURVIVORS

'Hey, Jo, we're not in China anymore,' I shouted and told her off, 'start watching where you are going!'

We had successfully made the pleasant ferry journey from Quingdao to Incheon, and were quickly trying to adapt back to life in a modern, developed society. The ferry ride alone had been a huge cultural transition, and it soon became clear that we were no longer in Asia as we had known it. There had been no pants hanging from the handrails, no thick clouds of smoke by the no-smoking signs, no puddles of spit collecting on the stairs, just the warm and welcoming smiles from the delicate Korean staff.

On land, it was no longer safe to coast through red lights, weave in and out of moving traffic and cycle on the wrong side of the road. It had been such a long time since we had experienced fast aggressive drivers, hiding behind their 'right of way', and as a cyclist I was already beginning to miss the casual mayhem of previous countries.

One positive of such a clean, organised society was that we were able to join a fantastic and picturesque bike path for the final two hours into Seoul. This winding river route was a haven for athletes, sports teams and people out walking their tiny dogs, and we had rarely been treated to such a spectacular introduction to a country. A thin layer of ice had formed over much of the water, and on this, a scattering of snow had settled, creating an incredible winter backdrop as we pedalled, chatting and processing our memories of crossing the entire width of China.

Thanks to Nick Horton, a captain in the US Army and Seoul Survivor winger, we had an address to head for and a place to stay for a long weekend in the capital. Nick had just finished work, and as he jogged across the road to greet us, we both stood in awe at his most pristine and sublime military uniform. He was every bit the model officer, tall, broad shouldered, clean shaven and immaculate from his short and tidy hair, right down to his dark shiny boots.

'Welcome to Seoul!' said a cheery Nick, 'I'm sorry for running late, I just came from a meeting.'

We looked him up and down, admiring his stripes and staggering tailorship of his jacket, before glancing back at ourselves.

'That's okay Nick,' I said, as I motioned to my own disgusting attire, 'we've just come from three months in a large communal toilet.'

'Well then, I expect you could use a beer!' he offered, 'But first I'll let you use my shower!'

As we relaxed in the local ex-pat pub, Nick ordered the beers and we admired a glass cabinet containing the recent history of the Seoul Survivors and Seoul Sisters rugby clubs. From several photos and shields we could make out that they had played fixtures against many Asian sides, most amusingly, another Korean based ex-pat club named the Busan Bastards RFC. Sadly we learned that the Bastards no longer played.

We sipped the extortionately priced beer and Nick proposed a toast to our journey, he was as hospitable a bloke as he was smart a captain. Short of it becoming cheaper to open their own pub, I suspected the entire bar of drunken ex-pats would pay practically anything for a pint of their favourite beer.

Richard, the Seoul Survivors captain, came to join us later that evening, and before long half the Seoul Survivors squad had popped in to say hello.

'I had a really good think about your World in Union scroll,' he said to us, as he ordered another round of drinks from the waitress. 'I've invited a guy called Jaesub to come and join us later. He's your man!'

'Thanks Rich! We really appreciate that,' I said, 'to be honest, it's been getting harder and harder to make the right contacts over this way.'

'Where else do you need contacts?' offered a New Zealand born Survivor, Kiwi-Nick.

'We've got a contact in Hong Kong,' I told them. 'A guy called Rocky, but we haven't managed to breakthrough to Japan at all.'

'Stop calling him Rocky!' Jodie told me off, 'His name is Rambo!'

'They were both great films,' Kiwi-Nick laughed. 'Anyway, I'll see what I can do about Japan.'

He pulled out his iPhone and tapped into the screen as a young looking Korean man approached our table.

'Jaesub!' Richard greeted him, 'Come and meet the cyclists!'

Jaesub Choi was one of the very few domestic Korean players to have proficient English and socialise with the ex-pat community. He had a good relationship with the Survivors, and performed relationship functions for the Korean Rugby Union that required his strong communication skills. He had a huge passion for rugby, and in addition to having earned caps at national level, he had also taken considerable time to piece together a study on the Korean history of the sport. By coincidence Jaesub was exactly our age, although he also described how being Korean, he technically had two ages.

In Korea, you were immediately considered a one year old the moment you were born. Your subsequent ageing was then measured on how many new calendar years you had experienced. If you were born on December 31st in 2009, then on January 1st 2010 you would either be two days old in real time, or two *years* old by Korean standards. Jaesub was twenty-nine and ten months old, or thirty-one and one month, depending on what view you took.

'Can you sign our scroll?' I asked Jaesub, changing the subject and wondering how such a seemingly simple question had caused my brain so much work.

As we celebrated another legend on our scroll, Kiwi-Nick brought over yet another round of drinks.

'Hey Tom!' he said, 'John Kirwan just e-mailed me back, he said he'd love to meet you both, I've forwarded you his details.'

Suddenly, cycling to Mount Fuji appeared an inspired decision.

*   *   *   *   *

Nick gave us a goodbye hug and saluted us off in full military uniform. We were sad to part company so soon, but our schedule was now quite tight, and the conditions not entirely favourable to covering large distances. Although the Seoul river path had been kept quite clear, once outside the inner city, we soon found ourselves forcing our bikes through a foot of snow.

The severe cold in China had caused our plastic ground sheet to shatter, opening up many cracks and rendering our tent vulnerable to damp, cold floors. All around us the ground was frozen, and although we had discussed ways of keeping the tent floor dry and warm, we couldn't guarantee picking up cardboard boxes and other such things out in the Korean hills.

We both assessed the situation as we pushed our bikes towards the main road. Although it was a clear 20 degrees warmer than in Central China, our original schedule had not included Korea or Japan, and would have taken us directly to the warmer areas of South East Asia. Feeling so emotionally close to warmer times, it now seemed unfair and unjust that we should continue to suffer.

'Hey Jo!' I said, as snow flakes settled in my beard, 'I've got a suggestion for our cycle through Korea.'

'What is it?' she asked, keeping her eyes on the road ahead.

'It's called - Operation Fuck the Budget.'

'What does it involve?' she asked, a little curiously.

'It involves not sleeping in the snow tonight,' I answered.

'I like your operation.'

Thanks to a Dutch settler in Busan called Jan Boonstra, we had been sent an idyllic bike route cutting through the length of the country from Seoul to Busan. It proved to be the only time on our entire trip that we had such detailed information of our environment, and thanks to him, not only did we enjoy the most spectacular Korean scenery, we were always able to plot exactly how far it was to the next cheap 'love motel'.

True to its name, our operation delivered everything that it promised, although by normal standards, most travellers would have viewed it as a bargain. For around $16 a night, we were able to check ourselves into a softly lit love shack with under floor heating and electric blankets. The bed sheets were often flamboyant, with silky soft covers providing the perfect comfort as we boiled our noodles inside the bedroom.

Fancy and erotic accompaniments came as standard, and we would pillage whatever toiletries and coffees we could find along the way, yet by far my favourite thing was the 'love motel' TV. Asides from a news channel, we also had an English speaking film channel, and no less than six channels of Korean porn.

'That looks like *our* room!' I joked, on the first night, as I flicked through the six channels.

'Well then I hope they changed the sheets!' Jodie replied, shaving her legs with the free razor. 'We're not watching that while we're eating please.'

We ate our noodles, savouring the comfort of a soft bed and warm room, then settled down to watch 'Kung Fu Panda'. Jodie drifted off to sleep midway through the action so I watched the end by myself, then flicked over for a teeny bit more Korean porn.

'It *is* our room!' I thought to myself, looking around my head for cameras.

Perhaps the excitement of that night's film, or not having to scout for hidden camp spots made the seven day journey vanish before us, but despite the incredibly tough hills in parts, we made reasonably light work of the 600 km journey to Busan. Jan's directions had been to the letter, and as Jodie often reminded me, if I had only followed *all* of these letters, I wouldn't have taken us on an unessential detour of 40 km through a procession of tight hairpins. Nevertheless, our short stay in Korea had been an absolute holiday, and as we bedded down on the ferry to Japan, we knew that whatever the weather, we would be camping again for the coming weeks. 'Operation Fuck the Budget' had finished.

CHAPTER 24
CHASING MOUNT FUJI

Yes, it was pissing down with rain, and yes, the port of Shiminoseki was as uninspiring as James Blunt singing Coldplay, but it didn't matter, we were in the magical and mystical land of Japan. Nothing had happened, and yet it was like nothing that we had ever experienced before. This was nothing, standing in the pissing rain in Japan!

As we cycled away from the drizzly port, things got better and better, and although still on a tight budget, we began to experience the finer things that Japan had to offer. In the morning we pushed our bikes up to an ornate Japanese temple, and at lunchtime we browsed a supermarket before gorging ourselves on the cheapest and most delicious sushi. Our afternoon completed the illusion when we discovered that, at the touch of a button, we could jetwash our bums for free in the 7/11 toilets. Sadly, with one rim problem fixed, another was just about to begin.

Having had to carry such a heavy load across the world, each bicycle part had been consequently subjected to more pressure than usual. In my situation, having to apply heavy force through the V-frame brakes had caused the worn brake pads to shear a fine dent into the wheel rim. In Japan, this pressure had finally caused my wheel to develop a trademark wobble.

'Oh bugger!' I said, staring closely at my worn rim, 'How did it look when I was cycling?'

'It was wobbling quite a bit,' Jodie answered.

'A bit or a lot?' I asked, hoping to hear that it could hold out until Tokyo.

'Well, you know that day you came home after the England vs All Blacks match.'

'Yep, bloody hell that was a big day out.'

'Well, it was wobbling more than you did.'

If that was indeed true then it probably wouldn't last until the next 7/11 bum wash, let alone Tokyo. It wasn't going to dampen our spirits however, so we continued on our way, rounding off an incredible day by camping in a soft, mossy orange grove behind a small village.

Perhaps with the contention of Georgia, Japan represented the biggest rugby country on our journey so far. I discounted France from our travels feeling that I never needed a strong reason to dismiss the French from anything.

Japan had a solid professional league structure in place and a massive history in the game behind them. They had participated in every single Rugby World Cup, and had been champions of Asia since the Asian Five Nations (A5N) structure had been introduced in 2008. With such limited time and no language skills, meeting with any of the top league sides across the country was an impossible dream, but we were pedalling to meet former All Black, John Kirwan, and quite frankly, that was worth pedalling from London for, let alone Shiminoseki.

After a handful of days on the road, it soon became clear that Japan was a very tourist friendly country to travel. Wild camping, whilst not encouraged officially, appeared to be respected as a necessary part of budget travel. We utilised public parks, beaches, and even the outer grounds of Osaka Castle to get an undisturbed nights rest. Only one morning did we encounter any drawbacks to our new found freedom camping.

'Right, that's it!' I proclaimed, 'I can't hold it any longer!'

'Have one for me too!' Jodie moaned from the comfort of her sleeping bag.

The previous night we had celebrated Valentine's Day by ducking into the budget, and treating ourselves to a couple of bottles of local plonk. Enjoying the rare treat on the road, we had stopped early and guzzled our way to intoxication, pitching our tent on a public playing field overlooking the sea, a stone's throw from a public toilet. Such a position was a strategic victory as it provided us with cooking and drinking water, a place to wash up our cooking utensils, and a more private place to take a wee during the night. We could still make out the crashing of the waves not far beyond the coastal path, and it was as romantic a location as one could wish for, save for the close proximity to a 24 hour public toilet.

As I unzipped the tent door I heard what sounded like a stereo being turned on not far to our right. It was only 5:30 a.m. and as I stood up straight, wearing only my pants, I stopped to rub my eyes. Either I was still very drunk, or a flash mob Tai Chi class was being held around our very tent.

No less than fifty old age pensioners were scattered over the playing field around us, limbering up and stretching. I too had a stretch, but realising I was still a tracksuit short of the correct dress code, I dived back in and grabbed some shorts and a rugby jersey.

I walked to the toilet, trying to look as dignified and unfazed as possible, and returned to give Jodie the great news. With puffy eyes and tent hair, she waited a full hour for the class to finish before dashing to the toilet. The romance of St Valentine had officially disappeared for another year.

We had managed to pick up a map of Japan, detailed enough to show most main roads through the country, but as we found out in the hardest possible way, there is a good reason people invest in real topography maps. One road from Osaka to Nara looked short and more or less direct, a clear winner over a much longer route that backtracked from a point further down the road. An easy agreement, we decided to take the quieter, more immediate turning and slowly cycled up into a small village.

Without warning, the road all but disappeared, replaced by cobbled stones of ever increasing gradient. Soon, it was so steep we were struggling to even move the bicycles, and keeping at least one hand on the brakes was a necessity for the frequent rests. To our right were beautiful views of waterfalls and a series of well maintained national park walkways. Halfway up the hill, three workmen were standing by a van, parked facing uphill on the narrow slope. They smiled and waved to us as we stopped once again to gather our strength. Minutes later, a tractor driver pulled over, chatted to the guys with familiarity, and joined up the vehicles with a stretch of towrope. As he pulled them up the hill, we realised that this procedure must be the usual way to ensure the van didn't simply plunge backwards into the village below.

'What about us?' I cried in vain to the man in the tractor.

Three hours after our estimates we were approaching the small town of Nara, screeching down a long winding descent with our brakes on full lock. We took a small tour to get our bearings and then located a youth hostel where we could wash the rest of our bodies to the standard of our bottoms. It was the cheapest hostel in town, but yet for a two night mattress on the floor, we had to hand over nearly two entire weeks' budget. We were going to have to recoup some of this in South East Asia or we would run out before New Zealand.

Nara was an exquisitely absorbing city, and by chance, we had arrived at the right time to enjoy a literature festival. During the day we walked around town, enjoying the curious deer in the park, and photographing the most ornate and traditional Japanese temples. By evening, the huge gardens scattered all around the town were decorated with millions of fairy lights, and a stunning firework display capped off the celebrations.

To add to the day's success, I received the perfect e-mail from Tokyo.

From: 'Rich Freeman'
To: 'Jodie and Tom'

'Hi Jodie and Tom
I am the rugby writer for The Daily Yomiuri in Japan
as well as the Japan correspondent for Rugby World
and New Zealand Rugby News.
JK has pointed me to your page and all the great
work you are doing. Was hoping we could meet up when
you get to Tokyo so I can do a feature and let
others know what you are doing.
If you need somewhere to stay here in Yokohama, our
Club President Simon Litster has offered to open up
the club facilities and a room in his own house for
you. Just let me know and I'll put you in touch.
Cheers
Rich'

I immediately typed a response as Jodie hurried to take advantage of
the ninety minute evening bath time. Not only did we have to sleep on
the floor, for the cost of a week's budget each night, we also had to
share our bath water with all the other guests too. I asked Rich for a
little help in organising Jodie's upcoming birthday, then joined some
naked Japanese men in the male tub of water. Breaking all the house
rules, we then shared a can of shandy and ate discounted sushi in the
bedroom.

While Jodie packed up our panniers the next morning, I snuck
downstairs and downloaded the e-mails before leaving. To my delight,
Rich had already replied back to me.

'Tom,

Very happy to hear Jodie will be turning 30 here in
Yokohama. I have suggested an itinerary if this
sounds like her type of thing.

Jodie can open her presents then I can come and
collect you and take you to the Chichibunomiya
Stadium. I have arranged two VIP tickets for the Cup
Semifinal, and you will both be hosted by the JRFU
while you are there. In the evening I'm playing
guitar with a band at our local pub. You are very
welcome as long as you don't laugh at the guitarist.
Simon will be arriving there direct from London so
easy to go back with him after.

Cheers, Rich

PS - I know a great lady who makes the best
chocolate cakes, I'll have a word for you.'

*   *   *   *   *

Almost as a consolation, when my wheel rim finally fractured on an innocuous stretch of coastal road, we caught our very first glimpse of a miraculous vision on the horizon. Deep in the distance, the giant volcanic body of Mount Fuji rose up from the meandering coastline, capped with a head of snow for all to admire.

'Bloody hell look!' we both stopped and stared at it together.

As it turned out we had plenty of time to admire the still active volcano, and despite spotting a number of 'Shimano' signs (a well known Japanese bicycle part manufacturer), we discovered that none of them could help with my fractured wheel. The first four Shimano outlets were entirely dedicated to fishing reels and rods, providing us with numerous false horizons as we pushed the wobbly bicycle for four hours along the coastline.

Finally, after alternating between pushing and trying unsuccessfully to pedal standing up, we reached a large enough town to ask around and find a real bike shop. With much relief and even achier legs, a brand new rim was fitted to my wheel, and we were ready to get back on the road.

For two entire days the majestic Mount Fuji grew in stature, causing the same jaw dropping response each time we glanced up at it. Eventually, after over 150 km of coastal cycling, we arrived at its feet and stared in awe at its quite perfect formation. Without doubt, this was an isolated highlight of the entire trip so far.

These memories kept us smiling through to our finishing point in Japan, where we arrived, wet but happy, at the Yokohama Country & Athletics Club (YCAC) and were shown to our bedroom by the club General Manager, Paul Murakami.

'You can have the bench Jo,' I offered, as we investigated around the lifeguard's hut, 'I know it's not exactly the Hilton.'

'It's fine Tom, don't worry!' she replied, 'It's not quite how you'd picture waking up on your thirtieth birthday, but considering what we've been through this year, I'd say that my expectations have been successfully managed!'

We laid our mats on the floor and settled down for what turned out to be a surprisingly good night's sleep. We looked back on our ride across Japan, remembering the snow, rain and wind, before realising that we had only taken a single day off in over 2,000 km of pedalling. Now, with a five day stay around Tokyo, a few days in Hong Kong and a few more in Hanoi, we wouldn't touch the bicycles again for over two weeks, the longest break since our flood relief work in Lahore over four months ago.

*　　*　　*　　*　　*

'Happy birthday to *you*! Happy birthday to *you*!' I sang, as I woke Jodie up with a cup of tea.

Jodie's birthdays were sensitive moments at best, and she openly disliked them more than a trip to the dentist. One year I had considered buying her dental vouchers as a joke, but on advice from her entire family, it was pointed out that I already made enough mistakes naturally, without deliberately adding to it. At least this year, whatever I was able to arrange would exceed her non existent expectations.

Jodie's mum, dad and brother had posted some small presents ahead to Tokyo, as well as a parcel containing some of her favourite smart-casual clothes from back in London. If I was going to drag her around, watching rugby in VIP lounges and going to gigs, I assumed she'd prefer not to do it dressed in waterproof trousers.

Jodie's expression lit up as she opened a container of Ferrero Rocher from her mum and dad, and enjoying her tea and chocolate breakfast, she was then reunited with her favourite jeans, choice of tops and a smart pair of soft shoes.

My personal contribution didn't amount to more than a photographic birthday card from Moonpig, but I *had* gone to great pains to maintain the rugby and cycling theme from our journey.

'To the Hooker from Harlow!' it began.

'Oi!!' she tried to elbow me, 'I'm from Stansted!'

'But you *were* happy with the 'Hooker' part?' I asked, just for clarification.

What the lifeguards hut lacked in bedroom comforts, it made up with ample showering and changing facilities. We felt ready to take on the day as Rich Freeman turned up to join us, right on queue.

'Happy birthday Jodie!' he greeted her with a peck on the cheek, 'Have you ordered any breakfast yet? I'm starving!'

Rich sensed us hesitating over the menu prices, the YCAC was a beautiful and modern clubhouse and the restaurant catered for a distinguished group of members.

'Simon's tab is your tab!' he laughed, 'He's very happy to host you here. Get in there and order something.'

'But we haven't even met Simon yet!' Jodie insisted.

'Bacon, eggs, sausage, beans, toast!' I squealed in delight, 'Thanks Simon!'

The breakfast was delicious, and only when Rich waved to the kitchen, did I remember that I was about to enjoy it even more. Out walked Paul, dressed in his usual immaculate suit, carrying a rich, dark chocolate cake glowing under the soft light of thirty candles. We all embarrassed Jodie with a little more singing and waited for her to dish out the cake.

'Where's the rest of it?' I said, staring at my slice, 'Rich is half my size, and his piece is twice as big!'

Rich Freeman had come to settle in Japan as a rugby correspondent, following a good amateur rugby background captaining the Old Pauline RFC in London. Formed in 1871, Old Pauline is officially the oldest 'Old Boys' rugby club in existence today. Rich himself was a hugely unfazed individual, great fun to be around, with a very easy sense of humour. He was the sort of bloke that always *appeared* to be on his best behaviour. That's not to say that his behaviour was always commendable, but you sensed that in the right, or wrong circumstances, it could probably be a lot worse.

'Right guys, I have to head off to work,' Rich said, looking at his watch, 'would you like me to show you the way into town?'

Rich was playing along with a thoroughly convincing performance, so much so, that I was actually a little worried he'd forgotten that he was organising us tickets. A nod and a wink behind Jodie's back set my mind at rest, and so we collected our day pack and followed him down to the subway station.

'So, this is my office!' Rich pointed up at the huge Chichibunomiya stadium, 'Follow me this way, I want to introduce you to someone.'

Rich led us towards a smart South American looking man, standing by the main gate.

'This is Gilbert,' Rich introduced us to the man, 'he is the JRFU marketing manager, and your host this afternoon.'

For a very microscopic moment, the whole situation felt like an episode of Jim'll Fix'it - 'Jodie, today is your birthday, and we've fixed it for you to eat chocolate and watch a Japanese cup semi-final!'

'Is that your real name?' I asked Gilbert as he led us to our corporate box.

'It's actually quite common in South America,' he replied, probably answering the question for the thousandth time.

'Maybe, but we've been carrying a mascot called Gilbert all the way from London!'

I waited for an expression of sheer surprise, but I realised it was a connection only really of interest to us, and at a stretch, the manufacturers of 'Gilbert'.

'Allow me to introduce you to the board of the JRFU,' Gilbert seamlessly integrated into his tour of the VIP lounges.

The ever polite group of dignified Japanese lined up and 'Kon-ee-chewa-d' us, before wishing Jodie a happy birthday and presenting her with a bag of even posher chocolates.

'Did you like your birthday card?' I asked Jodie, feeling a little outdone by the performance.

'Mustang Sally now baby!' sang the lead singer of Rich's band, dressed in a bright blue Elvis costume, his third outfit change of the night.

'These guys are good aren't they!' I turned to Jodie, who was stood at the foot of the stage passing a pint of Guinness up to Rich.

'Jo, wait until they've finished the song!' I tried to insist, without disrupting the performance.

Rich shook his head vigorously in disagreement, eagerly stretching out his strumming hand to accept the pint.

'Bloody hell! He's a pro!' I commented as Jodie returned to the bar stool. Rich was now only strumming along in the verses, using the distraction of Elvis's theatrical chorus to guzzle his pint mid-song.

'You must be Jodie and Tom,' a tall man said, now standing beside us at the bar. We knew it had to be Simon Litster.

'Happy birthday Jodie,' he said, 'now, what can I get you? It looks like Rich needs another Guinness already!'

Simon was in great shape for his 50s, and having started playing back row in England, had then spent several years in Hong Kong, representing Valley RFC as well as the national team in both 7s and XVs. With many fond memories he had finally relocated to Japan where he captained the YCAC rugby section, before most recently becoming President.

'That's some journey you've had Jodie,' he turned to her after ordering the drinks.

'I know,' I replied, 'I can't believe she's thirty already!'

'I was referring to the bike ride Tom, not her life!'

'Who's life?' Rich said, as he jumped down from the stage with an empty pint glass.

'Jodie's life,' Simon laughed, handing Rich another Guinness.

'I know!' Rich replied, 'Doesn't she look too young to be thirty?'

'Thanks Rich!' Jodie beamed, 'that's the first time anyone has said that today.'

'Hey! I said that to you this morning?' I intervened.

'No Tom! Actually, you said I didn't look all that bad for an older woman!'

Simon and Rich both turned to face me, shaking their heads in unison and rolling their eyes in sympathetic disappointment. It was an unspoken man-to-man expression to imply, 'Come on mate, that was a simple one!'

'Isn't that what Rich just said?'

'Hey, has Rich put you in touch with Eddie and George yet?' Simon steered me away from the icy thin subject.

'No, I was going to mention that tonight,' Rich replied.

'Are you talking about Eddie Jones and George Gregan?' I asked, clarifying that he was referring to the Suntory Sungoliaths, and not the two guys serving behind the bar.

'Yes, I can put you in touch if you like, they might be able to free some time up to meet you.'

'That would be amazing Rich! I didn't think we would end up meeting any world record holders!'

'You've already met one tonight!' Rich replied, allowing me the chance to look around the bar, 'You're standing next to him.'

Our host Simon Litster, as far as we can tell, is still the oldest player *ever* to have played at the 7s Rugby World Cup finals. In 1993, at the inaugural Edinburgh tournament, he represented Hong Kong less than two weeks before his thirty-eighth birthday, a full year older than Waisale Serevi had been when he won the tournament with Fiji in 2005.

'I don't think you should be talking about Serevi and I in the same breath!' he laughed.

'Really?' I answered, still in awe, 'Just how good were *you*?'

*　　*　　*　　*　　*

To my surprise, when John Kirwan strolled into Dean & Delucca's coffee shop, his second office, I managed to say hello without sounding like a twelve year old schoolgirl. Jodie later assured me that I behaved like a much older girl, but I think that she was just bitter about having a boyfriend still in his twenties.

John Kirwan should need no introduction, but for those who can't remember before 1994, when Kirwan retired from international rugby, I will provide a little justification for my nerves.

In all, John Kirwan played in ninety-six matches for the All Blacks, including sixty-three Test matches and two Rugby World Cups. He scored thirty-five Test tries, sixty-seven in All Black appearances and was joint top try scorer at their victorious campaign in the 1987 Rugby World Cup.

After finishing his illustrious playing career, he stepped into coaching, taking a struggling Italian side to their first big victories in the Six Nations competition, and then Japan to several successive A5N titles.

'Black coffee please Mr Kirwan,' I answered, as the legendary All Black offered me a drink. I had been drinking black coffee all morning and the last thing my heart needed was another shot of caffeine.

'So... ' I hesitated, suddenly realising that there was nothing I could tell this man that he didn't already know. 'How's it all going?'

'Good thanks guys, but I should be asking you the same question. I bet you've had some incredible experiences along the way.'

'It's a funny old world,' I offered, looking to Jodie for help and almost burning my lips on the scalding hot coffee.

'We've met with a lot of great rugby people,' she spoke quite freely, 'and there have been strong communities in every single country. We really couldn't have done it without them.'

'That's good to hear,' he acknowledged.

John listened carefully, and nodded in approval as we chatted away about chicken ice-cream, Islamic female rugby players and everything we could think to tell him about Pakistan. He admitted to having a strong interest in other languages and cultures, and despite already speaking both Italian and Japanese, we sensed that there were many more untapped plans inside John's head.

'Thinking of riding back to England for 2015?' I asked him, sensing a bike sale might be on the cards.

'I'm not sure what my family would make of that!' he laughed, 'But who's to say? If I did, I'd be asking you for advice!'

Soon the great JK was joined by his coaching staff and it was time for him to head off for winter camp. I was very sad for my coffee experience to be over, but at the same time I knew that they were some ground beans I would never forget.

'Right then Jo, what have we got on this afternoon?' I asked her, as we strolled away in the crisp bright air. She pretended to look at her diary.

'Let's see. Oh yes, we have Eddie Jones and George Gregan at 2 p.m.'

'Oh yeah!' I pretended to have forgotten, 'Let's see if we can squeeze them in!'

*   *   *   *   *

'How about that for a present?' Eddie Jones joked, as he offered me his very own Barbarians coaching jacket. 'Here, why don't George and I sign it for you too.'

The pair signed the jacket neatly in front of us and I accepted it with a bewildered expression of confusion and pleasure.

'This is... amazing,' I stuttered. It wasn't the first time that I had managed to understate my feelings towards a situation.

It *was* amazing, it was *very* amazing, but to receive a personal gift combining such history as Eddie Jones, George Gregan and the Barbarians, meant so much to me as a fan, that somehow it had regretfully become completely indescribable. As I searched my brain for some more suitable words, it suddenly dawned on me that I had spent too many years butchering the appropriate superlatives.

Present company excluded, I decided that I had no choice but to blame my Australian friends for this entire predicament. Much like the Irish, the Australians are very comfortable travellers, and it seems that wherever they migrate to, they embed themselves into their new community. It would take a very cold heart not to warm to their charisma, and before you could say 'fair dinkum', you'd left your lovely civilised bar to sing 'Men at Work' songs down at the sticky floored Walkabout pub. Sadly, associating with such people brought a downside, and despite their infectious optimism, the Australian integration had dealt a rather large handicap to my English vocabulary.

As I continued to stumble for a suitable word, I realised that I had spent my recent years following their example, and wrongly applying superlatives to 'regular' or perhaps just 'mildly good' events.

'Do you like my poem?'
'Does my bum look big in this?'
'Is the dinner okay?'

My answers had become autopilot, but incorrect.

'It's fantastic!'
'You look outstanding!'
'This food is incredible!'

The Australians simply have no words to describe 'bad' situations. Ask our Australian mate Chris what he thought about the Queensland flooding and he'd answer 'Jeez, not so good'. Going a notch up the scale and he'd describe their performance at the 2010 Ashes Cricket Tournament as 'Mah, pretty ordinary'. If this was his starting point, then it should come as no surprise that a Subway meal deal was 'awesome', and the London Transport oyster card was 'legendary'.

'Thanks guys, this is really, great,' I said, not finding a fresh new word. My brief word vacuum had come to an end, and although it wasn't a jaw dropping announcement, I had meant it. It had become painfully obvious that some language housekeeping was required, and to free up some space at the business end of adjectives, I would begin to wean myself away from giving unnecessary flattery. It wasn't an easy place to begin though, both Eddie and George were both worthy recipients of any accolade I could think of.

As a coach, Eddie had taken the Brumbies to a Super 12 title, before guiding the Wallabies to the 2003 Rugby World Cup final. He had then taken a role in the UK with top Premiership club Saracens, and was subsequently appointed as Technical Advisor to Jake White's victorious Springbok side in 2007. Even in Japan, he continued to deliver results with a return to his former club Suntory Sungoliaths.

'I really can't thank you guys enough for meeting us,' I said to Eddie and George, as they walked us to the foyer with a pile of energy snacks from the club stores.

'No need to thank us,' Eddie insisted, 'it was our pleasure.'

'Hang on a moment,' George added, as he made a dash to the changing rooms, 'I'll grab you something to put all those bits in.'

He disappeared into the changing room, reappearing a few seconds later with an empty boot bag. We stood dumbstruck, mouths wide open.

'Is this *your* boot bag?' I asked, realising that today would now eclipse the rest of my life into complete insignificance.

'He doesn't need it,' Eddie laughed, 'he's hanging his boots up after Sunday's final. I just need him to do me one last favour first!'

'Well, look. It was great to meet you both,' George smiled, 'I'm off to do my homework now.'

'You have homework?' I asked, glancing at his coach. Eddie Jones had been a school principal in a former career, and I wondered whether setting homework had been part of his winning secret.

'I'm going to go through the semi final video again,' he explained, 'the opposition's number 9 is a very useful player.'

The pair wished us good luck a final time, turned, and headed back up the stairs in their white slippers. It was clear to us that to become the most Test capped player in rugby history, he had needed to be the most professional one along the way. George had epitomised this, with his pleasant attitude in dealing with scruffy cyclists, the Japanese media, and through his mentor role to younger players at Suntory

Sungoliaths. It really was an entire galaxy away from grassroots rugby as I knew it, and I felt hugely privileged to have had time in their company.

'That's not homework!' I scoffed, as we stepped into our pre-paid taxi, 'I can watch videos all day long!'

The taxi gently pulled away to finally conclude our big day.

'Hey, what bastard stole my boot bag?' yelled an unidentified voice through the changing room window.

Back at Simon's house we joked with him, laughing in disbelief at what had been a remarkable experience, and following kisses by so many legends, Jodie's pledge never to wash her cheeks again.

'So, nothing new there then Jo?' I teased, guarding my ribs in the nick of time.

We sat down at the table while the oldest Rugby World Cup 7s player in history, served up some dinner and opened a bottle of red wine.

'Sounds like you guys had an extraordinary day!' he commented, filling our glasses.

'Out of this world!' I agreed, deciding to start my language housekeeping tomorrow.

'Simon, this bolognese is sensational!'

*   *   *   *   *

From: 'Rich Freeman'
To: 'Rugby Asia Channel'
cc: 'Jodie and Tom'

'Semi,
Am currently with Tom and Jodie, showing them the joys of Japanese rugby etc. They leave here on Thursday for a few days in Hong Kong and I said you were the man when it came to rugby in HK and Asia. They have been to a heap of countries playing in the A5N and I am sure would be worth a video clip!!

Cheers, Rich'

CHAPTER 25
DON'T DROP THE BALL

Catching up with an old work mate in Hong Kong was one thing, but catching up with an old rugby fanatic work mate to watch the Six Nations in Hong Kong, was quite another.

Thanks to Irishman and Leinster fan, Eoin Tormey, Jodie and I enjoyed the most spectacular of locations to base ourselves for our six day visit. Perched high in a twenty-sixth story 'mid-levels' apartment, we plotted and planned an itinerary that involved eating dumplings, but didn't involve unpacking the boxed bicycles in Eoin's front room.

The Irish pub was heaving, and thanks to Eoin's familiarity with the angles, we secured a pivotal position to catch all the action. Eoin reached over our shoulders and passed us a glass of white wine and a pint of Guinness. Not enjoying the Guinness, I finally allowed Jodie to swap with me for my glass of wine.

We were sat shoulder to shoulder on adjacent bar stools, with the formidable presence of former second row Eoin stood immediately behind me. To all of our surprise, Jodie's back was being shadowed by none other than kickboxing action hero, Jean Claude Van Damme, who we later learned had a quiet interest in rugby.

As we all cheered the kickoff between Ireland and Italy, I weighed up the odd situation. Van Damme's hometown may have rhymed with 'muscles', but I knew that if my head was at the bottom of a ruck, I had the better man standing behind me.

If there was one thing I could guarantee with Eoin, it was that we wouldn't be having an early night. Following the two evening rugby matches, he kicked off a 'Tormey tour' of Hong Kong, taking us to all the 'must drink' sights. For a grand finale, he took us for a drink at the most prestigious nightclub in the city.

'Eoin, I'm sorry, it looks kind of expensive here,' I looked at the Ferrari parked at the front door.

'Come on Huddo, I expected more from you. I said let's *have* a drink at the club! Not *buy* one!'

He strolled across the street before returning from the 7/11 with three cold beers. The entire front of the club had been slid open and many people were now enjoying the fresh air, sipping their overpriced drinks out on the same stretch of public pavement.

'I just saved about $45 and ten minutes in a queue!' he explained. 'That guy knows it too, but he can't do it because he'll look cheap in front of the Soho Sweethearts.'

'He does have a lot of attractive women around him!' Jodie observed out loud.

'Yes, but those girls drink here *every* week. Once that guy settles the tab and hands back the rental car, he'll go home and spend the rest of the year paying it off.'

'I never liked reality shows much,' I admitted, 'but this is quite fun!'

*   *   *   *   *

I had the opposite of fun the very next morning, when Jodie dragged me out of bed to drop in our visa application at the Vietnamese embassy. Thankfully the office was desolate, and only waiting behind Jodie, I found the queue to be pleasantly manageable.

The little man behind the counter was idly stamping away at passports, application forms and anything else that seemed to come within reach. I certainly had no intention of leaning too far over when I handed in my application.

'Xin chào! How fast is your express service please?' Jodie asked the man behind the desk, noticing the laminated sign on the counter surface.

'Wait one moment please,' the man replied politely. Clearly we had caught him at a most busy time.

'What did you just say?' I whispered in Jodie's ear.

'I asked him how fast the express service is.'

'Did you honestly think I was asking you to explain the English bit?'

'Oh sorry, 'xin chào' means hello!' she replied, finally remembering that I had been raised in South East London and not South East Asia.

'Xin chào!' the man looked up from his pile of passports.

Rather than the standard three days, the express visa, depending on his stamping responsibilities, could be available in five minutes. I suggested that it was probably worth the extra few dollars, and rightly pointed out that we might easily have to wait five minutes for the lift back down. Jodie agreed that an express visa was the right choice, but also insisted that it wouldn't kill me to consider walking down a single flight of stairs. We took our seats and stared at the reception clock as two older ladies walked in through the doors.

'Jodie, look!' I grabbed her attention before they came too close, 'Two cougars on a hen party to Saigon!'

Although I found it to be a little childish and immature, it was a game we always played, mainly to keep Jodie entertained.

'Nope,' she replied, dismissing my opinion, 'just two friends going on a long girly weekend together.'

'G'day, how yer going?' the first cougar said, with a degenerative form of English.

'Xin chào!' I said, temporarily raising the level of intellect, 'So are you two ladies off to Vietnam then?'

The illusion had been quickly shattered, realising that unless they were dropping off sandwiches to the man behind the counter, there was little other reason to have found themselves in the Vietnamese embassy.

'Yes, we're heading over for a short holiday,' the second cougar replied, with a much more pleasant dialect.

'Oh how lovely,' I tried to sound gracious, as Jodie gave me a discreet but victorious nod.

'It's actually more of a holiday in Laos,' she continued, and I feared I was about to hear their whole itinerary, 'but we have to pop over to Vietnam for a hen party first.'

'What a great plan!' I cheered, a little too loud for the circumstances.

'Visas are ready!' came a call from our counter man. He had smashed the five minute deadline and was now enjoying a sandwich, 'Have a happy holiday!'

'That was suspiciously easy,' I thought to myself.

'We just came from the Laos embassy,' the first nasally voice cut back into my ear, 'they do express visas there too.'

I thought about it for long enough to remember I was hung over, but the suggestion did come with advantages.

'Shall we?' I suggested to Jodie, 'It would save a lot of running around on my next hangover.'

'Actually, that's *not* a bad idea,' she said, somehow managing to turn an expected compliment into a mere absence of stupidity.

Outside the office we waited ten seconds for the rickety lift before Jodie led me down the stairs by my ear. The stairs reminded me of my physical capabilities that day, but after a successful two hours in downtown Hong Kong, we had now picked up enough visas to see us through to Bali.

* * * * *

As I arranged a meeting with Robbie McRobbie, an alarming sight caught my eye. Either I was still suffering from drinking with an Irishman, or I could see two young boys standing on the bamboo scaffolding outside Eoin's twenty-sixth story window. I ran over to investigate and could see that they were untying the lashings holding together the scaffolding, climbing quickly and steadily towards the ground. These boys were only in their mid teens, and it would have been a very poor family to have to send their children to do such a dangerous job, instead of going to school. By no coincidence, this was the very focus of our planned meeting with Robbie at the Hong Kong Rugby Football Union (HKRFU).

As a former policeman, Robbie McRobbie had come across from the UK, playing many seasons for the Police Rugby XV, and even representing the Hong Kong 'A' XV. Combining his knowledge of rugby culture with a social awareness developed through his profession, Robbie had been one of the key contributors to a scheme known as 'Breakthrough'.

Although not just offering rugby, the 'Breakthrough' project aimed to focus the efforts of children who had strayed onto the wrong side of the law. Rugby fitted their model perfectly, teaching children the importance of honesty, integrity, team work and responsibility for others. Hundreds of children had benefited from the scheme, few more than a young lad from the notorious Tin Siu Wai housing estate.

Ivan, an overactive 14 year old, was doing particularly poorly at school and was keeping with some bad company. He was placed into the scheme by his school principal, who was worried he would become further caught up in the area's destructive social problems. Domestic violence, juvenile crime, single parent families, and high levels of unemployment meant that strong role models were an extremely rare commodity.

Ivan became one of the very first inductees to the rugby section in early 2004, and despite never having seen a rugby ball before, began to enjoy the activity, forming strong relationships with other boys and the 'Breakthrough' officers. After being wrongly connected with a robbery, he realised the time had come to choose between the rugby project and his criminal friends, he chose correctly.

As a player, Ivan showed great potential, and after a few seasons he was not only representing the Hong Kong U20 side, but playing 1st division rugby with Valley, one of Hong Kong's most elite clubs. To add to his achievements, Ivan then helped develop younger children by coaching rugby at the 'Breakthrough' project.

As amazed as I was by his turnaround, I still didn't fully understand. When I was a troublesome 14 year old, my mum got me to behave by threatening me *with* rugby! Perhaps this is where the HKRFU got the idea for their project 'Don't Drop the Ball'.

Not trying to put unnecessary pressure onto children's handling skills, the project instead tried to tackle problems before they happened. Their aim was to steer children away from the lures of illegal activities, targeting any areas where there was a known Triad gang presence, and offering the children a choice upfront. The project was a suspected abbreviation of the concept, 'Don't drop the ball or we'll put you in Breakthrough!'

$$*\quad*\quad*\quad*\quad*$$

If being called 'Rambo' wasn't already enough achievement, being the first ever Chinese born player to represent Hong Kong certainly clinched it.

With his playing days over, Rambo Leung was now one of the most active figures in developing Asian rugby. He had invited us to meet him at a busy Chinese restaurant, heaving with smart businessmen on working lunches, we were the only western faces in the room.

'Why don't *you* order?' we both suggested to Rambo, realising by the fourth perusal of the menu that we definitely couldn't read Chinese.

'Would you care for Dim Sum?' he asked us, contemplating a range of dishes on the menu.

'If he asked me to, then yes, I probably would,' I chuckled on my own.

'Ow!' Jodie kicked me under the table and gave me a very multi-faceted stare. I covered all bases.

'Yes please Rambo, Dim Sum would be wonderful!'

Rambo's primary work was in China, but over the years he had made many friends, picking up coaching experience and assisting local development wherever he could. We had first heard of him through K in Pakistan, and Rambo's patchy English rugby e-mails had become so familiar across Asia, that his own special phrasing had been dubbed 'Ramb-lish'.

'My biggest aim is to try to find more Chinese people like me!' he explained, pointing out that 7s was distracting too much attention.

'Like you?' I clarified, 'You mean broad shouldered, for the front row?'

'No neck and little legs,' he laughed.

Rambo's biggest obstacle had been trying to overcome the perception that Asian genetics meant smaller and weaker people. He was adamant that with the right diet and training, they could compete with other national sides, in both speed and strength. I'd like to think that I deliberately played devil's advocate.

'I guess some people are just not suited to fifteens?' I offered.

Rambo lowered his chopsticks and turned to me with utmost seriousness.

'You know, I spend a lot of time learning about anthropology!' he explained, and I was shamed that a Chinese man knew an English word that I didn't, 'I ask people, how do you think Maori's came to be in New Zealand, how Fijians came to Fiji, how Samoans came to Samoa?'

I turned to Jodie for help, I still didn't know what anthropology was, and if I couldn't point to Fiji on a map, I'm pretty sure I wouldn't have found it in a boat.

'Long long time ago, many of these people came from Malaysia, from Taiwan and spread out through Polynesia and Micronesia. Over time, diet and competition for food changed their shape, but the roots are same DNA.'

'I guess that explains Sumo wrestlers!' I threw out there, trying to think of anything bigger than the Samoan, Trevor Leota.

'Genetics have changed in Asia, I'm not telling people they are still the same. They need to learn their own style of rugby, but they are not limited by their DNA.'

'It's actually interesting!' I said, realising that I had probably worked out the meaning of anthropology.

'Hey! You eat like Sumo wrestler!' he gasped, pointing at the two empty trays of dim sum in front of me, 'How come you not fat!'

'It must be my DNA!' I laughed, reaching for my third tray.

*　　*　　*　　*　　*

The city of Hong Kong had been like nothing I had ever seen before in my life. In many ways, it was heavily Chinese and reminded me of our recent crossing, but from another angle it was a very internationally modern city.

Somewhere in-between the gleaming office towers and the cramped bustling Asian side alleys, there were also still the reminders of previous generations under British colonialism. Nothing was more evidential of this time than the Hong Kong Football Club, our last invitation thanks to a local DHL manager called Ray Peacock.

Leading us to the members bar, Ray wasted no time in buying a round of drinks.

'Tom, Guinness. Jodie, white wine. There you go! Cheers to both of you.'

'Ah thanks Ray!' I smiled, seeing that he too had ordered a Guinness. I loved connecting with someone over a pint of Guinness, it was one of the few inexplicable joys of life. Jodie had tried to have one once, but having to hold it with two hands made me feel like I was drinking with a pet monkey.

'You've come at a good time guys! We're celebrating our 125th anniversary this year.'

'You're looking pretty good for it Ray,' Jodie replied, teasing the little Scotsman.

'Thank you Jodie,' he laughed, 'you know, I've always said there's nothing wrong with a girl showing a bit of cheek!'

I giggled into my pint, imagining Jodie with a little hole in the bum of her jeans.

Ray Peacock was a short, but an extremely athletic guy, not just for a man in his fifties but even compared to two cyclists. He was every ounce the model clubman, fanatical about every sport, and an ever present supporter of the club functions. He was also, to put it plainly, a stand out bloke.

'You know Tom and Jodie, I've been having a think about your trip from here onwards, and I think there might be something we can do to help you.'

'Well look, we were supposed to be cycling, but if Jodie's keen then I'm already in.'

'I'm just saying that there'll be things that you need help with, and we have lots of DHL offices along the way. I'll have a think and let you know if we can help.'

'That's really nice of you Ray!' Jodie answered on our behalf.

'Excellent, well look, it's Tuesday night and I insist you let me buy you the club's speciality pizza.'

'That's *really* nice of you Ray!' I came to the party with a few notches more enthusiasm.

*   *   *   *   *

From: 'Rugby Asia Channel'
To: 'Belly - Bangkok'
Cc: 'Jodie and Tom'

'Hey Belly, Semi here. Met with Tom and Jodie at huge minis tournament in Hong Kong, filmed a great piece for Rugby Asia Channel. Great couple, please show them the love in Bangkok.

Cheers, Semi'

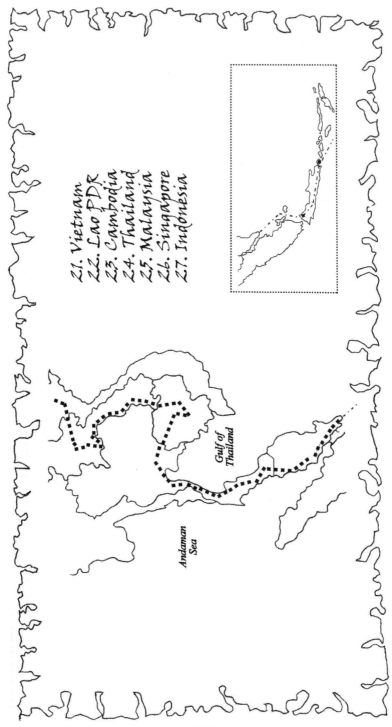

21. Vietnam
22. Lao PDR
23. Cambodia
24. Thailand
25. Malaysia
26. Singapore
27. Indonesia

Gulf of
Thailand

Andaman
Sea

CHAPTER 26
THE DRAGONS' LAIR

Admittedly, much like other parts of the world, I knew very little about mainland South East Asia. Thailand was perhaps the better known of the holiday destinations, home to the 'Bangkok lady-boys', and from watching an off-the-wall documentary on talented animals, also 'Ruby', the famous painting elephant. At first these stories might have seemed unrelated, but on further consideration, I suspected that it wasn't only Ruby's trunk that had raised a few eyebrows.

As we looked first to Vietnam I became hugely excited at the prospect of discovering mainland South East Asian rugby. The problem however, was that we would only be able to cross into each country on a 'single entry visa', meaning that once you left a country, you weren't allowed back. Given that 'Ruby', our elephant friend, had apparently been tasked with drawing up the borders in South East Asia, it meant a challenging few weeks for us to visit all the rugby hubs by bicycle.

Although Saigon RFC had kick started the modern era of Vietnamese rugby in 1992, due to geographical location it sadly looked unfeasible that we could include them on our tour. It was just too far south for us to have U-turned back to Vientiane to visit Maggie in Laos. We searched instead for a rugby presence further north in the country, and to our delight found a side in Hanoi, the 'Dragons', captained by Aussie front rower - Stuart 'Fergo' Ferguson.

After receiving our e-mail, he had extended out a warm invitation for us to come and stay at their lair, and so it came that Hanoi was to be our official gateway into mainland SE Asia.

'I've arranged for a taxi to collect you from the airport,' Fergo had advised, 'I've already paid them so don't hand them any money okay!'

With a short and painless flight from Hong Kong behind us, we both gazed out through the steamy taxi window and watched farmers tending to rice, knee deep in their flooded paddy fields. It looked extremely hard work, and although it reminded us how rural so much of our planet actually was, it hinted that flat, dry camp spots might also be tricky to find.

'We'll worry about that next week,' I said to myself, 'we've got five days with the Dragons first!'

My Wiki-research on Hanoi had taught me that although it had recently celebrated 1,000 years of official existence, the area of Hanoi itself had been inhabited for around 5,000 years. On hearing this, it came as no surprise to find the ancient city had been known by many names over the years, my favourite of which had been 'Long Đỗ ' -

'The Dragon's Belly'. Perhaps by a bizarre coincidence, or through a peculiar sense of destiny, we were welcomed by a man personifying this exact description. It was Fergo himself, the very reincarnation of the 'Long Đỗ'.

Although the Dragons had been born in 1994, just two years after their Saigon rivals, Fergo had captained the side ever since his arrival. He was an English teacher by trade, but with a fanatical passion for rugby running deep through his veins, we could tell immediately that if the Dragons echoed even a smidgin[*] of his enthusiasm, we were in for a very fun five days indeed.

Sitting down with Fergo over a cup of tea, we chatted about the Dragons before being joined by his girlfriend Lauren. If you have ten things to do before you die, cancel the bungee jump and replace it with a visit to Fergo and Lauren. You won't regret it.

'Fergo, there are only two teams in Vietnam aren't there?' I asked, 'So do you play in a league or a cup?' I thought this to be quite amusing seeing as either format would surely produce the same outcome.

'It's a cup mate,' he answered, not thinking it a daft question at all.

'Oh?' I said, 'How does that work then?'

'The main comp is the Indochina Cup, it's a mixture of teams from Thailand, Cambodia, Laos and here.'

'No way! That's pretty cool, is that every year?'

'Yeah mate, it's pretty good fun,' he explained to me, 'we won it last year, so ended up celebrating all night. Didn't stop until the next morning. Then, about half ten, Wicksy our fly half fell into a swimming pool still holding a bottle of champagne. We decided that was probably enough. Didn't go down too well, they were doing swimming lessons at the time.'

Outside of the senior side antics, Fergo is one of the many Dragons to actively promote rugby to the young Vietnamese locals, many of whom now attend the Dragons youth training sessions. Although most of his students show little interest in the sport, he's taken great pleasure in convincing them of his monumental personal achievement - to become the first pregnant male on the planet, a joke that never fails to break down the international culture barrier with the kids.

---

* Author's note: The definition of a 'smidgin' is an old English unit of alcohol most accurately ordered by, 'Just a tiny drop for me please... oh, no... go on, ... a bit more... little bit more... don't be shy now... aaaaaannndddd... stop. Lovely stuff... good lad.'

As expected, it was a full on week in Hanoi, and we were treated to a few good nights out with the Dragons. We even managed to watch a handful of Super Rugby matches thanks to some flexible interpretations of the law, combined with live internet streaming. Fergo and the team were extremely kind hosts and gave us a good, honest insight into Vietnamese rugby.

The real obstacle preventing the development of rugby lay with finding a genuine Vietnamese candidate to recognise the benefits of the sport, and then push for its integration into schools. Until this can happen, it will continue to be viewed as a pastime of the ex-pats and possibly worse, a throw back to the days of French colonial rule. Perhaps some hope for Vietnamese rugby can be found in the success of the French national player, François Trinh-Duc, whose little known heritage goes back to a Vietnamese man named Trịnh Đức Nhiên, his paternal grandfather.

*　　*　　*　　*　　*

'Hey Julien,' I said, hopping down from his moped, 'this is crazy! I love it! Thanks for bringing us here!'

After five days of talk we had finally arrived at 'Chicken Street', a crowd favourite with many of the Dragons, including our French hosts Julien and Sophie. Sophie pulled up next to us with Jodie on the back, and we parked up at the end of the colossal queue of BBQ stalls. Somehow, in the carnage, our French friends had coordinated to meet two further Dragons, as if it were just a casual afternoon in the park. I glanced back down the street to see our entrance had vanished beneath a carpet of bones, claws and greasy sinew. This was a genocide level event, and if I had not known better I would have feared for the survival of the species.

Old haggard women trampled over the piles of carcasses with handfuls of wooden sticks, some containing wings, some the gnarled claws, nails and all. Hundreds of plastic crates lay stacked up alongside the vendors, who each employed a porter to keep the supply stocked, in order to meet the relentless demands. To intensify the heat they pointed handheld fans directly at the coals, and the alley flickered with explosions of flames as oil dripped onto the white hot embers.

'It looks like the road to the underworld,' I whispered to Jodie, who was already desperately trying to capture the moment on her SLR. We piled onto one of the heaving tables, then sat down on tiny plastic chairs, raising us only inches above the rising tide of chicken corpses.

'I'm so glad I didn't wear thongs!' I said to Julien as he laughed at our faces.

'Ah,' he replied, looking down at my shoes, 'I should have mentioned that. Sorry!'

We both laughed, the thought of playing footsie with a thousand dead chickens was a little bit gross.

'What would you like to eat?' he asked.

'What fish do they do?' Jodie responded, as straight faced as she could manage.

'Only what's on the menu,' he chuckled again.

'They have a menu?' we both asked.

'Oui, yes of course,' he answered, 'it is by your feet.'

We both looked down, and fell about laughing. This was already the most unique meal of the trip.

'I'll have whatever doesn't have toes please Julien, other than that, I'm easy,' I declared.

'Okay, I'll order something for us all.'

He shouted over some Vietnamese instructions to the chicken lady, and ten seconds later food arrived on the table - three different types of chicken on a stick, and an odd but agreeable accompaniment of grilled honey glazed bread.

'That's not fast food, that's practically *instant* food!' I said, already reaching for an unidentifiable piece of chicken meat. We destroyed the first tray of chicken, discarding the bones on the floor around us as we did, then ordered another tray.

'Sure you don't want to try a foot?' Julien's friend, Christian, asked us. 'They're very good!'

'I feel like I should,' I said, looking for any excuse not to, 'but it just looks a bit pointless. There's barely any meat on them, and if you think about it, they've spent most their life marinating in chicken poo.'

'It's not that bad,' he laughed, 'you want to hear something really disgusting?'

Christian proceeded to explain a bit about his business role in Vietnam. One particular contract had taken both him, and a female colleague, to a remote village in the north of the country. Their role had been to secure a deal with the local chief that would prove mutually beneficial to both company, and locals. So happy to be doing business with them, the village chief had thrown on a traditional Vietnamese meal, saved for elders and prestigious figures in the community, as the highest sign of respect. As the pair sat with the tribe, two bowls of red soup were brought out and I suspect, not through choice, it was explained to them what was presented to them for dinner.

The below is an exert from the best selling business lunch cookbook 'Vietnamese Deals & Meals',

Hedgehog 'deal clincher' Soup

Ingredients: 1 Hedgehog
Preparation Time: 8 hours

'Take one whole hedgehog, a pestle & mortar, and an old lady with a strong stomach and eight hours on her hands. Have the old lady grind the entire hedgehog into a bloody pulp until prickles, nose and bum hole are no longer separately distinguishable.

Serve at the natural temperature for a hedgehog that's been dead for eight hours.'

'I had to eat two bowls,' he said, 'my colleague couldn't eat it once she knew.'

We both stared at him in a state of shock.

'I have to admit, those chicken feet sound bloody lovely now!'

*   *   *   *   *

Cycling out of Hanoi was not half as bad as people had suggested. In fact, sometimes it almost felt easier cycling in these cities than it would have driving a car. We were going slow by design, everyone else was going slow by necessity, therefore it could be considered that the ball was in our court.

If you got to a roundabout and stopped to wait for a gap, the likeliness is that the world would stop spinning long before the circle of traffic ever did. The best option was to have a quick look, but more importantly to smile as you swung out. If you looked someone in the eye, not only were they thrilled to see two 'tays' (westerners) riding heavily laden bicycles, but they'd be more than happy to have the privilege of letting you out.

The alternative was a local method which still involved pulling out into heavy traffic, but just not the looking. It might sound dangerous, but if everyone else had seen you pull out without looking, they knew that it was now in *their* hands to avoid a collision. In our time in Vietnam, we saw very few incidents.

In my waterproof case we carried a generic map of South East Asia, covering our entire journey from Hanoi down to Singapore. A map this small was no use for specific roads, but we could use town names and the compass to loosely guide us. For the next two months, we could hope to progress about four centimetres of print each day.

We also carried a paper napkin on which we had scribbled down directions to find the correct road out of Hanoi - we weren't taking the usual route down to the south of the country, but wanted to cross over to Laos via a more remote mountain crossing, predominantly used by locals.

That day, we felt just a tinge of nerves, having had three weeks off the saddle, it occurred to us that we'd begun to slip out of our 'road mentality'. 'Road mentality' could be best described as a state of mind where you biologically separated your brain from your decision making process. Whether you were cycling along the inner lane of a motorway, or about to throw your tent up under a bridge in the middle of town, 'road mentality' helped mute any sensible advice your brain was trying to offer. Everything that you had learned about self-preservation and responsibility had to be replaced with a firm belief in 'c'est la vie' (the French for 'shit happens').

While I'm on the topic, I ought to point out that 'road mentality' was only beneficial in areas of heavy civilisation, once we got back to rural or country areas, it paid to switch back on and take matters into our own hands again.

I guess at one point in time, most of us have driven out to the hills and thrown up a tent, intent on enjoying the thrills of the outdoors. You normally cook a crap meal, but enjoy it because you managed to heat it without using a microwave oven - primitive entertainment but one of life's simple pleasures. It then starts to drizzle, and so you go to bed six hours earlier than usual because it's cold outside, and you remember that without TV and beer, evenings are actually pretty bloody boring. That's all good, and so long as there are no werewolves or landslides you'll probably live to face another day, either way it 'feels right' to do such a thing, just like it does returning to civilisation and finding all of life's comforts back inside your four walls.

The polar opposite of this feeling is to arrive at a city in the early evening, knowing that you don't have enough daylight hours to traverse it. There are thousands of people hurtling around on mopeds, cars, buses and trucks, and so before it gets too late, you try to find a hidden alley, underpass or deserted building to bed down for the night.

Some cities will never sleep, with locals shopping at the night market, or socialising with friends away from the stifling daytime humidity. Often you will find a place you believe is hidden, and once you have packed down your panniers into the tent, you will be approached by the usual men that wander dark alleys at night.

On countless occasions we've had to appraise the situation in just a few seconds, before asking each other the question, 'Should we move?'. Thankfully, we had always been able to fall back on 'road mentality' - it'll probably be fine, and even if it's not, the only other option is to throw in the towel and blow your budget on hotel rooms.

So into the hills we headed, and our new purchases were immediately called into action. If you are considering your own tight-budget bicycle tour, rather than buying expensive western equipment, we'd recommend using whatever the local people use to deal with the conditions. In Vietnam, this meant buying $3 'moped ponchos', available in four funky colours.

The nice thing about 'moped ponchos' was that in addition to your own built-in waterproof hat, there was a hole for a second rider to sit behind you, a little like a waterproof Chinese Dragon costume. The extra hole didn't serve much use for us on the road, but it did provide us with a bit of entertainment that evening, performing our own four legged conga dance around the tent.

That same night, camped in a lay-by high in the hills, a mighty thunderstorm swept across the country. Giant claps of thunder echoed all around us as torrents of howling rain beat down on our thin tent.

'Do you think we're safe?' Jodie asked. It was normally me that was worried about lightning, maybe a genetic instinct that all tall people have.

'I have no idea,' I replied.

We'd been caught in a few lightning storms, sometimes inside forests, sometimes in open fields. Often we'd be on high ground, adding to the fear, but in reality when you were trying to sleep inside a small metal frame, lightning belting down all around you, talking about the laws of averages rarely made you feel safe.

'It might not be as close as you think,' I offered, 'you have to count in-between the lightning and thunder to see.'

FLASH!

My 'one' was cut short by a loud BANG! followed by the sizzle of evaporating tree sap, then a secondary thud.

'Okay, I think the storm is pretty close,' I concluded, burying my head into my pillow of spare underwear, socks and a rugby jersey, 'but don't forget the laws of averages.'

The only time that I had ever insisted on moving during a lightning storm was in Turkey where we had camped adjacent to a lighthouse, built on a pier about three hundred metres out at sea. In the middle of the night, I had got out and slid the tent a clear twenty metres from the building, not knowing whether it would make an ounce of difference or not. We didn't die that night so maybe it had, who knows.

It was still raining the next morning, and reluctantly we dragged ourselves back out of the tent to push on over the hill. At the first corner, a giant branch lay blocking the narrow road. I turned around and looked back at our camp spot, it was about forty metres away.

'I suppose it makes sense really,' I pondered, 'the laws of averages I mean. I wonder how many surfers have come within forty metres of a shark?'

People love to say things like, 'Dude, the odds of getting eaten are like, a thousand to one!', but I've always wondered one thing. If I handed them a gun with a thousand round chamber, then told them there was just a single bullet in it, would they put the gun to their head and pull the trigger? Most surfers probably would, and I guess that's what separates them from me. Raw courage, and not having to live with half their body weight in their girly backside.

Whether it was that night's thunderstorm, the rain, or just that I was now noticing things going wrong, but my bike seemed to have developed a problem in the rear axel, a slow grinding feeling each time I turned the pedal. I had never explored the inner mechanics of a bicycle wheel, but despite that, I believed that inside there would be something called bearings.

I suspected this because a few years before, my car had developed an awful 'shearing' sound when I drove around gentle right corners. I showed this fault to my friends, who, after an unusually mature discussion down the pub, had come to the unanimous decision that it was a problem with my bearings. They assured me that bearings were simple things to replace, but I shouldn't let them get too worn, or it might cause further damage to the cylinder.

Thankfully the conversation quickly returned to girls' bottoms and the evening wasn't a complete write off. Several pints and a sambuca later, and the only thing I took home from that evening was a doner kebab wrapper. Three years later the shearing sound had completely vanished, and so I assumed that given enough time bearings could slowly heal themselves.

'I think it's the bearings,' I stated quite profoundly.

Jodie looked at me with a mixture of suspicion and admiration. It was a special type of 'transition' look that only women could pull off, a look that could go two ways. This look implied, 'Go on, you may have impressed me, but you might still be the idiot I believe you to be.' I know this because I myself had tried that look, when Layth at work had announced he'd been down to the gym at lunchtime.

'Did you hear what I said?' he'd asked, as I'd sat staring at him across the desk.

'I thought you were going to continue,' I'd explained, 'like you ran a marathon or it was closed or something?'

He'd stopped shuffling papers and locked me in a stare of his own, maybe I had upset him.

'Why would I tell you I went down the gym if it was closed?'

'I don't know,' I'd said quite slowly, suddenly remembering why speaking, then thinking, was often the wrong order to do things, 'but just to clear up any confusion, does that mean you *wouldn't* tell us if the gym was closed...?'

'The bearings,' I modestly explained, 'are small spherical things, that rotate in the wheel like so.'

I made a twisting motion of my fist inside my palm. The motion in no way represented how a bearing might operate, although if they were indeed operating like that, it might explain the sound coming from my wheel. Nevertheless, after two further and equally poor demonstrations, I had managed to convince Jodie that I was on top of the situation and would get it addressed at the next bike shop.

'It isn't a problem,' I finished, 'but I should get them fixed before I do any further damage to the cylinder.'

Later that afternoon we came into a small town a day or so from the border. In the main street was a shop selling children's bicycles and small tropical birds in cages. I took off my rear wheel and walked in to investigate.

Inside, the lady smiled and gestured to a yellow bird hanging from the ceiling. I looked up and nodded.

'What a lovely bird,' I said.

She reached for a stick leaning against the wall, it had a tiny hook at the far end. She was about to try and sell me a budgie.

'No, no bird,' I said, 'bicycle problem, you fix?'

She squinted at the wheel before shaking her head. I looked around at the walls, there were a few spare tyres, bicycle pumps, bells and budgie food.

'Okay, thank you!' I said, as I walked back towards the door.

'Mister, one moment!' she suddenly called back, she was now on the phone. She said a few words that all sounded the same, then put the phone down and gave me a sign to wait five minutes. We did. Two minutes later, two younger boys in their teens arrived on a moped and came to us.

'You need fix?' one boy said to me, pointing at the wheel.

'Yes!' I smiled, 'Let me show you.'

With the help of Jodie's freakish vocal ability, we showed the movement that caused the problem, and the sound it was making on the bicycle. I drew a small picture of the bearings and showed them that we needed new ones. They nodded their heads in agreement and took the wheel.

'Ten moments!' the first boy said, as they hopped onto their moped and whisked away.

'There you go Jo, easy as that. It'll all be done in ten moments.'

Jodie, ever the sceptic, remained less convinced. She'd spent ten years in London, working in financial compliance, which in short, was a team with the role of cutting through layers of bullshit to determine whether the underlying intentions were honourable. I had come from an alternative environment, one where nothing I ever did seemed to make the slightest fucking difference. It certainly led to an interesting split of opinion when it came to these matters.

'We'll see,' is all she needed to say.

The boys returned on their moped with the wheel, and a hand scribbled docket.

'Excellent!' I said as I got my wheel back. Jodie had planted a few seeds of doubt ten minutes ago, but now all seemed well. They handed me the docket with several lines of scrawled Vietnamese, besides each of which was a price, in US Dollars, not Dong. The total had been summed to $58, a quite exact price although it seemed extraordinarily expensive for such a little town. Normally these sorts of works would not cost more than $3-4 at tops.

'Hang on a minute,' Jodie said, as she spun the wheel, 'it's not even fixed!'

I tried the wheel too, and there was no noticeable difference from before. Had they even taken the wheel apart? We went through the whole routine again, this time the two boys appeared to understand the manner of the problem.

'Ten moments!' they said as they whisked away on the moped again.

'We have to follow them,' Jodie insisted, 'this is *not* right!'

This time I didn't argue, and we ran after them, flip-flopping down the street in our sandals. They turned down the adjacent alleyway, and only for a heavy crowd of market dwellers were we able to keep them in our sights until the next junction. We snaked around one turning, then another, before we came to a busy cross roads, but we had lost them.

'Did you see which way they went?' I asked, knowing that if either of us had seen over the crowd it was me.

'I lost sight of them in this road,' Jodie said a little panicked.

I crossed the road and looked down the street ahead of us, the boys would be long gone, and this town was now a thick maze of avenues and alleyways.

'I think we've lost them,' I called across to Jodie, who it seemed was now edging her way along the street opposite me.

'Wait, hang on... there! I see them!' she called back, and I sprinted across the road. Somehow, in amongst the hundreds of parked mopeds, she had picked out the exact one the boys had been riding.

We marched up to the open garage door.

'Hello,' I said, as the boys looked up in horror, 'I thought you might like some help.'

The first boy had the docket in his hand, and was making adjustments with a ballpoint pen. Inside the empty concrete garage was a solitary chair in which sat a very old man. A half smoked cigarette hung from his mouth, and beneath him on the floor were his tools, three screwdrivers.

'He hasn't done any work to the wheel!' I thought to myself, but there was no way I was going to let him start now, not with screw drivers. If anyone was going to mangle my equipment it was me, and I'd do it for free.

'Where is your tool to open the wheel?' I asked the boys who were shrugging at the same time. They thrust the wheel to the old man, and he quickly picked up a screw driver.

'No, no, no,' I stated clearly, '*bicycle* tool?' and I pointed to the shape of the fitting.

They seemed out of ideas, and with the ball temporarily back in our court we grabbed back the wheel and made speedily off through the market.

'You have to be so careful don't you,' Jodie said, 'I've been to Vietnam three times and it's always the same here. You'll find Laos much easier.'

'I bloody hope so,' I said, 'otherwise these bearings will have to heal themselves too.'

*   *   *   *   *

In the event of closed roads, detours or anything out of the ordinary, we had written down a few town names to keep us on track. A previous road sign had indicated 10 km to Mai Chau, a small town on our route to the border. At a subsequent branch in the road, one sign had been knocked so that it pointed about halfway between both paths. One went down into a small village, another went high into the hills. A big part of us sensibly suggested that at some point we would inevitably need to climb hills, but a more persuasive part of us said, 'Why climb hills when we don't need to?'

When one young boy on a bicycle insisted that the lower road led to Mai Chau, we both conveniently took the opportunity to believe him. He pedalled down the road ahead of us and watched us ride past from his family's driveway. When we had taken the decision to cycle his way, he'd squealed like a hyena, and must have called his family to come out and watch us. We waved back but after ten kilometres of pedalling through farmland and villages, we began to suspect the intent of his directions.

Common sense indicated that at some point, we would be able to circumnavigate the hill range, and approach it from a different side, but not knowing how long the journey would take, we were being constantly bugged by the ever growing distance should we have to turn around. Knowing that each additional hour of pedalling was only adding to our time in Vietnam, our spirits grew weaker and we were soon pushing up over steep gradients with no exact knowledge of our location.

We checked the compass, we were heading north, and we needed southwest. Although we reminded ourselves that you couldn't rely on the compass on weaving roads, it was still a horrible situation, made worse that another poor encounter with a Vietnamese local had further soured our opinion of the country. In Hanoi, we had come across several aggressive confrontations with taxi drivers, and only a day after our fiasco with the opportunist bicycle mechanics, we had finally been sent in the wrong direction by a ten year old for his family's entertainment.

After six long hours, and a detour of an additional 65 km through the hills, we finally approached our town from the other side. Thankfully, on priceless advice from Julien and Sophie, we were at least able to unwind in a $3 homestay with a home cooked meal to boot.

By now, we longed to reach Maggie and the team in Laos. Three days into our South East Asian cycle, the novelty of the rain had long since worn off, and it was becoming increasingly difficult to keep on the right road. Very few of the junctions had any road signs, and we had regularly become disorientated by the winding hills.

There was a substantial river running through a valley, acting as a landmark, but soon it was joined by many others and it became a lottery as to which single path lead to the border village of Na Meo. Never before had we been so frustrated by the lack of signs, and we made several mistakes, each adding hours to our journey. After what felt like an eternity of detours and pushing, with some kind help from locals, we were finally set on the correct road to leave Vietnam and continue our rugby exploration of South East Asia.

CHAPTER 27
LITTLE BLOSSOMS

To my disappointment, there was very little to celebrate about our new landscape. The fields were still under a foot of water, the slopes were still windy and steep, and if anything, the roads were a little more broken than they had been in Vietnam. What had changed was the new cheery culture, and even the Laos greeting forced your cheeks into a fitting smile.

'Sabai Dee!' the screaming kids called to us from across the adjacent fields.

'Sabai Dee little Lao dudes,' we called back, much to their obvious delight.

The youngsters were like sharks, pouring out of the fields to chase us, apparently sensing our presence from many miles away. In stark contrast, when we passed through the farming villages, we noticed a rather inverted pace of life.

Up on the porches of stilted wooden huts, adolescent young males swung lazily on their hammocks, forcing their tired arms into a slight raise of acknowledgement as we rode past. Beneath them, in the communal areas, groups of women sat idly chatting around steaming bamboo baskets of sticky rice, all highly entertained by our arrival. This however was clearly still too much for the men, who judging by their absence, were probably still fast asleep in their beds. It was a fair analysis to describe the Laos culture as a nation of surfers without a coastline.

We pushed on into the winding hill roads, climbing for hours, then losing it all in minutes. As fatigued as we became, we realised that it wasn't only us struggling to deal with the conditions. Small buses carrying the locals regularly overtook us, only to screech to a standstill at the nearest clearing. Waves of green looking Lao families poured off the bus, hurling projectile vomit onto the grassy banks. Judging by the bus windows, and the stains on their shirts, they hadn't always managed to wait for the stops.

Finally arriving in our first proper town, Sam Noua, I took the opportunity to assess my increasingly noisy bicycle wheel, and make an educated call on the most sensible course of action.

'Tom, I really don't think you should be doing that!' Jodie issued a token piece of advice.

After doing what every man would do in such a circumstance, I took my bicycle tool and started to unscrew parts at random. In just three minutes, I had pleasingly managed to make several pieces fall to the ground, either side of my wheel.

'See, I told you that warning was a waste of time,' I announced, glancing back at the advice around the hub - 'Do not open unless properly trained.'

I stared down at the six parts in my hand and wondered why I still hadn't found any bearings. There was one serious looking locking nut still left, an irresistible challenge.

'It's jammed!' I said, putting all my weight into the wheel and tool.

'Tom, I really don't have a good feeling about this! Maybe you should put it back together and we'll get proper help.'

Without the right tool I realised that I was fighting a losing battle, and after another minute's more force I conceded defeat. It took another three hours before I finally managed to align the parts so that the wheel could actually spin again. I sank back onto the bench, wiped away my sweat, and felt a huge sense of relief that the wheel only sounded marginally worse than it had done before.

'It's not my fault!' I defended my actions to Jodie, 'The notice was the wrong way round.'

'But it told you not to open it!' she scolded me anyway.

'Well, it should have said, don't *put together* unless properly trained. Opening it was easy!'

Having lost over three hours of pedalling already, like most things, we decided to take it as a sign. The town boasted a large food market, and if we checked into a cheap guesthouse, we knew we could spend the remaining afternoon taking in some of the sights and soaking up the culture. Agreeing five dollars for a room with a cold tap seemed like a bargain, so we cheered our good fortune, dumped our gear, and made our way down to the main attraction.

Under a huge steel roof, long lines of connecting tables had transformed into stalls for scores of local market vendors. Fishermen proudly displayed their 'catch of the day' from muddy streams, while tiny women tended to their shimmering piles of fruit and vegetables. The market had a great sense of energy, and if they weren't spraying their fruit or fanning flies away from their produce, they were straightening the line of dead rats that lay tidily in their display.

'It's the Rat-o-meter!' I motioned to Jodie, 'Look, that stall's a champion grocer!'

'I think these ones are for sale Tom!' she laughed.

The presence of rats in amongst the fruit and vegetables in some ways at least prepared us for the meat stalls. On large wooden boards lay the carcasses of several different beasts, in many varying states of butchery. Some animals had been more popular than others, and many were now unrecognizable. Everything that could be cut off and sold seemed to do so, and as such, very little went to waste. Now at the end of the day, only the heads of the dog and donkey were left, presumably not a local favourite for boiling into stock.

'I know they're making the most of what they have,' Jodie said, 'but I just couldn't eat dog. Could you?'

I looked down at his gnarled little face.

'Not at that price Jo! It's way over budget!'

Instead, I treated myself to a one dollar pre-prepared chilli noodle dish. The cling film had kept off most of the flies, and the lady seemed very happy to be doing business with me. Initially very happy with my choice, I began to have second thoughts when I picked up the scent of a BBQ across the street. Deciding that a sausage or two would be the perfect accompaniment to my noodles, I begged Jodie to join me and take a look. A big fan of BBQs herself, we strolled over to investigate and peered through the crowd. Although there was no board we could identify that we had two options; a kebab of donkey offal, or a whole barbecued rat, presumably cooked midway through a press up. Judging by his face, he'd been holding that position for some time.

'I'm good with my noodles Jo,' I decided quite quickly, 'what are you having for dinner?'

'I might go and see if he's got any of that dog meat left.'

Maybe it was the distraction of my relentless squeaking, or maybe I had just taken my eye off the kit maintenance, but Jodie's brake pads had now worn thinner than Bilal Butt's little toenail. Having cycled over 17,500 km, rather than check the equipment more thoroughly, my irregular inspections had now been reduced to a gentle tap of each tyre with my foot.

During yet another relentless procession of steep gradients, the hilly mist finally eroded the last of Jodie's brake pads, and she began to hurtle uncontrollably down the hill.

'Use your feet!' I screamed at her, as I released my own brakes to try to catch up.

By now, Jodie was gambling on no oncoming traffic and taking each corner in the line of a Formula 1 driver. Down to her right was a steep bank into the forest, and to her left, an unforgiving rocky cliff face. For what seemed like an eternity she ploughed ahead, slamming down both feet as best she could, and hoping to stay on the road. Eventually, the road settled into a shallow enough gradient for her to finally bring her terrifying slalom to a finish.

I knew how she had felt, and I had suffered the same problem on an icy pass in Korea, but to see Jodie so helpless in front of me was the worst feeling of my life. I dropped my bike and rushed to her, giving her the biggest hug since she had bought me a drinking helmet for my day out at Twickenham.

Whereas Jodie's bicycle was clearly showing signs of wear and tear, my bicycle was now several weeks past that stage. It didn't last much longer, and as we finally pulled our way through the hills, my wheel rim split wide open for a second time, leaving us stranded in the drizzle, a clear ten hour walk to the capital.

Faced with two miserable choices and wet to the core, we pushed for a couple more hours before finally throwing our gear onto the projectile vomit bus.

*　　*　　*　　*　　*

Although Chris Mestaglio, stand off and all round Lao rugby superstar was away at the Hong Kong 7s, it was business as usual as we wheeled up to the Lao Rugby Federation (LRF) office.

'Congratulations guys! You made it!' welcomed Megan, our beautiful American host, as she invited us into the colourful room.

Megan Knight was originally from Colorado and had chosen to explore Asia after completing her studies. Having worked for US Rugby back home, she had not lasted long in Central Vietnam before becoming frustrated at the lack of rugby activity. When the opportunity arose to lend her skills to the LRF, she had not hesitated.

Being something of a language guru she had picked up comfortable Laotian in only a few months. This not only helped her communicate with her girls at the Lions RFC, but also shout instructions when assisting to coach the men's national team. Many unions would have fallen over backwards to have got Megan, but after seeing the leggy blonde in a pair of rugby shorts we doubt they'd have been solely interested in her coaching skills.

Although meeting with Megan, it had been another girl, and yet another American, that had first extended a warm invitation so many thousand kilometres ago. Maggie Dillon, from Detroit, was now only nine months into her contract as Operations Manager for the LRF, and like Megan, had already picked up a solid fluency in the language. Maggie had kept a close ear to the rugby ground ever since arriving, and was always looking for new ways to get the word out on the street.

'I can't believe you're actually here!' smiled Maggie, as we finally met face to face.

'There are so many things to show you this week,' Megan announced, as she grabbed a timetable from Maggie's desk.

Although we had only just arrived, our five day schedule was already crammed. In addition to meeting the local clubs and national team, we had three visits to 'Champa Ban' sessions, and an inaugural sevens match at the local drug rehabilitation centre - one of their outreach venues.

'Hey girls, I need you to do me a favour,' I asked, though perhaps without appropriate phrasing.

'Sure what do you need?' Maggie replied.

'If possible, I need you to suggest a local born representative for the World in Union scroll. Someone who you regard as integral to the Lao rugby culture.'

'Noui!' they both agreed in excitement, 'She is the captain of the national team, she coaches, she deals with the press, organises the marketing, the media, she... '

'What if it had to be a man?' I interrupted, before they started listing her super powers. It was like I'd walked in on the Spice Girls.

'Oh, we'll have to think about that. Can we let you know?'

'Sure, no problems,' I breathed a sigh of relief, after all, I'd nearly been asked to put a girl on the scroll.

As we unpacked our panniers in Megan's spare room, Jodie chose to open a rather familiar line of conversation.

'Tom, I was just wondering,' she threw out casually into the air.

I froze. Never in the history of mankind has a girl ever 'wondered' about anything. 'Wonder' was just another way of saying, 'I want something, and I'm going to phrase it in a way that you'll get it for me'. A bit like when Eve 'wondered' what an apple might taste like.

Megan's room only had the one door, and while I suspect it constituted a fire hazard, I was rather more immediately concerned that Jodie now stood blocking my quick exit strategy.

'Why does it have to be just men signing the scroll?' she finally revealed what she had been wondering all this time.

'Because it's a *man's* Rugby World Cup!' I explained, 'The girls played a few months ago.'

'Yes, I know that, but what about what the tournament stands for? Shouldn't you be delivering the person who contributes the most to that country's rugby culture?'

It sounded like a valid enough point, but all of Jodie's points sounded that way. You couldn't live your life listening to *every* solid argument your girlfriend made, or nothing would get done as you intended.

'It has to be a man because... well... it should be a man because... oh shit!'

'Can I take that as - it should be a man because there's no good reason?'

We both realised that she could indeed.

'Oh no, now I feel really bad, I just never considered it before. I know, we'll bring the scroll back to the office tomorrow and ask Noui. She can be the first girl to sign it!'

'That's okay Tom, being sexist isn't your worst fault.'

'Good, as long as you promise me that's true, then I completely agree, Noui should absolutely be our legend.'

'Tom, I promise you that it's true!'

To get to know Noui a little better, we accompanied her on one of her 'Champa Ban' trips. 'Champa Ban' meaning 'Little Blossom', was a flagship programme heavily pushed by Maggie and the team to bring the benefits of team rugby into the poorer outreach areas around the capital. With no federation transport available, Jodie and I were left to hang onto the back of two mopeds, while we clutched a bag of balls, cones and training bibs.

The road was horrendous, and if my leather saddle hadn't already given me odd shaped balls, the two hour moped ride certainly did. Even though it would have taken two days, I seriously considered walking the 80 km back.

What impressed me most about Noui's session, was not the accurate passing and careful hands displayed by the kids, but the equal level of interest shown between both boys and girls. Half of the children played in school uniform, most in bare feet, but out in this isolated stony paddock we had stumbled upon the textbook mixed rugby session. The kids adored Noui and in return, she took a passionate and genuine interest in each one of their developments, nobody was excluded and everyone smiled. The 'Spice Girls' had been correct, she really was the perfect role model, and we were proud to ask her to be the first woman on the scroll.

I don't know if it was the fun of the session, or just the fear of the moped, but either way it was all over too soon. We took a group photo with the smiling kids, and before I could say 'pothole', I was once again holding a bag of balls and left clinging onto my space hoppers.

Having cycled through many Lao villages en-route to Vientiane, we had learnt enough about Lao motivation not to be fooled. The children at Champa Ban may have been fuelled by Noui's spirit, but we suspected the men's national team would be another thing entirely.

To further promote the sport, Maggie had organised a national fitness training session at Patuxia, or Victory Gate, a local version of Paris' Arc de Triomphe in the middle of the city. It was a prime tourist area, and the natural curiosity of Asian culture meant that many people would begin to chat about what they had seen.

Having to operate with such a low budget, Maggie used many alternative strategies to get the word out there, like convincing the local pizza chain to rebrand their 'Calzone' pizza to the 'Rugby' pizza, due to its shape. To our amusement, our presence at training further captured the public interest. Upon seeing two westerners snapping away at the group, dozens of locals whipped out their cameras in an effort to capture a group of people who 'might possibly be famous'.

An ex-military English coach, Ian Melhuish, dispatched the boys around the huge square for two warm up laps. The sun was shining brightly and admittedly it was still a little on the hot side. A couple of the more athletic boys made good time, completing the circuits after six or seven minutes, but most struggled back to the huge colonial arch many minutes later. When the loose-head prop returned fifteen minutes later with an ice cream, Ian tried not to laugh and instead punished everyone with press-ups. As I understood no Laotian, it was difficult to know whether they were complaining about the press-ups, or that he wouldn't let the whole team get an ice cream.

Having watched the reluctant fitness session, I finally understood why the Lao Rugby Federation relied so heavily on women, it was the only way anything would get done in this country.

*   *   *   *   *

As we sat sipping our cocktails staring out to the Mekong River, we thought back over our five days and remarked at how much we had uncovered. Thanks to the fantastic team at the Lao Rugby Federation, we had managed to get round to visiting everyone in the rugby scene. Not only had we trained with the Buffalos, the Hogs and the Lions, we had witnessed a historical and thrilling sevens match at the drug rehabilitation centre, several 'Little Blossom' sessions and seen the national boys and girls at work.

'Sorry about all the bugs,' Maggie apologised as if she'd brought them along herself.

Outside the bar, millions of moths were collecting in thick clouds and literally blocking all street light to the entrance.

'That's why we do all our training during daylight this time of year!'

'It's crazy!' I laughed, looking out at the eerie sight.

'Although, when we *have* done evening sessions, we usually notice a better attendance from the locals.'

'Oh, why's that Maggie?' Jodie's curious little brain ticked away.

'Because the locals bring along their nets and eat them,' she answered, shuddering at the thought.

Oddly, as we looked across the river, we could see the lights of Thailand reflecting in the calm water. No matter how close they may have seemed, we knew that first we had a long ride south, heading for Phnom Penh where we would explore rugby with Laos' 'Mekong Cup' opponents, Cambodia.

CHAPTER 28
PICH OF THE BUNCH

Although most advice had been to pay for a ferry transfer into Cambodia, we decided instead to explore the border road described by one round the world cyclist as 'the worst he'd ever cycled on.' It wasn't in our budget, or morals, to pay for unnecessary transport, and even if it took all day, we knew we'd make it to the nearest town, Stung Treng by dark.

Sadly, there were many tears at the border, and whereas Jodie's had been to avoid the fraudulent two dollar exit charge, mine had been real from nearly severing my big toe in a cycling accident.

Since Hanoi, we had consciously decided to cycle in open topped sandals, most importantly to reduce the odour of sweaty feet in the tent, but also because it enabled us to keep our only pair of shoes dry during the regular showers. One of my front panniers had developed an annoying habit of bouncing backwards off my rack, at regular intervals during the day. For thousands of kilometres, I had refused to pull over safely, opting instead to push it back on with an outstretched foot. I must have saved myself entire minutes over the course of a year.

As we approached the border, not only was I about to end my time in Laos, but I was also about to end my usage of this technique. As I stretched out for one final time, my foot slipped on the rack and wedged itself between the spinning wheel spokes and my pannier. In agony, I tried desperately to brake using a more conventional method, but in wedging my foot, I had also served to lock my steering ability. Finally, bringing down my cruising speed of 20 k.p.h to zero with a painful cry, I collapsed from my bicycle onto the red dust below.

My foot was in torture and with panic immediately setting in, I fully expected to look down at a missing digit lying somewhere in the dust. Thankfully it wasn't missing at all, in fact it had actually doubled in size, and turned African. It was the sort of pain that very nearly put me off my food for weeks.

Jodie had vowed never to concede to corrupt border officials, and would sometimes dig deeper than a coalminer looking for sufficient tears to allow justice to prevail. For fear of drowning, the Lao border guard finally gave in, and as we walked across no-man's land to the Cambodian officials I congratulated Jodie for once again playing the part of 'girl in distress'. While I insisted several times that I really hadn't been acting, she congratulated me on my 'intellectually challenged' performance, and I was happy for the compliment.

'One dollar each!' the Cambodian man smiled, moving our passports and his stamp out of reach.

Jodie collected herself, then searched inside for one last tear. She was all cried out.

'Fine, seems fair enough,' she said, pulling out two dollar bills that hadn't existed five seconds ago. Across the border, I turned to see the Lao guard yelling and jumping up and down on his hat.

'But *you* are going to give me a Cambodian lesson!' she instructed, in her fair but firm instructor voice. It remained the one and *only* time that Jodie ever agreed to an illegal charge.

Satisfied that she'd received two dollars worth of value, we packed away our passports and prepared ourselves for the 'worst road in the world.'

'It's not that bad is it?' I joked, realising as we coasted along the smooth tarmac that it must have been recently laid.

Whilst the road surface was good, as expected with no history of regular traffic, there wasn't a single shop, house or even signpost for 50 km. Realising this in the early afternoon, we decided to make use of the only structure we had seen since crossing the border. Across a field was a simple farmer's shelter, a raised wooden platform with a roof.

Having received Jodie's history lesson about the Khmer Rouge, I was now paranoid about landmines in these rural areas, and although I knew most had been cleared in the crowded parts, I didn't much fancy pushing the bicycle off a road that had only just been laid. At my insistence, we tiptoed along a line of cow prints into the field, then cut a direct angle for the shelter. There were no obvious signs of craters or animal remains, and unless a spiteful cow had actually buried a landmine, I had to guess that the odds were on our side.

With such a nice new road laid for us, the remainder of the day was for once, much easier than we had allowed for. We arrived at Stung Treng in plenty of time, checked into a nice basic five dollar hostel overlooking the river, and perched ourselves outside to watch the world go by while cooking our noodles.

Being one of only two hostels in town, it wasn't that unusual to see two French people turn up minutes later, but what did grab my attention was their lovely shining white tandem bicycle.

'Gorrrr! Look at that bicycle Jo!' I stood and pointed as the couple pulled up beside us, 'That's brilliant!'

Ever since Jodie had suggested cycling across the world, I had tried my hardest to make it happen on a tandem. Less traction meant less effort, and if I got to sit at the back I could finally achieve my dream of doing exercise while partially asleep. Jodie insisted that she didn't want my backside to block her view of the world, and didn't trust me enough to let her backside block mine.

As it turned out, our new French friends had been half an hour in front of us all day, only coming off the road before us to most typically get naked and have a wash in the river. As we sat down together, conversation quickly came round to the border crossing earlier that day.

'Did you have to pay at the Laos border to leave the country?' Gregoire asked innocently, having recently landed with their bicycle from South America.

'No, Jodie told them we weren't going to pay Gregoire,' I explained.

'Oh? What about the doctor?' he asked again.

'What doctor?' Jodie exclaimed, nearly choking on her noodles.

'The ear doctor?' he hesitated.

'We didn't think it seemed very professional,' Sybille cut in as she leaned back and elegantly smoked her cigarette, 'they just pointed a thermometer gun near to our ear and charged us five dollars. We didn't know what to do.'

'Right, here's what you do next time,' I explained, 'Sybille, you have to cry, and Gregoire, you just act casual.'

'Look like you're intellectually challenged Gregoire,' Jodie laughed.

'Hey! I wasn't doing that!'

The following morning we packed up ready to leave, but tried our luck once more at changing the one hundred dollar bill that we had picked up in Islamabad. I remained adamant that it was real, but was apparently in the minority of people in South East Asia that shared this opinion. We took a shower, put on our smartest non-cycling outfits, and walked round to the bank as a model British couple.

On the fourteenth exchange attempt it was passed between several hands, under magnifying scopes, held under ultra violet lights before finally a huge stack of Riels were pushed in our direction. We walked hand in hand, slowly away from the CCTV cameras, turned a corner and ran skipping back to the hostel like we had just won the lottery. This was easily enough money to last until Thailand.

Although I have always maintained that the worst decisions are made when you're either hungry, or really need a wee, I was later forced to add 'winning the lottery' to that list. Overcome with the success of finally shifting the Pakistani note, we opted for the more scenic winding river road over the main inland route. We could see it was nothing more than a thin black line on our map, but the traffic on the dusty track was busy enough to suggest it led through to our next town, Kratie.

The road deteriorated quite fast, and although the traffic was still steady, we began to suspect things were not quite right as we crossed more and more small bridges.

When we arrived at the first of three fallen bridges, we should have cut our losses, but seeing the dried channel river bed, we instead chose to follow the locals' lead, and push down and up the bank. Many hours later, long after the traffic had evaporated, we were being fuelled more by hope than brain cells. Sadly, both ran out at the same time, when the road disappeared into a small rabbit burrow.

We were completely lost and to make matters worse, another bridgeless river now indicated our only choice was to swim or turn back. We turned and pedalled back past the amused faces of several small villages, before eventually gambling on an inland dirt track - the only junction option we had seen all day. After another two hour cross country effort, we finally clawed ourselves back to the main road, only to find that we were barely 40 km outside Stung Treng. We had pedalled over 90 km already, in seven long, hot, stressful hours, and if we'd only have taken the main road, we'd have done it in two. We were now seriously low on spirits, and even lower on water.

Where there was no clean flowing water, the locals stored their own water supplies in huge ceramic pots, refilled by passing water trucks.

'I think we'll wait until we get to the next town,' I suggested, as I looked down at our only water source. Beneath us, down the dusty bank, was a large reservoir of brown water, home to a herd of buffalo happily bathing away insects and farting.

Jodie jumped off her bicycle to snap the jacuzzi dwellers in action, but as she did, a passing water truck pulled over in front of us. A man jumped out from the cab and unravelled a tube from the rear engine.

'Oh, they're not!' I said. But they were.

Fuelled by our buffalo bath water, we powered down towards the capital, only for the road to disintegrate once more. This time, the passing lorries and trucks were enough to encourage us onwards, but after several hours the choking red dust began to stain our clothes, our skin and even our teeth.

Sleeping at night had already become an intolerably difficult thing to achieve in the humid March weather. We were not able to detach our thick outer tent layer, and to make matters worse, we then had to zip tight our inner bug layer, blocking off any hope of a passing breeze. Evenings were spent slipping and sliding off our sweaty ground mats, drying our damp faces, and wishing that the relentless Cambodians would electrocute themselves on their karaoke machines.

'I'm not going to bed like this!' I insisted, staring at my red body as we set up camp, 'It will turn to paint!'

With a quick glance around, we left our bicycles up on the bank and climbed down to the tempting sight of the Mekong. We had found the perfect spot, and as we bathed luxuriously for an hour in the gentle shallow waters, a year of dead skin was sucked off our bodies by a thousand tiny fish.

It was the first time we had truly 'skinny dipped' on the whole trip, and it will go down as one of our most unexpected pleasurable experiences, despite being selective over the areas I allowed to have cleaned.

*   *   *   *   *

In the 1970s, Cambodia had fallen under the rule of the 'Khmer Rouge', a regime engineered by Pol Pot to rid the country of its affluence and wealth. He had forced the country to regress to a simple self-sufficient rural lifestyle, ordering the genocide of 2.5 million innocent civilians along the way. Living under his constant watch, there was no freedom and independence, and if you ever forgot this you could turn on the government radio and be reminded, 'To keep you is no benefit, to destroy you is no loss.'

With nearly eleven months on the road we had pedalled 19,000 km, explored 23 countries, and were about to polish off our fourth glass of fifty cent beer in the sun. Sat at one of the many restaurant bars, we were thoroughly enjoying our freedom and independence, and reflecting on the ups and downs of the trip.

'Hey Jo, how come we always end up spending over our budget in the cheapest countries?' I asked her, before draining my glass.

'I don't really know,' she replied as she reached for the bowl of crisps, 'I haven't really thought about it.'

'See, look there, we *never* order crisps! But we decided to here?'

'We can afford it here.'

'But that's just the thing. We can't afford to do it, we've spent most of our day's budget in the last two hours.'

I wasn't complaining, I had been keeping a close eye on the budget the entire journey, and Phnom Penh had been our first real opportunity to sit down and treat ourselves without depending on the hospitality of others.

'I know, but look around you. This is the right thing to do.'

'Yes... it... is!' I articulated, in approval of our current activity. We had finally arrived at a place to sit and enjoy the same activities as everybody else.

Independence is sometimes described as 'the direction of one's own affairs without interference' and can often be a prerequisite of freedom, 'the power to determine action without restraint'. We had survived for nearly one year, living in a tent, eating food most students would turn their nose up at, and cooking all our meals using regular petrol, a cheap fuel available across the entire world. Many would argue that we had enjoyed nothing *but* freedom and independence.

The reality of living on such a limited budget meant that we had been simply watching the world pass us by, whilst trying to spend as much time as we could 'in-between' places. When we finally pulled up at our mini-destinations, we'd see tourists waving around wads of cash, couples checking into hotels and walking hand in hand to enjoy dinner in a restaurant. We, on the other hand were free to do whatever we liked, just so long as it didn't cost anything. Nobody would influence our decisions, and there was complete freedom of choice, do nothing or leave.

Going from a steady income, to surviving on three times less than a UK job-seekers allowance, it was funny to see how we reacted to our new social standing. We had been brought up in a western environment and when I saw someone order a beer or a pizza, I still believed that I was entitled to one too. The sad truth was, that when I ordered a beer back in London, it was my job that entitled me to have one - not who I was. Before we left I might have said things like, 'Yeah, I work in a bank, but it's not really *me*!' but now, I was beginning to realise that without my job at the bank, I actually had very little place in society.

Maybe real freedom and independence had been having the choice to throw yourself into an oppressive institution, take on commitments, and ever increasing your opportunity to change it all.

'Could we get one more beer?' I asked Jodie. We never bought a single thing without first discussing it together, not even a fifty cent beer. A man with a job would have said, 'I'm *having* another beer, would *you* like something to drink?'

'Maybe we could share one?' she suggested, 'Seeing as we've already overspent.'

'Okay,' I reluctantly agreed. It wasn't as I had hoped, but what more did I deserve? As the old saying goes, 'You are unique, just like everybody else.'

*   *   *   *   *

When Thomas, Gary and James Sterling first arrived in Cambodia, I doubt that they had turned up in an astro-turfed rugby tuk-tuk, their unique method of arrival to the national rugby trials.

'Do you wanna swap?' laughed Thomas Sterling, as the motorised grotto dropped them off in the car park.

I looked at their novel marketing tool, then back to my worn bicycle, and a small part of me hoped that he wasn't joking.

The stocky siblings had moved to Phnom Penh when they had relocated their project management business the previous year, but had barely furnished their office when they took on their first project, the Cambodian Rugby Federation.

As the boys began to run through some warm-up drills, we enjoyed the shaded protection of a pitch side dugout, and chatted to Thomas about the history of Cambodian rugby.

'A French man called Phillipe Monnin had already laid down some good foundations, but there's an awful lot of rebuilding to be done in society before you see them at the Rugby World Cup.'

'They *are* quite small!' I pointed out, in case this had slipped him by, even Rambo would have had his work cut out to convince me otherwise.

'That's just it, and we won't be fixing it overnight,' he sighed.

Under Pol Pot's regime, many of the estimated 2.5 million victims had been educated, pro-active city dwellers, the brains behind business, and often nutritionally the healthiest sector of society. Over four years of genocide, the national average height is thought to have fallen by a staggering 10 cm, a difference that takes around one hundred years of human evolution to gain back.

As I stood, contemplating the scale of such destruction, a smartly dressed Cambodian boy began to head our way.

'That's Ratana!' James pointed out, 'The boy I suggested for your scroll.'

'The guy from the centre?' I recalled from James' e-mail, now thankful that I carried the scroll everywhere.

In 1995, a French couple, Christian and Marie-France des Pallières, witnessed children living and working through the rubbish dumps in Phnom Penh. Starting only by feeding these children, they returned to France to raise awareness of the situation, and began collecting donations to assist with their work.

By 1996 they had expanded their visions and had created 'Pour un Sourir d'Enfant (PSE)' - 'for the smile of a child' as an official school to educate the children. By 2011, the project had grown beyond comprehension, providing housing, healthcare, nutrition, and education to over 6,500 children and their families.

Like many children, Ratana's childhood had been spent working on the rubbish dump, attending the local school by morning and sifting through piles of hazardous refuse and waste in the afternoon. By the age of sixteen, his family could no longer afford the loss of income, and he had dropped out of education to begin a full time struggle for food.

Ratana's luck changed in 1998, when Christian des Pallieres stumbled upon the boy and had personally brought him into the PSE. He was now seventeen years old, had just a simple education, and spoke only Khmer. Under the wings of PSE, Ratana quickly progressed, learning English, French and completing a further education in Business Studies. Further still, he had learned one more thing, something that had finally led to our meeting at the touchline of national rugby trials.

In 2000, Philippe Monnin, a volunteer in the PSE centre, initiated a school rugby session, capturing the interest of other volunteers and children alike. Soon the attendance was so strong that they could field several sides at each age group, the children called the game 'bal arb' – 'a ball to carry'. Ratana smiled and recalled how he had first started playing.

'One day I saw some boys throwing around the bal koi (broken ball). I thought, I must understand this game! It must be important if a French man is teaching it!'

After attending the training, Ratana discovered that it was also played in many English speaking nations around the world, and recognised that rugby might help connect him with other cultures. Most importantly he enjoyed the teamwork, and was surprised at how much he enjoyed playing. As Ratana and his friends finished their education, many of them continued to play rugby for a senior PSE rugby side, and soon Philippe created the Cambodian Federation de Rugby (CFR).

In 2005, Ratana got his first overseas experience, travelling to Hong Kong to play scrum half in their first ever international fixture. As an undercard to Hong Kong vs Korea, the boys from Cambodia took to the field weighing an average 35 kg less per player than their Macau opponents. Despite losing, the team left the pitch to a standing ovation from the Hong Kong crowd, amazed by the relentless effort and spirit of the tiny Cambodians.

An ever present part of the Khmer rugby family, Ratana became captain, and went on to become the most capped national player and top try scorer. Having been pulled from the rubbish dump at seventeen, Ratana's achievements were incredible, first leading his country, and now guiding the next generation as the new rugby co-ordinator at PSE.

'Can you sign here please!' I asked Ratana, never more sure of anything in my life.

CHAPTER 29
BROKEN IN BANGKOK

'How you doing Tom?' Belly asked me at my bedside. It was good of him to visit, not just because he'd traversed the calamitous city streets of Bangkok to do so, but because I'd nearly knocked over his table of beers when I'd collapsed two nights before. My drinking session with the Southerners Rugby Club had lasted a pitiful ten minutes, or half a small beer. It wasn't my finest hour.

'I'm feeling much better, thanks.'

'Good stuff, so what drugs are they giving you?' he asked.

'Some green ones, some blue ones and some white ones,' I answered, looking at the line of pots next to my bed.

'Do you know what they're all for?' he questioned.

'They're to make me feel better,' I explained, thinking he might be quite new to medicine.

'And the drip?' he looked up at the tube running into my arm.

'It's fluid and antibiotics for gastroenteritis,' Jodie called from the bathroom, before I could make something up.

'Okay, listen guys, I'd be very careful about what they give you here.'

'Honestly Belly, they're treating me so well!' I tried to explain.

'Mate, I know, that's just the problem. This is the best hospital in Bangkok, and the reason everyone speaks English is because it targets ex-pats on health insurance.'

We hadn't found this subject easy to address before leaving London. Most insurance brokers had hung up at the mere mention of 'Pakistan', and all we could find was a very generic cover with an extortionate excess of $2,500. Belly voiced his concerns that we may already have reached it.

'Seriously guys, I've seen it all before. You've practically got a hotel room here, and I bet those little Thai girls in their hot uniforms have been leaning over you, taking your temperature all night. I swear half of these patients aren't even sick!'

'I was really sick!' I tried to justify, as Jodie walked back into the room.

'Look mate, we could all see you were in a bad way, but you won't feel any better when you get the bill!'

He did have a point. I had my own en-suite, a state of the art hospital bed, nurses at my bedside every hour and even Sky Sports. That very morning I'd managed to watch Sri Lanka vs UAE in the A5N.

'What time did you check in Jodie?' Belly asked her, rather than myself. I'd been unconscious at the time.

'Tim helped us down here about midday,' she replied, checking the paperwork.

'Listen, if you're feeling well enough to sit back at the apartment, I strongly recommend you check yourself out at 11:59 today.'

We took Belly's advice, and even though I was still spraying chocolate milk every half hour, my soaring temperature and racing heart rate had returned to normal, and I was feeling infinitely better than twenty four hours before. The doctor agreed to sign me out and so we followed him to reception to settle the account.

'How much was it?' I asked Jodie, as she took back her Mastercard and paperwork.

'In Baht or dollars?' she replied.

'In dollars?' I answered, 'I can't keep up with all these exchange rates.'

'One thousand,' she replied calmly, 'but the main thing is that you are better. I was so worried about you!'

One thousand dollars was an extortionate amount to pay whether you were on a budget or not. Even though it had been put on a credit facility, it still represented over four months of our funds. I was distraught, not just at spending so much money, but that I had been far too sick to even enjoy it. Worse still, I realised that my dreams of buying Jodie a Thai nurse's outfit were well and truly finished. If it was being paid for by insurance, I now understood why most ex-pats stayed the extra day or two. Or six.

The compensation for checking out early was that we could now manage a dinner appointment with the ARFU chairman, Khun Adisak. Through his son, Nattapol, we had been able to arrange the meeting, specifically intended to get our targeted Thai scroll signature.

As we arrived at the Royal Bangkok Sports Club for the dinner, we were welcomed by an entire table of Khun Adisak's friends. One familiar name was Pat Cotter, who had invited us to visit his IRB awarded rugby project. Pat, who was living in Phuket, had tirelessly built a rugby platform to help care for hundreds of children orphaned by the 2005 Boxing Day tsunami, and it was our first planned rugby stop out of Bangkok.

The menu was an 'all you can eat' buffet, with lavish tables of local and imported foods spread all around the edge of the room. We plotted a method of recouping some of our one thousand dollars as we scanned between Thai curry, roast beef and Yorkshire pudding, crab and lobster platters, Mediterranean salads and European cheeseboards.

Whatever I started with on my buffet bonanza, salad was now a rare commodity, and was an absolute certain side dish with each main.

'Bloody hell Jo, is there any smoked salmon left?' I looked at Jodie's plate, it was like she had been hunting with a grizzly bear.

'You can talk!' she laughed, looking at my two plates.

'I need to get my strength back!' I said, before trying to get Jodie to bite, 'I didn't get much sleep last night... !'

Although we weren't able to discuss rugby with the current Thai Rugby Union (TRU), many of our present company had once been national players and members of the TRU. Khun Adisak, Khun Nakornthap, Nattapol and Major Apirak had become so frustrated with the meagre three month domestic structure, that they had decided to focus their energies on the rugby projects at the prestigious Vajiravudh College.

'Guys, if you are free tomorrow,' Nattapol asked, 'we'd really like to show you our school.'

'Sounds great,' I replied, reaching for a Yorkshire pudding on my auxiliary plate.

Over lunch they explained how their former school, Vajiravudh College, had given birth to the origins of true Thai rugby. When former monarch, King Rama VI, had returned from his studies at Oxford University, he chose not to celebrate his reign with a Buddhist temple, but by commissioning an English style boarding school instead.

Having experienced rugby in England, Rama insisted that his new school would play what he believed to be 'the sport played in heaven'. Being brought back by the King himself, it quickly became a game of principles and integrity, and grew in popularity. Even to this day, the school remains the primary contributor to the national squad, and all inter-house rugby matches are preceded by the singing of a Thai hymn meaning 'sportsmanship'.

'Is rugby growing outside of the college too?' Jodie asked.

'A little,' answered Khun Nakornthap, 'but it's tough because most parents still view rugby as unsafe.'

'It is unsafe!' Major Apirak spoke up, 'I got struck by lightning.'

The table fell into laughter, as did we, but as he went on with his story, we found it really had happened. The Major is thought to have been the only national rugby player to have ever been directly struck by lightning and survive. The unfortunate incident had happened as he was coaching the national side prior to a tournament in Singapore. Knocked unconscious by the strike, he was rushed to hospital where he could proudly show off the burn mark of a metallic Buddhist pendant around his neck.

'It was supposed to bring me good luck,' he laughed, 'but I'm still not sure if it saved me or caused it!'

Jodie had already fetched her dessert, and I now strolled between the apple crumble, mini pavalovas, passion fruit cheesecake, made to order crèpes and enough varieties of ice cream to give the tasters at Häagen-Dazs a headache. I ducked into the bathroom considering the most extravagant way I could end the meal.

'I can't believe you're having another main!' Jodie laughed, as I sat back down with a plate of shellfish.

'That's the good thing about having a gippy tummy, I *just* made some more room.'

'Too much information!' she paused, staring down at her bowl of chocolate custard.

*   *   *   *   *

'Congratulations guys, you made it!' Eddie wasn't referring to Bangkok, but finding his sportswear business on the complex network of industrial estates.

The former Canadian prop, Eddie Evans, was very modest about his own playing abilities, preferring instead to talk about his slum-kid rugby project, Nak Suu Tigers. If I had played in three Rugby World Cups, beaten a star studded France *and* scored a try against England at Twickenham, I would have talked about nothing else.

'Can you remember who was playing for England in 1994?' I asked Eddie, like a five year old in a sweet shop.

'Unfortunately I can,' he laughed, 'they were a bit too good for us.'

I cringed as Eddie described spending the best part of eighty minutes buried under the bodies of Martin Johnson, Jason Leonard, Brian Moore, Martin Bayfield and Dean Richards. When considering the pacey England back line included Will Carling, Jeremy Guscott and both the Underwood brothers, I felt the Canadians had performed well to keep the deficit to forty-one points.

'You did well to score three tries!' I offered in consolation for digging up the painful experience.

'We had Norm,' he stated, as if the matter was self-explanatory. 'Here look at this, you're probably too young to remember.'

Eddie swung round to his computer and pulled up several old articles on his teammate. By no coincidence, second row, Norm Hadley, had been present during a time of particular Canadian forward strength. At the 1991 Rugby World Cup, Canada had asked many questions, defeating Fiji, then a strong Romanian outfit, before missing out on top pool spot with a narrow six point defeat to France.

Although knocked out by the All Blacks in the quarter final, many saw the 29-13 defeat as Norm Hadley's finest hour, unanimously agreeing that the Canadians had completely destroyed the All Black pack. He had subsequently been selected for the World Barbarians against champions Australia, and went on to play four subsequent matches for the Barbarians.

When playing rugby for London Wasps with Lawrence Dallaglio, Norm had grabbed the headlines for conclusively dealing with two armed hooligans on the London Underground. Such was the uncompromising bravery of his actions, that not only did his carriage give him a standing ovation, but he was publicly praised by the Prime Minister, John Major, in parliament the following week. Why they threatened the 6'7", twenty-one stone lock I have no idea, but one can't help to think they'd have been safer throwing their insults at the London Transport Police.

'Would you like to meet him?' Eddie asked, quite bluntly.

'Sure,' I hesitated, planning to be on my best behaviour if the time ever came, 'will he be at the Rugby World Cup?'

'I don't know,' Eddie replied, 'why don't we call him downstairs and ask.'

*　　*　　*　　*　　*

Having spent the Nak Suu Tigers training session unconscious in hospital, we were keen to find out more about Eddie's slum-kid project. When relocating to Thailand, Eddie had become acquainted with two Samoan rugby brothers, running 'Ark International' social projects in the slum areas of Bangkok. The Christian missionaries, Sopo and Lea, had worked with Eddie to co-found a rugby project that could further their efforts and provide another level of social activity to the children. The 'Nak Suu' Tigers (meaning 'Warrior Tigers') were born.

Travelling out to two of the slum areas with Sopo, we were quite shocked by the living conditions so close to the capital city. Many of the communities were of Cambodian origin, left to survive in small living spaces built on stagnant flood lands. The stilted homes were very cramped, and we learned that the water levels would often rise so much that many of the houses became flooded with the contaminated water. In one recent emergency, Sopo had rushed to help a family to move accommodation, after two huge anacondas decided to set up home in their tiny living space.

As we passed one shack, Sopo called out and a little lad rushed out to greet us. We had carried 'Gilbert' all the way from London, but as I peered over the edge of the narrow decking walkways, I had doubts whether his journey might be about to end.

As we threw the ball around in a little circle, I began to question Sopo's coaching. The little lad had a hard and accurate throw, but seemed to prefer an American football style pass, using my testicles as his wide receivers.

'His name is Bum,' Sopo introduced, as I was doubled over for the third time.

'Bum from the Slum!' I wheezed. It was good to put a name to the pain.

We'd seen many poor areas on our journey across the world, many forgotten, many ignored, many publicly splashed across the news for all to see, but it was comforting to know that Eddie's 'Nak Suu' Tigers project was reaching out to the most needy, bringing hope and joy to a new generation of little ruggers.

*　　*　　*　　*　　*

Cycling south out of Bangkok we finally hit an entire year on the road, followed soon after by the computer ticking over to 20,000 km. As the Rugby World Cup became a more imminent event, we started to turn our thoughts to targets further afield. One eye now focused on Darwin, and allowing ourselves enough time to reach Melbourne for the final transfer. Despite not yet reaching Malaysia, we also realised that Singapore was just 1,000 km away. Under the new routine, 1,000 km no longer presented a challenge, and we had smashed out the last thousand in just over a week.

Early morning starts were followed by long lunch breaks, hiding in large Tesco Lotus stores to soak up the crisp, free air-conditioning. Despite following the perceived east coastal path, we rarely caught sight of the sea, and there was little to distract us from progressing quickly towards Malaysia.

The rare entertainment under such conditions came from watching TV in the Tesco restaurants. As I munched on a Pad Thai we managed to watch Will and Kate's royal wedding, while on another occassion, midway though a Thai omelette and chilli sauce sandwich, we learned of the death of Osama Bin Laden.

'Hang on a minute! Abbotobad? Didn't we cycle there?' I nudged Jodie, as a satellite map appeared on the screen.

'Look, yes, that's the road down from Murree!' she confirmed, as we looked at each other in amusement.

We later found that not only had we cycled within 1 km of his compound, but had more or less circled it, even stopping for a water

265

break on the corner. It was the same evening that we had been driven back to spend the night inside police barracks.

'If only Scott knew how close we had come!' I thought to myself, wondering how Osama had been keeping himself warm in winter.

CHAPTER 30
POT BELLIED PIGS, SOME COBRAS & A PENGUIN

Crossing into Malaysia was the smoothest and easiest transition of the whole journey. A cheerful, if not gappy toothed lady, welcomed us to her booth and was overjoyed by our intention to cycle through her country. At no charge, our passports were stamped, and the new open road was soon as idyllic as riding through a Teletubbies set.

For a long time I had wondered what Malaysia would be like, and as expected, my imagination had not been all that close to the mark. Firstly, I had not realised that it was an Islamic country, and with nearly two million Indians living there, I also found myself having more conversations about the English cricket team, than the Rugby World Cup.

Away from the white sandy beaches, it seemed that the entire country was one big palm plantation, and although the roads were smooth enough to make easy cycling, the hills were long, the view was tedious and the air increasingly sweaty. If not for a warm invitation to stay in the capital, we would already have been counting down the days to Singapore. Perhaps Jodie was anyway, because now missing rugby so much, I was taking every opportunity to chat to her about my life back in the low rural league rugby clubs. If you have never experienced the joys of rural league rugby, it would be my pleasure to give you a small insight.

A typical structure would see half of any given squad being old friends from school, none of whom ever progressed to better standards, and who were now well into their thirties or forties. Under the guise of exercise, they were still enjoying the opportunity to socialise on a Saturday, whilst simultaneously clinging onto those final years before trying to sneak a local golf course subscription past the wife.

Around 10% were formed of retired players in their mid fifties, guys who had enjoyed their 'retirement' drinks so much, that they now went in and out of retirement every season. A further third, usually the sons of club members, or friends of these sons, did the lion's share of the work, and were in the prime of their life, late twenties. This left around 5% which was commonly filled by something known as the 'Youth Policy' - my gateway to the world of rugby.

An organised 'Youth Policy' is an essential ingredient in any low-league senior side's armoury. Too many youth players and the game might be played at an unreasonable pace, too few and you may find it won't be played at any pace at all. In one recent Kent league match, it was reported that both sides had moved so little in the first forty minutes that neither could recall which end they should switch to at half time.

Financially though, the 'Youth Policy' is nothing more than a drain on resources. Most suitable teenagers had the metabolism of a horse, requiring constant feeding, organised transport, free membership and infinite beer as a prerequisite of not wasting away the weekend hours in their girlfriend's bedroom.

To be part of a club's 'Youth Policy' was nothing to be taken lightly, and usually no more than two players could be supported in a scheme at any one time, one on each wing. Although potentially a multi-faceted role, you had one primary function - to look young and quick. It wasn't even necessary to *be* quick, but based on the assumption that 'perception is reality', this was usually enough to get you marked, hence reducing the opposition involved in the real game - the one that involved the actual rugby ball. The wiser heads in the team often distracted you with words like 'development', 'future player base' and 'squad balance' to keep your spirits high on a Saturday night, but it was a mythical beast and one that needs to be explained in a little more detail.

In reality, a 'Youth Policy' is essentially the rugby equivalent of a poker bluff, giving you the option of an expansive attacking game, but one you wouldn't consider using if your remaining thirteen players were struck by lightning. Ironically, the ploy was normally negated before kick-off, on seeing that your opposition had turned up with the same set of cards, two young and quick looking teenagers on the wings.

Under a rural league's gentlemanly agreement, it had been decided that it was in nobody's interest for a youngster to take the ball into a breakdown eighty metres away from either pack. At many rural levels it had even been made a penalty offence to pass the ball into such capable hands. In *my* home league, eighty metres represented the aggregate movement for my forwards during a match, and often you'd see them still loitering on the halfway line, while the opposition standoff was converting his own try. It certainly made for an interesting situation come match day, and one in particular still sits painfully in my memory.

'He's *my* man,' I shouted, pointing to the young quick looking boy opposite me. We were defending a five metre scrum.

'Oh, is he now?' came a deliberately camp taunt from the sidelines.

This wasn't the first time I had heard it, and until I could work out a new call, it probably wouldn't be the last - but it was my opportunity to stamp my mark on the game. He knew he wouldn't be getting the ball, I knew that he wouldn't be getting the ball, and in turn I'm pretty sure he knew that I knew that. Still, he had to play along with the pretence, shuffling a metre or so from side to side, trying to get a bit of space, and show to all his agility and potency in attack.

In defence, I shadowed his movements, keen not to be outperformed in the amateur dramatics department, and armed with the usual comfort of mind that I wouldn't be required to make an actual tackle. Nevertheless, it was me who would ensure that my opposite number didn't score, and after the match, I would be bought many beers and praised that I had 'negated' their wide attacking threat.

'Touch, pause, engage!' The referee's call echoed far away to my left.

Unfazed, I stared ahead, directly at my opposite number, who now seemed a little uncomfortable with the special attention he was getting. By now I was even pointing out my man, in case there was any confusion over who I was taking out of the game. He held his ground and prepared himself for a theoretical but unimaginable ball out wide. The crowd responded to this little battle with a huge cheer, and I applied even more diligence to the performance, now practically down in a sprint block position.

'Tom!' came the call from my outside centre, 'Get back on the line!'

'No way,' I thought, I was like a coiled spring, ready to do something like the human equivalent of un-coiling.

Not breaking my concentration for a second, I continued my stare at the young lad opposite me, who was now carrying a confusingly smug expression, and walking towards the middle of the pitch. I followed him across to the middle determined not to let him score.

'Who did he think he was?' I thought to myself, upset that he no longer considered my imminent proximity a threat.

'Tom, get back on the bloody line will you?' my centre yelled again, 'They've already scored the try!'

I looked across, and sure enough their number 8 was walking back from our line, ball in hand, before tossing it casually to my opposite number. As my young adversary slotted over the conversion, it dawned on me that perhaps the previous cheer had been for the try, and not my defence, but the fact remained, the little sod had now scored two points in the match, and I knew I wouldn't match this all season.

No matter how mediocre I was, I reminded people that it had taken many seasons to reach that level, sometimes training two, three or even four times per year in conjunction with my Saturday afternoon experiments. In my early senior days I often struggled with my rugby strategy. It no longer seemed suitable to just kick the ball to my opposite number, knowing that the thirteen year old with cold wet hands would drop it straight to the floor. I sometimes tried evasive running, which did bring some temporary relief, but the pitch was only wide enough to buy you a few seconds. It was a tough old game, and I was still in the bounce back relationship from football.

My captain back then was a warm and popular man, and a good hooker too, his name was Simon Britten. Each Saturday night he would perform his dutiful responsibilities at the bar, as I would mine. He mixed with the team, praising us individually for our positive contributions that afternoon, and I would drink my free beer and agree to come back next week. It was a working relationship, I couldn't afford to insure my Fiesta and drink that much beer, and they would have someone to look young and quick in the back three.

My practiced method of trial and error was proving unsuccessful during matches, and so I would often use these bar sessions to delve a little deeper into the hidden secrets of rugby. I had many unanswered questions, like what should I do when I get the ball, where should I stand when the big men are throwing haymakers, and does anything really happen in the front row?

As a hooker, Simon said that I was far too young to understand the complexities of the front row, and that I was fine to remain where I was during the unscheduled but very necessary scuffles. After further clarifying my first issue, that I was never sure when to pass, run or kick, he told me something that has stayed with me to this day.

'Tom, when you have the ball, the *only* wrong decision is the one that you don't commit to.'

It was simple but quite beautiful advice, and it suddenly felt as if the code had been cracked, the secrets of rugby were finally laid bare. I could now block out the touchline screams of 'Kick it off you knob-end!' as I ran from my five metre line, and I would ignore the groans as I employed a 'chip and chase' in front of all potential contact situations. The world of rugby had finally swung open its doors to me, and at last I was ready to play. Until he continued that was.

'But generally speaking, us forwards would prefer it if you kicked to touch from inside the twenty-two, other than that, it's usually better to run... or pass... but you should run, because you are young and fast. Basically, just don't listen to anyone, including me, and commit to whatever you do. That's the *right* decision.'

It brought a very confused tear to my eye. I wanted to recap, but it was too late. I had drifted off temporarily into a land of wild and unpredictable decisions that I could now justify with 'commitment'. It was like I had been handed a full licence by the captain himself, but at the moment of signing, he'd handed me the small print. These new clauses were quite unnecessary in an otherwise extremely potent contract. It really had become like the third party insurance on my Fiesta. I was completely insured for damage on my car, as long as I didn't crash it. Perhaps I had missed the point, but surely this was when I would most need my insurance money.

*   *   *   *   *

Being hosted by Neil and Pat in Kuala Lumpar, we had the perfect base to get out and explore Malaysian rugby. Pat was a local girl of Chinese-Malay origin, but her partner, Neil, was an English rugby man having travelled all around Asia on high spec engineering contracts. Although he had been forced to retire early from the game through knee injuries, his first point of call at any new project was to introduce himself down at the local rugby club. In Kuala Lumpar, that had meant heading down to the oldest and most prestigious of all Malaysian clubs, the Royal Selangor Rugby Club.

His most recent project had been down in Brisbane, but when an opportunity had presented itself in Kuala Lumpar, he had decided to sell everything, buy a small boat and sail all the way to his new job. With a small crew, he had survived for four months, sleeping in shifts of two, three or four hours, so Neil certainly understood what it meant to blindly throw yourself into a challenge.

To welcome us to the capital, the dynamic couple suggested a drink at the unofficial rugby base, 'Sid's Pub'. At such short notice, Neil explained that he didn't need to arrange anything, all the guys would already be there. He was certainly proven right.

'Welcome to Sid's Pub,' said Geoff, the confusingly named owner.

'Two Guinness and two white wines please!' Neil wasted no time in ordering, 'We'll have these, and then I'll introduce you around. It might take all night though!'

Graham, a passionate Scotsman, was first to join us and it didn't take long for the conversation to get round to his local rugby project, the Bintang Rugby Club. Originally formed out of another local youth side, the Cobrats, Graham and Englishman, Ian Johns, had established a club focused specifically on developing the local Malay youth. After only four seasons, they already boasted 250 players, but their greatest success had been in creating the annual Bintang International Rugby 10s.

Designed just to offer the local kids a fun weekend and some opposition, somehow the tournament had blown out of all proportion, with the last event attracting 1,800 kids, from 123 teams around the world. Already it ranks as one of the biggest youth tournaments on the planet, not at all bad for a bunch of dads without their own pitch or clubhouse.

'That's an incredible achievement Graham, I'd really like to buy you a drink,' I said, in admiration.

'Oh thanks, I'll have a Guinness please,' he replied.

'Er, sorry Graham, I said I'd really *like* to buy you a drink, but I spent our budget on Thai girls in Bangkok.'

'That's perfectly understandable,' he laughed, 'in that case, let me buy you both a drink and we can discuss Scotland's chances at the Rugby World Cup.'

I suspected that more than one drink might be required to entertain that notion, but being in the same pool, it was risky for an England fan to be verbally bashing the 'Sweaties'.

'Let's ask Ian!' Graham suggested, introducing us to our next rugby face.

Ian Taylor was an IRB certified referee, and had gained vast playing and refereeing experience all around South East Asia. He shared some amusing memories from his tours with the 'Pot Bellied Pigs' - an invitational Asian touring side, formed almost entirely of front row forwards. Sadly one of these tours had led to a more sombre story.

'Let me get you a drink first,' Ian suggested, 'I don't want to be blamed for sobering you up.'

The Bali 10s was a tournament designed as an island social event, and to raise funds to develop rugby in the community. In 2002, Ian had toured with the Pigs, relaxing at a table in Kuta, when a suicide bomber detonated his backpack in the crowded bar. Instinctively, Ian had ducked his head to try and shield himself from the blast, but as the dust around him settled, he looked up to see those next to him had not been so lucky.

Ian was rushed to hospital with severe burns to his face and body, doctor's attributing his lucky survival to a baggy silk shirt that contained enough flame retardant properties to avoid fatality. Like many people in Sid's Pub, Ian had lost many good friends on that day.

'There you are!' called Neil, 'I've been looking all over for you.'

I looked back at Neil who was still standing at the bar, he hadn't even moved. Neil was six foot five and the pub was only twelve foot wide. It would have taken all of three seconds to scan the horizon and find us.

'There's two more drinks waiting for you at the bar,' he called, 'and Geoff's brought out two Ben Nevis burgers for you.'

'Hmmm... Tom maybe?' Ian analysed us, 'But Jodie? No chance!'

'You said that to the wrong girl!' Jodie growled, failing to recognise she was just half a full size person. Unlike the mountain of dust in Pakistan, she barely made it to base camp.

*   *   *   *   *

Sometimes, just sometimes, I believe that rather than sit on a natural acronym, some people with too much time to kill have just gone looking for one. I first suspected this when I applied overseas for a 'Bachelor Of Oiled Breast Studies', and again when the 'American Rude Studies Elementary School' stamped my rejection letter, but when we arrived at our next club, my suspicions were finally proven right.

The Combined Old Boys Rugby Association (COBRA) was formed in 1967 with its main objective to sound great, and to encourage young Malaysians to continue playing rugby after finishing school. Asides from fielding one of the strongest senior sides in the country, COBRA Rugby Club is most famous for inventing what has now become a widely recognised format of the game.

At the time of COBRA's inception, a group of Kuala Lumpar ex-pats challenged a group of local Malaysians to a game of rugby. Understandably the lean, quick footed Malays wanted no part in packing down with fifteen fat blokes, and likewise the ex-pats had little interest in chasing them round in a game of rugby sevens. The haggling commenced and it was finally agreed that each side should field just ten players. The format of the game became an instant success, allowing the lighter Asian players to compete on a level playing field with the bigger and heavier ex-pats. Rugby 10s was born.

Although the coach of the Malaysian national team had only just returned from Dubai, he had agreed to come directly to the club to chat about rugby in the region. Deano Herewini, second cousin of former All Black, Mac Herewini, was a former Hong Kong international and Waikato prop, and a charismatic individual. He was a passionate advocate for developing grassroots rugby and believed, without doubt, that the potential of any national team only ran as deep as its core roots in the culture.

'It's easy for me to get good players to play good rugby, but the trick is finding a system that pushes through a pool of players to pick from.'

I nodded in understanding of Deano's analogy, then offered what I hoped would be a recognition of my agreement.

'Too many structures work from the top down, it needs to be the opposite to have any lasting effect.'

Deano gave a huge grin of contentment, and it was clear that I had found a common wavelength.

'Tom, that is spot on, I couldn't have said it better myself.'

I was pleased. I didn't even know what it meant but Lawrence Dallaglio had said something similar about the RFU once and I figured it could apply to just about anything. 'Always start at the bottom and work up!' - I said it about climbing mountains, getting dressed in the morning, everything except what order you should dry yourself with a towel. There you should always finish with your bottom, just in case.

Asides from his coaching responsibilities, Deano was a regular feature in a charitable grassroots programme carried out by the HSBC Penguins, and prior to his work in Malaysia, he had been an integral figure in the formation of the Indonesian Rugby Union.

In 2002, he too had been coaching a side in Bali, and only for a last minute alteration of plans would have been in a taxi that claimed the lives of many of his team. Delayed only by a few minutes after a match, he was on the scene just moments after the blast, and still risked serious injury bravely trying to get help to many of the victims. Hearing this story for the second time that weekend brought home just how close many rugby players in Asia felt to the tragedy. Deano was a man who gave everything to his passion, and thanks to him, we were also sitting besides our Malaysian scroll legend.

Not from Kuala Lumpar, but born in the small coastal town of Melaka, Boon Hoon Chee had first learnt rugby by watching the Fijian Military play through the barrack fences. Although typically modest about his playing abilities, one has to assume that to be selected at number 8 for the national team from 1976 to 1989, he must have shown a particular pedigree on the field. Boon captained the national XV for four years, and was an ever present selection in the Malaysian sevens side throughout his career. After retirement, he became national sevens coach and after all international duties, concentrated his efforts at COBRA, most recently becoming president in 2010.

It had been another intensely short rugby break, and we found it incredibly hard to wave goodbye to our Kuala Lumpar hosts. Pat didn't even play rugby, and Neil hadn't touched a ball in years but they'd gone to every length to support our cause, driving us from one meeting to another, and treating us every step of the way. We had stayed with many ex-pats on the journey, and many generous locals too, but receiving such hospitality from a combination of the two, made us finally realise that there is no such thing as a hospitable country, culture or religion, only hospitable people. Through the rugby family we had now met some of the very best, they didn't feel an obligation to help us, just a desire to.

'We wish there was some way we could thank you both,' we insisted to Neil.

'Guys, I've had my share of hospitality over the years, just pass it on.'

CHAPTER 31
AN UNLIKELY STORY

As we crossed the busy bridge connecting mainland South East Asia to Singapore, I looked down and noticed that 21,000 km had just ticked over on the computer. We still gave 'high-fives' to celebrate every 100 km, and I usually waited for a break in traffic to pull alongside to do it. Overcome with the combined excitement of reaching a new 1,000 km mark, and recently discovering that Singapore even counted as a new country, I chose to celebrate the achievement on the bridge at 35 k.p.h., very nearly plunging headfirst into the Singapore shallow end.

It was a huge moment on our trip because it marked the furthest overland point we could pedal away from Calais. From Singapore, we would have to take a combination of ferries, planes and squeeze in some scattered cycling before finally touching down in our new home, Australia.

It had taken us three months to cycle the width of China, Singapore took us ninety minutes to cross, arriving at our Singapore Cricket Club ('SCC') hosts, Duncan and Ali, just before the Friday afternoon tropical downpour.

That evening, Duncan and Ali took us to the historical SCC for a 'light social', with some of their friends from the vets side 'The Growlers'. Now home to twelve different sports, the SCC was first initiated as a cricket club in 1852, but by the 1880s, the club had also established facilities for tennis, football, hockey and rugby. The SCC International 7s tournament has picked up a particularly high reputation, attracting the likes of Jonah Lomu and Tana Umaga amongst other legends to play at the club.

Life on the road seemed very surreal at times. Only that morning we had pulled on our sweaty cycling gear in a ten dollar Malay motel room, and now we stood in borrowed clothes, holding a cold beer in one of the most historical sporting clubs in the world. There could not have been a better venue to celebrate the end of a continent.

'If Rusty doesn't destroy you two tonight, you should try to get down to watch the Centaurs train tomorrow morning. Liam will be playing,' Duncan said with an unnervingly wry smile.

Liam was their five year old son, and was in his first year with the Centaurs minis section. I had no intention of missing out on this opportunity, but worryingly it sounded like the decision could end up in 'Rusty's' hands and not mine.

'As long as you're driving and not me!' I said.

'Actually, Ali will be, I have boxing training.'

'Boxing? On a Saturday morning? You're a bit keen aren't you?'

'I'm helping some guys train for a white collar boxing event in August. Have you heard of white collar boxing?'

I had, and as it turned out, our host Duncan was a reigning white collar boxing champion. Winning his first ever bout the previous year, he was now helping to train some friends for another Singapore Barbarians fundraiser.

The Singapore Barbarians were an invitation side formed in 2003, to showcase a combination of ex-pat and local Singaporean talent. They had achieved XVs victories over Singapore, Hong Kong and Western Australia, but it was in the sevens and tens that brought them most success, often touring the Pacific to raise money for local orphanages.

Holding up the 'Barbarians' reputation, they had attracted some high end coaching names, firstly New Zealand sevens star, Owen Scrimgeour, then later Phil Greening, the former England sevens captain, England hooker and British Lion.

'Phil Greening?' I said, 'That's a coincidence. He's now coaching at my old club, Footscray RFC!'

'Yep, the same Phil Greening. Phil's a great bloke, but don't say his name too loudly here mate.'

'Why? What happened?'

'Come on, let me introduce you to Rusty, he'll tell you. Tom and Jodie, this is Rusty.'

'Ah, the mad cyclists!' Rusty welcomed us with enthusiasm, 'Lovely that you're here! How are your bottoms?'

Russel Chalon, or 'Rusty', was an instantly uplifting character, the type that women wanted to be around, and as a result, that men wanted to be. He was sat at a bar stool while an attentive audience gathered around waiting for his next story - it was immediately apparent why he had been appointed as social secretary and 'Tankards' captain.

'Hey Duncan,' he said, 'if you and Ali are still busy tomorrow night, we'll look after Tom and Jodie for you.'

There was a collective laugh as Rusty tried on an angelic smile.

'Hey,' he said, making out that he was misunderstood, 'they're our guests, there's just a couple of places I want to show them.'

The crowd let off another groan in recognition of what this implied. 'Easy on them Rusty!', 'Careful guys!', 'Better wear your drinking boots!' came some comments among the laughs.

'It'll be nice to take in some sights of Singapore!' I joked with him, 'Thanks very much!'

'Now, Duncan said to ask you about Phil Greening? He used to coach here didn't he?'

'Hey, easy there,' he emphasised, theatrically looking over both shoulders, 'keep your voice down. Look, Phil's a great guy, we had good fun with Phil. Just don't say his name too loud.'

'Why?' I whispered, 'What happened with Phil?'

Rusty paused in thought, as if about to explain.

'Ahhh,' he hesitated, 'you'd better ask Shoe about that. And while you're at it, ask him to tell you the firework story. Shoe, Shoe!' he shouted, 'Come and meet Tom and Jodie.'

A man walked across the room with a bucket of ice and beers, I waved and met him halfway.

'How you going?' said Shoe, as he put the bucket down on the table, 'Here, help yourself to another beer. Really amazing journey you guys are having. Are you off to Batam next?'

I looked for Jodie to answer but she wasn't there.

'Oh, I'm not really sure,' I answered, 'I just know we're heading for New Zealand!'

'No problems,' he laughed, 'you'll either go to Bintang or Batam, they're the nearest stops, and you can catch ferries onwards from there.'

'Thanks,' I said, 'I'll ask Jodie which one she's looked at.'

'Don't go to Bintang,' he advised, 'it's pretty full-on, just full of bars and clubs. I went there last year with Rusty… ' he trailed off as if reliving the experience, then shuddered.

'My advice is go to Batam, I have a serviced apartment there that you can stay in for free.'

'Really?'

'Of course, honestly no problems at all, you'll have the whole place to yourselves. I'll let the owners, Doug and Mike know you're coming, they'll look after you. I won't be there because I'm going on rugby tour with Rusty and the boys.'

'Oh right, where are you going?' I asked.

Shoe looked over at Rusty and shook his head again.

'He's making us go to China dressed as Japanese ninjas,' he sighed.

'Sounds like fun!' I said, beginning to worry about tomorrow night.

'So Shoe, Rusty said to ask you about a firework story?' I remembered.

'Ah! I might save that story for later,' he said, eyeing up the full bucket of beers.

'Fair enough,' I laughed, 'and why do they call you Shoe?'

'Oh! Might have to save that for tomorrow night,' he fidgeted again.

'Blimey,' I thought to myself, 'what an earth do these boys get up to?'

277

'Okay, but surely *you* can tell me what happened with Phil Greening can't you?'

'Shhhh!' he panicked, 'Keep your voice down! You have to be careful using that name round here!'

'Why does everyone keep saying that? What happened with Phil?'

Shoe prepared to explain the situation, then with a change of heart, picked up the beer bucket and shaped to walk off.

'I'm afraid you'll need to ask Andy about that, and while you're there, tell him it's his round.'

Shoe gestured over to the bar. Towering over a small arc of guys was an absolute pillar of a man, with broad shoulders and a deep Middlesbrough accent. It was Andy Douglas, the captain of the SCC 1st XV, and former Singapore national prop.

'Ah, hello Tom! Really pleased to see you got here safely,' Andy said to me, 'I couldn't believe it when I heard about your trip from Charlie Chelliah in KL, what an amazing journey!'

'I assume that Jodie is one of those girls?' he said, pointing at the five girls now draped over Rusty.

'Do you think they've got tangled?' I replied, laughing and staring at the knot of women on Rusty's arms.

'Yep, quite possibly,' he replied. 'It wouldn't be the first time.'

'Now Andy,' I whispered quietly, 'can you please tell me what on earth happened with Phil Greening?'

'Ah that!' he laughed, 'I suppose the boys have been making a little song and dance again? Look, Phil was a great character to have around the club, he was a good coach and a cracking bloke, we were all sad to see him go home… and the matter is all cleared up now by the way… but the boys clearly still go on about it.'

'Go on about what?' I despaired.

'Well, Phil had a tab behind the bar for the two years he was with us,' he explained.

'And?'

'*And* he still had a tab two years after he left!'

I smiled, trying to imagine what Phil's two year tab would have looked like, and how many of the drinks Rusty had added to that tab in the subsequent two years.

'*But*, despite what the boys might say, I should say that from an official perspective, the matter has been completely resolved! Listen, I have to disappear off home now, but hopefully I'll see you properly tomorrow night! Tell Shoe it's his round will you!'

As the beer buckets were refilled and the rugby hospitality flowed, we talked about rugby tours, about Asia and on a darker note, again about the Bali incident which now seemed closer to home than ever before.

'Did you notice how many guys were just stood around Andy Douglas at the bar?' Duncan asked me.

'It's hard not to isn't it. He's definitely a man's man if you know what I mean,' I replied.

'There's a very tragic story associated with that I'm afraid.'

'Does it have anything to do with Bali?' I asked, having talked with Ian and Deano in Malaysia already.

'Exactly right,' he explained, 'the poor guy. He was stood against a pillar, just as he was tonight, with a crowd of people stood around him in an arch. Next thing he knew, the bomb had exploded not far behind him. The pillar took a lot of the impact but not one of Andy's friends survived. Despite all that, he still managed to help carry quite a few injured people to safety outside.'

'I've heard too many bad stories about those bombings,' I said, 'I hope we never find out what it was like for them.'

'You know the thing that annoys me the most? Those terrorists killed innocent people just to try to cause panic and divide people. Look at the rugby world and think of everyone who has lost a friend there. You try telling me that our community isn't now stronger *because* of it!'

The commemorative plaque on the clubhouse wall was a permanent reminder of all those members and friends that were lost to the Bali bombings. Yet despite the tragedy and the horrific accounts that day, the prevailing feeling was of lasting admiration for how the communities had responded. It made us even prouder to be part of the rugby family.

Many hours later, and quite worse for wear, we stumbled outside and into a taxi back to Duncan and Ali's. It had been a great introduction to the SCC boys, but I couldn't help wondering through my drunken haze how we were going to fare at Centaurs training the following morning.

*   *   *   *   *

Against all odds it was Jodie that shaped up better the next morning - not because she had drunk any less alcohol, but because she had only woken up *after* we'd arrived home from training.

Still quite heavily sedated, I had clawed myself into Ali's car without even time for a shower. Soon I was at the old Singapore Racetrack, outside in the rain, breathing in the sweet aroma of bacon rolls and chatting to founder and chairman, Tim Lambert. With the quite magnificent Singapore Grandstand as a backdrop, he explained how in 2002, he had started by training just twenty children. Now, in front of me were over five hundred boys and girls, running around in a cloud of morning mist and my Tiger beer breath.

'Bacon roll Tom?' Ali offered me.

My eyes must have given her all the answers, and she came over with two.

'Don't worry, Rusty will go easier on you tonight, I promise.'

Our session with Rusty and the Singapore Cricket boys, didn't last just one more night, but most of the weekend. It had been the biggest test of stamina since pushing up the Himalayas, and we soon found ourselves staggering around Sentosa beach, sipping from jugs of sangria and watching pretty people make us feel even more of a disgrace.

It was late Sunday afternoon, and we could tell the guys had found another gear, this time we were determined to let them hit the straight on their own.

'Oh my God! Jo!' I struggled to focus, 'Is that...?'

'Will King!!' Jodie screamed, and threw her arms around our confused friend's neck.

As we had dropped back our last empty jug, we had bumped into our Putney friend, settling up his tab, with a very pretty young lady beside him.

'What on earth are you doing here?' we both asked him together.

A lot had happened in one year since walking out of Will's front door. He was still working in London, but had met the stunning Anna on a work trip, and as we had been pedalling, he had since flown over our heads twelve times to see her.

'We were just heading off to dinner,' he explained, extremely animated by the coincidence of our meeting, 'but now we're taking you for drinks instead!'

CHAPTER 32
CAPTAIN KIRK

Whereas my growing lack of knowledge of the world came as no surprise, I'm still more certain than ever that Indonesia provided me with my biggest cultural shock. Considering we'd already cycled through one country I didn't even know existed, and several more that I couldn't have pointed to if they were labelled on a map, it indicated that in this case, my imagination really had been wide of the mark. I had pictured desert islands, deck chairs and hundreds of girls wearing grass skirts, serving cocktails in half coconuts. In reality, it was nothing like Hawaii.

Indonesia, far from being a quiet chain of islands has the world's fourth largest population, with around 238 million people. Seeing that it is also home to the largest Islamic population on the planet, the hope of seeing skimpy grass skirts was also an unrealistic expectation. Traffic across Indonesia was nothing short of chaos, and where the roads weren't completely falling apart, they were barely wide enough to allow passing for the millions of four wheel drives.

It was all looking good though as we stepped off at the Batam ferry port, the bikes had made it off at the other side, and we were even sold a *real* visa on arrival. Now we could relax at Shoe's 'Smiling Hill' apartment, exploring our onward options with the invaluable help of Australian manager, Doug.

'No way!' I gasped at Jodie, as I scanned the internet, 'Guess how many Indonesian islands there are!'

'I don't know Tom,' she said. Jodie liked guessing numbers less than she liked being asked to guess them.

'17,500!' I read out loud, 'Oh no, we didn't promise to cycle them all did we?'

'I don't think that anyone would expect you to, no,' she replied, frantically scrubbing the tent in Shoe's shower.

Jodie was getting things cleaned prior to the DHL collection in Jakarta, having been warned that the Australian quarantine process had no sense of humour.

I checked back to our charity mission statement with a little concern, for as much as I didn't fancy cycling across 17,500 islands, I also didn't want anyone to think we had moved the goalposts. As I pored over our vague and carefully evasive wording, I soon realised that no such promise had ever been made, and that reasonable transport could be seen as flying from Jakarta, rather than rowing from East Timor.

Considering that there were 17,500 islands, I was as confused as Jodie that we only had two realistic ferry options. One was to head a week's cycle in the opposite direction back towards London, the other, head a week's cycle forward, direct to Jakarta. We had assumed we might be able to head somewhere in-between, but I also assumed that the ferries would leave more than once a week. I was wrong on both accounts, and we'd just missed it.

The ferry ride to Jakarta was an entirely new experience, and when we arrived at Sekupang ferry port, we spent a full twenty minutes staring up at the giant vessel and conjuring a plan.

The harbour was clearly too low for such a large ship, so rather than lower a standard boarding ramp, at regular intervals the crew would lower a flimsy rigged stairwell, balanced half on the port, half over the water. No fewer than two hundred porters jostled for position on the cramped docks, fighting for the short window to heave stacks of cargo onto their shoulders, and up onto the deck. It was clear that they would be paid for what they managed to load onto the boat, as clear as it was that not everyone would get the opportunity - it was a complete free for all.

The stairs lowered for no more than a few seconds, allowing around five to push on, but were immediately hoisted back up whilst porters, presumably carrying grand pianos, were still ascending. As the solitary entrance rose time and time again, guys with smaller parcels leapt onto the moving target, holding on beneath by a solitary rope. I didn't fancy my chances holding my own body weight, let alone 120 kg of equipment.

Being English wasn't buying us much credit in the world of porters, and after gently mingling in at the back of the group, we had achieved nothing in over half an hour. In front of us, men and women were being knocked to the deck, as members from the crew piled into the mob, forcing them back from the raising stairs. As the situation got more intense, we started to feel the heat of the late morning and we needed a new strategy, or a slice of luck.

Perhaps by luck, Jodie stumbled on a new strategy. Moments later we were edging our way towards the front, protected by porters leaning back on the crowd and lifting huge boxes out of our way.

'Amazing what a pair of boobs will do,' I laughed, as Jodie zipped back up her top.

We had secured a prime position, and when the next opportunity came our way, I counted to three and managed my first squat in over a year. Ignoring the burning pain in my shoulder, I powered up the stairs, threw the bicycle into a corner, and returned to find they'd held open the stairs for me. From the porters' shouts, word had clearly got round to the crew that there was a very important bikini trying to board.

Purchasing an 'economique' ticket had done nothing to raise our status once on board, whatever the position of Jodie's zip. For sixty dollars each, we had bought the lowest class of ticket, getting a small waterproof mattress amongst a thousand other passengers on the bottom deck. The under-bed drawers were full of crumbs, dirt and hair, and the toilets were something best used towards the start of the 38 hour journey. Fathers were already sparking up, leaning against the no-smoking signs, and when their young teenage children came to join in, I once again hated being poor.

Normally a sound sleeper, I could have pushed aside the permanent fluorescent lighting, hideous karaoke, and stench of clove cigarettes, but I found the insistent tickling of cockroach antennas around my face the hardest thing to ignore yet. We finally forced ourselves to get some rest, knowing that as soon as we had docked at 3 a.m. on Friday morning, we would have little time to clean our bicycles for collection, then head directly for our Indonesian rugby dinner.

Despite the unsociable hour, Bill Ryan had arranged for his driver to collect us, bikes and all, and bring us directly to his house. I was tired and extremely grateful, guessing that navigating Jakarta on little sleep, in the middle of the night, was not listed as one of the top ten things to do before you die.

Known across South East Asia as 'Indo Bill', the Secretary of the Persatuan Rugby Union Indonesia (PRUI), has been involved in Indonesian rugby since arriving in the mid 1990s. The warm and animated American greeted us on the stairs in his pyjamas, just an hour before intending to head out on a morning jog. It was clearly paying off, and we could see from the hallway photos that Indo Bill was literally half the man he used to be.

*   *   *   *   *

The annual Indonesian rugby dinner was by coincidence being sponsored by our very own new sponsors, DHL.

Thanks to Ray in Hong Kong, when we'd blown our budget in Bangkok, he'd rallied the offices around the Southern Hemisphere and we were now having our equipment transfers cared for, free of charge. In fact, as we walked into the black tie event, wearing shorts and a polo shirt, the bicycles were heading somewhere across town in a red and yellow van.

Milling around the hotel foyer, trying to avoid attention in our beach clothes, we finally met our other Indonesian contact, Steve Barber. 'Barbs' was a kiwi by birth, but raised from a young age in

Brisbane, he now felt Australian by nature. He was not only one of the original founders and the PRUI Chairman, but even risked his own neck at second row for the national fixtures.

The guest speakers that evening were former Wales and British & Irish Lions, Scott Quinnell, former World Cup winning Wallabie, Owen 'Melon' Finegan, and very much current emcee and auctioneer, Justin 'Sambo' Sampson. To say that we were excited was like saying the Indonesian ferry had been a little grubby, and when Scott came over to say hello in the pre-dinner drinks, it topped off an incredible ten month Asian rugby experience.

The main doors opened and we shuffled in behind Bill to our table.

'Hi guys, I'm Owen,' Owen Finegan said, as he took his seat next to me.

'Oh! Hi Owen,' I jumped in surprise.

'Hello again!' Scott Quinnell laughed, as he sat beside Jodie.

'Are those seats okay?' Steve tapped me on the shoulder with a face of pretend concern.

The evening kicked off and the locally brewed beer began to flow. I had never been to a rugby dinner of this sort, and after seeing Sambo in action, I now understood why Kate from Dubai wouldn't leave Rob alone at these events. I wanted to buy everything.

'How about that!' Kirk congratulated us after the dinner. Kirk Aditya Arundale was the captain of the Indonesian national team, and was not only referring to our trip, but at us being called onto stage at a black tie function, wearing shorts and velcro sandals.

'Bill told us no-one would notice!' I sighed, still quite embarrassed, 'I'm going to have a word with him about that!'

'You might have to wait until tomorrow!' Kirk laughed, 'I saw someone put him in a taxi about an hour ago!'

'I wondered why he didn't come back for dessert!'

'He still thinks he can drink like he could when he was fat!' Kirk explained, 'He's lost about five stone since he started running.'

'We're supposed to be staying with him!' Jodie panicked, 'I can't even remember where he lives.'

'Don't worry guys, there's loads of places you can stay tonight, just come out with us.'

With no place yet to go home, refusing such an offer from 'Captain Kirk' seemed more ridiculous than buying the 'economique' ferry ticket. After polishing off the last of the event's beer, we meandered next door into the plush hotel bar.

Stood at the first table were Barbs, Melon and a few of the union sponsors, thoroughly engaging themselves in the spirit of the occasion.

With Kirk and his Indonesian 'Rhinos' team mates, we joined the group and spent many more hours 'exploring the sport'. One couple sponsoring the dinner were Australians, James and Michele Brown, who not only bought us a congratulation drink, but went on to host us for the duration of our Jakarta visit.

*   *   *   *   *

With the entire rugby community of Bali now in Jakarta for the upcoming A5N tournament, we anticipated a degree of skepticism over our next short rugby stop. Some more cynical heads would suggest that it was nothing more than self-indulgence, others that we were now paying for two flights where one would have sufficed.

As fate would have it, direct flights from Jakarta to Darwin were so extortionately over-priced, that spending a few days relaxing on the 'Island of the Gods' actually managed to save us a large chunk of cash. Thanks to Bali Rugby Club President, Nick Mesritz, we also had his wife, Kelli, waiting to look after us in their family home.

Hopping onto our no-frills flight, we touched down in the early hours with the chance to wrap up our Asian rugby leg with a visit to the Bali bombing memorial. The same afternoon, as we took a long walk around the district of Kuta, we finally found our way to the original site of 'Paddy's Pub', a name now ingrained in our memories. In its place stood a monument dedicated to all the 202 victims, many of whom were close friends of people we had met on our journey.

That morning, we had left the house of the Bali 10s tournament director, thinking about the Australian outback and the challenge that lay ahead. It would be a test of patience and endurance, but at least we had the chance to try. Now stood at the polished marble, we were solemnly reminded that at this very spot, many rugby journeys had been finished long before their time.

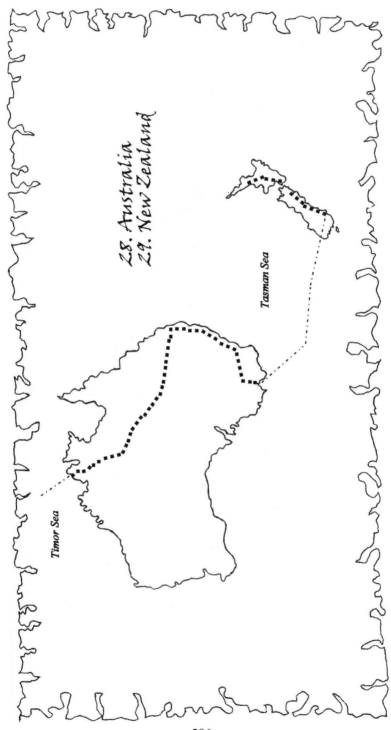

CHAPTER 33
AUSSIE MOSSIES

The three of us sat in the silent DHL office sipping our coffee.

'Welcome to your new home Jo,' I announced triumphantly, as we looked outside at the darkness.

Steve looked up from his desk, 'You've a little way to go yet guys, I thought you were heading for Melbourne?'

Steve Kent, the Territory's Freight and Forwarding Manager, had collected us from the airport terminal at 5 a.m. Now 5:30 a.m. and he was already working on getting our bicycles processed through the rigorous customs and quarantine inspections.

'I guess so,' I said, 'but it feels like Melbourne is just at the other end of the road.'

'True, but it's a bloody long one!' he laughed.

A reflex glance at the wall map of Australia reminded us how right he was. What were we thinking?

When booking our transfer from Bali, we had been faced with a few options. Firstly, we had to decide where we should begin our Australian leg, realistically Perth, Darwin or as many people suggested, Brisbane. Brisbane would have left us a relatively short cycle to Melbourne (around 2,000 km), whilst Perth would have offered the Nullabor Desert experience (around 3,500 km). Both were easily achievable in the 77 days we had before our flight to New Zealand.

Our biggest obstacle now became our principles. When previously traversing any 'wet bits' we had always agreed to take the shortest transport based on time, cost and visa accessibility. As such, neither Brisbane, nor Perth fitted in line with our principles, and so Darwin became our default choice.

With Darwin now pencilled in we then had to decide on a route to Melbourne. At this point, two main options presented themselves, either 3,800 km via Adelaide in South Australia, or 5,800 km via Brisbane and Sydney on the East coast.

Our friends waited for us in Brisbane, the rugby communities awaited us in Sydney, and we began to wonder whether we had any input in this trip whatsoever! The challenge had been laid down: 77 days, 5,800 km to pedal, rugby to be explored in four states, and to sink as many beers with our friends as we could.

With the bikes in government lock down over the weekend, our Darwin hosts, Andre and Maryse, helped assist us with the later components. Andre cracked open four beers, and as we relaxed out on the porch, he chatted about his rugby roots with Mid-Canterbury and the Junior All Blacks. I checked the beer label, it said 5% alcohol. Had I heard him correctly, or could I not handle Australian booze? The Junior All Blacks academy?

'It was a long time ago!' he added modestly, 'I was in the same year group as Carlos Spencer. Carlos didn't stick around at that level for long, he was a different class. It was great fun though, and quite a few of us enjoyed many years in rugby after that. I got to travel about England, Wales and Australia picking up semi-professional contracts wherever I settled down.'

'I'm trying to retire Tom!' he joked, 'I'm really enjoying my coaching roles here, but I always end up playing! One minute it's my club, Souths, then it's the Mossies, I'm thirty-six years old and I've played a *lot* of rugby!'

After a further explanation, we learned that 'Souths' referred to South Darwin, an early club of Eddie Jones, who competed in the Darwin A-Grade competition. The 'Mossies' were in fact the Territory representative side, 'The Mosquitos', who competed against interstate and rural representative sides.

Maryse disappeared into the kitchen, presumably to butcher an entire cow, because twenty minutes later she reappeared with four of the biggest steaks we had ever laid eyes on.

'Welcome to the Territory!' she presented to us proudly.

'We rented an apartment in London smaller than that,' said Jodie.

'You've got a long way to cycle guys! You'll need it!'

'It's honestly not that far,' I said, wondering who I was trying to convince.

'Tom, did you know that there are four rugby teams down in Katherine?' asked Andre.

'Actually, now that you mention it, I had seen something about rugby in Katherine.'

'They have their *own* competition down there, because it's *so* friggin' far away,' he laughed 'and they're not even halfway to Alice Springs!'

Andre did make a good point, the outback stretch was a long way. The leg to Brisbane alone was around 3,500 km, and we were attempting to do that part in 34 days, not allowing a single day's rest. It seemed easy to talk about it, but without Maryse's juicy steaks every night for dinner, would it be a realistic target after all? One day at a time I told myself.

'She'll be right,' I said, tucking into my steak.

On Sunday morning we borrowed Maryse's ute and drove ourselves down for a chat on the ABC Radio breakfast show. Forgetting that Darwin was comprised of just two roads, we arrived early at 10:30 a.m. instead of the scheduled 11 a.m. slot.

'We might take the chance to have a quick walk around Darwin,' I said to the producer, 'we'll be back in twenty minutes or so.'

She looked at me confused, but let us back out through the one way doors anyway.

'See you in a bit!' I said.

First we'd stop in at the bike shop, then the military surplus store, then maybe find somewhere to get some more sunscreen - we were going to need it.

'Quiet isn't it,' I pointed out to Jodie, after we'd crossed a small block.

'I think we've become too used to Asia,' she replied.

'You're right!' I agreed, 'But it feels very laid back here doesn't it. Quite civilised!'

Just then, two men appeared from round the corner, both wearing singlets and walking down the pavement with bare feet. Their feet were dry, cracked and filthy. I looked up at their faces, and there wasn't much improvement.

'I don't even recall seeing that in Jakarta?' I thought to myself, 'Why wouldn't you at least wear flip-flops?'

Technically Darwin was a city, even the capital of the Territory if there should be such a thing, but it in no way compared to the recent calamities of Hanoi, Bangkok or Jakarta. Even in the poorest of these places, we had noticed the locals keeping as smart as circumstances would allow them to. After so many months in Asia, it now felt quite unfamiliar stepping back into a fully western environment.

'It's shut?' I uttered in genuine surprise, 'What's the time?'

'It's 10:40,' Jodie replied.

'Let's have a look when it opens and we'll come back later.'

A timetable on the door read: Sunday - Closed.

Are they serious? Back in London, Sunday shopping was an absolute necessity. The working week was a complete write off with the long office hours, and if you played any sport on a Saturday afternoon, you'd rely on Sunday to get all the necessary jobs done for the week.

'Ridiculous,' I said, 'let's go and check out the military store.'

'Closed!' I read again, 'What is going on with this place?'

'Look back down the high street!' Jodie pointed out, 'What do you see?'

'Not much,' I said, 'It's empty?'

'That might be a clue,' she explained, 'I think *Darwin* is closed on Sundays.'

We ambled back to the radio station, realising that we were about to address the entire Darwin population, tucked up in bed at home.

*   *   *   *   *

It was Monday morning and the bikes had successfully cleared inspection, only Jodie's baby-formula milk had been disposed of meaning black tea that morning. As we pedalled a little nervously away, she swerved, just avoiding the fresh carcass of a large brown snake caught immobile in the crisp morning air.

'Bloody hell!' Jodie shouted behind her, 'Should we be worrying about snakes?'

'Not that one,' I reassured her, looking back over my shoulder. It could be mistaken for two snakes.

'Which way?' she called again, taking the brunt of the stiff headwind in our new shift pattern, we were now on the solitary road south from Darwin.

'It's basically straight ahead here, then turn left,' I called again.

'When do we turn left?'

'About Tuesday or Wednesday next week!'

Tennant Creek was the closest town to our left hand turn at Threeways - the signpost read 980 km.

'Not too bad,' I reassured myself. I looked down at the bicycle computer, it read 9 k.p.h. We always knew that getting out of Darwin would be tough, and we were trying to stay positive that the conditions would ease over the coming days.

Temporary respite came when a family from the Swampdogs Rugby Club hosted us in Humpty Doo, then a rugby playing park ranger in Katherine, but three days into the journey and we were out in the desolate Territory, on our own.

Although it spans an area five and a half times larger than the entire United Kingdom, it houses only 0.3% of the Australian population. It should go without saying that personal space was not a commodity out there, and we suddenly found a huge amount of time to reflect on our trip.

'Welcome to Mataranka, Capital of the Never Never!' a hand painted sign read.

'Territory's Tidiest Town 1991 & 1994!' another proudly displayed.

We were only a day inland from Katherine, and I had already begun to sympathise with their need for fabricated entertainment.

'Territory's Tidiest Town Awards!' I read silently, 'How might that work?'

I pictured imaginary scenes from the morning of the grand inspection. Irene would be by the town's water pump, frantically sweeping up leaves, while Roger applied a glossy new coat of paint to the community hall fence. Reggie and Dora would be desperately trying to turn the pile of buckled wagon wheels into installation art, and everyone piled pressure onto cattle farmer, Alf, to change into some more presentable trousers. With an hour to spare, Ted from the little post office, would plead with the local rubbish authorities to arrange a special collection.

'I know it's only supposed to be twice yearly!' he'd cry down the phone.

As nice an idea as it seemed, I felt sure that it could never catch on back at home. Tactics in South East London would almost certainly be to sabotage neighbouring boroughs rather than tidy their own backyard. It wouldn't take long for gangs of hoodies to coordinate 'drive by trashings', and have unmarked packages of litter delivered through rivals letterboxes. A 'tidy town' competition back home would have quite the opposite effect.

The best part about the TTT awards, was that even if you lost to a tidier town, there were many other genuine accolades to take home - 'Best New Tidy Towns Entrant', 'Best Dust Suppression Initiatives', 'Best Landfill Site', 'Best Medium Community' to name just a few. The last of these briefly raised concern, when staring defeat in the face, a medium sized town tried to enter 'Best Small Community' by hiding all their old people in a nearby cave. To prevent a similar situation happening again, they became the first recipients of the new award 'Best Cave Retirement Facilities'. It soon became clear that every town would leave with something.

We left the two time champions as quickly as we had arrived, and camped up in a road side picnic stop. Dinner had now become a shared meal on rations of one carrot, some cabbage, and three packets of two-minute noodles mixed with two sachets of cup-a-soup. Dessert was an even more depressing affair, being just the leftovers from a daily supply of six biscuits each. Out in the small towns, a single loaf of bread would cost the entire day's food budget, and so we were forced to carry enough supplies to last until Mount Isa, and another cheap supermarket.

The evenings were short and the nights long, but if you woke up and could brave the cold, you would be treated to a quite spectacular view of the entire galaxy. With such an unspoiled spectacle, we would regularly gaze up at the billions of shining stars, having the clichéd conversations of how meaningless everything really was - especially long bicycle rides. Hit by this stark realization, the 'Territory's Tidy Town' awards very nearly paled into insignificance.

A giant road train passed us by, the driver giving a polite toot on the horn as he gave us plenty of berth. As he pulled back in, we saw the trademark arse wiggle, as fifty metres of carriage, loaded two tier with cattle, tried to straighten out. There would be no stopping a unit of this size, and we had chatted with several road train drivers at rest stops who wanted to ensure we stayed safe on the road.

'Listen, the guys will always give you as much space as they can,' one man explained, 'but if they hold down the horn, don't think twice, please just get off the road because it means they can't move for you. They're not being rude or aggressive.'

'How much do these things weigh?' I asked in wonder.

'Look mate, this one here might weigh about 100 tonnes, but others can be 120, 140, sometimes upwards depending on where you are.'

I was hit by a sudden attack of 'quantity irrelevance' - he could have said one tonne and it would have been easily sufficient to have me leaping for cover. My brain wasn't able to comprehend cycling into a 120 tonne truck or a 140 tonne truck. Would I even notice a difference?

'What about your set-up?' he looked at our bicycles.

'Ah, maybe 50, 60 kg,' I said. 'Sometimes upwards, depending on how many chocolate biscuits we have left.'

'You bloody crazy poms,' he laughed, 'where did you start from?'

'We started our ride in London,' Jodie answered, going through the motions, 'we've cycled across the world to get here.'

He looked at us with a little bewilderment. 'But where did you start from in Australia?' he asked.

'Darwin,' I answered, knowing exactly what was about to happen next.

'Darwin!' he shouted, 'That's bloody miles away!'

*   *   *   *   *

'Welcome to Adelaide River - Territory's Tidiest Town 2000!'

Another town, another new winner, but the sign was eroding in the elements, causing flakes of paint to collect in a small pile on the floor. Although the weather was tepid, it indicated how severe the conditions could get at other times of the year.

'It'd be ironic if that sign had actually cost them from defending the title,' I said to Jodie, who had long since lost interest in the outback, and was now counting down the days until Brisbane.

The previous night, a storm had passed over us, giving the whole outback a good soaking in the process. Although the road had quickly dried in the morning sunshine, we were now hit by a much more serious hurdle.

Hundreds of decaying kangaroo carcasses, that had previously been tolerable, had now begun to react violently with the overnight rainfall. The stench in the outback was now tenfold, and every new wisp of headwind carried the musk from the next decomposing victim.

Perhaps the only thing worse that the smell of a decaying kangaroo with its intestines spread out on the smouldering tarmac, was the one in our tent at night. Our repetitive diet was now taking its toll, causing us to produce a gas similar in toxicity to carbon monoxide. Although equally potent, it wasn't odourless, and had the type of smell that could literally melt your face. On many occasions we both woke up clutching at our throats, and on one particularly windy night, I actually felt our Terra Nova tent trying to float away. Our guts had begun to erode, and as the cycle progressed, I started to fear for the lifetime warranty on my Brooks saddle.

A long wet season had also meant a much greener outback, and combined with the pleasant temperature, circumstances now led to any even more eerie experience on the road.

'What is that?' I pointed ahead, 'It looks like the road goes underwater.'

As we got closer, the shimmering surface no longer looked like water, but was the hatchlings of millions and millions of little wood lice.

'Oh, no! That's disgusting,' I said, as our tyres kicked hundreds of the hatchlings up against our bare legs. 'Look, it just goes on and on!'

'Slow down a bit,' Jodie instructed, 'you're back wheel is flicking them all up at my face.'

We slowed down, and although it reduced the numbers we disturbed, it now became harder to hold our breath past the decaying kangaroos. Before we had managed to clear the bugs, several motor homes flashed past us, coating us in waves of antennas, legs and wood louse juice.

'Fucking hell!' I yelled, shaking them out of my helmet, 'This is ridiculous! Really Jo, when you thought about what it was going to be like cycling through the outback, did you imagine this?'

Jodie was quiet.

'I didn't!' I yelled again, answering the question for her, and trying to pick out the last of the woodlice from my gums.

*   *   *   *   *

'Look Jo!' I laughed, pointing to a colourful wooden board at the side of the road, 'Those Australians just can't help themselves!'

'What do you mean?' she turned trying to make out the semi-circular chart.

'Do you remember what I said about the Australian's murdering our superlatives?'

'You said they didn't have enough words for regular situations?'

On our left was a large six-stage fire-risk scale, not in itself very amusing, but then neither were bush fires. It was the thought behind the scale that made me slap my forehead in sheer disappointment.

'Look at the scale!' I insisted again, the arrow was pointed at 'High Risk of Fire'.

'If I said to you, Jo don't eat that, there's a *high* risk that you might die. Would you still eat it?'

'Depends how chocolatly it was I suppose! What are you trying to say?'

Although only stage two on the danger scale, if 'High Risk of Fire' wasn't enough to stop you flicking cigarettes into the bush, the third stage 'Very High Risk of fire' would surely sound some warnings. Put into another context, I've yet to meet a man willing to do something with a 'Very High Risk' of, say, losing his testicles.

I didn't think the scale warranted anything stronger, but stage four bent me over and pulled down my pants - 'Extremely High Risk of Fire'. Logically, we then needed 'Severely High Risk of Fire' for those who did extreme sports just for kicks, but if someone really required 'Catastrophically High Risk of Fire' - the final stage, I feared that they were probably the type to do it anyway.

At the *safe* end of the scale the warning read 'Low/ Moderate Risk of Fire'.

'Look, *low* and *moderate* have to share a segment!' I pointed out again, now killing the subject.

'Maybe there is no such thing as a low risk of fire here,' Jodie suggested sensibly, trying to bring back some logic.

'Jo, wasn't the whole area just under six foot of water?'

As the weeks began to slowly slip away, so too did our patience with the huge road sign distances. After nearly four weeks in the Australian outback, with a full thousand kilometres still left to Brisbane, we both agreed that we were 100% bored.

'You know what Tom?' Jodie finally concluded, 'Sometimes there is just *too* much bush.'

There was a pun in there somewhere, but I was too fed up to even bother looking.

CHAPTER 34
THE RUGBY COAST

If you are going to separate two best friends, both girls and both chatterboxes, you'd be right to expect a fair amount of gossip once the magnets were reunited.

'So tell me all about it!' Sam squealed, as they squeezed the life out of each other. Naturally there was a short delay to summarise fifteen months on the road,

'... and that's why we were half an hour late,' said Jodie, seven days later.

Luckily for me, in that seven day hurricane of gasbagging, I was pulled to safety by King, Sam's Brisbane fiancé, and Chris, our ginger haired Australian mate - responsible for at least half of our hangovers back in London. We maintained a steady flow of beers, and kept our conversation to strictly 'manly' topics like 'Where were the scariest wild animals?' and 'Which girls had the nicest boobs?'

The Queensland Reds had just brought home the first ever Super 15 title, so it became a perfect location to kick back for a week, talk rugby and sink a few cold ones while we planned the East Coast itinerary. Somehow, I even managed a visit to North Brisbane rugby club, unexpectedly stumbling on the Greek national coach, Michael Bishop, in the process.

Prizing the girls apart for a second time was harder than changing a flat tyre in minus 25 degrees, and so it was lucky for us that the Gold Coast Eagles RFC welcomed us with such hospitality.

Former SAS man, Austin Whittaker, and his family ensured we enjoyed a very safe night at their house, and we were still wearing the Eagles' jerseys when we arrived at Ballina RFC the following evening.

Despite Australia's clear success at national level, the crafty buggers still love to convince you that they 'don't play union'. Let me tell you now, they *do* play union, and there are literally tens of thousands of players, they have more rugby union clubs than in New Zealand. The underlying and unresolved problem is that the country is just too large to produce a cost efficient domestic competition to feed up into Super Rugby franchises. It is therefore left to the devices of each state to run domestic competitions, and bring through the best players. The highest quality regional league has traditionally been in Sydney, but it is still a huge step down for players looking to gain match time in-between either international duty, or Super Rugby. This belief was confirmed when we met former Waratahs coach, Chris Hickie, coaching down at his old club, the 'Sea Horses' in Ballina.

After another comfortable night inside a rugby clubhouse, we started to hit our stride down the East coast. Still on track for my 30th birthday in Sydney, our strong progress was unexpectedly tested when we arrived at Doug Anderson's sugar cane farm in the picturesque town of Yamba.

'It's a real shame that you're heading off so soon!' he said, 'My wife's away for the weekend and my old team are playing a big derby match across the bay in Iluka. It would be quite an experience for you both to see it.'

'And you think there are still tickets available?' I laughed.

'I'll check of course, but I think there are still dog walking tickets available. The type that let you watch from anywhere around the pitch.'

That evening, the more Doug topped up our wine glasses, the more I considered a day off to watch some rugby, not to mention the added lure of Australia playing New Zealand on the TV. I looked at Jodie who had sensed my wavering thoughts long before even myself.

'Look, you know I don't mind at all, as long as you're happy with the schedule to Sydney, then so am I.'

I turned back to Doug. 'It's a deal!' I said.

'Excellent!' he replied. 'The standard won't be much to write about, but I promise you, you won't have seen anything like it before.'

'Well great!' I said, 'If you're happy to put us up for another night, we'd love to hang out with you and chat about rugby!'

Doug nodded contently and pulled a tray of sizzling meat from the oven to serve up some dinner.

'It's a pleasure to have you here. My son's over in the UK at the moment, and I'd like to think he's being looked after in the same way.'

We sat at the table and he opened a third bottle of wine.

'So look, anyway, there's something I've really been waiting to ask you,' he said, a little tactfully.

'Sure, what is it?' I replied.

'What exactly *are* you selling?'

It was the morning of the big local derby, the Yamba Buccaneers vs Iluka Cossacks. Many years ago, the Iluka squad had been a 3rd grade side within the Yamba Buccaneers, but after a period of apparent repression and social inadequacy, they had decided to cross the waters and set up independently on the less preferential 'North Shore'.

Exiled into what the locals had coined as Siberia, they became known as the 'Cossacks', and still to this day vowed to silence the 'noncing posh southerners' whenever the tribes clashed.

Morning came, and as the sun rose, we stared out over the bay in wonder of what barbaric hordes awaited us on the far side. Droplets of resentment splashed against the bows of Yamba yachts, and a spray of bitterness blew up off from the gentle waters to wet our cheeks. The waves glimmered red with the innocent reflections of the sunrise, but instead I imagined a shoreline teaming with the burning effigies of Yamba rugby players, as delirious Cossacks danced in frantic circles wielding huge axes. I looked down at my third coffee that morning.

'Do you have any decaf, Doug?' I asked.

Although only about a kilometre apart, the two grounds were separated by a 50 km road trip, leading inland to the west and across the only bridge. Today, it was Yamba's turn to make the journey.

'Why do they resent you guys so much?' I asked Dave Fleming, one of the Yamba supporters, as we docked up his beautiful speedboat on the Iluka shores. The exhilarating journey had taken only two minutes, and the entire team had been able to traverse the waters in four of their shiny new boats.

'Ah look, don't ask me Tom!' he answered, 'For some reason, they still see us as the rich guys on the posh shore. If you ask me, it's about time they let go.'

As a team mate helped secure his boat, he smiled and passed up a makeshift floating cheese board, with a bag containing a fancy selection of French cheeses.

'For the after-game bath,' he explained, 'now do me a favour would you, and pass me those bottles of Merlot, they're under the seat.'

We arrived at the battlefield to a gathering crowd and the team kitted up. Iluka numbers swelled, and soon it felt that the entire township had come to witness the encounter. The pitch side seating had filled, and the BBQ tent was in full operation, as crowds of locals sat on their pickups swigging crates of VB. Finally, a young teenage referee took to the field, followed by the two teams and the wait was over. The ceremonious handshaking between the teams convinced me of nothing, it was all on the line and this was to be much more than just another rugby game.

Perhaps due to struggling player numbers, or quite possibly malnutrition on the less preferential shore, the Cossack side gave away huge concessions in both size and body weight, particularly in the pack. In sharp contrast were the gym chiselled Yamba players, who proudly displayed the results of their protein enriched diet and personal training plans.

Although Yamba took the points quite comfortably winning 54-0, many aspects of the game were closely contested. Most impressive was the good discipline showed by the Cossacks, especially considering that 90% of the players were serving lifetime bans for fighting, amongst themselves, in their own pub. It was the perfect old fashioned local derby, and perhaps fittingly, the more refined Buccaneers were swiftly destroyed in the after match boat race.

With a great day of rugby finished, I pondered over our experience on the speed boat ride back to Yamba. The Cossacks and the Buccaneers certainly hadn't burned any bridges over the years, but perhaps in their situation, it was probably better they hadn't built one.

Thanks to Doug, we left Yamba the next morning with another roof and a bed waiting for us. Gary Munday, his old friend, was co-founder and now life member of the Kempsey 'Cannonballs' Rugby Club. An extraordinarily passionate man, Gary had been instrumental from the very beginning, even creating their first pavilion by wheeling down an entire house from a nearby village.

The New South Wales weather had now become more fitting to South Wales and we were hugely thankful for such a tight Australian rugby community of mates.

$$* \quad * \quad * \quad * \quad *$$

From: 'Charlie Buchanan'
To: 'Jodie and Tom'

'I have just become aware of your epic and inspiring venture. I take my hat off to you - almost there! I am from a big rugby family (UK) but been settled in Sydney now for 9 years. My husband and I have been lucky enough to travel the world and been welcomed into homes of the global rugby family.
I'd love to extend an invitation for you to stay with us in Sydney for as long as your schedule will allow. Look forward to meeting you.

Kind regards
Charlie Buchanan'

$$* \quad * \quad * \quad * \quad *$$

Only one more appointment now separated us from a very welcoming invitation in Sydney, it was scheduled with the Port Macquarie Pirates.

'Sounds great mate!' Wilbur had told me by phone, 'I'd love to show you around the club, but there's no training that night as we lost in the semi-final last weekend. Our season's finished now.'

'Smashing!' I'd replied, 'We'll get down there at 5 p.m. and wait around for you. Cheers Wilbur!'

At 4:45 p.m. it began to rain, and although we had found the communal sports park, we had to pedal around the complex several times to locate the correct locked pavilion. Sheltered under a concrete balcony, we lit the cooker and prepared a cup of tea, it was nearly 5 p.m.

A tall athletic man appeared from around the corner and strolled towards us with intent.

'Bang on time!' I said to Jodie, and strolled out into the rain towards the man.

'Hi there!' I said.

'Oh, hello,' the man replied, a little surprised, 'do you speak English?'

I nodded, now realising that he was carrying a tennis racket.

'I hope you don't mind me coming over,' he continued, 'but I saw you both cycling around the complex and thought you might need some help.'

'Oh, thanks,' I replied. 'We're actually due to meet someone from the rugby club here, they're going to show us around the club quickly.'

'Were you planning to camp on the pitch?' he asked, glancing across at all of our gear.

'Er, yes, we were actually!' I said, 'We can't camp inside the clubhouse - apparently it's a shared facility.'

'Listen, I'll completely understand if you don't want to, but I would like to offer you both to spend the night with my wife and I. We've just got back from a ten week camping trip around Spain, and I *really* understand how nice it is to have a hot shower and a bed!'

'Really?' I said to the man, 'We have a quick tour to do here when our Pirate arrives, but after that we'd love to.'

'Great!' he replied.

'We're doing a bit of a rugby themed cycle tour you see,' I continued, 'rugby union that is. Are you into rugby union at all?'

I reached into my pocket and handed him a soggy business card.

'Oh thanks, and yes, I like rugby union,' he said, glancing down at the mushy card. 'Tom, listen, I'll write down my address and phone number for you, and don't worry at all if you change your mind, I won't be offended. I'm Peter by the way.'

'Great, really nice to meet you Peter. Thanks, we'll come over to you as soon as we're finished.'

I shook his hands, realising that I'd made him stand in the rain through the whole conversation. We drank our tea with a big smile and waited for Wilbur to arrive, he was running late but it now didn't matter in the slightest.

'What a really nice bloke!' Jodie reflected, 'He didn't even care what we were doing, he just wanted to help us.'

Wilbur arrived and opened up the pavilion for a private tour.

'Do you fancy a beer?' he smiled, pointing at the fridge behind the bar, 'I have the keys.'

'Haha, you know that any other day and I would have!' I laughed, 'But we have a 10 km cycle after this, better play it safe!'

I looked over, allowing Jodie to acknowledge her pride in me, but she managed to hide it with almost military precision.

'No worries, as you wish,' said Wilbur, 'so come on, bring your bicycles in out of the rain and I'll show you around.'

'How long have you played rugby for?' I asked him, after all he was the club captain.

'I honestly don't know how it all happened!' he laughed, 'I didn't start playing until I was thirty-six years old, when I got asked to join the vets side. I played a few games, but I was being used as a tackle bag so much I *dropped down* to the seniors. After my first season, they voted me as club captain! I only joined last year!'

'Sounds like rugby logic to me Wilbur!' I said, 'Come on, let's get some photos wearing pirate gear.'

Despite leaving before dark, it was pitch black by the time we finally closed in on Peter Lumsdaine's house. As we pulled up, he was delighted to see that we had accepted his invitation.

'Did you ever play rugby Peter?' Jodie asked him over dinner.

Peter didn't need to answer as Kate's laugh was one of a true rugby widow.

'I used to watch Peter play *every* single week,' she smiled, 'but they were such good boys, we all had a lot of fun'

'Really? Did you? Who did you play for Peter?'

Peter Lumsdaine not only played rugby, but progressed to captain one of the strongest club sides in the country, Manly RFC in North Sydney. I was beside myself, we had literally stumbled across a great grassroots story by chance, and the little devil hadn't mentioned a thing. He may have just grilled the sausages, but that wouldn't be the last of the grilling that evening.

'Come on Peter! Tell me some stories. Who was the best player you played with?'

'Okay, well look, if I tell you some stories I want you to remember that I was not playing at their level by any means.

'I understand.'

'Tom, these men really were *fantastic* players. You can't go around saying that I was a fantastic player, okay?'

'Peter, I promise.'

Peter was a fantastic player, possibly not quite as fantastic as some of his opponents, but nevertheless, about as good as one could get without wearing their country's colours.

Peter had played for the Australian Barbarians, and against France for a South West Pacific XV, but insisted that this had reflected the limits of his powers. Peter's refusal to proudly admit his talent supported everything that I remembered and loved about grassroots rugby - that great players talked themselves down, us crap players talked ourselves up, and somehow at 5 p.m. we could all stand together and enjoy a drink.

'The best player I ever had the fortune to play with was a good friend called 'Slaggy' Miller.'

Tony Miller, commonly known as 'Slaggy' after a rugby tour near the slag heaps in Wales, was once Australia's most capped national player. At a time when very few tests could be arranged, he managed to represent his country forty-one times over sixteen seasons, only missing two tours through injury and commitments to his young family.

Slaggy was a tough, rugged lock and later prop, who not only played one hundred times for New South Wales, but an incredible 346 first grade matches for Manly RFC too. When he played his final test match against the All Blacks in 1967, he was 38 years old and remains the oldest Australian ever to have played in a test match.

Peter Lumsdaine was 1st XV captain at Manly while Slaggy was playing at the end of his career. In his very last match, Peter found himself being interfered with at a line out, and at Slaggy's own advice, had thrown out an elbow to even out the situation. He heard the crunch of a nose being displaced, and turned in horror to see blood pouring down Slaggy's chin. Slaggy was furious, not because Peter had broken his nose, but that he didn't want people to think the opposition had got one over him. Slaggy's wife, Joyce, was equally critical of Peter's aim, complaining that after all those years of rugby, he could have at least broken it in the other direction and straightened it back up.

'Luckily we got on very well!' Peter laughed, 'He was my coach for many years after that.'

'Okay, what about the best player you played against?'

'That's an easy one. I'd have to say Ray Price. He was a horrible man on the pitch, but as usual, an absolute gentleman off it.'

Ray Price, often referred to as 'Mr Perpetual Motion', was a hard, intimidating and very direct player. He proved so effective in the

1970s that he was selected several times for the Wallabies, before transferring to rugby league and becoming a regular fixture in the 'Kangaroos' - the national side.

'Oh Peter, tell them about the prop you played with against France,' Kate encouraged him, as did we all.

'Okay, okay,' he agreed, smiling as he reminisced about the overseas experience in New Caledonia.

In 1972, Peter had been invited to play in a match featuring Fijians, Tongans, Samoans, three All Blacks, three Australians and a scattering of locals. For France stood a full line up of stars, including Joe Maso, Pierre Villepreux and both Claude and Walter Spanghero. Considering that Sir Colin Meads later identified Walter Spanghero as his 'toughest ever international opponent', I began to understand how horrible it would have been to face Ray Price.

Amongst Peter's pack were two All Black props, Richie Guy and Keith Murdoch, and an Australian Number 8 called Greg Cornelson. In Auckland, several years later, Greg became the only man to score four tries against the All Blacks in a single test, another record that still stands today.

Iron hard prop, Keith Murdoch, was a 17 stone man mountain and had an appetite fitting to his build. Never satisfied by a regular meal, Peter joked that in the posh French hotel, he had repeatedly placed his giant hand on the waitress' arm, and signalled for three or four more portions.

'Later that year, Keith toured the UK with the All Blacks but there was an incident and he was thrown off the tour.'

'God, what happened?' Jodie asked, as I tried to imagine my own frustration at small fancy French dinners.

'Keith scored the only try beating the Welsh, then went out to celebrate with some of the guys. Later that evening he was found with his hands in the hotel fridge, and when both security and tour manager tried to stop him, he knocked one of the guards out. He never even returned to New Zealand.'

'That's awful!' I said in shock, 'I can't believe they tried to stop him making a sandwich.'

I woke up from our second night at Peter and Kate's, knowing that Sydney was only 400 km away. As a carrot for arriving inside four days, it would coincide with my own 30th birthday, and Jodie had been busy organising a surprise celebration through Charlie and Jim.

'It's not a surprise, if you've already told me!' I explained to Jodie, as I sulked in the pouring rain.

'Oh cheer up Tom! You don't even know who's coming to your drinks!'

As interesting as it all sounded, we were four hard days away and now cycling on a very exposed part of coastline. The wind whipped in, the rain lashed down and progress had become soggy, turgid and unpleasant. Now completely drenched, we pulled up under the small overhang of a surfers' changing room, hoping to sit it out - there was to be no relenting.

Two depressing hours later, we finally gave up hope, pushing back into wave after wave of gruelling showers.

Naturally, the following morning nothing had dried out, and we faced pulling on our wet gear and making up for the lost ground. The pattering on our tent roof told us all we needed to know about our fortune.

'We can't pedal in this for eight hours!' I insisted to Jodie, who was now disappointed that her plans looked on the ropes.

'I know, but we can't sit here all day either.'

As much as I hated to be reminded of the reality, Jodie was correct and we faced two simple choices; either wait illegally, camped in a public park and miss my birthday by a country mile, or leave now, miss my birthday by a day and get very wet in the process.

Eating smash and fried chicken schnitzel in the rain three days later, we can tell you that we attempted the second option.

'Happy birthday honey!' Jodie said, trying her very best to raise our spirits.

We were again camped in a small public park, hiding down towards a nearby river, on a ground saturated by days of persistent rain. As a rare treat, we had considered checking into a hostel to celebrate my birthday somewhere dry, but the cheapest room was more than a week's budget and there was no longer any time ahead to save it back. We were now down to nine dollars a day.

'Jo, seeing as we're still 60 km outside of Sydney, you might as well tell me what I've missed out on.'

'Really? You don't think that will make it worse?'

'No, I'd like to know. It's the thought that counts.'

'We were all going to the pub with Phil Kearns,' she answered, believing every word that I had just said.

'*Nooooooo!*' I cried, shedding tears into my smash.

CHAPTER 35
A DAY IN NOBODY'S PANTS

True to her word, Charlie Buchanan, former England rugby schoolgirl, had indeed come from a very big rugby family. Her father, former England rugby schoolboy, John Jeavons-Fellows, was previously the chairman of the RFU and a representative on the IRB.

Perhaps his most crucial contribution to rugby came as a 4th official in the 1995 Rugby World Cup, when he made the decision to allow South Africa to contest the semi-final against France. Had this decision not been made, France would have gone through by default, and Matt Damon would never have been miscast so horribly in Invictus.

'I can't turn up to another dinner wearing thongs and boardies,' I moaned to Jodie, suddenly taking an interest in my appearance at the age of thirty.

I wasn't pretending to be comfortable with using terms like 'thongs' and 'boardies', but during my short time in Australia, I had forced myself to adopt the local dialect. Saying 'flip-flops' in Australia, not only made you sound like a five year old grandchild of the Queen, but it usually led to people wetting themselves and spilling their cheap tasting beer all over you.

Once I'd taken my first tentative step into their beach culture, I then felt obliged to see it through, never again using the correct and accurate names for many day to day items. Trousers had become 'pants', pants were displaced to 'undies' in turn relegating undies to 'G-strings', ruining any chance of listening to Johan Sebastian Bach's masterpiece again without sniggering.

In any case, I had nothing to wear and we were going to another DHL sponsored rugby lunch. With Sambo back as emcee, there was every chance we'd become at least a brief inclusion into the itinerary, and with bare knees on display this could lead to a little embarrassment.

Charlie's husband, Jim, returned back from work, and it didn't take long to realise that we were made of different genetic compositions. He had a little more genetic evolution around the belly area, and at the same time, my head was further away from the floor than his. At a push, the shirt could fit well enough to say a few words, but the trousers looked like I was trying to advocate a male version of the three quarter length suit, the polar opposite of the word 'power'.

It would be our first opportunity to mingle with legends such as South African coach, Jake White, and former All Black, Stu Wilson, not to mention former Wallaby and leading rugby writer, Peter

Fitzsimmons. With my fingers crossed, the Buchanans phoned around their friends and colleagues in search of some 'pants'. By 9 p.m. we were still in situation 'pants down' as all their taller friends appeared away on holiday, direct to voicemail or off the radar. The outlook was bleak and time was running out.

'Aren't you meeting John Eales at breakfast tomorrow morning?' Charlie turned to ask us.

'Yep! We're meeting him around 9 a.m. at the Australian Rugby Union HQ,' I answered, although casually, still secretly ecstatic that we were meeting John Eales the following day, 'but it's just an informal meeting, I was only going to wear my trackies.'

'I wasn't asking what you were going to wear to meet him, I was wondering what *he* would be wearing to meet you!'

'Charlie, are you seriously suggesting that we ask John for his pants? If I walk away wearing his pants, he's going to look a bit daft in his morning meetings?'

'If you ask him *before* you meet him, maybe he could bring a spare pair for you.'

'Charlie, I've never even met John, he just confirmed the meeting by text.'

'Then text him back and ask.'

'I can't text him back.'

'Text him back.'

'I'm not texting him back,' I insisted, 'there must be someone else you know, what about your neighbours?'

'Listen here!' Charlie stepped into her 'sports marketing' mode, 'You need pants, we know he is taller than you, and he's the last person you will be meeting before the lunch. Just send him a text. What is the worst outcome? He says no?'

'Charlie, I can't. It's John Eales for God's sake. You don't just ask people like John Eales for their pants. We're lucky enough to... ' I stopped mid sentence.

She looked at me and I realised that despite the lunacy of the suggestion, Charlie did in fairness appear to be presenting a logical argument. Sure, he would probably say no, but with the haphazard nature of our trip, and John was quite aware of this, he probably wouldn't take offence at the request either. Not only this, but the idea of wearing a pair of John Eales pants to a rugby debate had now crept into my thoughts - there could be no better pants to wear to such an event.

'... oh bloody hell!' I conceded as I nervously started to type a text. Jodie, Charlie and the kids fell about laughing.

'HI JOHN, REALLY SORRY TO ASK YOU BUT WE'RE GOING TO A RUGBY LUNCH TOMORROW AT SYDNEY STADIUM AND I CAN'T FIND ANYBODY TALL ENOUGH TO LEND ME ANY PANTS. IF YOU ARE ABLE TO LOAN ME A SPARE PAIR AT OUR MEETING THAT WOULD BE REALLY HELPFUL. SORRY AGAIN AND LOOK FORWARD TO MEETING YOU'

The backlight glowed, 'MESSAGE SENT'.

'Done,' I breathed a sigh of relief, it was out of my hands now.

'Really? Did you actually just ask John Eales for his pants?' Charlie asked, laughing at me in apparent disbelief.

'What?... Hang on... You said...' I panicked, 'It was *your* idea!'

I realised that she was winding me up and I collapsed down on the sofa in exhaustion.

'What are you watching Jakey-boy?' I asked, seeking refuge with the youngest of the Buchanans.

'Tri-Nations repeat,' he stated very confidently, 'Australia win.'

Jake Buchanan was only six years old, and last year he had depressingly achieved more in a single week than I had in my entire career. As 'Top Try Scorer' and 'Most Valuable Player', he'd played his final match for the Sydney side, Mosman Juniors, before flying back to England for the remaining half a season. After touching down, he'd attended a midweek rugby camp with Worcester Warriors, winning 'Most Promising Player', and playing his first match for Strourbridge RFC the very next day, upholding a long and proud family tradition.

Having spent a full season and a half inside a tent, matching my wits against a six year old rugby expert were nervy times. He already knew most things there was to know, following all levels of rugby in both the Northern and Southern Hemisphere. Jake was by far the biggest and youngest rugby fan I had ever met, but although he was in love with rugby, I reminded myself that he was also just six years old. I had clear mental and social superiority, I could tie my own shoe laces, I didn't have to go to school, in fact I didn't have to do anything I didn't want to - not unless Jodie said so.

'Who do you want to win the World Cup Jake?' I asked him.

'Australia,' he answered, with little consideration at all, 'Curtley Beale plays for them. He's the best.'

Although Jake was born in England to English parents, in recent months he had reached a tipping point where he felt a greater following for the Wallabies. Jake would probably give you specific and technical reasons for the change of heart, quite possibly the more dynamic and attacking back line in the Southern Hemisphere, compiled with the disillusionment at the heavy one dimensional direction of the English side. When I was six, I liked to pour marmalade onto the carpet.

'Yep, sounds fair enough Jake. Curtley is a pretty good player.'

'Who do you want to win?' he fired back at me.

'England of course!' I said, trying to shame him with my patriotism.

'Shall we have a bet?' little Jake turned to me.

'Not sure if I should be encouraging you to bet Jakey-boy. Mummy Buchanan might kill me.'

'No gambling your pocket money Jake Buchanan!' Charlie called from the bedroom.

'One dollar!' he whispered to me.

'One dollar?' I replied, 'I'll have to think about it.'

Jake turned back to the match, he seemed very comfortable and his legs barely stretched over the edge of the seat. He might have been sitting pretty with a piggy bank full of dollar coins, but we had recently dropped to an eight dollar a day budget. One dollar could now be the difference of having beans on toast for lunch, or just toast. There was definite risk involved, but due to an unidentifiable patriotism, I almost felt obliged to throw a dollar of support to the boys of the red rose. I doubted that Australia could beat New Zealand at Eden Park, and in any case, I wouldn't have to square up with Jake until the World Cup final. If I put aside two cents per day until the 23 October, my lunch might already be covered in the result of a loss.

'Okay, you're on Jakey-boy,' I decided, 'but if neither of our teams win the World Cup then the bet is null and void... It means we don't pay each other.'

'I bet you one dollar that England win the Rugby World Cup,' I offered him my hand.

'And I bet you one dollar that New Zealand win the Rugby World Cup,' he said, as he shook mine.

'What? But you said you were choosing Australia?' I stammered, realising I had just offered a six year old evens on an All Black victory at home.

'No, I said I *wanted* Australia to win,' he replied, 'but now I'll get a dollar if they don't.'

'You little... ' BEEP - my phone received a text.

'TOM, WHAT WAIST SIZE ARE YOU? JOHN EALES'

* * * * *

308

'Thanks for guiding us out of Sydney Dylan! You definitely know your way round on a bicycle.'

'It's my pleasure guys, it's what I do.'

'Great stuff, hang on... What do you mean it's *what* you do?'

'My company 'Ride and Seek'?' now *he* sounded confused, 'Didn't I tell you?'

We had been speaking with Dylan Reynolds for over one year, and he had not once mentioned that he ran a cycle touring company. I considered the notion, that quite possibly, this information would have been useful over the previous 26,000 km of pedalling.

'I thought you just did charity tours with the Tag Rugby Trust?' I despaired.

'That might help other kids Tom, but it doesn't pay for mine!'

'Well then Dylan, if that is indeed your real name, thanks for all your help!'

'No problems guys,' he laughed, waving us off. 'Listen, have fun and go easy on Nobody's trousers!'

'Nobody?' Jodie frowned, 'Why are you calling John Eales nobody?'

Dylan kept a straight face.

'Because *nobody's* perfect Jodie. Just look at Tom.'

So many people were full of good advice when it came to the subject of long distance cycling. Based on the fact that last year they borrowed a friend's mountain bike to enter a 50 km charity fundraiser, they somehow felt qualified to criticise our route decisions. Despite the coastal route being over 100 km longer, and as easy to cycle as a sheet of corrugated iron, most people desponded at hearing that we were taking the Hume Highway to Melbourne. We'd always tried to remind them that our bicycles weighed 50 kg and we needed to be there in nine days, but they'd still walk away shaking their heads in disappointment.

'It's not what I'd do, that's all I'm saying.'

'Well, if it's that fucking great, then why haven't *they* cycled it?' I'd usually turn to Jodie, waiting until they had left.

As it turned out the Hume Highway was, in parts, a very pleasant road to cycle. The weather inland proved a lot more stable, the gradients were more gradual, and tickling along at such a leisurely pace, some of the views were immense. Novelties did wear off however, and after eight days of 'getting away from it all' we were ready to 'go back to it' in the form of old mates, Freeway and Kristy.

After eight consecutive days of over 100 km, we pulled up at a petrol station to let the guys know about our impending arrival. I logged onto Skype and gave Freeway a call at work.

'I can't wait to have a shower,' Jodie smiled, as the phone began to ring.

'Hey guys!' answered Freeway in his diluted Derby-Kiwi accent, 'How are you travelling?'

We gave him the rundown of progress and our estimated time of arrival, we were now just hours away from finishing a mammoth 6,000 km Australian leg.

'Listen guys, what do you want first? The good news or the bad news?'

'The good news please!' I answered without hesitation.

'Well, the good news is that there is a gym at the end of our road, and we've got some free passes for you!'

'Fair enough,' I answered, pulling a face at Jodie. There was no way in a million years that I was going to be going down the gym. 'What's the bad news?'

'The bad news is that if you want a shower, you'll have to use them. Ours is broken.'

'So guys! Only one more country and you're finished!' Sambo said to us at the Victorian Rugby Union grand final.

Since wearing John Eales' trousers, and reuniting with the former prop at the Sydney rugby lunch, we had stayed a night at Sambo's Victorian farm and got to see our auctioneering celebrity in a very different light. Far from being just the quick witted comedian we had known on stage, we slowly unearthed a full spectrum of his rugby experience through many countries.

As a player, Sambo had progressed through the New South Wales leagues, finally captaining the NSW Country representative team where he played matches against both the All Blacks and British & Irish Lions. He later captained the Northern Suburbs side in Sydney, before becoming one of the first professional Australian players to play in Japan.

After his retirement, he became coach of the Singapore national side, consultant to the Indonesian national side, and lastly became a leading rugby presenter and commentator on ESPN Star Sports - Asia's leading sports channel.

I couldn't think of ways to talk up my rugby experiences, so now stood quietly enjoying the climax of the Victorian regional competitions.

'Well, I don't really know,' I tried to explain to him, 'we will kind of feel like we've made it when we land in Dunedin.'

Sambo gave me a stern look, he had been following our progress since our meeting in Jakarta and clearly didn't approve of our premature ending.

'What?' I tried to justify to him, as well as myself, 'England are based down there for the pool stages and we will have cycled *to* the Rugby World Cup.'

'Ah bull crap,' he rubbished our idea, 'that doesn't count. You get yourself up there for the final, you can't cycle half way across the world and not even make it to Auckland.'

Funnily enough, that's exactly what I thought we could do. My family had emigrated to Dunedin several years ago, and currently that represented the only accommodation we would have during the seven week tournament. Cycling out aimlessly into one of the wettest countries on the planet, would show that after a year on the road, we had really learned very little at all.

'I don't know, we'll see what sort of response we get to the New Zealand Herald article, and take it from there.'

CHAPTER 36
THE RUGBY WORLD CUP

From: 'Wayne Jackson'
To: 'Jodie and Tom'

'I was wondering if you would like tickets to both quarter finals in Auckland? If not, I have two spare tickets...as a gift of course... Best wishes for the rest of your journey... Wayne'

From: 'Greg Lim'
To: 'Jodie and Tom'

'If you need a place to stay in Auckland (for free) we have a self-contained unit available - 10 minutes walk to Eden Park. No fridge or oven, but has Sky TV which has 24 hour Rugby Channel... Cheers Greg'

From: 'Rachel - DHL'
To: 'Jodie and Tom'

'I am just confirming the tickets we have for you: 2 x AU vs USA (corporate box Wellington) & 2 x Fiji vs Wales (corporate box Hamilton)... Cheers, Rachel DHL'

From: 'Neil Beckett'
To: 'Jodie and Tom'

'Are you all sorted for places to stay in New Zealand? We're in Wellington and happy to put you up. It's an amazing thing you're doing.... Neil'

From: 'Tessa & Walt'
To: 'Jodie and Tom'

'We live in Palmerston North, if you need a bed on your way through you are very welcome indeed... Best regards Tessa & Walt'

From: 'Rich Freeman'
To: 'Jodie and Tom'

'Guys - reckon you can make it to Napier for the
Japan vs Canada match... I've got two tickets
waiting for you... See you there! Rich'

*   *   *   *   *

'Does that mean we have to keep cycling?' I asked, a little nervous of the answer as I looked out at the Dunedin rain.

'Maybe,' she suggested, 'but you'll have to work out whether the match dates are actually realistic.'

As 'Chief of Route Planning', I agreed to look over the map of New Zealand later that night, but first there was a significant event we had to attend.

In Sydney, both Nick Farr-Jones and John Eales had happily put pen to parchment, adding two World Cup winning captains to our collection of legends across the world. In a few hours time, another World Cup winning captain, Martin Johnson, would be leading the England team to Dunedin Town Hall for their capping ceremony. If we could find a way to add him to the scroll, we could think of no better way to fulfil all of our wildest expectations.

'Martin!' I called across the chairs, down at the town hall.

The England team hadn't even arrived, and yet I'd already spotted an opportunity. I rushed around the lines of empty chairs and waited patiently behind another fan that had beaten me to him. Up close, he was even bigger than I had imagined. The former England and British & Irish Lions second row looked down on me from such a height, that I worried he wouldn't notice Jodie at all.

'Hello Martin!' I said, introducing myself and nervously handing him a homemade business card, 'We've cycled across the world to try to raise awareness of rugby culture, and we wondered if you could help add a signature to our list of legends.'

He looked at the lopsided card and smiled, 'Congratulations to both of you, that's a very impressive achievement. I'd be more than happy to help.'

'Great,' I replied, 'I need you to get us Martin Johnson's.'

'That Martin Bayfield is such a nice guy!' I said, for the sixteenth time as we left the town hall, 'He used to be a policeman you know.'

'I only know because you already told me fifteen times. You're delirious!'

'I'm so happy!' I said, skipping back to the bicycles chained besides a church. 'We just met Martin Johnson and Martin Bayfield at the *same* time!'

Back at the house, we opened a bottle of celebratory wine, and I started to plan out a cycling route of New Zealand. The quickest and flattest route would be to hug the East coast the entire way round to Picton, then hop on a ferry to Wellington, and cut straight through the North Island to Auckland. It was only about 2,000 km, which allowing seven weeks, wouldn't prove any difficulty at all. No matter how I juggled the numbers though, there just seemed no realistic way of accepting the ticket offers and still getting around solely on bicycle.

Thanks hugely to Wayne, an extortionately generous rugby fan, we actually had tickets to Eden Park for both the quarter finals and therefore something specifically to head to. We would have to be at Greg's accommodation at least a day before to allow for problems, so our schedule would now see us travel the length of the two islands, in just five weeks.

'We can cycle some bits,' I decided, 'but we're going to have to ask for some help too.'

With no rugby being played between Dunedin and Nelson, cycling the full 900 km would mean missing a large chunk of the pool stages, and remove our chances of watching any of the 'tournament colour' games. Instead, we focused our energies on cycling to Christchurch, with the hope of meeting Richie McCaw at the team's special visit to the earthquake damaged city.

A fantastic young lady called Rachel, from Destination Marlborough, had already extended an warm invitation to the famous wine region in the north of the island, and if we needed assistance getting there from Christchurch, she had also offered to look into putting us onto the scenic coastal train. This sounded like a fair compromise for cycling four days into the battering Otago wind and rain.

With the help of a couple of rugby writers from the New Zealand Herald, we were put in touch with Joe Locke, the media manager for the All Blacks. This was the great thing about New Zealand, not only was the rugby community very tight, but at many levels the entire country. Considering the acreage is larger than the United Kingdom, it staggered me to think that their population was still significantly smaller than even Scotland's.

Joe patiently explained that although he usually answered the phone to a thousand requests a day, he wasn't able to facilitate most of them, after all, how many fans *didn't* want to meet Richie McCaw for an autograph? After listening to our project, he promised to make every effort to create a small window for us. Clinging onto that faint hope, we pushed up high into the hills of Dunedin as a huge rainstorm tried to force us back.

Although dripping wet as we emerged the other side, once through the steep hills we really believed that we had overcome the worst of our battles. A further day into the ride saw us reach the huge Canterbury plains, and we knew that it would be flat cycling from here to Christchurch. The disadvantage of such a flat landscape was that if the wind wasn't blowing your way, there would be very few places to hide, and following in our poor fortune with the winds, we spent two days heading directly into a stiff northeasterly.

Several thousand fans packed into Centennial Park, eagerly awaiting the arrival of their national team. We pedalled up to the event, completely unsure what to do or where to put ourselves, and finally decided that if we waited in the car park by the empty team bus, at least they'd have to walk nearby to get out again. I sent Joe a text as the team emerged from the sports pavilion and took their place on a giant temporary stage.

Midway through an entertaining audience participation with the team, Joe Locke came to the car park to find us.

'Come with me guys! I can squeeze you in.'

Moments later, we found ourselves up on stage to ask Richie McCaw, in front of thousands of adoring fans, to officially bring our 'World in Union Scroll' project to a close. He gave us a polite smile, suggesting that it wasn't the weirdest thing he'd ever been asked to do, and happily completed our little piece of rugby history with a careful squiggle. We had deliberately targeted World Cup winning captains at the end of our project, and were now pinning our hopes on Richie to deliver the perfect finale.

After an incredible pool stage experience, watching matches in four different venues along the way, we were soon in Auckland and eagerly awaiting the knockout stage of the tournament. Thanks to Neil Beckett, who had opened up his house in Wellington, the prestigious Ponsonby Rugby Club had also heard about our journey, and had offered to help accommodate our intended display amongst their new collection of All Black and club memorabilia.

Auckland's oldest, and most successful club, had been home to many famous All Blacks, starting with the first All Black captain, Dave Gallaher, through to Va'aiga Tuigamala, Carlos Spencer and more recently, Ali Williams. We couldn't have wished for a more fitting location to exhibit the results of our rugby research.

Peter Thorp and Chris Clews, two board members, showed us around their cabinets and identified a spot for our display.

'It doesn't look very good,' I pointed out, gesturing towards our shapeless pile of rugby jerseys on the floor.

'Don't you worry,' Chris replied, 'I might be able to help you with that!'

Not for the first time on our journey, our good fortune inside the rugby family left us completely speechless. By chance, Chris Clews owned a staging company called DE Group, and was perfectly happy to help us in the name of grassroots rugby. Not only that, but former captain Dave Atkins, owned the Rugby World NZ magazine and a printing company called Image Centre. In just two days, we had a professional exhibition showcasing the most inspiring rugby stories from around the world, and an unbroken chain of twenty-eight signed national jerseys.

We proudly manned our exhibition for the best part of two weeks, mingling in with Ponsonby's many rugby events, and enjoying the festivities of the Rugby World Cup. One regular, and very familiar face around the clubhouse, belonged to the Director of Rugby, Bryan Williams, a former All Black winger and the current President of the NZRU.

On our first weekend, England had been sent packing, as had the Argentineans, South Africans and Irish, and a few days previously, a nervous Ponsonby had seen their countrymen dismiss Australia. In the other semi-final, almost fittingly, France had again progressed to face New Zealand in what would be a replay of the 1987 tournament final.

Now, with just a few days left to kick off, the club was hosting a group of French supporters, led by none other than French legend, Philippe Sella.

On Thursday afternoon, after four years of waiting and six and a half weeks of international action, the competition was about to boil down to one final confrontation. With France and New Zealand both through to the World Cup final, Philippe Sella reached for a microphone and prepared for a 'sing off' with NZRU President, Bryan Williams.

Philippe was off to a flying start, and in a typically French and exuberant performance he had the tour party in the palm of his hand, raising their glasses and singing along to the unpronounceable lyrics. Ignoring the pressure, Bryan didn't bat an eyelid, and just when we feared that he was dead and buried, he slid in under the posts with a magnificent hip-swaying rendition of the Kiwi classic, 'Ten Guitars'.

With two striking performances it wasn't conclusive who had won, but if the final proved to be half as entertaining then we were all in for a great weekend.

CHAPTER 37
THE GARDEN OF EDEN PARK

Thanks to our Singapore 'Growler', Duncan McGilligan, a former Esher team mate of John Inverdale, we had the chance for a quick BBC Radio 5 Live interview a couple of hours before kickoff. John arrived at our house armed with a microphone and a set of questions. The excitement was now building around the city, and from Greg's balcony, we sat outside with a clear view of the fortress that is Eden Park.

'Where are you going to watch the game?' John asked us, before the interview.

'Ah, we're just going to watch it with some friends,' I explained, 'they're having a barbecue!'

I was looking forward to catching up with some kiwi friends for the tense final, but I had concerns that most of the food would already be scoffed by the time we arrived.

'I can't believe you've come *all* this way and you're not going to be there!' he laughed.

After a hundred interviews throughout the year, ranging from local newspapers and radio stations, up to international TV sports broadcasters, it was now just Jodie and I, with John Inverdale, and a single producer. Only hours before the biggest match in the history of the All Blacks, I was sat a stone's throw from Eden Park, chatting rugby with the man who brought back my very first memories of the sport. To me, John was always the face of UK rugby, and it's a memory that will never disappear.

'It's moments like these,' he paused, as he reached into his pocket, 'that are sadly lost to radio. But when I found out about Tom and Jodie, I asked around some friends and we've found them a couple of tickets.'

John handed us two plastic sleeves, passing them at such an angle that they literally glowed golden in the late afternoon sun.

'They are the best seats in the house,' he added. 'Congratulations to you both, from everyone!'

'Guess what Greg!' I said, as John and the producer left for the match.

'You're going to the game?' he smiled, opening the door and spoiling my fun.

'How did you know?'

'What else was it going to be Tom? Guess what - Countdown's running a special on processed cheese slices?'

'Are they?' came my automatic response, we hadn't been able to afford cheese for ages, 'I might pick some up after the match.'

Due to the excitement, we arrived half an hour late at the Michael Jones statue, but predictably, so too did our Mosman friends, Charlie and Jim.

Perhaps the casual greeting could be put down to the fact that both parties were still suffering from the previous evening's antics, necking jager-bombs and singing inappropriate rugby songs in a local bar. It had been great fun though, with at least three hours of singing ably led by Jim and his old rugby friends.

Some songs I had known from back home, but most songs had seemed unfamiliar to Jodie, who bopped along to the new tunes, joining in with the chorus' at the second time round.

A rather fetching rendition of 'Old MacDonald' clearly hit the mark with Jodie, and I speak for everyone in the bar that night when I say that the proceeding barrage of farmyard noises couldn't possibly have come from such a little mouth. One would indeed be forgiven for thinking that Old MacDonald had sold his farm and transferred into the abattoir business.

'Hey guys, this is Greg, our host,' I rasped, pointing to the only other man standing with us.

Greg was excited, but incredibly nervous and had bought his match ticket a long time ago.

'Nice to meet you,' came many a response, and there were handshakes all round.

It was a lovely moment on the brink of a Rugby World Cup final, two independent members of our new 'global rugby family' meeting for the first time.

Suddenly, another man appeared and thrust out his hand. Instinctively I grabbed it, thinking there was little else I could do with such a gesture. I had never been 'ghetto' enough to partake in any slapping or tickling of fingers, and to offer a 'knuckle on knuckle' scenario was now not my choice to make. I shook the new hand with the traditional method, and looked up at the stranger who was sporting a baseball cap and prickly stubble.

'Hey, how you doing?' I asked him, noting how much smarter it was to shave one's face.

Since clean shaving just moments before leaving for the game, I had felt like a new man. The crisp air licked at my bare skin and it felt as if my top lip had finally been released of its shackles. Not that I needed to, but if I wanted, I could finally 'pucker' without the feeling of forcing a caterpillar up each nostril. Perhaps I was doing this too much, or maybe Jodie just didn't recognise me, either way, every time I glanced at her she was laughing.

'You don't remember us do you?' our new friend brought my trail of thought back to Auckland.

I now looked at him without distraction, he was sporting a rugby cap and wore a rather trendy pair of glasses, he looked a little Italian. We hadn't been to Italy.

'You don't remember *us*' he had asked me. Was that a clue? Maybe I would find his accomplice and piece together this great Italian rugby mystery once and for all. A boy now appeared at his side, with no misleading stubble, he was a very familiar face indeed. I looked back at the father who was smiling in amusement, I *did* recognise him. We had stayed with this family for a single night somewhere on our journey, but was I going to remember where in time?

'Yes, of course I remember you!' I exclaimed in delight, trying to buy myself a little more. It didn't help.

'... but where from?' I added, almost rhetorically, despite trying desperately not to be rhetorical - I really was looking to prevent further embarrassment and be politely reminded.

'We're from Humpty Doo,' Swampdog Chris said, introducing himself to Auckland Greg, then the Buchanans from Mosman.

'These guys are from the Swampdogs Rugby Club in Australia,' I finally added, not really disguising my failure.

'Humpty Doo? Is that a real place?' Jim asked, it was a fair question.

I had actually been there, but yet some mornings I woke up wondering if it had all been in my imagination, a little like my visit to the Neverneverland Rugby Football Club. Peter Pan had been awarded 'Player of the Year' after a fantastic season in the U14s, and although senior rugby was an unlikely dream, he had been looking forward to winning the U14 award again the following year.

'Certainly is, it's in the Territory,' came a voice from behind us. It was Steve 'Barbs' Barber from Indonesia.

'No way!' came Jodie and my simultaneous response. Maybe the *whole trip* had been a dream.

*   *   *   *   *

Inside the stadium we followed directions from security, edging us closer and closer to the halfway line. As we stood overlooking the players' tunnel, Jodie stopped and peered down at the first two seats by the aisle.

'Jo, are you sure these are *our* seats?'

'That's what it says, look!' she pointed to the seat number.

'And it's definitely for *this* match?' I double checked again, this couldn't be real. I looked behind me, noticing a list of name tags pinned onto seat covers.

'Bloody hell Jo! We better not stand up too often or we'll block the Prime Minister's view!'

Seated immediately behind us was our new friend Bryan Williams, with Bill Beaumont, John Key and many other familiar names. Further behind them, was Lawrence Dallaglio with his commentary team and just to the left was Sir Richard Branson, wearing a 'Sir Richie' All Black jersey in his private box.

'This is crazy! I can't believe we are sitting here at the final!'

'I know, this is really it, there's no more rugby after today. Come on, let's have a drink to celebrate.'

I grabbed the bag and ducked out to the private bar area, most guests were still sat enjoying their dinner in the VIP lounge, but two attentive bar tenders stood waiting to take my order.

'How much for a glass of white wine and a beer please?'

'That's fifteen dollars.'

'Oh, what about two beers?'

'Fifteen dollars.'

'One beer?' I clung to the hope that somehow this might be a cheaper way of getting the drinks.

'Seven dollars fifty.'

Bugger. I looked down at our little purse, we had six dollars and fifty-five cents.

'Is the tap water free?'

Sipping our icy tap water, and waiting for the stand to fill, we absorbed the moment and turned our thoughts to the match itself.

'Who do you think will win?' Jodie asked.

'It has to be New Zealand Jo, there's no way I can see past them for this.'

At Eden Park, the All Blacks had an unparalleled record. Since the game went professional in 1995, they'd won *every* single Test match. Not only had they also won their last twenty-six consecutive matches, but had only lost one match there since the 1987 Rugby World Cup kicked off over twenty-four years before.

'Can I give you some stats?' I asked Jodie, 'I was doing some reading on Eden Park earlier today.'

'You normally just tell me anyway?' she pointed out correctly, and I wasn't at all interested in her answer.

'In the ninety years of using Eden Park,' I began, 'the All Blacks have scored in *every* single match, only losing three times by more than seven points. Ninety years!' I repeated, entirely for myself, 'The odds are in their favour... '

'Who was the last team to beat them here?'

'I knew you were going to say that!'

'Why? Who was it?

'France.'

As we sat through what was one of the tightest and most competitive finals yet, I noticed a gradually changing attitude and atmosphere at the stadium.

Prior to the tournament, many of our very own kiwi friends, had warned us not to get disappointed with the New Zealand crowd - 'They won't sing, they won't applaud failure, and they will start getting frustrated if they're not winning'.

At the quarter final with Argentina, we learned that all these things had been true. A small pocket of Puma fans, engulfed by a sea of black, had created more atmosphere than the rest of the stadium put together. Despite scoring the only try of the first half, an Argentinean drop goal attempt was met with 'booing', and although their valiant performance only pushed the kiwis for 50 minutes, this was enough time for several All Black fans to actually get themselves arrested for aggressive and drunken behaviour.

These people weren't 'fans', they had simply come along to watch the All Blacks win. Of course they cheered them when they scored, but what spectators didn't? Real fans were people who got behind their team more when they were down than when they were up. When I thought back to days at Twickenham Stadium, I didn't think of glorious England victories, or stunning performances, I remembered the camaraderie, the songs and more importantly, the atmosphere!

Although All Black Tony Woodcock had been a surprise early try scorer, when French captain Thierry Dusautoir slid under the posts, a simple conversion took the game back to within a single point. The French were playing out of their skins, and the All Blacks digging as deep as ever before. Fourth choice fly half Stephen Donald had been called onto the pitch after just thirty-four minutes, and when star man Piri Weepu, partially responsible for the French try, was pulled off with half an hour to go many began to fear the worst.

With a chance to take France into the lead, part Vietnamese Trinh-Duc, pushed a penalty marginally wide and the All Black fans finally found their voice. The notorious 'silence' of Eden Park was swept aside as every subsequent pass, ruck and tackle was being joined by the all important '16th man'.

When Richie McCaw was out for the count, floored with a huge blow to the head, 40-50,000 fans urged him to his feet for the final minutes. It was like watching a dramatic slow motion scene from Rocky.

After an agonising final passage of play from the French, the All Blacks retained possession, booted the ball into touch and the final whistle was drowned out by the biggest celebration in New Zealand's history.

'They earned that!' I cheered with Jodie, 'Text everyone!'

After such fantastic New Zealand hospitality, we felt overjoyed for all of our new friends. We sat soaking up the lap of honour, the presentation and then for almost another hour, watching the stadium of happy fans chatting on the stairs, hugging and smiling.

'They have never really understood what it was to lose before,' I tried to explain, 'they always go around winning everything for four years, then fall over in the knockout stage and walk away scratching their heads and making excuses.'

'They deserved to win, they were the best team all tournament,' Jodie replied, speaking far too concisely for my liking. I certainly wasn't going to leave it there.

'This year was different, they lost to Australia, they lost to South Africa and today, they lost half their players and nothing went to plan. The fans genuinely responded and realised that you don't just walk in and take a World Cup, you have to fight for one and earn it.'

'Very philosophical!' Jodie mused, tolerating my verbal passion for rugby.

'Except for 2007' I added, 'South Africa did walk in and steal that one.'

Asides from a rather coincidental encounter, bumping into Rambo, as we bought a six dollar bottle of wine in Countdown, we returned straight home and sent a big 'thank you' e-mail to everyone who had supported us through our project.

We had found strong rugby communities every step of the way, and as we had hoped in Christchurch, the World in Union scroll *had* been finally completed by the new World Cup winning captain, Richie McCaw.

Exhausted by the excitement, we guzzled our wine, congratulated Greg for the fiftieth time, and then finally fell into a deep and well needed sleep.

*   *   *   *   *

```
From: 'Tom Griffiths'
To: 'Jodie and Tom'

'The World Cup winning captain is good, but it's not
a Head of State. Bad luck guys, mine's a Vindaloo.'
```

'Shit bums, how is that fair?' I moaned, 'We cycled halfway round the bloody world, met with over 100 rugby communities and now he thinks we owe *him* a curry. This is all Stefan's fault.'

'Don't blame Stefan Tom, if it wasn't for him, none of this could have ever happened.'

'I *know*. That's what I just said!'

Stefan Watts was our new friend in London, the founder of 'Study Options', and the man who had organised everything for a painless enrollment in our Australian college courses.

When we had first visited Stefan, our plan had been nothing more than an intoxicated decision, but with his encouragement, and a few carefully directed e-mails to friends, he had not only opened up doors, but also our own imagination. *Bastard*

'Tom, hurry up and get changed. We have to be there in one hour.'

We had been invited to the annual IRB Awards, and to our delight we had been sat beside Chris Rea, the soft hypnotic voice of IRB Total Rugby - not the husky English singer. By coincidence, Chris had also been one of the founding brains behind the awards, organising the ceremony over the previous ten years.

'You know!' he said to us, in his soft Scottish tilt, 'We first held the awards in a wee theatre in Mayfair, there were about one hundred guests and we had to go elsewhere for dinner! Just look at it now.'

I looked around us, watching as over one thousand guests enjoyed the prestigious black-tie event. It was too much for me to take in, and I was still confused at how the ice sculpture was not melting all over our table.

Chris was no stranger to rugby in New Zealand, the former Scottish centre had toured with the British & Irish Lions in 1971, which still to this day remains the only Lions side to have won a Test series in New Zealand. Asides from having the most soothing reading voice, part of me suspects that he was selected partly as a lucky mascot. Having already played for Scotland in victories over Australia, South Africa, France, and back to back successes over England, he was certainly a man to bring in for the big occasion.

To a standing ovation, Richie McCaw entered the hall, brushing my shoulder as he walked the centre channel, carrying the William Webb Ellis trophy. The ceremony kicked off, and to our delight the pre-recorded introductions were from the very man sat beside us.

Midway through the dinner, sports presenter Tony Johnson again took to the stage as the huge screen behind him introduced the next award - 'IRPA Special Merit Award'.

'Now most of you will have chosen to fly with Emirates,' he said, strategically dropping in the tournament sponsors, 'but one young couple instead chose to cycle across the world, raising £30,000 for charity... '

'Oh dear God,' I gasped.

He gave a further, albeit brief explanation of our trip, before inviting us to stand and receive a round of applause from the hall.

'Just smile and give them all a wave,' Chris calmly guided us, still sat in his seat. I can't speak for Jodie, but I was shitting myself. Thankfully, we weren't required to give a speech.

'Wow, it's great that they gave you an award,' John Eales congratulated us after the dinner.

'Er, I don't think they did?' I laughed, 'Didn't George Smith win it?'

John was the tenth person to congratulate us, and amusingly, it appeared that nobody was really sure what had happened, and this time I *mean* nobody. George Smith had indeed received the 'IRPA Special Merit Award', only a minute after our round of applause, but whatever the situation I was sure I could at least celebrate winning an 'IRB Special Mention Award'.

John glanced down suspiciously at my trousers before saying a final goodbye, it finally dawned on us that this was it, our great rugby trip really was coming to an end. On his way out of the hall even the Prime Minister, John Key, caught our eye and stopped to personally recognise our journey.

'Jodie and Tom,' he said, as he shook our hands, 'I really want to congratulate you on a truly amazing achievement. What you have done to promote rugby across the world deserves real credit and if there's anything, *anything* I can do to help, please let me know.'

I thought back to Tom Griffiths' last e-mail.

'Well Mr Prime Minister, you know, there is just *one* small thing...'

It has been impossible to mention all the people who have made our journey possible, the strangers who have fed, watered and housed us, the people who have taken a chance on us, the people who have passed us on our message, and the people who have supported us. To all our new family, thank you everyone.

Our hosts - Will King (Putney), Mum & Pops Burton, Gilles Vandeweerd (Royal Liege RFC), Werner Wehmeier & family, Robert & Regina, Adam Taylor (SC Neunheim RFC), Eduard & Maria Krutzner, Vitek Petras (Tatra Smichov RFC), Tomas Cerny (Prelouc RFC), Daniel Benes (Brno Brystrc RFC), Eva and her homebrew (CZ Rep), Paul Duteil & family (Vienna), Renee & Tini Carmine (Austrian Rugby Union), Balasz Bohm (Erzstergom RFC), Dave Alpert (Budapest Exiles RFC), Pal Turi & Gica (Kecskemet RFC), Simon & Timea (Gyula RFC), Claudiu Moga & family (Romania), Radu & Anca Constantin and Max (Romania), Pavel & Stella (Bulgaria), Pavel's grandmother (Bulgaria), Zabi Ahmadi, Hakan & Esbie Unsal (Istanbul Ottomans), Mustafa Sagir, Deniz Krom & John Henry-Rees (Samsun Sharks), Hakan's cousin - Ufuk (Turkey), Uta Beyer (Georgia), Eldegiz Rafibeyli (Azerbaijan Rugby Union), Mike (Iran), Rahim & Farideh (Iran), Darush (Iran), Amir, Ali & family (Iran), Ashkan, Christian, Mahiar (Shiraz RFC), Rob & Kate Cotterill and the boys (Dubai), 'K' & 'Jay' Haroon and family (Lahore RFC), Matt & Binosche Barratt (Pakistan), Hamid Hussein & family (Pakistan), Nick Horton (Seoul Survivors), Kenji (Japan), Simon Litster & family (Yokohama RFC), Eoin Tormey (Hong Kong), Fergo & Lauren (Hanoi Dragons), Julien & Sophie (Vietnam), Megan Knight & Maggie Dillon (Lao PDR Rugby Federation), Guilan & Elizabeth Lavoisier-Brasset (Stade Khmer RFC), Tim Hanson (Southerners RFC, Bangkok), Neil Ankcorn & Pat Yong (RSC RFC, Kuala Lumpar), Graham Donald (Bintang RFC, KL), Duncan & Ali McGilligan (SCC RFC), Will King & Anna Kaisharis (Singapore), Doug, Mike & crew at Smiling Hill, James & Michele Brown, Steve 'Barbs' & 'Indo Bill' (Persatuan Rugby Union Indonesia), Nick & Kelli Mesritz (Bali Rugby Union), Andre Thomas & Maryse Batenburg (Souths RFC), Chris Howard & family (Swampdogs RFC), Chris Binney & Kirstin Meinschaefer (Katherine Gorge), Sam 'the Snake' Stokes & King de Guia (Brisbane), Chris 'Fraggle' Halsall & Kirsty le Juge (Brisbane), Austin & Janet Whittaker and 'muppet' (Gold Coast Eagles RFC), Al Barrett (Ballina Sea Horses RFC), Doug Anderson (Yamba Buccaneers RFC), Garry & Sue Munday (Kempsey Cannonballs RFC), Peter & Kate Lumsdaine (Port Macquarie), Bev (Newcastle), Charlie & Jim Buchanan (Mosman RFC), Justin 'Sambo' Sampson & family, Paul 'Freeway' & Kristy (Melbourne), Elaine, Derek & Claire Hudson (Dunedin), Johnny 'the Fox' (Palmerston), Dot (Riverstone Kitchens), Gareth Morgan (Holmes Station Homestead), Astrid & Heiner (Christchurch), Neil Beckett & family (Wellington), Wayne & Belinda Jackson (Wellington), 'Tess & Walt' Glass (Palmerston North), Phil Fry 'the Spy' (Auckland), Greg Lim & family (Auckland). Thanks to you all!

Further thanks to - Stefan Watts (Study Options), Tom Griffiths (Gapyear.com), Alastair Humphries, Simon Mattick (Saracens RFC), Chris Lis (Blackheath RFC), Scott & 'Ma and Pa' Richards, Brian Rowe, Dany Roelands (Belgium Rugby Union), Rudi Glock, Andreas Shwalbe (Austrian Rugby Union), Dr Martin, Rama and Claus-Peter Bach (SC Neunheim RFC), Zoltan Heckel (Esztergom RFC), Pete 'the Welshman', Beth Coulter (IRB), Richie Dixon (Georgia coach), Chris Thau (IRB), Ivan Ivanov (Bulgarian Rugby Union), Vassil Varbanov (Murphys Misfits), Hasan Akman & Ozer Onkal (Istanbul Ottomans), Remo, Maia (GRU), Minoo, Mr Sadeghi, Alireza, (Iranian Rugby Federation), Wayne Marsters, Hamza Girache, Ghaith Jalajel (Dubai Exiles RFC), Fawzi, Arif, 'Grouse' (Pakistan Rugby Union), Billal Butt (Islamabad Rugby Club), Luna (Qingdao Sharks RFC), James (Hairy Crabs RFC), Richard Jarvis, Kiwi-Nick & Jaesub Choi (Seoul Survivors RFC), Jan Boonstra (Busan), John Kirwan, Eddie Jones, George Gregan, Takako Matsudaira (Suntory Sungoliaths RFC), Takamasa Okado, Rich Freeman, Gilbert Gozalez (Japan Rugby Union), Taji Chosa, Steve Jones (Hong Kong Football Club), Ray Peacock (DHL), Robbie McRobbie (HKRU), Rambo Leung (IRB), Leah & Davey Brown (Hanoi Dragons RFC), Alastair Crozier (Hanoi), Noui (LRF), Chris Mastaglio (LRF), Larry (Billabong Hotel), Dan Parkes (Sisowath Knights RFC), James & Thomas & Gary Sterling (CFR), Jean-Baptiste (Siem Riep RFC), Eddie Evans (Nak Suu Tigers), Stephen 'Belly' Bells (Southerners RFC), Nattapol, Khun Adisak & Khun Nakanthorp (Bangkok), Sopo & Lea (Nak Suu Tigers), David Pine (Kuala Lumpar), Charlie Chelliah (Royal Selangor RFC), Shoe, Craig & Sarah Mounsey & Andy Douglas (SCC RFC), David Taylor (Jakarta), Steve Kent (DHL), Drew & James (NT Rugby Union), Dave Barber (Norths RFC), Grant Anderson (Gold Coast Rugby Union), Glenn Fletcher (Port Macquarie Pirates RFC), Alastair Gaisford (Canberra), Tom Jeavons-Fellows (Mosman RFC), Everyone at Fox Sports - The Rugby Club (Sydney), John Eales, Dylan Reynolds, Trevor and Martin (Tag Rugby Development Trust), Andre Van Der Schee (Footscray RFC), Martin Bayfield, Joe Locke (NZRU), Jim Locke (Wellington), Robert Antonin (Romania coach), Stephen Berg (NZ Rugby Museum), Vaughan (Palmerston North), Rachel Brown (Blenheim), Aimee Hodge (Hamilton), Shona Cobham & Claudia Tasker (Auckland), Steve Hawkes, Craig & Kelly Nimmo (Auckland), Bede Brittenden (Onehunga Rotary Club), Bryan Williams (NZRU), Ces Williams, Chris Clews, Peter Thorp, Dave Atkins, Frazer, Tyrone, Ian (Ponsonby RFC), Gary Edmunds (Gilbert), Paul Morgan, Sarah Mockford, Chris Rea, James Williams, Franc 'talk to Frank' Visser, John Inverdale, Ben and Hannah, Adam Hudson, and *everyone* at DHL worldwide, we'd still be haggling down at an Indonesian ferry port if not for you.